THE BALLAD OF

JOHN AND YOKO

THE BALLAD OF

JOHN AND YOKO

THE EDITORS OF ROLLING STONE

EDITED BY JONATHAN COTT AND CHRISTINE DOUDNA

ART DIRECTION BY BEA FEITLER

A ROLLING STONE PRESS BOOK

MICHAEL JOSEPH – LONDON

DESIGN BY BARBARA RICHER

First published in Great Britain by Michael Joseph Ltd
44 Bedford Square, London WC1
1982

ISBN 0 7181 2186 4 (hardback)
ISBN 0 7181 2208 9 (trade paperback)

Printed and bound in Great Britain by
Billing & Sons Limited
London and Worcester.

TABLE OF CONTENTS

ACKNOWLEDGMENTS

The Ballad of John and Yoko is the result of a collaborative effort that has spanned nearly fifteen years. This book reflects not only the contributions of those who have worked during the past year to create it, but also a history of work by the editors and staff of *Rolling Stone*, where much of the material contained here was originally published.

At Doubleday, thanks are due Jacqueline Onassis for having faith in and sponsoring the project, and Lindy Hess for shepherding it through. Those who directly coordinated and edited *The Ballad of John and Yoko* were Jonathan Cott and Christine Doudna (coeditors of the book), Bea Feitler and Barbara Richer (art director and designer of the book) and Sarah Lazin and Patty Romanowski (director and associate editor of the Rolling Stone Press). The Press staff included Peggy Allen, Marion Baker, Sydney Cohen, Jim Nettleton, Linda Perney, Carol Sonenklar and Pat Stuppi. The editors and entire staff of *Rolling Stone* worked tirelessly after John Lennon's death to create the January 22, 1981 special memorial issue, much of which is republished in this book.

Special thanks must be given to Barbara Moore, Gary Victor and Michael Roseman for their generosity in allowing us access to their rare photographs, record albums and memorabilia; to Elliot Mintz for sharing his memories of John with us; and to Jann S. Wenner for his diligence and advice in overseeing this book, which is dedicated to the remarkable human being and artist who inspired all of our lives.

FOREWORD

O<small>F</small> the many things that will be long remembered about John Lennon—his genius as a musician and singer, his wit and literary swiftness, his social intuition and leadership—among the most haunting was the stark, unembarrassed commitment of his life, his work and his undernourished frame to truth, to peace and to humanity.

In the beginning, we could not see the depth of what the Beatles were about or would become, nor what different parts each of them played. Yet they came to stand for, gave form to and helped re-create in those who saw them a notion of community, an ideal of friendship, a spirit of joy. Here was a simple benchmark by which we could measure ourselves, better ourselves and believe in ourselves.

As the Beatles broke up—during the two years between The White Album and "Lennon Remembers"—the images of innocence, unending harmony and communal equality gave way to the understanding that John Lennon was the leader of the group, that he had a uniqueness, a personal vision and energy, that was not only the largest part of the foursome, but also something that could not be contained within the group; and finally something that could not be contained within himself.

In John there was an energy always at peak level. His innate volatility and constant motion was in part a response to the lack of a resting place, a home, during his earliest childhood; and, as an adult, the capricious departures, again and again, of those people in his life he wanted to rely on.

The breakup was not an intentional act, but the consequence of the fact that John could no longer be John Beatle. The group, like the atom, had been split, from which was released John Lennon, pure and uncontrollable.

Few of us saw the fundamentally transforming and irreversible nature of the changes that took place then—what occurs when the stakes are so high—and the potential power being formed. Few of us saw the risks and daring were then at their greatest and those things that came later, which seemed far more chancey, were not that difficult for John and in fact, by that time, had become rather natural and obvious to him.

How John finally became John Lennon was a crucible whose enormity must be remembered: a beloved hero leaves wife and child, and openly admits adultery; as a lover he takes a foreigner. He then turns his back on all financial rules and commandments by leaving the Beatles. He stirs the anger of a world which cherished the Beatles, taking on its disappointment, its hatred, its need to strike back. And then he and his lover—John and Yoko—photograph themselves naked; not seriously affronting decency, but confronting that ninety-nine percent of the population who have lived in fear because they have small penises or the wrong kind of breasts.

I cannot think of an individual or a pair of individuals who in our times risked so much—not just once, but again and again, until finally running out of strength, opportunity, and inner sanctuary in 1976.

I always found it unnerving, sometimes frightening, in various degrees, to be with John or with John and Yoko. At first, it was in telephone conversations from San Francisco to London in 1968 and 1969, being entrusted with increasingly frank interviews without warning. The frankness was unnerving; having to handle the trust without any guidelines or rules was frightening.

A personal involvement with them—as I had on and off from 1970—was intense and transfixing in a way that forever engaged one with their lives. And I think this is what happened to everyone who encountered them—however briefly—or who saw their work at a distance.

To lose John as a friend, as a treasure, as a part of our lives, as a good person—it broke our hearts.

A great man was lost. Great work and music to come was destroyed.

To have loved, and to be in great debt to, his music, his vision, his fight and his friendship is what remains, for us to hold against the wind.

—Jann Wenner
New York City
February, 1982

The royalties from *The Ballad of John and Yoko* are being shared among Rolling Stone Press, editors and the Foundation on Violence in America.

The Foundation on Violence in America was incorporated in 1981 as a non-profit organization, whose goal it is to facilitate a noticeable, meaningful and sustainable reduction in handgun violence in the United States. (The address is: The Foundation on Violence in America, 745 Fifth Avenue, New York, New York 10151.)

PREFACE

T HE beginning of John Lennon and Yoko Ono's romance and life and work together coincided with the birth of *Rolling Stone*. John was on the cover of the magazine's first issue in November 1967. One year later, after the *Two Virgins* album was released —and banned—the photograph of John and Yoko simply standing naked together became the cover and center spread of the magazine's first anniversary issue.

Rolling Stone was a privileged witness to and supporter of their romance and work, and ran articles or news about them in almost every issue. In 1972, at the urging of cofounder Ralph J. Gleason, the magazine took on the immigration fight in support of John.

As a starting point for our book, we selected the most important articles about and interviews with John and Yoko that were published in *Rolling Stone* during the fourteen years between 1967 and 1980. These articles and interviews describe John and Yoko's artistic, political and personal evolution, and at the same time give a documentary glimpse of the worlds and times in which they moved.

The last interview that *Rolling Stone* did with John Lennon took place on December 5, 1980, and his last photographic session on the morning of December 8. The magazine had been preparing a cover story on John and Yoko for its first issue of 1981, and, after the tragedy of December 8, devoted its entire issue to his memory. Most of the material that appears in parts IV, V and VI of *The Ballad of John and Yoko* was taken from that special issue of January 22, 1981, which was put together by the staff of *Rolling Stone* in the eight days and nights following Lennon's death.

In assembling our new tribute, we have also commissioned and brought together new essays—biographical and critical—about John's and Yoko's childhoods and personalities, along with assessments of their individual and collaborative work in film and music, and a look at their relationship as they presented it to the world.

John and Yoko were born and raised during the bombings of World War II. Half a world apart physically, they were also poles apart in their respective upbringings and in the way they developed creatively. Their lives, in fact, provide a study in contrasts—male/female, East/West, avant-garde/rock & roll. But their meeting and collaboration as marriage partners, artists and workers for peace equally provide a testament to the unity of everything that lives. Their final days and dreams together are remembered and represented in our book by many of the same hands and hearts that gave testimony to their beginnings.

—Jonathan Cott and Christine Doudna

JOHN LENNON: HOW HE BECAME WHO HE WAS

By Jonathan Cott

Do I contradict myself?   Say the word and be like me.
Very well then I contradict myself,   —"THE WORD"
(I am large, I contain multitudes.)   (JOHN LENNON AND
—"SONG OF MYSELF" (WALT WHITMAN)   PAUL McCARTNEY)

s there anybody going to listen to my story?" John Lennon asked in his song "Girl" on the 1965 *Rubber Soul* album. And it was one of the most ironic questions in the history of popular music, for it seemed as if everybody wanted to listen to his story—or at least to the ongoing story of the four Beatles.

"None of us would've made it alone," Lennon once explained, "because Paul wasn't quite strong enough, I didn't have enough girl-appeal, George was too quiet and Ringo was the drummer. But we thought everyone would be able to dig at least one of us, and that's how it turned out." In fact, each of the Beatles came to be seen and thought of symbolically—like the four evangelists or the four elements. And in an elementary sense, each Beatle—in the way each became defined by his face, gestures, voice and songs—took on an archetypal role: Paul, sweet and sensitive; John, sly and skeptical; George, mysterious and mystical; Ringo, childish but commonsensical (these roles were fixed forever in the film *A Hard Day's Night* and sanctified in the animation feature *Yellow Submarine*). But, at the risk of slighting the composers of beautiful songs like "Here, There and Everywhere" (Paul) and "Here Comes the Sun" (George), it seems clear on hindsight that there was one Beatle who embodied all of the above-named characteristics and qualities, and that was John Lennon.

The more he developed as a person and an artist, the more facets of himself he revealed. Alluding to the well-known image of the giraffe going by a window, he once said: "People are always just seeing little bits of it, but I try and see the whole . . . not just in my own life, but the whole universe, the whole game." He was both Nowhere Man and Eggman, he contained multitudes ("I am he as you are he as you are me and we are all together"), and of these one and all, he, like Walt Whitman, wove the song of himself. It was a song that included anthems ("Give Peace a Chance") and dream collages ("Revolution 9"), portraits ("Mean Mr. Mustard") and statements ("I Want You"), meditations

("Strawberry Fields Forever") and calls to action ("Power to the People"); it was a song of contrasting states of feeling and emotion—weariness ("I'm So Tired") and wakefulness ("Instant Karma!"), need ("Help!") and independence ("Good Morning, Good Morning"), depression ("You've Got to Hide Your Love Away") and elation ("Whatever Gets You Thru the Night"), reflective-ness ("In My Life") and anger ("How Do You Sleep?"), pain ("Yer Blues") and pleasure ("I Feel Fine"), toughness ("Run for Your Life") and gentleness ("Julia"); it was a song featuring different modes of expression—irony ("Happi-ness Is a Warm Gun"), primal screaming ("Mother"), sermons ("The Word"), political protest ("John Sinclair") and nonsense ("I Am the Walrus"); and it was a song manifesting different states of being—the tragic ("Isolation"), the comic ("Polythene Pam") and the cosmic ("Across the Universe").

As Walt Whitman knew, the art and life of a person who contains multitudes is usually filled with contradictions. John Lennon was a born leader. It was he who brought Paul into the Quarrymen (Paul brought George, and George, Ringo), and it was he who, early on, had a sense of being out of the ordinary ("I was hip in kindergarten. I was different from the others. . . . When I was about twelve I used to think: I must be a genius, but nobody's noticed"). But he was a leader who also unstintingly shared his creative powers in collabora-tion with Paul McCartney and Yoko Ono.

He was an unreconstructible rock & roller whose life was forever changed by "Heartbreak Hotel" ("When I heard it I dropped everything") and "Long Tall Sally" ("When I heard it, it was so great I couldn't speak") and who once thought that "avant-garde" was French for "bullshit." Yet he was always experimenting, even as a Beatle, with tapes played backward, tape loops, sound montages and nonnarrative eight-millimeter films; and he produced an avant-garde masterwork in "Revolution 9." He furthermore came to rhapsodize about Yoko's music ("She makes music like you've never heard on earth. . . . It's as important as anything we ever did . . . as anything the Stones or Townshend ever did"), and often used to compare some of her most *outré* songs to "Tutti-Frutti"!

He grew up not only tough and angry but also gentle and vulnerable ("I was torn between being Marlon Brando and being the sensitive poet—the Oscar Wilde part of me with the velvet, feminine side"). He was a compassion-ate, pacifistic human being who was so in touch with his feelings that he could lash out verbally at those he felt had acted hypocritically or who had abused him or, especially, Yoko ("People want me to . . . be lovable. But I was never that. Even at school I was just 'Lennon.' Nobody ever thought of me as cuddly").

He was sometimes insecure and sometimes boastful ("Part of me suspects that I'm a loser and the other part of me thinks I'm God almighty"). He was a trusting and believing person who frequently—and, as it turned out, prescient-ly—spoke of his sense of paranoia and mistrust ("The way things are going /

They're going to crucify me"). And if he occasionally seemed stubborn, he at the same time developed a high degree of flexibility that allowed him to move on, to take risks—personally and artistically—and to live continually in the present ("Some people like Ping-Pong, other people like digging over graves. Some people will do anything rather than be here now. . . . *I don't believe in yesterday*"). And, finally, he was a leader who renounced his crown and empire in order to be true to himself ("It's pretty hard when you are Caesar and everyone is saying how wonderful you are and they are giving you all the goodies and the girls, it's pretty hard to break out of that to say, 'Well, I don't want to be king, I want to be real' ").

"I left [the Beatles] physically when I fell in love with Yoko," Lennon said a short time before his death, "but mentally it took the last ten years of struggling. I learned everything from her." In fact, Yoko became his teacher, his guru, his soul guide (like Dante's Beatrice), and as he told us in "One Day (at a Time)," he was the door and she was the key. Simply, Yoko enabled John to become what he was.

After they met at Yoko's 1966 Indica Gallery show in London, John used to receive "instructions" from Yoko in the mail (BREATHE, HIT A WALL WITH YOUR HEAD); he was perplexed but intrigued. They became lovers in 1968 after he and she stayed up one night and, at dawn, created the lovely East/West musical symbiosis they called *Two Virgins*, for whose album cover they posed naked together. She had led him where he would not go. "I always wanted to be an eccentric millionaire, and now I am," John said a short time later. "It was Yoko who changed me. She forced me to become avant-garde and take my clothes off when all I wanted to be was Tom Jones. And now look at me." But he also said: "People have got to become aware . . . that being nude is not obscene. Being ourselves is what's important. If everyone practiced being themselves instead of pretending to be what they aren't, there would be peace." And on the Beatles' White Album, John, inspired by Yoko, sang his much-neglected, exhilarating song of liberation, telling the world of his newfound energy, fearlessness, and openness:

> *The deeper you go the higher you fly.*
> *The higher you fly the deeper you go.*
> *So come on, come on . . .*
>> —"Everybody's Got Something to Hide Except
>> Me and My Monkey" (John Lennon and
>> Paul McCartney)

John Lennon had surrendered to his love for Yoko Ono ("Yes is surrender, you got to let it, you got to let it go," he would sing later in one of his most haunting songs, "Mind Games"). And from the moment he and Yoko became a couple, John Lennon, Beatle, began to learn how to become "John Lennon" again. On his first solo album, for instance (*John Lennon / Plastic Ono Band*), he jettisoned the extravagant, pullulating imagery of songs like "I Am the Walrus" and "Come Together." As he once explained it:

> I started from the "Mother" album onward trying to shave off all imagery, pretensions of poetry, illusions of grandeur, [what] I call à la Dylan Dylan-esque. . . . Just say what it is, simple English, make it rhyme and put a backbeat on it and express yourself as simply [and] straightforwardly as possible.

On "Girl," Lennon had sung: "Was she told when she was young that pain would lead to pleasure?" But it was on this explosive new record—what I like to call his Howlin' Wolf album, inspired, in part, by John's and Yoko's primal-scream therapy with Arthur Janov—that he stripped down words and music and entered and explored, emotionally naked, an unmediated and undiluted world of pain. It became the subject of almost every song: "Don't let them fool you with dope and cocaine / Can't do you no harm to feel your own pain" ("I Found Out"); "God is a concept / By which we measure / Our pain" ("God"). And in a very real way, his pain was his waking up—from the world of personal illusion and the Social Lie ("As soon as you're born they make you feel small / By giving you no time instead of it all"—"Working Class Hero"). The record was certainly one of the most extraordinary creations in the history of rock & roll.

On his next solo album, *Imagine*, Lennon presented a more lyrical and accessible musical "package," but his songs were still unsettling and subversive, for his pain was still forcing him to open his eyes to everything—politically ("No short-haired, yellow-bellied son of Tricky Dicky / Is gonna Mother Hubbard soft-soap me / With just a pocketful of hope"—"Gimme Some Truth") and psychologically ("You can wear a mask and paint your face / You can call yourself the human race / You can wear a collar and a tie / One thing you can't hide / Is when you're crippled inside"—"Crippled Inside").

His pain could lead to anger, as in his attack on Paul McCartney for falling creatively asleep in the vitriolic "How Do You Sleep?" and as explanation said: "I felt resentment, so I used that situation, the same as I used withdrawing from heroin to write 'Cold Turkey.' " And he took on the subject of his own irrepressible jealousy—a subject he had dealt with in previous Beatles songs like "No Reply," "Run for Your Life" and "You Can't Do That"—and attempted to understand its ravaging power by entering into its realm and describing the manner and process by which jealousy manifests itself in our bodies and, in so doing, allowed it to be experienced as something rich and strange:

> *I was dreaming of the past*
> *And my heart was beating fast*
> *I began to lose control*
> *I began to lose control*

I was feeling insecure
You might not love me anymore
I was shivering inside
I was shivering inside

I was trying to catch your eyes
Thought that you was trying to hide
I was swallowing my pain
I was swallowing my pain

—"Jealous Guy" (John Lennon)

But pain also led him to see noble truths, as in his song "Imagine," one of the most beautiful visions—"antireligious, antinationalistic, anticonventional, anti-capitalistic," as John termed it—of our possibilities as human beings: "You may say I'm a dreamer / But I'm not the only one / I hope someday you'll join us / And the world will be as one."

The muse of the album was, of course, Yoko, whose cover design showed John's face in the clouds, and to whom he wrote one of his most heartfelt ("Oh My Love") and one of his most joyous ("Oh Yoko!") songs. But it was she who sent him on his way in 1973 for what he called his eighteen-month Lost Week-end, and also on a trip by himself to Hong Kong in the late Seventies where he wandered around the city on his own, waking up at five in the morning to see the dawn, and during which, in the middle of a bath one day, he rediscovered *himself.* "I just got very, very relaxed," he recalled. "And it was like a recog-nition. God! It's me! This relaxed person is *me.* I remember this guy from way back when! So I called [Yoko]. I said, 'Guess who, it's *me!* It's *me* here.' I was John Lennon before the Beatles, and after the Beatles, and so be it."

"Out of such abysses," Nietzsche once wrote—as if to describe the moment —"also out of the abyss of great suspicion, one returns newborn, having shed one's skin, more ticklish and sarcastic, with a more delicate taste for joy, with a more tender tongue for all good things, with gayer senses, with a second dan-gerous innocence in joy, more childlike and yet a hundred times more subtle than one has ever seen before." And in John and Yoko's last collaboration, *Double Fantasy,* they clearly revealed this joy and subtlety.

Aside from the beauty of individual songs like "Beautiful Boy" and "Every Man Has a Woman Who Loves Him," one might notice the mysterious little sound-collage segue on side two—it lasts less than a minute—between John's "Watching the Wheels" (a thematic variation on his wonderful Beatles song "I'm Only Sleeping") and Yoko's charming, Thirties-like "I'm Your Angel." One hears what seems to be a hawker's voice, then an arresting few seconds of Greek balalaika music, followed by the sounds of a horse-driven carriage and footsteps, then a door slamming and a few phrases played by a piano and violin in a restaurant. When I asked John about this collage shortly before he died, he told me:

One of the voices is me, going, "God bless you, man, thank you, you've got a lucky face," which is what the English guys who beg or want a tip say, so that's what you hear me mumbling. And then we re-created the sounds of what Yoko and I call the Strawberries and Violin Room—the Palm Court at the Plaza Hotel. We like to sit there occasionally and listen to the old violin and have a cup of tea and some strawberries. It's romantic. And so the picture is: There's this kind of street prophet, Hyde Park corner-type guy who just watches the wheels going around, pronouncing on whatever he's pronouncing on. And people are throwing money in the hat. (We faked that in the studio, we had people walking up and down dropping coins in a hat.) And they're throwing money in his hat, and he's saying, Thank you, Thank you, and then you get in the horse carriage and you go around New York and go into the hotel and the violins are playing and then this woman comes on and sings about being an angel.

And in "I'm Your Angel," Yoko sings: "I'm in your pocket / You're in my locket / And we're so lucky in every way." They must have had a guardian angel watching over their relationship, for, starting over after thirteen years as a couple, they seemed happier than ever before.

"All for love and the world well lost" has always been the motto of romantic lovers. But in the early years of their relationship John and Yoko might have said: "All for love and the world we'll win" ("Just a boy and a little girl / Trying to change the whole wide world" is what John did say in his song "Isolation"), as they performed their bag events and bed-ins for peace—"in the tradition of Gandhi, only with a sense of humor," as John put it. The *London Daily Mirror* described him as 1969's Clown of the Year, and he and Yoko were laughed at, patronized and scorned by many people. Taking off one's clothes, greeting journalists in bed, and planting acorns wasn't exactly the appropriate image for two great romantic lovers. But it was exactly their naive and comic behavior that made them so real and believable a modern romantic couple—only two fools could be so much in love! And in their own tongue-in-cheek way, and like few others in history, John and Yoko lived lives that acted out in the everyday world of archetypal dramas of the imagination. I have always thought of them whenever I read the letters of Abelard and Heloise, the ill-starred twelfth-century lovers—he a famous philosopher, theologian, poet and musician; she, his pupil, paramour, wife, then abbess of a convent. As she wrote to Abelard:

> You had besides, I admit, two special gifts whereby to win at once the heart of any woman—your gifts for composing verse and song, in which we know other philosophers have rarely been successful. . . . The beauty of the airs ensured that even the unlettered did not forget you; more than anything this made women sigh for love of you. And as most of these songs told of our love, they soon made me widely known and roused the

envy of many women against me. For your manhood was adorned by every grace of mind and body, and among the women who envied me then, could there be one now who does not feel compelled by my misfortune to sympathize with my loss of such joys? Who is there who was once my enemy, whether man or woman, who is not moved now by the compassion which is my due?

It is a letter that Yoko Ono might have written after John's death.

But John and Yoko also acted out the mythology of the gods and goddesses. Lennon once described Yoko as his "goddess of love and the fulfillment of my whole life." And in her song "Mother of the Universe," on *Season of Glass*, Yoko sings a hymn to the Mother Goddess, saying: "You gave us life and protection / And see us through our confusion / Teach us love and freedom / As it is to be."

It is interesting to find out that Yoko was deeply interested in Egyptian art and antiques—a large collection of which, including a full-size mummy in a case, she bought for their home. As she said: "I make sure to get all the Egyptian things, not for their value but for their magic power." And it is the ancient Egyptian goddess Isis that Yoko seems most to revere—the goddess who considered cows sacred to her (think of Yoko's interest in buying cows!) and who was at once wife and sister to Osiris, the supreme god and king of eternity (his name means "many-eyed") who was slain, dismembered, revived by Isis, and resurrected. In the words of William Irwin Thompson, Osiris is "a spirit of growth and transformation, expressing the transformation of barbarism into civilization. As the moon calls secretly to the plant to blossom, Osiris calls humanity away from savagery, cannibalism and human sacrifice to a new age of agriculture and the arts of poetry and music." And as Thompson also points out, "the figure of Osiris hearkens back to the old Neolithic religion in which Isis would be the Great Mother and Osiris her son-lover consort."

John's Isis was both mother and wife. "I occasionally call her Mother," he once said, "because I used to call her Mother Superior—remember 'Happiness Is a Warm Gun.' She is Mother Superior, she is Mother Earth, she is the mother of my child, she's my mother, she's my daughter. . . . The relationship goes through many levels, as in most relationships; it does not have any deep-seated strangeness about it." But the mythical Isis-Osiris resonance is there—as is the similarity to Heloise's famous salutation to Abelard: "To her master, or rather her father, husband, or rather brother; his handmaid, or rather his daughter, wife, or rather sister; to Abelard, Heloise."

And one further thinks of a seventeenth-century engraving of the "Soul of the World" that shows some of the symbols associated with Isis: long flowing hair; half-moon on her womb and one foot on water, the other on land. She is standing naked, chained to God, while man (pictured as an ape) is chained to her—and one recalls the photograph taken by Annie Leibovitz on the day

Lennon was killed, showing a naked John in fetal position clinging onto Yoko's body. "You've captured our relationship exactly," was what he said when he saw the test Polaroids.

John Lennon was a worshiper of the goddess. He was also a househusband for five years, while Yoko took care of all business and legal concerns. One thinks of Herodotus writing about Egypt in the fifth century B.C.: "Women attend market and are employed in trade, while men stay at home and do the weaving." The Lenonos—to use the name of John and Yoko's music-publishing company—seem to have run an ancient Egyptian household! Or a topsy-turvy nursery-rhyme one, for, as Lennon sang on "Cleanup Time": "The queen is in the counting house / Counting out the money / The king is in the kitchen / Making bread and honey."

Watching the wheels or baking bread, John Lennon had become who he was. Then, one night while at a disco in Bermuda in 1980, where he was vacationing with his son, Sean, John heard a song called "Rock Lobster" by the B-52's for the first time. It sounded like Yoko's music, so he said to himself: "It's time to get out the old axe and wake the wife up!" In Bermuda he also had taken Sean to the Botanical Gardens and come across a flower called a Double Fantasy. "It's a type of freesia," John said, "but what it means to us is that if two people picture the same image at the same time, that is the secret." So John and Yoko decided to return to the world of music and share their secret. The ballad of John and Yoko ended on December 8, 1980, but their romance will live forever.

The Ballad of John and Yoko is an account of John and Yoko's romance as it manifested itself in their life and art ("Our life is our art," John once said). Most of all, it is a tribute and homage to one of the most extraordinary artists of our century. Throughout his life, John Lennon never stopped taking risks; and, as he continued to develop and grow, he revealed to us what he had learned with humor, intensity and wisdom. In "The Ballad of John and Yoko," he sang: "Last night the wife said, / Oh boy, when you're dead / you don't take / nothing with you but your soul"—but he didn't leave it at that, for, pausing after the word *soul*, he added another word: "Think!" ("Oh boy, when you're dead / you don't take / nothing with you but your soul—Think!"). His message always was that each one of us should wake up.

"Produce your own dream," he said at the end of his life. "You have to do it yourself. . . . I can't wake you up. *You* can wake you up." But he pointed the way. "Why in the world are we here? / Surely not to live in pain and fear," he sang in "Instant Karma!" adding: "Well we all shine on like the moon and the stars and the sun. . . . Come on and on and on on"—and ending, in inimitable John Lennon fashion, "Yeah yeah, all right, ah ha."

CHILDREN OF WAR, EAST AND WEST

IN LIVERPOOL

By Jan Morris

OHN WINSTON LENNON was born on October 9, 1940, at latitude 53° 25' north, longitude 2° 55' west. And, though he was to become one of the immortals, and though his fame was to transcend all frontiers in the end, that date, and that fix on the map, made him what he was.

The year 1940 was a heroic landmark in the history of the British people—the year in which they alone defied the force of Nazi Germany and held that monstrous power at bay until the greater allies of East and West could combine to crush it. But if it was an epic year—a year so dominated by the colossal leadership of Winston Churchill that the newborn child was given a middle name in his honor—still, if the British had known it, 1940 was also the year that marked the beginning of the end of their grandeur. Never again, after 1940, would they occupy such a commanding place on the world's stage:

A national history that had lasted a thousand years and had culminated in the greatest empire ever known to man was about to enter its decisive decline. Before the infant John could walk or talk, Churchill's Britain had become a junior partner in the military alliance that won World War II. Before he was out of school, its once overweening confidence had gone and its character was irrevocably changed: from a semi-feudal aristocracy to a social democracy, from an empire to an offshore island, from terrific certainties to perpetual doubtful flux. In 1940 the turning-point was reached. And just then John Lennon was born.

As for that geographical location, it was as remarkable in British topography as the moment was in British history. Liverpool, which stands on the same latitude as Goose Bay, Labrador, and the same longitude as Timbuktu, was a city of profound and pungent individualism. In those days it was one of the great ports of Europe and, though it had been cruelly bashed about by German bombers (a raid was taking place at the moment of Lennon's birth), it was still

John, approximately eight years old, with his aunt, Mimi Smith, in Liverpool.

a place of irresistible vitality. It was in England but not exactly of it, being a boisterous and sometimes explosive mix of nationalities—Irish, Welsh, Chinese, African and many more—and it had been built upon the most ruthless kind of capitalist enterprise. A great slaving port once, Europe's chief transatlantic passenger port for decades, it was famous for its ships, its waterfront prostitutes, its football clubs, its stand-up comedians and its peculiar nasal accent familiarly known as Scouse. It was also the birthplace of William Ewart Gladstone, the most towering of Victorian prime ministers, whose family fortunes were based, as it happened, upon West Indian slavery.

John, at age seven, with puppy, Liverpool.

So it was in very special circumstances that John Winston Lennon came into the world: at a very special moment, at a very special place and to a destiny altogether unique.

When he was four years old the war ended, and Britain was left, shabby but heroic, to find its feet again. Though the conflict had done something to correct the social inequalities of the nation rooted in centuries of landed privilege, the intricacies of the British class system were inescapable even in Liverpool, and the infant Lennon was pitchforked into them with a peculiar intensity.

John, age ten, in front of Aunt Mimi's house.

The city had a powerful Tory upper crust of shipowners, insurers and finan-
ciers living often in agreeable half-timbered manors in the neighboring Lan-
cashire countryside. It had a huge working-class community, much of it Irish,
living in tough city slums and municipal tenements. And it had a relatively
small bourgeoisie, which had settled in a few well-defined residential suburbs
on the higher ground behind the Mersey riverfront. Subtle gradations of self-
esteem and aspiration separated these groups, and Lennon grew up anomalously
astride one of their several border lines. By origin he was certainly plain prole-
tarian. His father, Freddy, was a ship's steward, his grandfather was a salvage
worker and his first home was a small terrace house in the classic English
working-class mode—rather a nice house to modern eyes, far from a slum, but
still in those days not the sort of house a respectable middle-class housewife
would care to be seen scrubbing the steps of.

Freddy Lennon soon abandoned his little family though, his merry wife,
Julia, found herself another man and John was brought up by his mother's sister
Mimi, a woman with a much keener eye for the proprieties. Still a babe-in-arms,
he crossed the line between the working class to the petty bourgeoisie, from the
Victorian terrace house on Newcastle Road to Mendips, a genteel semi-
detached villa, in the mock-Tudor style, in the desirable suburb of Woolton. It
is true that the house was on the edge of the suburb, facing the heavy traffic
of Menlove Avenue, and that Mimi's husband, George Smith, earned his living
by providing milk for the grander detached houses behind. But it was a long
way from Newcastle Road and further still from the tough alleys of the Dingle,
Toxteth or the waterfront, where the Irish brawled, the tarts paraded and the
raw Liverpool humor fizzed.

So, on the face of it, Lennon's early boyhood was distinctly proper. Mimi
despised anything "common," and the little boy was brought up with a metic-
ulous care for manners and appearances. One of the great treats of the year was

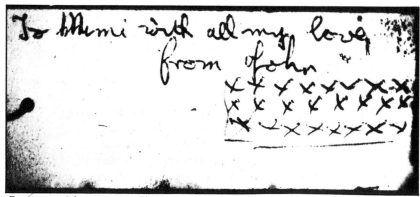

From a note John wrote on a Christmas gift to Aunt Mimi, 1953.

a visit to Strawberry Fields—a Salvation Army children's home just down the road from Mendips—for its summer garden party. When he went to his first school, Dovedale Primary, Mimi met him every afternoon beside the bus stop at Penny Lane. When he graduated to Quarry Bank High School, a much-admired suburban grammar school housed in a sham-Elizabethan mansion beside a park, Mimi had his black school blazer specially tailored and bought him a Raleigh bicycle, the very best, to ride there every day. And when he eventually went on to the Liverpool Art College, he briefly found lodgings in Gambier Terrace, a splendid row of early nineteenth-century houses looking directly across the road to the still-unfinished Anglican cathedral and down the hill beyond to the docks, towers and warehouses of the Mersey waterfront.

Mimi must have been proud of him, so clever with words and pictures, so loving—even the Scouse, so his father thought on one of his rare visits, all poshed out of him. But truth will out. If no suburb could be much more conformist than Woolton, no boy could be much less orthodox at heart than John Winston Lennon. As he grew older beneath Mimi's care, so he grew closer too to his own mother, now living with her lover in less decorous circumstances not so far away, and her harum-scarum influence, irreverent, funny, heedless, proper Liverpudlian, brought out his real character and made a wild, brilliant layabout of him. Defiantly disobedient at school, recklessly lawless on the streets, with no real father around to keep him in order, only dear, kind Mimi and irrepressible Julia, Lennon often dismayed the more proper neighbors along Menlove Avenue, and sometimes even taxed the patience of his ever-adoring aunt.

But it was this very confusion of his upbringing, its mixture of the raucous and the respectable, the deprived and the cherished, terraced house and timbered villa, runaway father and conventional grammar school, all wrapped up in the rowdy, effervescent, dingy, grand and unpredictable flavor of the old seaport, that turned him by slow stages into an artist.

With a little help, that is, from a distinctly mixed bag of friends. It was the age of skiffle, it was the spring of the young Presley, it was the dawn of rock & roll; and it was the beat of these new musics, proscribed over the cautious transmitters of the state-run BBC, that took the teenage Lennon out of Mimi's range, so to speak, and into the company of his kind. If the young tearaways could not listen to rock on British radio, they could hear it on records, or in the programs Radio Luxembourg beamed to Britain every evening: If they still went to school in blazers and gray flannels down in the city, where the seamen came ashore, they could glimpse the style of the new times, the drainpipe trousers, the winkle-picker shoes, the sideburns, the particular sort of swagger— like the defiance of cheerful nouveaux riches—that went with the Teddy boys.

By 1956 John Lennon, at least when out of sight of Mendips, was a proper Ted himself. He'd acquired the obligatory guitar and become at once obsessed with the idea of rock, and the practice of it. He got the right clothes. He devel-

7

oped the proper swagger. Sneaking out of Mendips with his guitar, he would call at his indulgent mother's house to change into his gear and then he and his friends would strut the streets authentically, get into fights or make their first tentative attempts at creating music together. Gradually, almost spontaneously, there came into being under John's inspiration a more or less permanent rock band.

Behind its extraordinary leader, as gifted in music, it now appeared, as he was with words and images, a shifting assortment of guitarists and drummers formed its personnel—boys with a natural Welsh musicality, as often as not, with names like Griffiths, Vaughan or Davis—and it had its own manager, and found its gigs wherever it could. "AVAILABLE FOR ENGAGEMENTS," said its business card:

COUNTRY. WESTERN. ROCK 'N' ROLL. SKIFFLE.

THE QUARRYMEN

The Quarrymen took their name from a phrase in the Quarry Bank school song—"*Quarry men strong before our birth*"—but they recruited players from other schools, too, and, as Lennon graduated from grammar school to art college, prospered moderately, playing at youth clubs and church halls, parading on a float behind the Boy Scouts, the Rose Queen and Cheshire Yeomanry band at the summer fête of St. Peter's Church, Woolton. Members of the band came and went, and its style was more eclectic than distinctive, but in 1957 there joined it a wide-eyed and innocent-looking guitarist and songwriter, sixteen years old, from the Liverpool Institute Grammar School. His name was Paul McCartney, and his arrival changed everything.

For now the particular chemistry was forming, of personality as of sound, that would presently project the leader of the Quarrymen, Lennon himself, through a fame almost inconceivable into a kind of secular martyrdom. No friends could differ much more than Lennon and McCartney—John so wild, so mercurial, so generous, so hot-tempered but so affectionate; Paul so calm and logical, so charming of manner, so controlled in talent. And Paul brought with him another institute boy, George Harrison, son of a Liverpool bus driver, who talked a particularly vivid variety of Scouse and added another dimension altogether—tough but rather enigmatic—to the nature of the Quarrymen. The group fluctuated in fortune and in name, calling itself at one time or another, in part and in whole, Johnny and the Moondogs, the Rainbows, the Nurk Twins and, finally, in a choice not universally admired, the Silver Beatles.

So, at the beginning of the Sixties, the Beatles were born. Ringo Starr, the drummer, came later but, already, impelled partly by his own gifts, partly by the circumstances of the time, partly by the lucky chance of these fruitful friendships, John Lennon had burst the bounds of his background and upbringing. The Beatles became proper professionals when, in the summer of 1960, they got a chance to play in the frenzied nightclubs of Hamburg, a wide-open city that gave them a chance to discover themselves. They first became famous in a shabby old cellar club at home in downtown Liverpool, the Cavern Club, which offered lunchtime rock sessions for secretaries and schoolchildren. Taken in hand by a manager of genius, their fellow Liverpudlian Brian Epstein, they entered the new decade lively, confident and unlike anybody else: And, more than any other people on the face of the earth, they made the Sixties their own.

By now Britain was in the depths of its postwar malaise. The achievements of 1940 were remembered chiefly in middle-aged memories and old war films resuscitated for TV and, as Dean Rusk, Kennedy's secretary of state once observed, the nation had lost an empire and failed to find a substitute. Into its drab uncertainties, relieved for the most part only by royal occasions and sporting victories, the Beatles burst like something out of another field of consciousness.

It is hard to imagine now their impact upon the tired old kingdom. They were something altogether new in British show business. They were neither posh, like musical-comedy performers or Noel Coward, nor mock-American, like the skiffle-boarders and the rockers; not soppy, like the balladeers, nor cloth cap, like the old comedians. They looked clean but raffish, irreverent but engaging; they talked in vigorous Scouse; they made a sound all their own, accompanying lyrics of a distinction almost unknown in their generation, and, dear God, they came from Liverpool.

Among the British at large Liverpool was little more than an unlovely legend. Hardly anybody went there unless it was to board one of the few remaining liners that still sailed from Merseyside and few came *from* there, either, except for the long line of comedians who had started their careers in its music halls — performers unknown elsewhere but household names of a risible kind in England. As for the rock music then sweeping the country, the fount of it all was London, the center of the entertainment business as of almost everything else. Liverpool! The very idea of sophisticated modern music emanating from that home of the Irish joke and the dockland rough-up seemed a contradiction in terms.

In fact Liverpool was a natural birthplace for the Beatles because of all the large cities of the United Kingdom it was the most naturally receptive to new ideas and alien influences. Even in the worst days of blitzed havoc, even in the hangdog Depression years, Liverpool had retained a freshness, a tautness, a liberty of thought and action unique in the country. That this freedom of spirit degenerated often into violence was not objectionable to the young: To the mixed bag of musicians, artists, poets and miscellaneous Scouse dilettantes who congregated in the purlieus of the university and the school of art in the Fifties, rebellion was the very breath of life.

More pertinent, Liverpool was in many ways an extension of the United

States, then in the full flood of its victorious confidence. The city's links with the Atlantic seaboard of America were immemorial and innumerable and had been greatly strengthened by the war, when thousands of American soldiers and seamen had passed through the port. In some ways Liverpool was more like an American city than an English one—more akin to Baltimore, say, or the Irish parts of Boston, than to Manchester or Birmingham. The whole climate of the place, its pervasive Irishness, its gusto, its sense of detachment from the rest of England, made it amenable to new ideas from across the ocean—and to new sounds, for in the clubs of Liverpool, during the years after World War II, many of the contemporary American musical forms were first heard in Europe.

It was partly the unlikeliness of it all that so startled the British when the Beatles burst upon their platforms, screens and radios—for many of them through the unlikely medium of a televised Royal Command Variety Perform-ance ("Those in the cheap seats, clap their hands," Lennon told the astonished audience, adding with a glance toward the royal box, "the rest of you can rattle your jewelry"). But for the Beatles' own British contemporaries their impact was, above all, a message of hope and opportunity. Young Britons, they seemed to be saying, need not, after all, be stifled by class, tradition, nostalgia or conformism. Nor need they all be imitation Yanks. They could be outrageous, rebellious, North Country British. They could all be, if they wanted to be, Liverpool, Class of 1940! "The first thing we did," said Lennon once, "was to proclaim our Liverpoolness to the world and say, 'It's all right to come from Liverpool and talk like this.' " It was not just show but part of his art, part of his truth, that he soon sloughed off the suburban English his father had detected in him at Mendips and reverted to his native Scouse.

Liverpool was not known as the most patriotic of British cities. Its big Irish population was not invariably devoted to Crown and Country, and even during the war Liverpudlian dockers and shipyard workers had sometimes seemed to officers of the Royal Navy more of a nuisance than a help. Julia's choice of a middle name for John had been a sudden topical whim, and he was cruelly teased about it at school. Yet by a marvelous paradox of place and time, nobody was to do more to revive Britain's flagging fortunes and spirits at the end of the Fifties than Lennon and his fellow Beatles.

It dawned slowly upon the British that in these disrespectful young pro-vincials they possessed an incomparable national asset, but that was because British self-esteem was still rooted in old conceptions of prestige—social splen-dors, imperial triumphs, royal occasions, victories in battle and masterpieces of literature. The Beatles offered them a totally different kind of national assurance, a cocky and iconoclastic verve. To the young they seemed to demonstrate that Britain need not be, after all, pompous and second best. To older people they seemed to represent a new national fulfillment of sorts, not as high-flown, indeed, as the Churchillian or imperial satisfactions but still patriotically in-spiriting. More than that, they were a healthily revolutionary force: Almost at a stroke, it seems in retrospect, the advent of the Beatles altered the entire national attitude toward class, toward appearances, toward achievement and the nature of success.

And abroad the Beatles truly transformed the reputation of their country. Suddenly a nation hitherto seen, especially among young people, as dignified but essentially stuffy, acquired a marvelously vivid and entertaining new image. The plummy upstage accent long associated with Englishness was challenged by lively Scouse, and the kingdom seemed to be rejuvenated by the audacious example of the Beatles. In all the long centuries of British history, there have been few decades more invigorating than the Sixties: the decade of the Mini and the miniskirt, the decade of Swinging London, the decade, above all, of the Beatles, when the country seemed to have found another winning streak at last and was full of artistic vitality, commercial success and newness—new colors, new rhythms, new ideas, new money.

In 1965, just a quarter of a century after John Lennon's arrival in the Liver-pool Maternity Hospital in Oxford Street, Queen Elizabeth II of England appointed him, with his friends, to Membership of the Order of the British Empire, the lowest rank of the last surviving imperial order of chivalry, more generally reserved for minor functionaries, long-service nurses or successful charity organizers. Mimi must have been thrilled; some of her neighbors along the avenue a trifle disillusioned.

He returned his insignia to the queen anyway, just four years later, just as he absolved himself of his patriotic middle name by deed poll: His mother had been killed in a traffic accident, his father was God-knows-where and, after buying Mimi a comfortable bungalow beside the sea on the south coast of England, Lennon left Liverpool forever, finally settling down with Yoko in New York City. Always, though, Merseyside was in his eyes, in his ears. Blue suburban skies shone forever over Penny Lane: Transformed by acid and tran-scendental meditation, Strawberry Fields—where that little boy of the Forties had gone to eat ice cream at summer fêtes—became a haunting image of no-where, of nihilism. *Nothing is real, nothing to get hung about* . . .

Britain soon returned to its querulous self, when the blaze of the Sixties died away, the royal family once more replacing the Beatles as the idols of the public, and even Liverpool itself has not been very permanently affected by the mete-oric passage of Lennon and the Beatles through its life. Lively, quirky and tough as ever, it is poorer than ever too, and more dangerous. The once-great port is half dead these days, and only the ferries cross and recross the Mersey, where once the Cunarders from Manhattan moored. Unemployment is terrible, vio-lence is rampant, successive schemes of reconstruction and revival all seem to come to nothing. That half-finished cathedral outside Lennon's student window is magnificently completed now and costs a dollar a minute to maintain. To this day, wide wastelands remain from the ravages of the blitz while the grim slum tenements are scrawled with obscene graffiti and window-blocked against vandals.

Lennon is scarcely a civic martyr in this unsentimental seaport. Far more tears were shed for him in New York, I fear, than in his native place. The Cavern Club closed long ago—a car park occupies its site now—and only a

John at fifteen with skiffle band, 1955.

sad little memorial on the other side of the street commemorates the beginnings here of the most astonishing careers in the history of entertainment: FOUR LADS, as it says on its inscription, WHO SHOOK THE WORLD. Liverpudlians are often ambivalent about the Beatles, and in particular about Lennon, always the most controversial, as the most visionary, of the four. Some resent his rejection of the queen's honor. Some think of him as in some way a traitor to his origins. Lennon's acid period, of the guru and the bed-ins, did not endear him to this down-to-earth citizenry. There is no municipal memorial to the most celebrated of all Liverpool's sons (just as there is none either to the runner-up, Mr. Gladstone, another Liverpudlian who got away . . .). All the municipality offers is a map, The Beatle Trail, sold for sixty cents a copy to dedicated Beatle pilgrims.

And even the pilgrims, actually, are fewer nowadays. You see them sometimes sauntering down Penny Lane or hanging around the ghost of the Cavern, but they are aging now: They grew up with John Lennon and the Beatles; they saw themselves in the Beatles' sometimes wistful, sometimes hilarious, sometimes harsh, sometimes crazy art and, with the murder of Lennon, I suppose, they recognized the end of the affair. The legend is fading: Only the music echoes still across Merseyside—and even it is prettied up, as often as not these days, with saccharine arrangements so that the hard, strange lyrics—those unforgettable messages from other times, other dreams—sound wry and bitter by comparison.

IN TOKYO

By Donald Kirk

OKYO. The sirens screamed the air-raid warnings around bedtime on March 9, 1945, as the largest single armada of B-29s deployed so far in what the Japanese called the Pacific War began dropping thousands of incendiary bombs over Tokyo. At dawn, as the last plane disappeared on its way back to Saipan, the island taken by U.S. marines four months earlier, a quarter of the city was in ashes or burning and 83,000 people were dead. For Japan, it was a day of infamy, one to be recalled every year, an anniversary only slightly less notorious than the two dates the following August, when the dreaded B-29s dropped the first atomic bombs on the unsuspecting cities of Hiroshima and Nagasaki.

No sooner had the first sirens started wailing than Isoko Ono and her last two or three servants—the others had all been pressed into military service or into factory jobs—gathered together her three small children and vanished into the sanctuary of their nearby bunker. For the elite of the capital, the suffering during the attack was hardly comparable to that of the vast majority of urban residents squeezed into small frame houses or dingy apartment blocks without running water or flush toilets—or, in the later stages, gas or electricity. Mrs. Ono, thirty-four-year-old granddaughter of one of Japan's richest merchant princes and wife of a fast-rising bank executive, was ready for anything but a direct hit. There was a bomb shelter in the yard of her Western-style mansion in Azabu, then as now a well-to-do residential district, and enough food and water to survive underground for days.

During the bombing, Mrs. Ono had had to restrain one of the servants from poking her head out to view the eerie tableau of planes and searchlights over a night sky now turning fire orange with flames crackling from the hardest hit,

Emiko Hayashi aided in the research of this article and also served as translator and interpreter.

Yoko, not yet one, Tokyo.

most crowded neighborhoods near the fetid Sumida River, several miles to the east. The eldest child, Yoko, aged twelve, and her brother, Keisuke, three years younger, waited patiently, quiet and secure, while their mother comforted their younger sister, Setsuko, born two months before the attack on Pearl Harbor on December 8, 1941.

When they emerged, with the all-clear signals, shortly after daybreak, they discovered the metal cover of an incendiary device lying ominously in the garden. It was enough to convince Mrs. Ono that the time had come to join thousands of others—mostly those with enough money or goods to barter— in the flight from the capital. She might have gone already but for her desire to remain near her family, which included the descendants of Zenjiro Yasuda, founder of the Yasuda Bank, centerpiece of a powerful *zaibatsu*, or cartel, with interests ranging from real estate to insurance to manufacturing. Yasuda had first gone into money-lending in Edo, now Tokyo, before the downfall of the shogunate and the opening of Japan to the West in 1868, and he'd amassed a fortune of more than a billion dollars by the time of his death in 1921, when he was assassinated by a right-wing youth after refusing to give him a donation for a workers' hotel.

Mrs. Ono regarded herself as a member of the main branch of the Yasuda family since her father, Zenzaburo, had married Teruko Yasuda, the eldest of Zenjiro's five children, had adopted the family name as his own, had succeeded his father-in-law as head of the Yasuda Bank and had been inducted into the House of Peers, upper house of the Japanese diet, or parliament, in 1915. Some-time before he was killed, however, Zenjiro quarreled with Zenzaburo and passed on the main responsibility for the family fortune to his natural son, Zenjiro II. Zenzaburo, still enormously wealthy, retired and spent the next twelve or so years until he died, shortly before Yoko's birth, consorting with artists.

The youngest of Zenzaburo's four sons and four daughters, Mrs. Ono could still see some of them during the early years of the war in their homes in Tokyo, in other homes in Kamakura—a quiet town of shrines and temples some thirty miles to the south—or in the mountain resort of Hakone, east of Mount Fuji. She especially craved the associations after her husband, Eisuke, with the Yokohama Specie Bank—Japan's, and possibly the world's, largest foreign-exchange bank until the end of the war—had gone to Indochina in 1942 to serve as assistant manager of the bank's branch in Hanoi. The post was a critical one since the Japanese had more or less seized Indochina from the Vichy French two years earlier. It was the hub of their Greater East Asia Co-Prosperity Sphere, linchpin of a "southern strategy" that would take them south to the Dutch East Indies, now Indonesia, west to the borders of British India and east through the South Pacific. Around the time Eisuke Ono was flying to Hanoi on an imperial air-force plane, the Japanese were driving the British down the map of Malaya on their way to capturing Singapore and cornering ill-equipped American troops on the Bataan peninsula in the Philippines.

For Japan's merchant tycoons as much as its armed forces, the previous decade had been one of power and promise undimmed by serious thoughts of failure, much less total defeat. The Ono family, befitting its legacy, had participated in the ultimate dream—that of "catching up" with the West in high hopes of surpassing it with a great empire spanning all of Asia and much of the Pacific. Two weeks before Yoko was born on a snowy February 18, 1933, her father had gone to San Francisco in a junior post with the bank. The name Yoko, one not so common then for Japanese females as it is today, was a logical choice— it means "Ocean Child." Two and a half years later, mother and daughter crossed the Pacific for the first time to meet the hard-driving father.

For all her status and wealth, Mrs. Ono was a typical Japanese woman in her respect for the requirements of her husband's profession. She was also intensely proud of her husband for his own antecedents and accomplishments. While there might have been a tinge of the nouveau riche about the Yasuda family, Ono could claim a lineage purporting to go back to a ninth-century emperor. Yoko's great-grandfather, Atsushi Saisho, had been a viscount allied with a powerful clan in southern Japan in the campaign against the shogunate and then had served as a prefectural governor and member of the Imperial Household Council under the munificent Emperor Meiji, who moved his court from Kyoto to Tokyo after the last shogun's demise and oversaw the modernization of his country.

Saisho's lone regret was that he had no sons—a distinct misfortune in an irredeemably male-chauvinist society. Partly to compensate, he sent the eldest of his three daughters, Yoko's grandmother, Tsuruko, to study English and music at a Protestant college in the cosmopolitan Inland Sea port city of Kobe— an unusual education for a Japanese girl in those days. Having converted to Christianity, the faith of a scant one percent of all Japanese, Tsuruko then married another Christian, Eijiro Ono, on the faculty of a leading Christian college in Kyoto. The brilliant son of a proud but relatively poor family of samurai warriors, Eijiro had acquired his doctorate at the University of Michigan around 1890 with one of the best academic records ever achieved there by a foreigner.

Despite its scholarly accomplishments, though, the family had to have money, and the only way to make it was for Eijiro Ono to give up his samurai's abhorrence of trade and go into business—a decision that led him first to the Bank of Japan in 1896, and then to the presidency of the Japan Industrial Bank before he died, in 1927. Eijiro's third son, Eisuke—Yoko's father—went a traditionally elitist route with two degrees from Tokyo University—one in economics, the other in mathematics. Yet there was a difference. His talents, like his father's, weren't limited to business. An elder brother, caught in St. Petersburg at the

Yoko at two and a half, with her mother, Isoko, and father, Eisuke. San Francisco, 1935.

start of the Russian revolution, had married a Russian woman named Anna, an accomplished violinist and pianist, and almost everyone in the family took lessons from her. Eisuke was one of her best students and played the piano constantly during vacations at the family's sprawling summer home in Karui-zawa, holiday retreat for the Japanese upper classes, on a cool plateau some 100 miles north of Tokyo.

Eisuke Ono's love for piano playing helped make him a popular figure, and he entertained at least one eligible girl by playing duets with her. Among the most sought-after bachelors in the Karuizawa set, he met the future Mrs. Ono, eight years younger than he, not through the usual *omiai*, or arranged meeting, but socially around town. At first, Zenzaburo Yasuda was not altogether certain Eisuke was good enough for his daughter. She had a fortune that far surpassed his—when she was a little girl, her father had rewarded her with diamonds for good report cards and insisted she go everywhere by carriage or private car. In the end, however, Eisuke's impeccable pedigree, good looks, intellect and charm were enough to convince Isoko's father to sanction the match.

Mrs. Ono returned her father's love by caring for him until his death. With Eisuke in San Francisco, she took charge of her parents' home and nursed her mother, who by then was seriously ill. On a hill behind the grounds of the imperial palace, the house commanded a view of a third of Tokyo, a panorama now obstructed by high-rise apartment and office buildings. The style was prototypical Japanese with sliding screens opening onto rooms with tatami-matted floors and windows made of paper. A staff of thirty servants and gar-deners scuttled about, bowing deeply and respectfully to the orders of Mrs. Ono, known for a biting tongue despite her classically correct language and charming smile. Yoko's earliest memory, she told relatives years later, was of getting lost in the garden.

For Yoko, though, the servants were her warmest friends, the source of love and comfort in place of an ambitious mother who sometimes had little time for her. On an excursion to Yosemite Park soon after their arrival in San Francisco, Yoko stood in front of some elderly women in the dining room of their hotel and surprised her mother more than anybody else by singing Japanese children's songs that her parents had no idea she knew. She concluded with a polite curtsy, holding her skirt with two fingers of each hand and tapping the floor with her right toe behind her left foot—a fitting finale to a performance she could only have learned from her doting nannies. Yoko's mother promptly packed her off to a special private school where she began learning tap-dancing and Mother Goose.

The West Coast idyll explains much that followed. Mrs. Ono, Yoko and Keisuke, born in December of 1936, had to return to Tokyo in the spring of 1937 as Japanese troops swarmed over northern China and tension heightened be-tween the U.S. and Japan. A year later, Mrs. Ono enrolled Yoko in the kindergarten of the same expensive school from which she herself had graduated, placing her in the music group. Not convinced Yoko was getting the best, Mrs. Ono sent her the following year to the more prestigious Gakushuin, or Peers' School, then open only to those with relatives in the imperial family or the House of Peers.

Yoko had finished just one year at Gakushuin before her mother boldly sailed back to San Francisco in 1940 with her two children and took the train to New York to rejoin her husband, then in the bank's Manhattan office. She did it for fear the U.S. would stop all Japanese from coming, and she was afraid she might not see her husband again for years. Yoko studied at a public school near her home on Long Island—which solidified her grasp of English and, more important, gave her a certain brashness and cultural ambivalence that would forever distinguish her among her more conventional classmates. By now,

Yoko (front row, second from right), age eight, watching a school play in Tokyo.

though, the U.S. and Japan were on the brink of war. Mrs. Ono and children sailed from San Francisco for the last time in the spring of 1941, and her husband left several weeks later, and was next stationed in Hanoi.

Regardless of the boasts of the militarists now in almost total control, Japan was beginning to suffer from the hardships of a decade of fighting in China, hardships exacerbated by the cutoff of oil and other supplies by the ABCD powers—America, Britain, China and the Dutch. Housewives had to get along without cotton and make do with a synthetic rayonlike fabric that seemed to disintegrate in the laundry. There was almost no rubber for sale on the open market, no gasoline or oil for private use. Buses and taxis chugged along on charcoal-burning engines. With the onset of food rationing, farmers hawked black-market produce door to door. After Pearl Harbor, as the fighting expanded across Southeast Asia, an egg was, for most Japanese, a delicacy, fish a weekly treat and meat simply unavailable. Housewives learned to look for "edible weeds" by the roads, to pick weevils from their rice rations and to use the excrement of silkworms as a substitute for soap.

If ninety-nine percent of the Japanese population shared such hardships, though, Yoko was firmly entrenched in the tiny sliver that was largely immune to them until the final stages of the war. True, her mother had had to turn in her diamonds and platinum to her husband's bank for use in the war effort and scrape along with just a few servants, but the Ono family could always get enough food from friends, relatives and business associates around Karuizawa and Kamakura if supplies ran low in Tokyo. Nor did Yoko have to endure severe problems of adjustment from having been schooled in an enemy country: When she returned to Japan, her parents sent her to Keimei Gakuen, a Christian academy opened in 1940 specifically for children who had been educated abroad. They "are precious treasures to a nation," said Takasumi Mitsui, Oxford-educated founder of the school and one of the heirs of the Mitsui fortune, larger still than that of the Yasuda family. "The students' overseas experiences richly benefit their native country."

Mitsui and his wife, Hideko, both of whom had converted to the Church of England at Oxford, had no notion of indoctrination and encouraged students to speak English and other alien tongues in class. School officials grew accustomed to humoring the *kempeitai* or "thought police" during monthly visits that might have resulted in harassment and arrest for less highly placed objects of suspicion.

For three years Yoko attended Keimei Gakuen, on the Mitsui estate just a twenty-minute walk from her home, until, in 1944, the primary-school division was moved to another Mitsui family holding west of the city, as American planes began bombing with increasing frequency. At that time, however, Yoko's mother decided she wanted her at home. "If Yoko is going to die," said Mrs. Ono, "she should die with her family."

Yoko left her elementary-school teachers with a lasting impression of a strong girl who had her own ideas about art and drama—which were distinctly Westernized. The fact that the authorities banned popular Western music and movies made little difference. Her uninhibited laughter, her flair for dramatic gestures, her American-style skirts and blouses were all extremely unusual, even among the elite at that time.

In an autobiographical account published in 1974 by *Bungei Shunju*, one of Japan's most prestigious monthly magazines, Yoko wrote, "My father was always overseas on business trips," referring to his assignments in the U.S. and Hanoi, "and my mother was busy with her friends in Tokyo." Whatever money could buy, though, Yoko was likely to get: "There were several maids and private tutors beside me. I had one private tutor who read me the Bible and another for-eign tutor who gave me piano lessons, and my attendant taught me Buddhism."

Yoko complained that she was isolated from her family even at mealtimes: "I had every meal by myself, alone. I was told the meal was ready and went into the dining room, where there was a long table for me to eat at. My private tutor watched me silently, sitting on the chair beside me." At the country home of her mother's family in Kamakura, she found solace in picnic lunches alone in the garden: "It was so large that when the eight women who were hired to weed finished weeding all over the garden at once, the weeds were already grown where they started." In her loneliness she would seek out the daughter of the caretaker: "I would ask her what she wanted to play, and she would say, 'I would do whatever you wish to, miss,' or, 'What would you like to do, miss?'"

Not that Yoko's mother did not care for her. If anything, she may have sown the seeds of a mother-daughter conflict by being overly protective and proud. When Yoko was a baby, her mother asked her nursemaids not to rock her in their arms when they carried her for fear the motion would leave her brainless. "She also told them not to help me get up when I tumbled down because I had to learn to stand up by myself without help," Yoko reminisced. "I still re-member vaguely several women in kimono staring at me without offering a hand while I was trying to get up from the ground."

Mrs. Ono's ideas about child care were to have a bizarre influence on Yoko's sensibilities: "My attendants always carried absorbent cotton dipped in alcohol on an occasion like a family trip. They disinfected every place I was likely to touch on a train. That was because of my mother's partiality for cleanliness. Thus, I became sensitive to cleanliness too. Once I dropped a pencil I borrowed from a classmate sitting next to me because it was still warm from her body temperature. Even now I find it unpleasant to sit on a cushion or chair that still retains the temperature of somebody who had just been sitting there." Such compulsive maternal concern—similar to that of millions of other Japanese mothers bent on perpetuating rigid social standards and ensuring the best in education, marriage prospects and jobs for their offspring — doubtless weighed more heavily on Yoko than did the war.

If her mother's love was a burden, however, it also protected Yoko from any danger. Mrs. Ono did not hesitate to ask Yoko's school to list her as a primary rather than middle-school student even after she had passed her twelfth birthday in 1945. By that time, middle- and high-school students had to labor in munitions factories, targets of bombing. Keimei Gakuen had such connections that its students could work after hours in the Tokyo schoolhouse rather than go to a factory. Nonetheless, the building was wiped out by bombs on the night of May 24, 1945. Luckily, the students were at home.

The tragedy then befalling Japan did not become real for Yoko until her mother sent her, along with her brother and sister and one of the last Ono servants, to a small farming village south of Karuizawa after the bombing through the night of March 9. A friend had suggested the village as a congenial place, but by the time Mrs. Ono arrived several days later, after a slow ride on a crowded train running on an irregular wartime schedule, she knew she was far out of her natural milieu. Her image of the warmhearted yokels was shattered by the sight of ill-clad farmers and their children, clearly jealous and instinctively eager to gain revenge for centuries of social injustices at the hands of the high and mighty.

Farmers throughout the region unhesitatingly held up the Japanese elite for all the money they could get for precious foodstuffs, which the pampered rich had no idea how to grow on their own. Mrs. Ono claimed she had given all her jewelry to the government, but she had to sell expensive kimonos and other possessions for food. In one typical transaction, she got sixty kilograms of rice for a large German-built sewing machine. When her last servant was finally summoned to duty, Mrs. Ono had to carry her youngest child, Setsuko, on her back in Japanese style for the first time. She and Yoko got used to hauling a cart on their rounds to the homes of truculent farmers in search of food, and Mrs. Ono once had to pull the cart from the mud of a rice paddy — an edifying experience for a woman whose hands had never been callused before.

The Ono family also encountered firsthand a much more serious social problem — that of the Buraku, a subclass of butchers and leatherworkers victimized by discrimination for centuries. Yoko, Keisuke and Setsuko sometimes played with Buraku children, who struck Mrs. Ono as in no way inferior to the farmers. When a neighbor spied her one day buying a stack of sandals from a Buraku peddler, he demanded that her landlord expel her and her family from the farmhouse. The request might have been honored were Mrs. Ono not paying an exorbitant rent for the dubious privilege of staying there — and still more for the corn planted up to the front door.

Life in the local school was worse, if anything, for the Ono children. The farm children resented the presence of the educated Ono kids, and older boys teased them perpetually. They frightened Keisuke so badly by chasing him with a cow that he dropped out of school. Yoko, though, was made of sterner stuff. She stared them down and shouted at them. Indeed, to those who saw her she seemed to revel in the whole adventure. She braided her hair, went about in *monpe*—rough farmer's trousers—carried a rucksack on her back and appeared exhilarated whenever she showed up in that garb at her cousins' villa in Karuizawa.

The interlude in rural living did not end until several months after Emperor Hirohito had broadcast Japan's surrender on August 15, 1945—a message the Ono family missed hearing since they had no radio. Mrs. Ono, fearful of what the American conquerors would do, and far from certain if her husband was dead or alive in Hanoi, waited until she knew the occupation would be a benevolent one before she brought her children to her parents' home in Kamakura. They returned to discover much of Tokyo reduced to rubble in the final months of bombing. Half-starved men and women, their arms and legs thin as sticks, their faces drawn, lined up at flimsy stalls to buy American C-rations and whatever else they could find. Passengers piled on the roofs of jam-packed trains, and huge, well-scrubbed GIs directed traffic.

For all Japanese, however, the war's end brought profound relief. The Onos had not heard a word from Eisuke during the last year of the war, while U.S. planes and navy vessels were tearing apart Japanese shipping. Then, in early 1946, a bank official told them he was alive—and that he had won a promotion. For several months before the surrender he had been manager of the Yokohama Specie Bank's Hanoi branch—a post of sufficient stature to earn him special, if annoying, recognition. Interned by Nationalist Chinese forces who temporarily took over Hanoi, he was returned to Tokyo in the hold of a Japanese troopship and listed by occupation authorities among some 1,500 prominent executives who were to be expelled from any further position in business or industry.

The purge that caught Yoko's father in its web reflected the American view that Japan's *zaibatsu* and other big-business interests were as much to blame as the militarists for plunging Japan into war. Within weeks after the Supreme Commander Allied Powers, General Douglas MacArthur, arrived in Japan, on August 30, 1945, President Truman ordered "a program for the dissolution of the large industrial and banking combinations which have exercised control of a great part of Japan's trade and industry." Among the holding companies at the top of the list was the Yasuda *zaibatsu*, fourth largest after Mitsui, Mitsubishi and Sumitomo. The primary banking target was Ono's old Yokohama Specie Bank, which had dutifully served all the *zaibatsu*.

The next year, when ordered to purge all "active exponents of militant nationalism and aggression," MacArthur branded the industrialists and bankers as "feudalistic overlords" who had "held the lives and destiny of the majority of Japan's people in virtual slavery" and, "in closest affiliation with the military, geared the country with both the tools and the will to make aggressive war." The titans of the Japanese economy would now have to scramble through a turbulent period of drastic reorganization to survive. But they succeeded totally —initially by winning the sympathy of American diplomats and business leaders who recognized their abilities and permitted them to return to their old jobs. The *zaibatsu* emerged stronger than ever and, in 1947, Ono turned up at the headquarters of the newly formed Bank of Tokyo, successor to the Yokohama Specie Bank, first as behind-the-scenes adviser and then as a full-fledged executive.

The travail of Yoko's father was part of a national drama she could observe from afar, almost abstractly, after re-entering Gakushuin, the Peers' School, at the start of the new academic year in April of 1946. While millions of Japanese children attended classes in old barracks, Gakushuin, naturally, had the best that money and influence could obtain—the spacious grounds and facilities formerly used by the imperial palace horse guards several miles from the palace itself.

The character of the school broadened somewhat after a new Japanese constitution was adopted at MacArthur's behest in 1946. Among other things, the constitution did away with the peerage and ruled that only the emperor and members of his immediate family could retain their noble titles. The only students in Yoko's school left with titles were Emperor Hirohito's two sons— Akihito, the crown prince, in the same class as Yoko, and his younger brother, Yoshi, now Prince Hitachi, two years behind them. Recognizing new realities, the school withdrew its requirement that all students be of noble blood—a cosmetic change of no immediate impact on the students' lives.

In that kind of environment Yoko could flourish as oblivious to the throes of the American occupation and Japanese recovery as she had been to much of the war. The worst daily challenge she had to face was the two-hour train ride from the family home in Kamakura, where she lived until they moved to another fashionable neighborhood closer to the center of Tokyo. In the early years before full train service was restored, she and her friends sometimes jumped in and out of the windows to get seats, and they often ran the last fifteen minutes from the nearest station in Tokyo to the school. Some of the other girls were thin from the war—so thin they felt a tingling in their arms and legs—but Yoko was healthy, even beautiful.

From the start of middle school Yoko struck her classmates as more mature and worldly than most of them. She was, in fact, older than the average since she had fallen behind during the war. But she was also much more outspoken than the others—who had been brought up never to question, much less flout, the edicts of elders or teachers. Yoko was superb in both English and Japanese —she impressed teachers and classmates alike by reading widely from complicated books and plays in both languages. Gorky's *The Lower Depths* was among her favorites. Sometimes, too, she would amaze her conventional friends by writing a short novel when they were assigned merely to describe a class outing.

The center of attention, Yoko was both popular and feared by those around her. Yet she was also a conservative, well-spoken girl who seldom deviated far from the norms of her class or society. She might talk loudly and knowledgeably about exploits real or imagined, but she was no more likely than her classmates to violate the rules of either school or home. One afternoon on the way back to Kamakura she told a friend, now the wife of a doctor, that she knew how to handle men, smoke cigarettes and drink—all taboo for Japanese girls in their teens. When a man beside them on the train indignantly protested, Yoko calmed him down with a lengthy theoretical recitation of her views, expressed in the most cultured, polite language she could muster.

One of the marvels of the Japanese recovery, in fact, was that the war and occupation had remarkably little effect on fundamental social behavior. Like students in most Japanese schools, Yoko continued to wear a precisely regimented navy-style uniform and would bow respectfully before her teachers. Both her school and her family forbade her going anywhere so déclassé as one of the new coffee shops then opening up all over Tokyo, much less entering a nightclub or dance hall, and she spent much of her spare time giving English lessons to neighbors and reading. On her tight schedule she could contemplate some of what was happening around her: Luxury goods were showing up on black markets, bar girls and prostitutes were marrying GIs by the thousands, once-empty streets were filling with traffic and piles of structural steel and concrete were shooting up from the ruins. Japan was again prospering—from selling goods to U.S. forces fighting in Korea. But an hour sipping tea with girl-friends after school was the closest Yoko came to illicit adventure.

The sensitivities of Yoko's family conditioned her against the ill-mannered Americans in their midst. Isolated by the shogunate from dealing with foreigners for more than two centuries, Japanese instinctively harbor ambivalent feelings toward foreigners. The seventeenth-century shoguns viewed the early missionaries as apostles of war and conquest, and Japanese today are fearful of foreign attempts to penetrate their markets, spread their culture and control them militarily. For the students at Gakushuin, the famous picture of Hirohito in formal attire beside MacArthur, in open-necked shirt, taken at their first meeting at the American embassy in September of 1945, symbolized Japanese class against foreign gaucherie. They laughed at MacArthur for not wearing a necktie!

Yoko's mother had still more personal reasons for holding the newcomers in contempt. While few of them were murderers, rapists or bandits, they had the execrable taste to wear shoes inside the Ono family houses rented to them during the occupation, to tear up tatami mats and even knock down the walls of rooms that did not seem expansive enough. They showed what the Onos regarded as the worst middle-American touch when they got rid of exquisite furniture and replaced it with synthetic trash more appropriate for a hotel room. They also offended Japanese landlords everywhere by their habit of slapping white paint over subtly hued beige and brown interiors.

But the Americans were conquerors and could afford whatever they wanted. A few months' worth of rationed cigarettes could buy patches of real estate now worth thousands if not millions of dollars, and Americans rode free in their own special railroad cars while the Japanese scrounged for space in the rear. Such was the prestige of the Americans in those days that members of the Ono and Yasuda families attended a party proffered by an American marine renting one of their villas in Kamakura—and were embarrassed by his oafish manners and the social inexperience of his young American wife. The encounter typified myriad episodes that confirmed the sometimes-subconscious anti-foreignism of the most internationally minded Japanese.

Scrupulously shielded, Yoko pursued her own interests. When she tired of reading, she turned to the drama club at school to show off her good looks and sometimes extroverted personality. By the time she got to high school she was the star, director and often writer of most of the plays. "We decided who would do the leading roles by vote, and Yoko made us vote again when she couldn't get a good part," said one of her classmates. "She never felt happy unless she was treated like a queen." Through it all her mother supported her inclination to be different. "She used to tell me that even a woman could become a diplomat or prime minister if she was as bright as I," said Yoko. "She also said I should not be so foolish as to get married or that I should not be foolish enough to have children." But she was apparently dismayed by Yoko's later artistic inclinations. She may have seemed "rather progressive as a woman of those days," Yoko conceded, "but she preferred to see me as a successful woman in an existing society rather than as an underground artist." (Later, when Yoko was displaying her art in New York and London, her mother would remark, in polite understatement, "It's regrettable you do odd things though I know you are bright.")

As long as she was in Gakushuin, however, the Ono parents were delighted by her associations. In the final year of high school, the girls could appear in plays with the boys and rehearsed at the boys' school. One of her most ardent admirers was Prince Yoshi, who watched her rehearse and sometimes ventured to the girls' school to discuss her writing. Boys from the best families let it be known—discreetly, through their careful parents—that they would like to marry her. For her part, Yoko made at least one "unauthorized" trip to the boys' school and shocked her teachers by questioning the rigid rule against going there without permission.

Yoko's underlying rebellion was basically directed against her mother. Her

Yoko with design for poster announcing concert, 1961.

father was a mostly absent figure during her childhood—who never spoke harshly to her and encouraged her interest in art and music and proffered advice in whatever time he had to spare. It was a typical Japanese family split— mother and daughter knowing each other too well while the father remained a kind but remote figure, preoccupied with his man's world of business and success. But Yoko occasionally revealed how much she needed her father's blessing: When she decided to apply for admission as the first female student to enter the philosophy course at Gakushuin University in 1952, after having first planned to go to the Tokyo Music School, she cabled her father, then in New York with the Bank of Tokyo, for permission. Her loving father unhesi- tatingly assented. The desire to be closer to her father may explain in part why she dropped out of Gakushuin University after two semesters, moved with her family to her father's home in Scarsdale as she neared her twentieth birthday and entered Sarah Lawrence, in nearby Bronxville.

When she left Gakushuin, her former teachers expected nothing but the best from her. One of them, recommending her to Sarah Lawrence, wrote that she would be "a bridge between the United States and Japan." Prince Yoshi was sorry to see her go. He sent her an autographed picture of himself—and a *waka*, a traditional form of poetry that all members of the royal family are tutored to write:

> Let us ask the high wave from far away
> If the person I dream of is safe or not

So moved was Yoko that she kept the paper in which the picture was wrapped. Later, she was to amuse her classmates at Sarah Lawrence by con- fessing that she had never so much as held the hand of any of her boyfriends.

1966-1976

A CHRONOLOGY

By Ben Fong-Torres

John and Yoko's romance began at about the same time that Rolling Stone *started publishing, and their public years were thoroughly chronicled in the magazine. The articles in this section that follow the Chronology represent the highlights of that coverage.*

1966

NOVEMBER 9. John Lennon meets Yoko Ono at the Indica Gallery in London. John has had a hard day's year: He's gotten the Beatles into a popularity contest with Jesus; the band's had an album pulled off the market because of the cover (which had the Beatles as butchers in the valley of the dolls); they've been attacked by a crowd at the Manila airport after inadvertently insulting the president of the Philippines; their manager, Brian Epstein, has attempted suicide; the Beatles have played what will be their last concerts . . . and the first rumblings about a breakup have begun.

But they've kept making hits—so far this year four singles and two albums, the latest being *Revolver*. Recent albums have been rife with drug references and, just two years after conquering the teenyboppers of the world, the Beatles, along with the Stones and Bob Dylan, are overlords of the fast-flowering psychedelic scene.

All of this means very little to Yoko Ono, avant-garde artist. When John Lennon shows up at a preview of her exhibition in a West End gallery, she has no clue who he is. Lennon climbs the ladder in the middle of the room, peers through the tiny telescope she's chained to a canvas hanging from the ceiling, and likes what he reads through the spyglass: YES. Next, he spots a sign reading HAMMER A NAIL IN. He asks Yoko if he can, but she says no, the show hasn't officially opened yet.

"But," John says later, "the owner whispered to her, 'Let him hammer a nail in. You know, he's a millionaire. He might buy it.' And finally she said, 'Okay. You can hammer a nail in for five shillings.' So smartass says, 'Well, I'll give you an imaginary five shillings and hammer an imaginary nail in.' And that's when we really met. That's when we locked eyes and she got it and I got it and, as they say in all the interviews we do, the rest is history."

1967

SEPTEMBER. John, just back from a visit with the Maharishi Mahesh Yogi (a.k.a. Sexy Sadie), sponsors Yoko's

"Half-Wind Show" at the Lisson Gallery in London. Subtitled "Yoko Plus Me" (referring to John, who insists on remaining anonymous and doesn't attend the show), the exhibit consists of everyday objects—a chair, a washbasin, a pillow—all cut in half.

On the Beatles front, *Sgt. Pepper's Lonely Hearts Club Band* is just finishing up a fifteen-week stay at the top of the album charts when Brian Epstein commits suicide. The group will never quite be the same but nevertheless begins work on the film *Magical Mystery Tour*.

1968

Sexy Sadie what have you done.
You made a fool of everyone.

FEBRUARY. John and fellow Beatles go to India for a Transcendental Meditation course at the Maharishi's academy. After hearing talk about the guru trying to get into the vibes of some of the women students, the Beatles leave. John breaks the news to the Maharishi. "I said, 'We're leaving.' 'Why?' he asked, and I said, 'If you're so *cosmic*, you'll know why.'"

I want you / I want you so bad
I want you / I want you so bad
It's driving me mad, it's driving
me mad . . .

Before and during his stay in India, John gets cards and letters from Yoko, with directions like: BREATHE or HIT A WALL WITH YOUR HEAD or KEEP LAUGHING FOR A WEEK. Or, simply, to think of her. He does. "These crazy letters kept coming, driving me mad," he confesses later. "But it was great, too."

MAY. One night, with Cynthia away in Greece, John decides it's now or never, rings up Yoko and invites her over to his country home in Weybridge. Her husband is in France. "We were very shy at first," Yoko would recall. "I mean, he just couldn't say, 'Okay, let's make it.' So he said we could go upstairs to his studio and make some music or stay downstairs and chat." They go upstairs, John plays her a variety of his experimental and comic tapes and Yoko suggests a little do-it-ourselves. John picks up the story: "So we made *Two Virgins*. It was midnight when we started and it was dawn when we finished, and then we made love. It was very beautiful."

The ballad of John and Yoko begins.

JUNE 15. By now, Paul has told the world about the Fab Four's excursions into LSD; the band has taken a crack at post-Epstein business with Apple; and John has moved out of his house, and in with Yoko, in a London flat owned by Ringo.

John begins working with Yoko on artistic ventures. They participate in an exhibit of sculpture at Coventry Cathedral by planting two acorns in pots. "One faced east and the other faced west, to symbolize that East and West have met through Yoko and me," John explains afterward. "In fifty years' time people will understand what we're trying to say when there are a couple of lovely great oak trees up there rather than all those bits of old iron in funny shapes." But, in much less than fifty years the acorns are taken by fans, and when John and

Yoko replant new ones, the site is watched by a round-the-clock guard.

JUNE 18. A stage production of John's book, *In His Own Write*, opens at the Old Vic. John arrives with Yoko and reporters shout at him: "Where is your wife?"

"I suppose I've spoiled my image," he says. But he didn't care about cat-calls, from the press, from the fans or from fellow Beatles.

JULY 1. John puts on his own art exhibit. Called "You Are Here" and openly dedicated "To Yoko from John, with Love," it features a seemingly random display of charity collection boxes and a round white canvas. John opens the exhibit by releasing 365 white balloons, each stamped YOU ARE HERE, into the evening sky. "I declare the balloons . . . high!"

AUGUST 22. Cynthia sues for divorce. "My marriage to Cyn was not unhappy," John would recount. "But it was just a normal marital state where nothing happened and which we continued to sustain. You sustain it until you meet someone who suddenly sets you alight."

OCTOBER 18. Just before noon, a dozen police officers, followed by two huge dope-sniffing Alsatian police dogs, knock on the door of John and Yoko's apartment and arrest them for possession of an ounce or so of hash. They are booked at a nearby station and released on bail. John will later be fined 150 pounds after admitting to possession of cannabis resin. John insists the dope has been planted, and later says he pleaded guilty only to keep Yoko, who was pregnant, from

having to go through a trial. But the bust will cause trouble with U.S. immigration officials a few years later.

NOVEMBER 8. Cynthia gets her divorce. John and Yoko take out an ad in music publications in support of the Peace Ship, an independent radio station that broadcasts peace messages to the disputants in the Middle East. Yoko, who is expecting a baby in February, has complications and enters Queen Charlotte's Maternity Hospital. John camps at her side, in a sleeping bag. They make a tape recording of the baby's heartbeat. Two weeks later, on the day the White Album is released, Yoko miscarries.

NOVEMBER 11. *Unfinished Music #1: Two Virgins* is released. Recorded by John and Yoko that first night together, it's an abstract collage of electronic sounds. But what causes the most noise is the cover photo. The nude shot, says Yoko, was John's idea. "I suppose he just thought it would be effective. He took the picture himself, with an automatic camera. It's nice.

Unfinished Music No. 1: Two Virgins, 1968.

The picture isn't lewd or anything like that. Basically we are both very shy and square people. We'd be the first to be embarrassed if anyone were to invite us to a nude party."

DECEMBER 11. John and Yoko sing "Yer Blues" in the Stones film, Rock 'n' Roll Circus.

Bagism, Shagism, Dragism,
    Madism,
Ragism, Tagism, This-ism, That-
    ism, Is-m is-m is-m.
All we are saying is give peace a
    chance.

DECEMBER 18. John and Yoko appear at the Underground's Christmas party called the "Alchemical Wedding" at the Royal Albert Hall. But they don't actually appear; they're onstage, tied up and writhing inside a white bag. This, says Yoko, is "bagism," inspired by The Little Prince and its theme: "The essential is invisible to the eye." By staying hidden, she says, the force of what they are saying will not be misinterpreted by physical appearance. The press doesn't get it.

1969

JANUARY 2. As a group, the Beatles are pretty much over, but they meet a contractual obligation for a third film by letting cameras roll while they work on the "Get Back" sessions for what will become Let It Be. After more than four weeks and two hundred songs, they end it all with an outdoor set January 30, atop Apple's headquarters building. All together, John would confess, the sessions were "six weeks of misery." It's Paul who's

determined to keep the Beatles going, and who dominates the sessions. But Lennon still manages to come up with the punch line for the movie: "I hope we passed the audition."

FEBRUARY 3. The Beatles appoint Allen Klein as adviser. John is his champion; Paul, who's about to marry Linda Eastman (whose father and brother are lawyers) opposes the move.

MARCH 2. John and Yoko participate in an experimental jazz concert in Cambridge. While Yoko sings, John crouches at her feet, his back to the audience, and sends out electric-guitar feedback.

Finally made the plane into Paris
Honeymooning down by the Seine.
Peter Brown called to say,
You can make it O.K.,
You can get married in Gibraltar
    near Spain . . .

MARCH 20. After a holiday in Paris, John and Yoko jet to Gibraltar and marry. For the morning ceremony, witnessed by two Apple executives, Yoko wears a white minidress, a wide-brimmed white hat, white socks and white tennis shoes. John wears a white jacket and off-white pants with his white tennies. "We're going to stage many happenings," says Yoko, "and this marriage was one of them." But if the wedding is relatively private—Paul and Linda's a week before drew a mob of screaming girls, shrill shades of Beatlemania—the honeymoon is another matter, another John-and-Yoko event.

MARCH 22. The happy couple moves into the presidential suite of the Amsterdam Hilton for a week-long

"Bed-in for Peace," wide open to the press. John explains: "Just suppose we had wanted to go to Capri for a secret honeymoon, like Jackie Kennedy had. The press would have been bound to find out. So we thought we might as well do something constructive with the publicity."

1969 is the year of Richard Nixon's inauguration, of campus riots over Vietnam, of black unrest in the wake of Martin Luther King's assassination —and of John and Yoko. "We are both artists," says John. "Peace is our art. . . . We stand a chance of influencing other young people. And it is they who will rule the world tomorrow."

The newspaper said,
She's gone to his head,
They look just like two Gurus
  in drag . . .

The press visits—and attacks— this eccentric pair sitting up in bed talking about world peace. Some reporters zoom in on Yoko and call her ugly. "I don't think she's ugly," says an upset John, "I think she's beautiful."

Memo to area secretaries from headquarters of the Beatles (U.S.A.) Fan Club, Ltd., on the occasion of the wedding:

"Please try to understand that we should at least give Yoko the same chance we are going to be giving Linda and that Maureen and Patti got! I know this news is shocking, but I suppose if it will make John happy, we should all be very enthused too."

John and Yoko continue to blitz the media on behalf of peace and art. For a press conference introducing their first

joint venture in filmmaking, called *Rape* (*Film No. 6*), they perform "bagism" on a tabletop. Later, they announce a "Nuts for Peace" campaign. They've sent acorns to fifty world leaders, and they suggest that said leaders hold peace talks inside a giant bag. John gets his middle name officially changed from Winston to Ono, in a ceremony on the site of the Beatles' last performance, on top of old Apple.

MAY 5. John and Yoko buy Tittenhurst Park, a Georgian mansion on seventy-two acres in Ascot, in the hilly English countryside. But they are by no means homebodies. In mid-month, they try to join Ringo, Peter Sellers and a group from the promotional tour for *The Magic Christian* aboard the Queen Elizabeth II in order to cross to the United States for a bed-in. But John fails to get a visa.

MAY 9. John and Yoko's album, *Music No. 2: Life with the Lions*, is released. The album comprises their March jazz concert and the recorded

Unfinished Music No. 2: Life with the Lions, 1969.

heartbeat of the baby Yoko lost in November.

During the month, they've seen two other Beatles at a *Magic Christian* party, and John records "The Ballad of John and Yoko" with McCartney on piano, drums and harmony. But in his own mind, John is long past the Beatles. He and Yoko have formed Bag Productions for records, films and books, and in late May they perform a "Lie-in for Peace" in the Bahamas, then fly on to Montreal for a ten-day bed-in. During the event, they record "Give Peace a Chance" on a mobile recorder with harmonic help from Timothy Leary, Tommy Smothers and the Canadian chapter of Hare Krishna. Released in July, it's John's first single without the rest of the boys.

JULY 1. As John drives through Scotland on a holiday with Yoko, her daughter, Kyoko, and his son, Julian, he loses control and the car goes into a ditch. All are treated for cuts and shock. After John recovers, he joins Paul, George and Ringo at the EMI Abbey Road studios. There, they manage to overcome personal and business disputes—Allen Klein and Lee Eastman are fighting for control of the Beatles' business interests—to come up with one more album.

You never give me your money
You only give me your funny paper
And in the middle of negotiations
*   you break down . . .*

SEPTEMBER. John hates *Abbey Road*; in Los Angeles courtrooms the Beatles are being connected—by song lyrics off the White Album—to the Manson family murders; Paul McCartney is rumored dead; Beatles business is a continuing hassle and John and Yoko have taken to sniffing heroin on occasion ("When we were in real pain. We got such a hard time from everyone," says John). But they haven't lost their humor. For "Two Evenings with John and Yoko" at the New Cinema Club in London, including the premiere of *Self Portrait*, a slow-motion film of John's penis, the Lennons hire a man and woman to substitute for them. Hidden inside a bag, the surrogates show up at the theater in a white Rolls-Royce. To the accompaniment of flashbulbs, they hobble down the aisle and sit on the stage, chanting "Hare Krishna" while various John and Yoko films unspool. John captures the audience's reactions on film.

In midmonth, John and Yoko—the real ones—pop up at a "Rock 'n' Roll Revival Concert" in Toronto, joining a band including Eric Clapton and Klaus Voormann. "I can't remember when I had such a good time," John says afterward. "We did all the old things from the Cavern days in Liverpool ["Blue Suede Shoes," "Dizzy Miss Lizzie"]. Yoko, who you can say was playing bag, was holding a piece of paper with the words to the songs in front of me. But then she suddenly disappeared into her bag in the middle of the performance and I had to make them up because it's so long since I sang them that I've forgotten most of them. It didn't seem to matter." He wants to go back to playing rock onstage, he says, but not with the Beatles. He's told McCartney and Allen

Wedding Album, 1969.

Klein about his intentions to leave the group, but he's been convinced to keep it quiet. "Business-wise, you know."

OCTOBER 20. "Cold Turkey," written during the summer, is released as a single, credited to John Lennon and the Plastic Ono Band. Also out: John and Yoko's *Wedding Album*, a boxed set of two records, a booklet of press clippings, a postcard, a photo of a piece of wedding cake and several wedding pictures.

NOVEMBER. *Live Peace in Toronto*, an album of John and Yoko at the rock-revival concert, is released. It'll hit the charts in January and stay on for almost eight months, peaking at Number Ten. In late November, John returns his M.B.E. medal to the queen.

DECEMBER 15. John and Yoko wind up the year with a Christmas peace campaign pegged to the slogan, "War Is Over! If You Want It." They kick it off with a concert at the Lyceum Theatre in London to benefit the United Nations Children's Fund. Guests include George Harrison, Keith Moon, Eric Clapton and Billy Preston.

DECEMBER 16. John and Yoko fly to Toronto to announce plans for a peace-and-music festival the following July in nearby Mosport Park. They set up headquarters at singer Ronnie Hawkins's farm, hosting reporters and other visitors. Three phone lines are installed for calls to radio stations around the United States. While in Canada, John signs over four thousand of his erotic lithographs (they're handed to and taken from him bucket-brigade style), talks with Marshall McLuhan on CBS television and has lengthy meetings with the Le Dain Drug Commission and with Prime Minister Pierre Trudeau. The Lennons are getting through. Trudeau expresses support for the festival and, at home, A.T.V. names Lennon a "Man of the Decade," along with John F. Kennedy and Chairman Mao.

"Henry Ford knew how to sell cars by advertising," says John. "I'm selling peace, and Yoko and I are just one big advertising campaign. It may make people laugh, but it may make them think, too. Really, we're Mr. and Mrs. Peace."

1970

JANUARY. John and Yoko begin what they call "Year One for Peace" with a new look. They get radical haircuts and donate the trimmings to Michael Abdul Malik, a.k.a. Michael X, who uses the proceeds from the hair sale to start up a black-culture center in London. (Months later, the Blackhouse will burn down, and Malik will be arrested for robbery. In 1973 he will be convicted and hanged for two murders.)

JANUARY 15. John's lithographs are displayed at the London Arts Gallery. The next day, Scotland Yard seizes eight of the prints for possible prosecution on grounds of obscenity and shuts down the gallery for a few hours. The drawings depict him and Yoko making love in various positions. Asked why there appeared to be an emphasis on cunnilingus, John smiles and says: "Because I like it."

JANUARY 26. John writes, records and mixes "Instant Karma!" in one day, with Phil Spector doing the production. "I wrote it for breakfast, recorded it for lunch and we're putting it out for dinner," says John.

FEBRUARY 26. John disavows any connection with the Toronto Peace Festival, which is in organizational shambles and, ultimately, doesn't happen.

MARCH 2. A bored Lennon has heard about primal screaming—therapy via trips back to babyhood—and he and Yoko soon hook up with psychologist Arthur Janov for four months of personal "get back" sessions in Los Angeles. Suddenly, peace, politics and other causes take a back seat.

MARCH 29. Yoko announces she's pregnant and expecting in October.

APRIL 10. Paul announces his split from the Beatles and releases his first solo album. John, who had privately told Paul that the group was finished a year before, calls Paul's statement a PR move. "I was a fool not to do what Paul did, which was use it to sell a

John Lennon/Plastic Ono Band, 1970.

record."

APRIL 27. John's confiscated lithographs are declared "not obscene" and returned.

MAY 13. The film *Let It Be* opens in New York and, five days later, the album, remixed and embellished with strings by producer Phil Spector, is finally released.

AUGUST 1. Cynthia Lennon remarries. John begins sessions for his first solo album backed by Ringo and Klaus Voormann, and with Yoko as coproducer. Later in the month, Yoko miscarries again.

DECEMBER 11. *John Lennon / Plastic Ono Band* is released. The first single, "Mother," is issued December 28. John and Yoko spend time in New York—"Yoko's old stomping ground," says John—with Jonas Mekas and make two films, *Fly* and *Up Your Legs Forever.*

DECEMBER 30. McCartney begins High Court proceedings to end the Beatles' business partnership. In spring, the court will appoint a receiver to handle the group's affairs, effectively ending Allen Klein's control. The decision is opposed by John, George and Ringo.

1971

> I don't believe in Beatles
> I just believe in me
> Yoko and me
> And that's reality.

JANUARY 21. John's let-it-all-out interview with *Rolling Stone* is published.

MARCH 12. "Power to the People," recorded in February, is released. The spring has been taken up with legal hassles over Beatles' business, with only a short respite in Japan, where John meets Yoko's parents for the first time.

JUNE 6. John and Yoko join Frank Zappa and the Mothers of Invention onstage at the Fillmore East. "I expected sort of a grubby maniac with naked women all over the place," John says. "The first thing I said was, 'Wow, you look so different. You look great.' And he said, 'You look clean, too.' He was expecting a couple of nude freaks."

JULY. John records the album *Imagine* with Klaus Voormann on bass, Nicky Hopkins on keyboards, Jim Keltner on drums and special guest George Harrison. John films the sessions. Later, George invites John to join him in New York for the concert for Bangladesh. John accepts, but drops out the day before the show after George refuses Yoko's request to appear onstage. It is *Let It Be* all over again.

AUGUST. John and Yoko go to the Virgin Islands in search of Kyoko—Yoko and ex-husband Tony Cox are fighting for custody—fail and decide to relocate to New York City. John has obtained a six-month nonrenewable visa. "Yoko and I were forever coming and going to New York," John would explain, "so, finally, we decided it would be cheaper and more functional to actually live here. Yoko sold me on New York. She'd been poor here and she knew every inch. She made me walk around the streets and parks and squares and examine every nook and cranny. In fact, you could say that I fell in love with New York on a streetcorner." John and Yoko look at one prospective apartment—in the Dakota—camp out at the St. Regis Hotel for a while and settle in the West Village. Later, they will go back to the Dakota and purchase several apartments there.

The Lennons get reacquainted with activist politics. While his soothing song "Imagine" gets airplay, he and Yoko join a protest by Native Americans in Syracuse, then John plays at a benefit at the Apollo Theatre for prisoners at Attica. In December John and Yoko appear at a benefit for John Sinclair, an Ann Arbor political figure imprisoned for possession of two marijuana joints.

1972

JANUARY. Unbeknownst to John, the Senate internal-security subcommittee of the Judiciary Committee submits a memo to Senator Strom

Thurmond regarding Lennon's involvement with such radicals as Jerry Rubin and Abbie Hoffman. John, the memo asserts, is part of a group of "strong advocates of a program to dump Nixon.'... The source felt that if Lennon's visa was terminated it would be a strategy countermeasure."

FEBRUARY. Thurmond writes to Attorney General John Mitchell, intimating that Lennon ought to be deported. "Headaches might be avoided," the senator says.

MARCH 1. A few weeks after cohosting "The Mike Douglas Show," John gets an extension on his just-expired visa. But that's the last good news he'll get for a while, as his fight to remain in the United States is about to begin.

From a press conference at the height of Beatlemania:

Q: How come you were turned back by immigration?

John: We had to be deloused.

MARCH 6. John's visa extension is canceled by the New York Immigra-tion and Naturalization Service director, at the instigation of the attorney general's office.

APRIL 29. John Lindsay, mayor of New York, asks federal authorities to halt deportation proceedings against John and Yoko.

MAY 8. John and Yoko have recorded an album, *Some Time in New York City*, with backing by a latter-day hippie rock band, Elephant's Memory. It's a stark and strident album. Says John: "I want to say whatever it is I've got to say, as simple as the music I like. And that's rock & roll."

MAY 11. On "The Dick Cavett Show," John says he's being followed by government agents, and his phone is being tapped. "I was so damn paranoid," he says later.

JUNE 12. *Some Time in New York City* is released. Two months later, John, Yoko and the band play the One-to-One concert at Madison Square Garden to benefit a home for handicapped children.

Imagine, 1971.

Some Time in New York City, 1972.

OCTOBER. Yoko records an album, *Approximately Infinite Universe*, with Elephant's Memory and others; she and John coproduce and the two-record set is out in January.

DECEMBER 23. The film *Imagine* is released.

1973

MARCH. U.S. Immigration authorities order John to leave the country, on grounds of his 1968 drug bust; he appeals. "Having just celebrated our fourth wedding anniversary," he says, "we are not prepared to sleep in separate beds." Elsewhere in the U.S. courts, Yoko wins custody of Kyoko, but Tony Cox disappears with the eight-year-old girl.

And John *still* manages to make music, writing a song for Ringo Starr's album and helping out on a session.

OCTOBER. The pressures keep mounting. After cutting the album *Mind Games*, John separates from Yoko and moves to Los Angeles. "It

Mind Games, 1973.

was like being sent to the desert," he recalls later. "I had to settle things within myself." It would take eighteen months. In L.A., John convinces Phil Spector to produce an oldies album. Spector, he says, was "fantastic, but it got madder and madder and it ended up breaking down and falling apart." So does John.

1974

JANUARY. John asks the queen for a royal pardon of his drug conviction so he can "be free as to travel to and from the U.S." The request is denied.

MARCH. John asks Yoko for permission to come home. "I would say, 'I don't like this, I'm getting in trouble,' and she would say, 'You're not ready to come home.' So, what do you say? Okay, back to the bottle."

At the Troubadour nightclub in Los Angeles, John is heard heckling the Smothers Brothers and is seen with a sanitary napkin on his head. He is ejected.

As the immigration news stays bad, John stays drunk, with help from friends like Harry Nilsson and Keith Moon. He produces Nilsson's album, *Pussy Cats*, and writes a painfully reflective song, "Nobody Loves You (When You're Down and Out)."

> Well I get up in the morning and
> I'm lookin' in the mirror to see,
> ooo wee!
> Then I'm lying in the darkness and
> I know I can't get to sleep,
> ooo wee!

JULY 17. The Justice Department orders John to leave the country within sixty days or be deported. John files an appeal. A week later, two thousand people attending a Beatles Appreciation Convention in Boston demonstrate in support of Lennon. A similar rally takes place later in New York.

AUGUST. John returns to New York with plans for a solo album, *Walls and Bridges*, and to attend immigration hearings. He finds time to back up Elton John in the studio on Elton's version of "Lucy in the Sky with Diamonds" and "One Day (at a Time)."

AUGUST 31. In federal court, John says the Nixon administration tried to have him deported because he helped organize an antiwar demonstration at the Republican convention in Miami in 1972.

SEPTEMBER. The Board of Immigration Appeals reaffirms the Justice Department's order to John to leave or be deported. He again appeals.

SEPTEMBER 26. *Walls and Bridges* is out. John gets to work salvaging the oldies tracks he'd cut with Spector and finishes up *Rock 'n' Roll* himself.

OCTOBER. "Whatever Gets You Thru the Night" is a Number One hit single for John.

NOVEMBER 28. Lennon joins Elton John onstage at Madison Square Garden to play "Whatever Gets You Thru the Night," "Lucy in the Sky with Diamonds" and "I Saw Her Standing There." In New York, he has continued to call Yoko, and backstage at Elton's concert they have a brief reunion. "There was just that moment," he would say, "when we saw each other and it's like in the movies, you know, when time stands still . . ." But John is still seeing former secretary May Pang and will spend the Christmas holidays with her and his son, Julian, at Disney World in Florida.

DECEMBER. *Rolling Stone* publishes details of the Nixon administration's conspiracy to deport Lennon. And a new single, "#9 Dream," is out.

1975

JANUARY. A London court dissolves

Walls and Bridges, 1974.

Rock 'n' Roll, 1975.

the last legal links among the Beatles. In the United States, a district-court judge rules to permit John and his lawyers access to his immigration-case files.

John cowrites "Fame" with David Bowie and plays guitar on Bowie's version of "Across the Universe."

FEBRUARY. Morris Levy of Adam VIII Records puts out *Roots*, an album of rough tapes from John's oldies sessions. Capitol Records rushes out the *Rock 'n' Roll* album Lennon himself completed and threatens legal action, stopping distribution of *Roots* at 3,000. Levy sues Lennon for $42 million, unsuccessfully. Lennon will later countersue and win a $35,000 judgment.

MARCH 10. A single from *Rock 'n' Roll*, "Stand by Me," is released.

John moves back in with Yoko at the Dakota, and the couple appear at the Grammy Awards, where John is a presenter. "I thought it would be a good opportunity to kill two birds with one stone," he says later. "(A)

Shaved Fish, 1975.

show that sometimes I'm sober and, (B) that I was back with my wife and that everything . . . was back to normal."

Later in the spring, the Lennons send a card to friends: "Here's a hard one for you to take," it reads. "Not only have John and Yoko got back together but they are expecting a baby due in October."

JUNE. John sues former attorney generals Mitchell and Kleindienst and various immigration officials over their handling of his case.

SEPTEMBER. He is granted a temporary nonpriority status by the Immigration and Naturalization Service because of Yoko's pregnancy.

OCTOBER 7. John wins. The U.S. Court of Appeals overturns the order to deport him, adding a layer of ironic frosting: "Lennon's four-year battle to remain in our country," the court writes in its decision, "is a testimony to his faith in this American dream."

OCTOBER 9. At age forty-two, after three miscarriages, Yoko wins. She gives birth to Sean Ono Lennon in New York Hospital on John's thirty-fifth birthday. "I feel higher than the Empire State Building," says John.

OCTOBER 24. *Shaved Fish*, a collection of Lennon songs from 1969 to 1975, is released.

Double Fantasy, 1980.

Season of Glass, 1981.

John and Yoko ended their period of seclusion with the release of Double Fantasy *in 1980; Yoko's album,* Season of Glass, *was released a few months after John's death.*

THE FIRST ROLLING STONE INTERVIEW

By Jonathan Cott/November 23, 1968

Unlike almost any other artist, John Lennon allowed himself to be interviewed at crucial points in his life in order to reveal and, perhaps, define for himself where he was in his world. In this first of four major Rolling Stone *interviews, John hesitatingly began to define himself as* John Lennon *and not just* Beatle John Lennon.

HE interview took place at John Lennon and Yoko Ono's temporary basement flat in London—a flat where Jimi Hendrix, Ringo Starr and William Burroughs, among others, have stayed. But the flat seemed as much John and Yoko's as the Indian incense that took over the living room. The walls were covered with photos of John, of Yoko, a giant Sgt. Pepper ensign, Richard Chamberlain's poster collage of news clippings of the Stones bust, the *Time* magazine cover of the Beatles.

We arrived at five on the afternoon of September 17, said hello to gallery owner Robert Fraser, who had arranged the interview, and to John and Yoko, sitting together, looking "*très bien ensemble.*" We sat down around a simple wooden table covered with magazines, newspapers, sketch paper, boxes, drawings, a beaded necklace shaped in the form of a pentangle.

John said he had to be at a recording session in half an hour, so we talked for a while about John's show at the Fraser Gallery.

When we arrived the next afternoon, September 18, John was walking around the room, humming what sounded like "Hold Me Tight"—just singing the song to the air. Old Fifties 45s were scattered about the floor, and John played Rosie and the Originals' version of "Give Me Love." We talked about the lyrics of Gene Vincent's "Woman Love." In spite of having slept only two hours, John asked us to sit down on the floor and begin the interview.

Any suspicions that John would be ornery, mean, cruel or brutish—feelings attributed to him and imagined by press reports and various paranoiac personalities—never arose even for the purpose of being pressed down. As John said simply about the interview: "There's nothing more fun than talking about your own songs and your own records. I mean, you can't help it, it's your bit, really. We talk about them *together*. Remember that."

I've listed a group of songs that I associate with you, in terms of what you are or what you were, songs that struck me as embodying you a little bit: "You've Got to Hide Your Love Away," "Strawberry Fields," "It's Only Love," "She Said She Said," "Lucy in the Sky," "I'm Only Sleeping," "Run for Your Life," "I Am the Walrus," "All You Need Is Love," "Rain," "Girl."

The ones that really meant something to me—look, I don't know about "Hide Your Love Away," that's so long ago—probably "Strawberry Fields," "She Said," "Walrus," "Rain," "Girl," there are just one or two others, "Day Tripper," "Paperback Writer," even. "Ticket to Ride" was one more, I remember that. It was a definite sort of change. "Norwegian Wood"—that was the sitar bit. Definitely, I consider them moods or moments.

There have been a lot of philosophical analyses written about your songs, "Strawberry Fields" in particular . . .

Well, they *can* take them apart. They can take anything apart. I mean, I hit it on all levels, you know. We write lyrics, and I write lyrics that you don't realize what they mean 'till after. Especially some of the better songs or some of the more flowing ones, like "Walrus." The whole first verse was written without any knowledge. And "Tomorrow Never Knows"—I didn't know what I was saying, and you just find out later. I know that when there are some lyrics I dig I know that somewhere people will be looking at them. And I dig the people that notice that I have a sort of strange rhythm scene, because I've never been able to keep rhythm on the stage. I always used to get lost. It's me double off-beats.

What is Strawberry Fields?

It's a name, it's a nice name. When I was writing "In My Life"—I was trying "Penny Lane" at that time—we were trying to write about Liverpool, and I just listed all the nice-sounding names, just arbitrarily. Strawberry Fields was a place near us that happened to be a Salvation Army home. But Strawberry Fields—I mean, I have visions of *Strawberry Fields*. And there was Penny Lane, and the Cast Iron Shore, which I've just got in some song now, and they were just good names—just groovy names. Just good sounding. Because Strawberry Fields is anywhere you want to go.

Pop analysts are often trying to read something into songs that isn't there.

It is there. It's like abstract art really. It's just the same really. It's just that when you have to think about it to write it, it just means that you labored at it. But when you just *say* it, man, you know you're saying it, it's a continuous flow. The same as when you're recording or just playing. You come out of a thing and you *know* "I've been there," and it was nothing, it was just pure, and that's what we're looking for all the time, really.

How much do you think the songs go toward building up a myth of a state of mind?

I don't know. I mean, we got a bit pretentious. Like everybody, we had our phase and now it's a little change over to trying to be more natural, less "newspaper taxis," say. I mean, we're just changing. I don't know what we're doing at all, I just write them. Really, I just like rock & roll. I mean, these [*pointing to a pile of Fifties records*] are the records I dug then, I dig them now and I'm still trying to reproduce "Some Other Guy" sometimes or "Be-Bop-A-Lula." Whatever it is, it's the same bit for me. It's really just the sound.

The Beatles seem to be one of the only groups who ever made a distinction between friends and lovers. For instance, there's the "baby" who can drive your car. But when it comes to "We Can Work It Out," you talk about "my friend." In most other groups' songs, calling someone "baby" is a bit demeaning compared to your distinction.

Yeah, I don't know why. It's Paul's bit that—"Buy you a diamond ring, my friend"—it's an alternative to *baby*. You can take it logically, the way you took it. See, I don't know really. Yours is as true a way of looking at it as any other way. In "Baby, You're a Rich Man" the point was, stop moaning. You're a rich man and we're all rich men, heh, heh, baby!

I've felt your other mood recently: "Here I stand, head in hand" in "Hide Your Love Away" and "When I was a boy, everything was right" in "She Said She Said."

Yeah, right. That was pure. That was what I meant all right. You see, when I wrote that I had the "She said she said," but it was just meaning nothing. It was just vaguely to do with someone who had said something like he knew what it was like to be dead, and then it was just a sound. And then I wanted a middle-eight. The beginning had been around for days and days and so I wrote the first thing that came into my head and it was "When I was a boy," in a different beat, but it was real because it just happened.

It's funny, because while we're recording we're all aware and listening to our old records and we say, we'll do one like "The Word"—make it like that. It never does turn out like that, but we're always comparing and talking about the old albums—just checking up, what is it? like swatting up for the exam—just listening to everything.

Yet people think you're trying to get away from the old records.

But I'd like to make a record like "Some Other Guy." I haven't done one that satisfies me as much as that satisfied me. Or "Be-Bop-A-Lula" or "Heartbreak Hotel" or "Good Golly, Miss Molly" or "Whole Lot of Shakin'." I'm not being modest. I mean, we're still trying it. We sit there in the studio and we say,

"How did it go, how did it go? Come on, let's do *that*." Like what Fats Domino has done with "Lady Madonna"—"See how they ruhhnnn."

Wasn't it about the time of Rubber Soul *that you moved away from the old records to something quite different?*

Yes, yes, we got involved completely in ourselves then. I think it was *Rubber Soul* when we did all our own numbers. Something just happened. We controlled it a bit. Whatever it was we were putting over, we just tried to control it a bit.

Are there any other versions of your songs you like?

Well, Ray Charles's version of "Yesterday"—that's beautiful. And "Eleanor Rigby" is a groove. I just dig the strings on that. Like Thirties strings. Jose Feliciano does great things to "Help!" and "Day Tripper."

"Got to Get You Into My Life"—sure, we were doing our Tamla Motown bit. You see, we're influenced by whatever's going. Even if we're not influenced, we're all going that way at a certain time. If we played a Stones record now, and a Beatles record—and we've been way apart—you'd find a lot of similarities. We're all heavy. Just heavy. How did we ever do anything light?

What we're trying to do is rock & roll, with less of your philosorock, is what we're saying to ourselves. And get on with rocking because rockers is what we really are. You can give me a guitar, stand me up in front of a few people. Even in the studio, if I'm getting into it, I'm just doing my old bit—not quite doing Elvis Legs but doing my equivalent. It's just natural. Everybody says we must do this and that but our thing is just rocking—you know, the usual gig. That's what this new record is about. Definitely rocking. What we were doing on *Pepper* was rocking—and not rocking.

"A Day in the Life"—that was something. I dug it. It was a good piece of work between Paul and me. I had the "I read the news today" bit, and it turned Paul on. Now and then we really turn each other on with a bit of song, and he just said "yeah"—bang bang, like that. It just sort of happened beautifully, and we arranged it and rehearsed it, which we don't often do, the afternoon before. So we all knew what we were playing, we all got into it. It was a real groove, the whole scene on that one. Paul sang half of it and I sang half. I needed a middle-eight for it, but that would have been forcing it. All the rest had come out smooth, flowing, no trouble, and to write a middle-eight would have been to write a middle-eight, but instead Paul already had one there. It's a bit of a 2001, you know.

Songs like "Good Morning, Good Morning" and "Penny Lane" convey a child's feeling of the world.

We write about our past. "Good Morning, Good Morning," I was never

49

proud of it. I just knocked it off to do a song. But it was writing about my past so it does get the kids because it was me at school, my whole bit. The same with "Penny Lane." We really got into the groove of imagining Penny Lane—the bank was there, and that was where the tram sheds were and people waiting and the inspector stood there, the fire engines were down there. It was just reliving childhood.

You really had a place where you grew up.

Oh, yeah. Didn't you?

Well, Manhattan isn't Liverpool.

Well, you could write about your local bus station.

In Manhattan?

Sure, why not? Everywhere is somewhere.

In "Hey, Jude," as in one of your first songs, "She Loves You," you're singing to someone else and yet you might as well be singing to yourself. Do you find that as well?

Oh, yeah. Well, when Paul first sang "Hey, Jude" to me—or played me the little tape he'd made of it—I took it very personally. "Ah, it's me!" I said. "It's *me*." He says,"No, it's *me*." I said, "Check, we're going through the same bit." So we all are. Whoever is going through that bit with us is going through it, that's the groove.

In the Magical Mystery Tour *theme song you say, "The Magical Mystery Tour is waiting to take you away." In* Sgt. Pepper *you sing, "We'd like to take you home with us." How do you relate this embracing, come-sit-on-my-lawn feeling in the songs with your need for everyday privacy?*

I take a narrower concept of it, like whoever was around at the time wanting to talk to them talked to me, but of course it does have that wider aspect to it. The concept is very good and I went through it and said, "Well, okay. Let them sit on my lawn." But of course it doesn't work. People climbed in the house and smashed things up, and then you think, "That's no good, that doesn't work." So actually you're saying, "Don't talk to me," really.

We're all trying to say nice things like that but most of the time we can't make it—ninety percent of the time—and the odd time we do make it, when we do it, together as people. You can say it in a song: "Well, whatever I did say to you that day about getting out of the garden, part of me said that but, really, in my heart of hearts, I'd like to have it right and talk to you and communicate." Unfortunately we're human, you know—it doesn't seem to work.

Do you feel free to put anything in a song?

Yes. In the early days I'd—well, we all did—we'd take things out for being banal, clichés, even chords we wouldn't use because we thought they were clichés. And even just this year there's been a great release for all of us, going right back to the basics. On "Revolution" I'm playing the guitar and I haven't improved since I was last playing, but I dug it. It sounds the way I wanted it to sound.

It's a pity I can't do better—the fingering, you know—but I couldn't have done that last year. I'd have been too paranoiac. I couldn't play dddddddddddd. George must play, or somebody better. My playing has probably improved a little bit on this session because I've been playing a little. I was always the rhythm guy anyway, but I always just fiddled about in the background. I didn't actually want to play rhythm. We all sort of wanted to be lead—as in most groups—but it's a groove now, and so are the clichés. We've gone past those days when we wouldn't have used words because they didn't make sense, or what we thought was sense.

But of course Dylan taught us a lot in this respect.

Another thing is, I used to write a book or stories on one hand and write songs on the other. And I'd be writing completely free form in a book or just on a bit of paper, but when I'd start to write a song I'd be thinking *dee duh dee duh do doo do de do de doo*. And it took Dylan and all that was going on then to say, oh, come on now, that's the same bit, I'm just singing the words.

With "I Am the Walrus," I had "I am he as you are he as we are all to-gether." I had just these two lines on the typewriter, and then about two weeks later I ran through and wrote another two lines and then, when I saw something, after about four lines, I just knocked the rest of it off. Then I had the whole verse or verse and a half and then sang it. I had this idea of doing a song that was a police siren, but it didn't work in the end [*sings like a siren*]: "I-am-he-as-you-are-he-as . . ." You couldn't really sing the police siren.

Do you write your music with instruments or in your head?

On piano or guitar. Most of this session has been written on guitar 'cause we were in India and only had our guitars there. They have a different feel about them. I missed the piano a bit because you just write differently. My piano playing is even worse than me guitar. I hardly know what the chords are, so it's good to have a slightly limited palette, heh heh.

What did you think of Dylan's "version" of "Norwegian Wood"? ("Fourth Time Around.")

I was very paranoid about that. I remember he played it to me when he was in London. He said, "What do you think?" I said, "I don't like it." I didn't like it. I was very paranoid. I just didn't like what I felt I was feeling—I thought it was an out-and-out skit, you know, but it wasn't. It was great.

I mean, he wasn't playing any tricks on me. I was just going through the bit.

Is there anybody besides Dylan you've gotten something from musically?

Oh, millions. All those I mentioned before—Little Richard, Presley.

Anyone contemporary?

Are they dead? Well, nobody sustains it. I've been buzzed by the Stones and other groups, but none of them can sustain the buzz for me continually through a whole album or through three singles even.

You and Dylan are often thought of together in some way.

Yeah? Yeah, well we were for a bit, but I couldn't make it. Too paranoiac. I always saw him when he was in London. He first turned us on in New York actually. He thought "I Want to Hold Your Hand"—when it goes "I can't hide"—he thought we were singing "I get high." So he turns up with Al Aronowitz and turns us on, and we had the biggest laugh all night—forever. Fantastic. We've got a lot to thank him for.

Do you ever see him anymore?

No, 'cause he's living his cozy little life, doing that bit. If I was in New York, he'd be the person I'd most like to see. I've grown up enough to communicate with him. Both of us were always uptight, you know, and of course I wouldn't know whether he was uptight, because I was so uptight. And then, when he wasn't uptight, I was—all that bit. But we just sat it out because we just liked being together.

What about the new desire to return to a more natural environment? Dylan's return to country music?

Dylan broke his neck and we went to India. Everybody did their bit. And now we're all just coming out, coming out of a shell, in a new way, kind of saying, remember what it was like to play.

Do you feel better now?

Yes . . . and worse.

What do you feel about India now?

I've got no regrets at all, 'cause it was a groove and I had some great experiences meditating eight hours a day—some amazing things, some amazing trips—it was great. And I still meditate off and on. George is doing it regularly. And I believe implicitly in the whole bit. It's just that it's difficult to continue it. I lost the rosy glasses. And I'm like that. I'm very idealistic. So I can't really manage my exercises when I've lost that. I mean, I don't want to be a boxer so much. It's just that a few things happened, or didn't happen. I don't know, but *something* happened. It was sort of like a ⟦*click*⟧ and we just left and I don't know what went on. It's too near—I don't really know what happened.

You just showed me what might be the front and back album photos for the record you're putting out of the music you and Yoko composed for your film Two Virgins. *The photos have the simplicity of a daguerreotype. . . .*

Well, that's because I took it. I'm a ham photographer, you know. It's me Nikon what I was given by a commercially minded Japanese when we were in Japan, along with me Pentax, me Canon, me boom-boom and all the others. So I just set it up and did it.

For the cover, there's a photo of you and Yoko standing naked facing the camera. And on the backside are your backsides. What do you think people are going to think of the cover?

Well, we've got that to come. The thing is, I started it with a pure . . . it was the truth, and it was only after I'd got into it and done it and looked at it that I'd realized what kind of scene I was going to create. And then suddenly, there it was, and then suddenly you show it to people and then you know what the world's going to do to you, or try to do. But you have no knowledge of it when you conceive it or make it.

Originally, I was going to record Yoko, and I thought the best picture of her for an album would be her naked. I was just going to record her as an artist. We were only on those kind of terms then. So after that, when we got together, it just seemed natural for us, if we made an album together, for both of us to be naked.

Of course, I've never seen me prick on an album or on a photo before: "Whatnearth, there's a fellow with his prick out." And that was the first time I realized me prick was out, you know. I mean, you can see it on the photo itself—we're naked in front of a camera—that comes over in the eyes, just for a minute you go!! I mean, you're not used to it, being naked, but it's got to come out.

How do you face the fact that people are going to mutilate you?

Well, I can take that as long as we can get the cover out. And I really don't know what the chances are of that.

You don't worry about the nuts across the street?

No, no. I know it won't be very comfortable walking around with all the lorry drivers whistling and that, but it'll all die. Next year it'll be nothing, like miniskirts or bare tits. It isn't anything. We're all naked really. When people

53

attack Yoko and me, we know they're paranoiac. We don't worry too much. It's the ones that don't know, and you know they don't know—they're just going round in a blue fuzz. The thing is, the album also says: Look, lay off will you? It's two people—what have we done?

Lenny Bruce once compared himself to a doctor, saying that if people weren't sick, there wouldn't be any need for him.

That's the bit, isn't it? Since we started being more natural in public—the four of us—we've really had a lot of knocking. I mean, we're always natural. I mean, you can't help it. We couldn't have been where we are if we hadn't done that. We wouldn't have been us either. And it took four of us to enable us to do it; we couldn't have done it alone and kept that up. I don't know why I get knocked more often. I seem to open me mouth more often, something happens, I forget what I am till it all happens again. I mean, we just get knocked—from the underground, the pop world—me personally. They're all doing it. They've got to stop soon.

Couldn't you go off to your own community and not be bothered with all of this?

Well, it's just the same there, you see. India was a bit of that, it was a taste of it—it's the same. So there's a small community, it's the same gig, it's relative. There's no escape.

Your show at the Fraser Gallery gave critics a chance to take a swipe at you.

Oh, right, but putting it on was taking a swipe at them in a way. I mean, that's what it was about. What they couldn't understand was that—a lot of them were saying, well, if it hadn't been for John Lennon nobody would have gone to it, but as it was, it was *me* doing it. And if it had been Sam Bloggs it would have been nice. But the point of it was—it was me. And they're using that as a reason to say why it didn't work. Work as what?

Do you think Yoko's film of you smiling would work if it were just anyone smiling?

Yes, it works with somebody else smiling, but she went through all this. It originally started out that she wanted a million people all over the world to send in a snapshot of themselves smiling, and then it got down to lots of people smiling, and then maybe one or two and then me smiling as a symbol of today smiling—and that's what I am, whatever that means. And so it's me smiling, and that's the hang-up, of course, because it's me again. But they've got to see it someday—it's only me. I don't mind if people go to the film to see me smiling because it doesn't matter, it's not harmful. The idea of the film won't really be dug for another fifty or a hundred years probably. That's what it's all about. I just happen to be that face.

It's too bad people can't come down here individually to see how you're living.

Well, that's it. I didn't see Ringo and his wife for about a month when I first got together with Yoko, and there were rumors going around about the film and all that. Maureen was saying she really had some strange ideas about where we were at and what we were up to. And there were some strange reactions from all me friends and at Apple about Yoko and me and what we were doing — "Have they gone mad?" But of course it was just us, you know, and if *they* are puzzled or reacting strangely to us two being together and doing what we're doing, it's not hard to visualize the rest of the world really having some amazing image.

International Times *recently published an interview with Jean-Luc Godard . . .*

Oh yeah, right, he said we should do something. Now that's sour grapes from a man who couldn't get us to be in his film [*One Plus One,* in which the Stones appear], and I don't expect it from people like that. Dear Mr. Godard, just because we didn't want to be in the film with you, it doesn't mean to say that we aren't doing any more than you. We should do whatever we're all doing.

But Godard put it in activist political terms. He said that people with influence and money should be trying to blow up the establishment and that you weren't.

What's he think we're doing? He wants to stop looking at his own films and look around.

Time magazine came out and said, look, the Beatles say "no" to destruction.

There's no point in dropping out because it's the same there and it's got to change. But I think it all comes down to changing your head and, sure, I know that's a cliché.

What would you tell a black-power guy who's changed his head and then finds a wall there all the time?

Well, I can't tell him anything 'cause he's got to do it himself. If destruction's the only way he can do it, there's nothing I can say that could influence him 'cause that's where he's at, really. We've all got that in us, too, and that's why I did the "Out and In" bit on a few takes and in the TV version of "Revolution" — "Destruction, well, you know, you can count me out, and in," like yin and yang.

I prefer "out." But we've got the other bit in us. I don't know what I'd be doing if I was in his position. I don't think I'd be so meek and mild. I just don't know.

GIVING PEACE A CHANCE

John and Yoko spent their honeymoon in bed for peace in Amsterdam —their first official "bed-in." They then focused their peace activities in Canada and decided to sponsor the biggest rock festival in history there. They began with enormous optimism in the face of much of the world's skepticism: All they needed, they thought, was love. The following four pieces chronicle the evolution and eventual disintegration of John and Yoko's dream. Ritchie Yorke wrote not only as a journalist but also as an active participant in the festival planning. John Lennon wrote his version of what happened at the request of Rolling Stone. Then several months later, Barry Ballister gave another insider's account of the events.

BOOSTING PEACE: JOHN AND YOKO IN CANADA
By Ritchie Yorke/February 7, 1969

TORONTO. Police were on duty along the corridors to hold back fans and to scrutinize the credentials of the fifty or so press representatives who turned up either to gaze in wonder at the most famous couple in the world, or to dismiss the visit as more weird stuff from the weirdest family around. It was the beginning of John and Yoko's second bed-in for peace and after their unexpected arrival, they had quickly called a press conference. Inside a crowded hotel suite, they sat peacefully holding hands, surrounded by pink and white carnations, record players, film equipment and busy phones.

"We're trying to interest young people in doing something for peace," Lennon said, toying with a white carnation. "But it must be done by nonviolent means—otherwise there can be only chaos. We're saying to the young people—and they have always been the hippest ones—we're telling them to get the message across to the squares."

What about talking to the people who make the decisions, the power brokers? suggested a cynical reporter. Lennon laughed. "Shit, talk? Talk about what? It doesn't happen like that. In the U.S., the government is too busy talking about how to keep me out. If I'm a joke, as they say, why don't they just let me in?"

Asked if there may be a better way to promote peace than to lie in bed for seven days, Yoko said: "We worked for three months thinking out the most functional approach to boosting peace before we got married and spent our honeymoon talking to the press in bed in Amsterdam. For us it was the only way. We can't lead a parade or a march because of all the autograph hunters."

"We're all responsible for war," Lennon continued. "We all must do something, no matter what—by growing our hair long, standing on one leg, talking to the press, having bed-ins—to change the attitudes. The people must be made aware that it's up to them.

"Bed-ins are something that everybody can do and they're so simple. We're willing to be the world's clowns to make people realize it."

Montreal bed-in, June 1969.

The next day they bedded down again—this time in Montreal, where Lennon devoted a good portion of his time talking with AM and FM stations all around the United States and Canada from his hotel-room phone. He happily counseled peace to KSAN-FM's San Francisco Bay Area listeners. The following day—the day of the big People's Park march in Berkeley—Lennon phoned KPFA-FM in Berkeley twice to inquire how it was going and to advise the demonstrators to use peaceful methods.

"When I first got the news it stooned me, absolutely stooned me,' he told the KPFA listeners, and assured them that people around the world were on the side of People's Park.

"But you can't do it with violent means. That won't accomplish anything. Keep it peaceful. Violence is what has kept mankind from getting together for centuries."

JOHN, YOKO AND YEAR ONE
By Ritchie Yorke/June 28, 1970

ORONTO. Snow was starting to fall in splashing flakes on the windows. Ronnie Hawkins yawned. Yoko Ono cuddled closer to John Lennon, took a drag on his Gitane cigarette and closed her eyes. The whole household was drowsily relaxing in the rambling old farmhouse on the outskirts of Toronto that Ronnie Hawkins and his wife, Wanda, owned.

Ed Sullivan's vacuous visage bounced onto the screen as Wanda came into the room and exclaimed: "Look, it's the Beatles on TV." John and Yoko came to life and Hawkins reached out to turn on the volume. Lennon leaped out of the sofa and knelt a few inches from the screen.

The long shot cut to a close-up of Paul McCartney singing "Yesterday, all my troubles seemed . . ." Lennon laughed, "Boy, was he shitting then."

Then a rerun of the group's first-ever appearance on the Sullivan show. Up came Lennon, short-haired and obviously nervous, strumming his axe and screaming into the mike. John had returned to the sofa and Yoko was laughing.

"Is that really my husband?" she teased. John shrugged.

Shea Stadium: John, leading the rest of the Beatles through the police guard and the cutaway shots of the crying, craving teenyboppers. "Yes, yes, yes," John bubbled. "I remember every moment of that. It was incredible."

A few minutes later, Sullivan was replaced by a Canadian network's public-affairs show, "W5," and Lennon was back on the screen. He was talking about peace and a massive pop-music festival for peace to be held in Canada next summer. His words were clear and full of conviction. The interviewer wanted to know if the rest of the Beatles would be there performing. "Yes, yes," he said impatiently. "I'm going to ask each of them. I can't say now that they'll play but I think they will."

John and Yoko's arrival in Toronto for the third time in less than a year was preceded by a large "War Is Over" campaign that had been simultaneously unveiled in twelve cities the previous morning. In Toronto, thirty roadside billboards went up, along with thousands of posters and handbills. Capitol Records of Canada took out newspaper ads with the same message.

The first press conference took place at the Ontario Science Centre.

"Well," announced John, "we've come back to Canada to announce plans for a big peace-and-music festival to be held at Mosport Park near Toronto on July third, fourth and fifth next year. We aim to make it the biggest music festival in history, and we're going to be asking everybody who's anybody to play.

"The whole idea of our new peace campaign is to be positive. You can't expect anybody to do anything for nothing. You must run things the way the Establishment does. The idea came from the Toronto people. They wanted to produce the biggest pop festival in history by the usual means, and then give a percentage of the gross to a new peace fund, which we're setting up. But it won't be the usual fund thing, and that's what we liked about the idea.

Holding "Bag of Laughs" at Montreal press conference, September 1969.

John and Yoko's billboards for peace. Top: Times Square, New York City; bottom: Sunset Strip, Hollywood; right: Shaftesbury Avenue, London. On December 15, 1969, the billboard campaign opened in twelve cities around the world.

"We are forming a peace council that will administer the fund as it sees fit. If we decide, for example, that we want to give food to starving children in Biafra, we won't use the traditional means. We'll hire planes and take the stuff there ourselves. We're doing away with all the old methods because they haven't worked very well from what we can see."

John spoke slowly, distinctly, choosing his words with evident care. Yoko, looking nervous, chewed a great wad of gum and, for the most part, only listened, smiling at John continually.

"One of our friends here in Toronto has come up with the idea that the new year should not be called 1970 A.D. Everyone who is into peace and awareness will regard the New Year as Year One A.P.—for After Peace. All of our letters and calendars from now on will use this new method.

"Along with the festival, we are going to have an International Peace Vote. We're asking everyone to vote for either peace or war and to send in a coupon with their name and address. This is going to be done worldwide, through music papers initially and, when we've got about twenty million votes, we're going to give them to the United States. It's just another positive step."

Why Canada and not the U.S.? According to John Brower, one of the team working with the Lennons on the festival and allied projects, Lennon feels that Canada has become the world's greatest hope for peace. "The political climate in Canada is completely different from any other country. The politicians here at least want to hear what young people think. They'll talk, and that is the important first step."

Riding a Ski-Doo at Ronnie Hawkins's farm, December 1969.

John and Yoko spent the next couple of days meeting press for personal interviews and occasionally frolicking in the snow on the Hawkins's farm.

On the Saturday afternoon before Christmas, John met Marshall McLuhan, Toronto's silver-haired communications prophet. The meeting was arranged by CBS television.

McLuhan: Can you recall the occasion or the immediate reasons for your getting involved in music?

John: I heard Elvis Presley.

McLuhan: Ah.

John: And that was it. There were lots of other things going on but that was the conversion. I kind of dropped everything.

McLuhan: You felt you could do it at least as well as he could?

John: Yeah. But I thought we better get a few people together, because maybe we wouldn't make it alone. So we did a team job.

McLuhan: The British are still more team-oriented than the Americans. In terms of performance. The star system doesn't play quite as well in England. The private star.

John: They have a reaction to that in England—treating their stars and entertainers like animals. We're not like the Americans, to be hyped by Hollywood. The attitude is be quiet, do a dance at the London Palladium, and stop talking about peace. That's what we get in London.

Professor McLuhan then outlined his theories about why rock festivals are becoming larger and larger. "Frustration creates bigness. And when people are frustrated, they feel the need to expand, to get more room and length. The man who gives up smoking gets so frustrated that he puts on huge amounts of weight, even when he doesn't eat anything.

"Frustration in organizations results in huge growth of cities, businesses, countries, territorial imperatives and so on.

"Frustration releases adrenaline in the system. Adrenaline creates much bigger muscles and bigger arms and legs and has tremendous weight on the political body.

"This is why dinosaurs ended in sudden death, because as the environment became more and more hostile, more and more adrenaline was released into their bodies and they got bigger and bigger and then they collapsed.

"It could happen to America; it already happened to the British Empire. Adrenaline just gave out. In fact, your songs represented the end of that big adrenaline flow. As far as the U.K. was concerned, Beatles music was the end of the adrenaline. And the beginning of peace and contentment."

McLuhan then switched to a more familiar topic: the medium as message.

McLuhan: Language is a form of organized stutter. Literally, you chop your sounds up into bits in order to talk. Now, when you sing, you don't stutter, so singing is a way of stretching language into long, harmonious patterns and cycles. How do you think about language in songs?

John: Language and song is to me, apart from being pure vibrations, just like trying to describe a dream. And because we don't have telepathy or whatever it is, we try and describe the dream to each other, to verify to each other what we know, what we believe is inside each other. And the stuttering is right—because we can't say it. No matter how you say it, it's never how you want to say it.

McLuhan: The moment you sing, you feel you are communicating much more.

John: Yes, because the words are irrelevant.

McLuhan: Rowan and Martin say "We don't tell jokes; we just project a mood." You're concerned with projecting a mood and defining it. Putting down some pattern so that other people can find the pattern, participate, and . . .

John: As soon as you find the pattern, you break it. Otherwise it gets boring. The Beatles' pattern is one that has to be scrapped. If it remains the same, it's a monument, or a museum, and one thing this age is about is no museums. The Beatles turned into a museum, so they have to be scrapped or deformed or changed.

McLuhan: They're in danger of becoming good taste?

John: They passed through that. They have to be thoroughly horsewhipped.

McLuhan: What do you think we're moving into in the way of new rhythms, new patterns?

With (left to right) Ronnie Hawkins, Wanda Hawkins and Dick Gregory at Ronnie Hawkins's farm outside Toronto, December 1969.

John: Just complete freedom and nonexpectation from audience or musician or performer. And then, when we've had that for a few hundred years, then we can talk about playing around with patterns and bars and music again. We must get away from the patterns we've had for these thousands of years.

McLuhan: Well, this means very much in the way of decentralizing our world, doesn't it?

John: Yes. We must be one country and stick together. You don't have to have badges to say we're together. We're together if we're together, and no stamps or flags are going to make anybody together . . . folks.

The snow was falling in great white sheets as John and Yoko left McLuhan's office and climbed into the Rolls for the drive back to the farm.

It was still snowing the next morning when they met Dick Gregory at the airport. Gregory entered the Peace Festival discussions with vigor, pulling out ideas about festival spinoffs and entertaining the household.

On Monday morning, everyone was up early and rushed to Union Station for the trip to Montreal. First came a press conference and then twenty-four hours of meetings with politicians and representatives of the commission investigating the legalization of marijuana in Canada.

Tuesday morning at 10:30, the press in Ottawa was stunned to learn of an impending meeting between Lennon and the prime minister. One of the conditions which the prime minister's office had imposed on Lennon if there were a meeting between the two, was that there would be no advance publicity of any kind. At precisely 10:55, John and Yoko were rushed by limousine to the Parliament building.

The Lennons' fifty-one-minute meeting with the PM was private and, afterward, they were besieged by the press.

"If there were more leaders like Mr. Trudeau," John said into a field of microphones and cameras, "the world would have peace." Later John told me Trudeau had talked about how important it was for him to keep in close contact with youth, and how he would like to meet the Lennons on less formal ground for further discussions.

From the PM's office, the Lennons were escorted to the ministry of health for a lengthy meeting with Health Minister John Munro and senior members of his department.

When the generation-gap subject hit the table, Munro seized the opportunity to get some Lennon advice. "Often when I talk with young people," he said, "I can't even get to open my mouth before I'm battered with placards and posters and catch phrases." Quipped Lennon: "Get your own posters together and fire them back."

Back in London, Lennon said: "It was the best trip we've ever had. We got more done for peace this week than in our whole lives."

THE PRESS CONFERENCE

There are a lot of people around the world now trying to promote world peace. Why do you think that you can succeed where they have so far failed?

That's like saying why bother keeping on Christianity because Jesus got killed. We don't think people have tried advertising before. Pretend peace is new then 'cause we've never had it. So you start advertising it: . . . Sell, sell, sell.

Are there any similarities between where the Beatles were during the Cavern days and this peace campaign now?

We do consider that we're in the Cavern stage; you know, we haven't got out of Liverpool with this campaign. And we've got to break London and then America. I feel exactly the same as I did then about the Beatles as I do about peace and what we're doing now. But I don't care how long it takes, and what obstacles there are. We won't stop.

Was there any one incident that got you into the peace campaign?

Well, it built up over a number of years, but the thing that struck it off was a letter we got from a guy called Peter Watkins, who made a film called *The War Game*. It was a long letter stating what's happening—how the media is controlled, how it's all run, and it ended up: "What are you going to do about it?"

He said people in our position and his position have a responsibility to use the media for world peace. And we sat on the letter for three weeks and thought it over and figured at first we were doing our best with songs like "All You Need Is Love."

Finally we came up with the bed event and that was what sparked it off. It was like getting your call-up papers for peace. Then we did the bed event.

Is it true that you were planning on going to Biafra a short while back?

Yeah. At the time, Yoko was pregnant and we decided not to go and she had a miscarriage. Then we thought and thought about it. But we're scared to go somewhere where it's happening. 'Cause we don't want to be dead saints or martyrs. I'm scared of going to Vietnam and Biafra and, until I'm convinced that I can do better there than I can do outside of it, I'll stay out of it. I'd go to Russia, but I'd think twice about China.

YOKO: I think we did a lot of good for Biafra when John returned his M.B.E.

You said you were going to have a peace vote. How do you answer accusations that that sort of thing borders on naiveté?

Let's see. If anybody thinks our campaign is naive, that's their opinion and that's okay. Let them do something else and if we like their ideas, we'll join in with them. But until then, we'll do it the way we are. We're artists, not politicians. Not newspapermen, not anything. We do it in the way that suits us best, and this is the way we work.

Publicity and things like that is our game. The Beatles' thing was that. And that was the trade I've learned. This is my trade, and I'm using it to the best of my ability.

But what is the point of having a vote for peace?

Why do people have those Gallup polls? If we get a vote from around the world with millions and millions of kids that want peace, that's a nice Gallup poll. We can wave those figures around. That's all. It's a positive move; all we want is a yes.

Will the Beatles play at this festival?

I'll try to hustle them out. Maybe I'll get on two of them, or something like that. I got George on the other night for UNICEF in London. I can't speak for the Beatles because I'm only me. But if I can get them, if I can get Elvis . . . I'll try. I'll try and get all of them.

Do you think this festival could become something like that recent Stones affair in California, where some people died?

The Stones' one was bad. I've heard a lot of things about that concert. I think it was just a bad scene. It won't be like that here. I think they created that either subconsciously or whatever, and that is the result of the image and the mood they create. I think if you create a peaceful scene, you stand a better chance. We have six months to prevent that sort of thing; the Stones thing was done overnight.

How soon can the world reach a state of peace?

As soon as people realize that they have the power. The power doesn't belong with Mr. Trudeau, Mr. Wilson or Mr. Nixon. We are the power. The people are the power. And as soon as people are aware that they have the power, then they can do what they want. And if it's a case of they don't know what to do, let's advertise to them to tell them they have an option. They've all got a vote. Vote for peace, folks.

Don't you think your long hair and your clothes may put old people off in your pursuit of peace?

I understand that. Many people say, "Why don't you get a butch haircut and a tie, suit?" and the thing is, that's what politicians do. We just try to be as natural as possible. Now, how many members of the public are gullible to politicians, with the nice picture of the family, the dog and the whore on the side? Now, I could do that, but I don't think people would believe it. That's the politicians' way, but youth certainly doesn't believe it anymore.

Have you ever thought of taking your ideas to someone like Henry Ford?

When we get a bit organized. You see, what we didn't want to become was leaders. I believe in that Wilhelm Reich guy who said, "Don't become a leader." We don't want to be the people that everyone says, "It was your fault we didn't get peace." We want to be part of it. It's like people said the Beatles were the movement; but we were only part of the movement. We were in-fluenced as much as we influenced.

And John and Yoko refuse to be the leaders of the youth movement for peace. That's dictatorship. We want everybody to help us. And then, if it takes time for this kind of news to get through to Henry Ford or Onassis or anybody like that.

When we get something functional happening and a few people that aren't John and Yoko, we can approach from that angle. We can then say we've got so much money, will you double it? 'Cause we know they all do charity for whatever reason.

Do you believe in God?

Yes, I believe that God is like a powerhouse, like where you keep electricity, like a power station. And that he's a supreme power, and that he's neither good nor bad, left, right, black or white. He just is. And we tap that source of power and make of it what we will. Just as electricity can kill people in a chair, or you can light a room with it. I think God is.

Don't you worry about being identified as a father figure?

I believe that leaders and father figures are the mistake of all the generations before us. And that all of us rely on Nixon or Jesus or whoever we rely on; it's lack of responsibility that you expect somebody else to do it. He must help me or we kill him or we vote him out. I think that's the mistake, just having father figures. It's a sign of weakness; you must do the greasing yourself.

I won't be a leader. Everybody is a leader. People thought the Beatles were leaders, but they weren't, and now people are finding that out.

What, in brief, is your philosophy?

Peace, just no violence, and everybody grooving, if you don't mind the word. Of course, we all have violence in us, but it must be channeled or something. If I have long hair, I don't see why everybody else should have long hair. And if I want peace, I'll suggest peace to everyone. But I won't hustle them up for peace.

If people want to be violent, let them not interfere with people who don't want violence. Let them kill each other if there has to be that.

Are there any alternatives?

You either get tired fighting for peace, or you die.

Don't you think the Peace Grease may be a substitute for the massive problem young people are having with drugs?

Well, the liquor problem is even worse. I think the drug problem is a hang-up and a drag, but if we hadn't had methedrine, and all the rest of it, the ones that are going to go through that trip would have been alcoholics. Everybody seems to need something in the way society is; because of the pressure. So it would have been alcohol or something. The problem isn't what they're on, it's what made them go on whatever they're on.

The best antidote for drug taking and liquor is hope, it seems to me. You're giving young people hope.

The only time Yoko and I took heavy drugs was when we were without hope. And the only way we got out of it was with hope. And if we can sustain the hope, we don't need liquor, hard drugs, or anything. But if we lose hope, what can you do? What is there to do?

John, would you have achieved that hope without the success of the Beatles?

The Beatles had nothing to do with the hope. This is after; I mean, the Beatles made it four years ago and they stopped touring and they had all the money they wanted, and all the fame they wanted and they found out they had nothing. And then we started on our various trips of LSD and Maharishi and all the rest of the things we did. And the old gag about money and power and fame is not the answer. We didn't have any hope just because we were famous.

You see, Marilyn Monroe and all the other people, they had everything the Beatles had, but it's no answer. So John and Yoko had the same problems and fears and hopes and aspirations that any other couple on earth does, regardless of the position we were in and regardless of the money we had. We had exactly the same paranoia as everybody else, the same petty thoughts, the same everything. We had no superanswer that came through Beatles or power. In that respect, the Beatles were irrelevant to what I'm talking about.

Getting back to how it started, how did you and Yoko initially find ground for this campaign?

Both Yoko and I were in different bags, as we call it. But both had a positive side—we were singing "All You Need Is Love" and she was in Trafalgar Square, protesting for peace in a black bag. We met, we had to decide what our common goal was, we had one thing in common—we were in love. But love is just a gift, and it doesn't answer everything and it's like a precious plant that you have to nurture and look after and all that.

So we had to find what we wanted to do together—these two egos. What they had in common was love; we had to work on it. What goes with love, we thought, was peace. Now we were thinking of all this, and planning on getting married and not getting married and what we were going to do and how we were going to do it and rock & roll and avant-garde and all that bit, and then we got that letter from Peter Watkins. And it all started from there.

A PRIVATE TALK WITH JOHN

You've been talking lately about the fact that the Beatles aren't the musical group they were two or three years ago—that you are now all pursuing completely separate directions—Yoko's and your scene, for example. In fact, you are virtually all competing with one another.

Yes, well, the thing is that because there's no room on an album, we've got to have other outlets and I'm using the Plastic Ono Band. George will use whatever, Ringo's got an album in the can and Paul's doing Mary Hopkin or whoever he decides to do on his own. We still might make Beatles' products—right now, I just don't know. But we need more room—the Beatles are just too limited. That's where the trouble is.

When you're working on a new Beatles album, how many songs would you personally come up with, and then how many would you get to use in the end?

Probably at least seven or eight each and there's only fourteen tracks on an album, so you can imagine what it's like. So you have to choose the ones you like best or the ones that are easiest to get across to the others. That's the trouble.

Do you dislike writing a song and not being able to record it immediately?

I can't stand it. I can't stand having songs lying around for years. It just annoys me, and I think it annoys all of us. I cut "Revolution 2"—the one that's on the album—and "Revolution 9" with them, but they went away, and I wanted it out as a single 'cause it was revolution and there was a lot of violence going on and I wanted to get it out fast. But the others came back from holiday and said we don't think it's commercial or not good enough or some crap like that. And we waited and waited and we got "Hey Jude," but we would have had both if we hadn't waited.

That kind of thing I can't wait for. They let me put "The Ballad of John and Yoko" out, but I wanted it out as news, not as something like the film of the event. I wanted the video of the event happening then and that's it really. I can't wait.

I offered "Cold Turkey" to the Beatles but they weren't ready to record a single, so I did it as the Plastic Ono Band. I don't care what it goes out as, as long as it goes out.

Have you ever thought of writing songs for other artists as another possible solution?

No, not specifically *for* them because if I write a particularly good song, or one I like, I want to do it myself. But I often think of giving somebody I like a song, or something like that, but I usually don't get around to it. But the thing is with all our songs, remixing it is as important as writing it.

When you are about to record a new Beatles album, do you feel very excited about it? Does that old excitement still permeate the sessions?

Oh yeah, sure, sure. Every time you go in the studio you get the whole thing all over . . . the nerves and the light goes on and everything. It's still the same battle every time and the same joy.

One gets the impression that you are the most active of the Beatles while the others are quite content to take it easy.

That's not always like that . . . only at the moment because I'm active in peace. For a couple of years, Paul was the one who was hustling us together. Saying, "C'mon, record" and we'd go, "Ah, c'mon, we don't feel like it," and all that. Now I've got something other than just recording to think about and that's what's made me active.

I was really losing interest in just doing the Beatles' bit and I think we all were, but Paul did a good job in holding us together for a few years while we were sort of undecided about what to do.

And I found out what to do and it didn't really have to be with the Beatles. It could have been if they had wanted. But it got that I couldn't wait for them to make up their minds about peace or whatever, about committing themselves, just the same as the songs, so I'd gone ahead and I'd have liked them to have come along.

Did you ever try to get them into the peace scene?

I did a little at first, but I think it was too much like Yoko and me and what we're doing and trying to get them to come along and I think they reacted. I hassled them too much, so I'm really leaving them alone. Maybe they'll come along, wagging their tails behind them, and if not, good luck to them.

If I just mentioned the Sixties, what sort of things come to mind?

I don't think in terms of that. The Sixties I suppose was, I dunno, my early twenties for me, and the Fifties were the good old days, your teenage days. That's what they are to me personally. I don't think much about it; I don't think about this or that decade until people start asking me.

What about new product . . . the Plastic Ono Band, John and Yoko, the Beatles.

Ah, well, the next thing that's sort of in the can is the next John and Yoko "freak" album and one side of it is laughing and the other side is whispering . . . so far anyway. We got John and Yoko and a few engineers—whoever was at EMI at the time—and the guy who cuts our records at Apple and the top EMI Beatles superengineer . . . and we put on funny noses and that and we got stoned and laughed for track over track. And, of course, all the guys, even the ones working for us but originally from EMI (we sort of infiltrated and took all the people we liked, the young people), they were all shouting their own in-jokes.

It's a scream just hearing the in-jokes. It's like when the Beatles used to have the sort of in-jokes. Everybody gets into that sort of humor if you're with them for a long time, so this is like we're sort of sending out that in-joke even though it's everybody's joke. And it makes you laugh, you know.

And then we started whispering the piece that Yoko had done. You like to whisper to one person and they have to pass it on to the next person and by the time it gets back it's gobbledy-gook. Yoko had done this at a theater and there were about two hundred or three hundred people and they passed the whisper right on through the theater, and the guy comes to her at the end to tell her what it is after climbing up the balcony and running all the way down, and she said, "Don't tell me." So that was a scream. And we were doing this whisper thing at the session, and they filmed us doing it. We just got screaming, you know.

People just couldn't get it together. They couldn't even pass a whisper along, they were laughing so much. So it really makes you giggle. It'll start Year One off with a laugh.

The Beatles' stuff is in the can. It comes out in February . . . *Get Back.* And I've got a couple of songs I'll try to make into singles for the Plastic Ono. I keep trying to finish the ones I have when I get an opportunity because I keep writing one line, which always gets me because I can't forget it and I have to keep going back to it. So I've got six or seven that I could call songs and another six or seven that are one or two lines or a thought. But it's getting around to them, with all this going on. But I'll do it, all right, because I like recording. It's something I need.

In the aftermath of the week in Canada with the meetings with Trudeau and Munro, how do you feel about the results?

Well, the meetings, of course, made it really well worthwhile. It was worthwhile anyway but there were about three big turn-ons—one was Dick Gregory, the other was Trudeau and the other was Munro and the other was the men from the drug commission. That's about four actually.

We felt that we'd made a communication with the Establishment and it was, like, surprising to find that they were straight. Of course, it is snobbery to assume that the whole Establishment is one big thing—like it is the same to assume that all Jews are this or all blacks are that. We all are guilty of that.

These people are trying and they're driving a very big machine and there's lots of copilots and they've got to be very careful how they do it.

But it certainly gives us hope that there are straights in there who are trying to communicate with us and all the youth. They do want to know, but they're not sure how to approach us, so we must stretch our hand as they're beginning to try and stretch theirs. No compromise, but, you know, communicate.

You were saying to Health Minister Munro that you were a little worried that talking to so-called Establishment people can appear to be copping out in the eyes of some young people and that you were worried about the danger of this.

It wasn't so much a matter of being worried as of being aware of it. It's just like when the Beatles left Liverpool. Some people thought we'd sold out by leaving Liverpool or leaving even one particular club—the Cavern. It worked even on a dance-hall level.

If you left one dance hall to play at another, you lost a few people. And so when we left Liverpool we lost a few but gained a lot more. And when we left London and England—we lost a few in England because they thought we'd sold out to America. So I'm aware that that'll happen. But we're just about at the stage—John and Yoko and the peace thing—where we're just about to leave England and have just done "The Ed Sullivan Show" and it's just beginning—Year One A.P.

Do you feel confident that the new year, Year One, is going to be a positive year for peace?

Yeah, well, like we think that this decade was a positive decade, not a depressing one. It's the decade of all the music, the generation, and the freedom and the sort of awareness and all the jazz and the moratoriums and the Woodstocks and the Isle of Wights and everything. This is just the beginning. What we've got to do is keep hope alive. Because without it we'll sink.

MARCH 6 1970

1). WHEN YOKO AND I WERE FIRST CONTACTED ABOUT THE PEACE FESTIVAL
BY RITCHIE YORKE/JOHN BROWER _ AS USUAL WITH ANYTHING TO
DO WITH PEACE - WE SAID YES AND HOPED IT WOULD WORK ITSELF
OUT AFTER. WE DID MAKE IT CLEAR THAT WE DIDN'T WANT
- AND DIDN'T HAVE THE ABILITY - TO HANDLE ANY ORGANISATION
- BUT WE DID WANT COMPLETE CONTROL - IF OUR NAMES WERE TO BE
USED TO HUSTLE THE THING TOGETHER. IN THE EARLY STAGES WE
WEREN'T SURE WHETHER THE SHOW WOULD BE FREE - OR NOT. THERE
WAS A LOT OF TALK ABOUT THE 'STONES DISASTER' AND WE WERE
SWAYED INTO THINKING MAYBE IF ITS FREE, PEOPLE WOULD HAVE LESS
RESPECT OR SOME SUCH BULLSHIT. HOWEVER BROWER AND YORKE
PERSUADED US TO COME TO CANADA AND 'ANNOUNCE THE PEACE
FESTIVAL' WHICH WE DID IN OUR USUAL WAY - WHEN THE PRESS
STARTED ASKING ABOUT IS IT FREE OR NOT - I SAID THINGS LIKE
'MAYBE IT WOULD BE BETTER TO PAY THE ARTISTS', 'BUT
NOTHING HAD BEEN FINALISED AND WE WERE GOING TO HAVE
FURTHER DISCUSSIONS WITH BROWER' ETC. WHEN THEY ASKED ME,
IF THE BEATLES WERE COMING. I ANSWERED THAT OF COURSE I
WOULD ASK THEM - IN FACT I WOULD ASK 'EVERYONE WHO WAS
ANYONE' WHICH I INTENDED TO - BUT ONLY WHEN I HAD A COMPLETE
RUNDOWN ON THE SHOW - HOW MUCH? WHERE? HOW? WHY? IN FACT I
WASN'T GOING TO ASK ANYONE I KNEW-EVEN VAGULEY, TO COMMIT
THEMSELVES UNTIL WE KNEW WHAT WAS HAPPENING. - WE NEVER FOUND
OUT! THEY TALKED ABOUT FOUNDATIONS AND WHAT THEY
COULD DO WITH ALL THE 'MILLIONS' WHICH WE WERE TOLD WOULD BE
EARNED. ALL THE TIME IN CANADA AND AFTER WE WERE GETTING
PRESSURE TO CORNER DYLAN - BEATLES - PRESLEY BUT WE STILL
DIDN'T HAVE ANY IDEA HOW BROWER INTENDED TO ARRANGE THINGS.

LATER WHEN WE WERE IN RETREAT IN DENMARK WE BEGAN THINKING -
WHY SHOULDN'T IT ALL BE FREE? - SURELY THEY CAN HUSTLE SOME FILM
FIRMS OR SOMETHING TO PUT UP MONEY? AND ANYWAY IT LOOKED LIKE
THE GOVERNMENT NATIONAL AND LOCAL WERE INTERESTED - WOULDN'T
IT BE A GREAT PLUG FOR 'YOUNG CANADA' - AND THE TOURIST TRADE?

The original manuscript.

"HAVE WE ALL FORGOTTEN WHAT VIBES ARE?"

By John Lennon/April 16, 1970

HEN the Toronto Peace Festival thing was look-ing like it was getting out of hand, I sent John Lennon a wire asking him to explain. John said he immediately sat down and wrote the following piece. After a week-long delay, here it is.

—Editor

When Yoko and I were first contacted about the peace festival by Ritchie Yorke and John Brower—as usual with anything to do with peace—we said yes and hoped it would work itself out after. We did make it clear that we didn't want—and didn't have the ability—to handle any organization—but we did want com-plete control—if our names were to be used to hustle the thing together.

In the early stages we weren't sure whether the show would be free or not. There was a lot of talk about the "Stones' disaster" and we were swayed into thinking maybe if it's free, people would have less respect or some such bullshit. However, Brower and Yorke persuaded us to come to Canada and "announce the peace festival," which we did in our usual way.

When the press started asking about is it free or not, I said things like, "Maybe it would be better to pay the artists, but nothing had been finalized and we were going to have further discussions with Brower," etc.

When they asked me if the Beatles were coming, I answered that of course I would ask them—in fact, I would ask "everyone who was anyone," which I intended to—but *only* when I had a complete rundown on the show: How much? Where? How? Why? In fact, I wasn't going to ask anyone I knew, even vaguely, to commit themselves until we knew what was happening.

We never found out! They talked about foundations and what they could do with all the "millions" we were told would be earned. All the time in Canada and after we were getting pressure to corner Dylan/Beatles/Presley, but we still didn't have any idea how Brower intended to arrange things.

Later, when we were in retreat in Denmark, we began thinking, "Why shouldn't it all be free? Surely they can hustle some big firms or something to put up money." And, anyway, it looked like the national and local government were interested. Wouldn't it be a great plug for "Young Canada"—and the tourist trade?

In Denmark, we'd had no phone for a few weeks, being in a far-out farm house. When we finally got one, all hell let loose (also, we had been fasting— meditating, energy exchange, telepathy—for days). We got the horrors when our personal assistant, A. Fawcett, rang, saying, "Disaster, disaster. Klein is frightening Brower off!—and the Canadian government doesn't like it and Brower won't touch the festival if Klein is involved!" And a lot more Aquarian paranoia.

We fell for it. I rang Allen and insulted him no end with the biggest, loudest verbal ammunition I could muster, screaming about what he had done to Brower at their meeting at Allen's office. Allen was hurt—but I even suspected that. (You can't imagine the shit about him we've had laid on us for the past few years, plus we were so sensitive and "clear" at just having had no contact outside the small group of us.)

Anyway, I shellacked him and told him we had tape recordings of his meeting with Brower (Brower told us he had tapes of conversations with Allen, etc., which proved this and that—this is before I rang Allen). And they had lots of "dirt" on Klein, connecting him with the Mafia and God knows what else. So I said, "Stop just telling me about it (having heard it all before). Show me some proof."

With (left to right) Kyoko (Yoko's daughter with Tony Cox), Tony Cox and friend Melinda. North Jutland, Denmark.

The situation seemed so desperate that we allowed Brower/Yorke to come to Denmark with their "proof." They arrived with a cassette player which had on it a fairly straight conversation between Brower and Klein about the festival. Yoko, me, Tony and Melinda all thought that the way Brower was phrasing his questions to Allen was more peculiar than Allen's answers, which were noncommittal. In fact, all Klein said was, "Come and see me and we'll talk in the office, not on the phone."

The so-called "dossier of dirt" on Klein—some supposedly from Canadian government sources, including something about him ringing the Danish king and queen—turned out to be a typewritten page of shit from people who obviously disliked Klein for many different and personal reasons—but all of it was *opinion*.

We both felt so ashamed of what effect this hearsay crap—all of this information had been gathered by them ringing people and saying, "What do you think of Allen Klein?"—had on Brower/Yorke and Fawcett. (I forgot to mention the look on Brower's face when we told him we definitely wanted to do the festival *free!* He asked for "time to think," etc., said he'd committed acts previous to contacting us—surprise! surprise!)

Then we asked Klein to come over so we could put them all together in one room and sort it all out. The meeting was tense at first but then relaxed a little. We talked and pointed out what their or anyone's paranoia had done or could do to them and sent them back to their hotel in Aalborg in what we thought was a better state of mind.

It didn't work. They spent the night prowling the corridors—Brower with a knife! Waiting for the Mafia to get them!

(A friend of ours who was also staying at the hotel, Dr. Don Hamrick—or Zee, to his Martian friends—sent them a love note which they interpreted as the Mafia death sentence! So you can imagine where their heads were at.)

We had decided to do the show free *before* they arrived—and were even more convinced after seeing them. We blamed the "bad vibes" on the fact that so much money was being talked about that people had lost their heads. It was resolved that Brower would go home to Canada and produce a proper plan of campaign: How we could do it free or why not.

We did mention one or two things had been said and done without our knowledge, e.g., Jerry Wexler, of Atlantic, was on the Peace Committee. And why hadn't we been informed—and why was he on it, in fact? This was put down to us having no phone for three weeks—which seemed reasonable. Another was an ad in *Billboard*, which was asking radio stations to join the Peace Campaign. We didn't like the style of the ad, so we drew out what we wanted. It *never* did happen the way Yoko and I wanted it. We were told it was "too late." Too late for what?

After they had all gone home, we decided we needed someone in Canada with Brower to keep his "vibes" steady. We still hoped that the larger concept of the peace festival and its karmic effects on the world had lifted him out of the bread hang-up scene and he would turn on to being a peace promoter.

Tony said he had a friend who had been at Harbinger with Zee and many others and who could probably go to Toronto and help. I don't know what happened, but two guys turned up at our Denmark farm—one said he'd had the peace-festival idea a long time ago and had all the plans and logos. So we listened, made music together and they went back to the hotel in Aalborg. We decided not to use them as they looked like they would confuse the issue even more. (The spokesman was a magician who was going to turn anyone who messed up the festival into a frog or something.)

They went back to Canada—with no instructions from us and moved in on Brower's scene to "straighten him out." The results we've been reading about in *Rolling Stone*, i.e., going to California and blabbing off about who was to be invited and who was not, etc.

(All this without any words to John and Yoko who had "complete control." That reminds me. On the tape between Klein and Brower, Brower kept saying he would give us "artistic control." Klein answered no to that. *We all know* that "artistic control" means very little and in fact we haven't even had that! They also had taped phone calls from Yoko which we inadvertently heard at the beginning of the cassette—just testing, I suppose!)

Since then, various whispers have reached us about the "impossibility of doing it free—the government won't let us, etc." Brower and Klein met again in New York, Klein telling him that John and Yoko wouldn't do it any other way but free. Meanwhile, Ritchie Yorke was doing some nice things 'round the world with Ronnie Hawkins (who, by the way, ended up paying for all the phone bills that had accumulated during our stay in Toronto, which was arranged by Brower. We'll look into it Ronnie, don't worry!).

Ritchie got to London sometime in late February and told us about his trip: How he had been hearing strange things about the festival, and Brower in particular. We said, "Yes we heard it, too, what shall we do?" We discussed dropping the whole idea before it was too late. I must admit to wanting "out" many times after Denmark. The pressure and the tale-telling was bringing me down but Yoko kept waking me up again, reminding me of our original intentions. Ritchie then went to Toronto to find out what was happening.

The latest news we got was that Brower was again in New York and so was Rabbi Abraham L. Feinberg—who sent us a telegram saying his name was at stake (don't worry, Rabbi. God will save you!). I'm not sure whether Klein saw Brower or not but one or two things came out from New York—*Village Voice, New York Times, Rolling Stone*—which, I suppose, were meant to make our position clear. But obviously they didn't because *here we are*—as a result of Jann Wenner's telegram! We've had only one call from John Brower over the past one-and-a-half months (we've been editing the Montreal bed-in film) and it came, surprisingly enough, *after* the articles mentioned above. Brower spoke to Yoko (I wonder if he taped it?). He said he was sending his plans to us. One and a half weeks has gone and still nothing. I rang Allen and he said he was still waiting for the plans, too!

In spite of everything—and you haven't heard *half*—Yoko and I would still like to be part of a peace festival in Canada or anywhere else. Our latest idea was to have everyone at the festival singing only *Hare Krishna*—including all those famous stars I'm supposed to be getting in touch with whom I'm sure will run a mile if I call them now, after all the shit of the last few months—anyway there wouldn't be any money involved in that! No chance! People would have to come for the right reasons whatever they are.

One thing in the *Rolling Stone* article which struck us: Someone said, "Do we need a festival?" Yoko and I still think we need it—not just to show that we can gather peacefully and groove to rock bands, but to change the balance of energy power. On earth and, therefore, in the universe.

Have we all forgotten what vibes are? Can you imagine what we could do together in the one spot—thinking, singing and praying for peace—one million souls apart from any TV link-ups, etc. to the rest of the planet. If we came together for *one reason*, we could *make it together!*

We need help! It is out of our control. Brower does not represent us any more than you do. All we have is our name. (Klein will help any way we want, but he won't let us be hyped.) We are sorry for the confusion, it's bigger than both of us. We are doing our best for all our sakes—we still believe. Pray for us.

Love and Peace   John and Yoko

In early 1970.

WHO AND WHAT KILLED THE TORONTO PEACE FESTIVAL?

By Barry Ballister/December 24, 1970

T was 2:30 in the morning early in December a year ago when the phone awakened me.

"Hi, Barry. This is Bruce. How are you? I heard you quit your job and moved on a farm. Far out. Beautiful. How are you?"

Bruce Newmark, I figured. Calling from Toronto. Two-thirty in the morning. Crazy.

"Yeah. Hi, Bruce. How's the shop? Good? Great! Really nice hearing from you . . . but Bruce, why two-thirty in the morning?"

"Did I get you up? Sorry, but it's really important. Can you fly up here first thing in the morning? There's somebody who wants to meet you. John Brower. He's a friend of mine and he's doing the Toronto Peace Festival with John Lennon and he wants you to do all the advertising and publicity and press relations and it's really beautiful."

I had heard the rumble about the Toronto Peace Festival and had wanted to do something like it after I left my job as Creative Director of Ted Bates and Company Advertising in New York. So after a few more middle-of-the-night calls, I finally arranged to go to Toronto to meet John Brower.

A guy named Hugh Curry met me at the airport. He was sorry, but John Brower had had to leave suddenly to join John Lennon in Denmark at a summit meeting. Lennon was at the farm where Yoko's ex-husband, Tony Cox, was living with a chick named Melinda. John and Yoko had been called there suddenly because Yoko's daughter, in Tony's custody, had taken sick. Brower had followed the Lennons a day or two later with a Dr. Hamrick and someone called Leonard. Hamrick called himself "doctor" but apparently it was a title he'd given himself as the founder of a psychic cult living at a place in California called Harbinger Springs.

When we got to the hotel I called my friend Bruce.

"Bruce, who's Hamrick? And a cat named Leonard?"

Bruce told me all he could about Hamrick, or Don, as he called him. Bruce said he had a fantastic mind, that he had written some psychic books or papers, and was in trouble with the law in some states. Leonard was one of Hamrick's disciples. They believed and preached that they and their Harbinger brothers were in contact with supernatural beings from another planet who would arrive on earth to save us from our own self-destruction. Melinda, who was now living with Yoko's ex-husband, was also a member of Harbinger and was a witch. There was a plan at Harbinger, Bruce said, by which the Harbinger people would "capture" the Beatles, obviously now through Melinda and her association with the Lennons. "The Beatles would be the earth force by which the supernatural powers and the Harbinger people could act in concert to bring peace to our chaotic planet."

The next day I went to the office of Karma Productions. It was a spot-on hippie office. Peace and pot posters and twenty-five people rapping and playing guitars. Curry showed me a map of the site. Mosport Park—an automobile road race track about forty miles outside of Toronto. The property included woods, streams, parking areas, buildings, water, power supply and access highways. Perfect.

Then he laid the Peace Network on me. Four hundred radio stations, including New York City's two biggest rock-music stations, were going to pump out a constant flow of John and Yoko Peace Messages and Peace Network Reports. Ultimately, everything would be directed toward promoting the biggest piece of "peace news" around: the Toronto Peace Festival.

If the Harbinger Springs thing seemed like pure fantasy, everything else I was seeing was real. Curry, Brower and their investors really had hold of something. They had four hundred radio stations eager to give away time and endorsement; millions of lines of free newspaper space and publicity and the festival was still six months away. They had the Canadian prime minister's de facto endorsement. They had secured the perfect site with a $20,000 bond and John Lennon was lending his name, his support and offering to bring over the other three Beatles. It could hardly miss.

Curry and I did some preliminary business. Then I asked: "How much do I make?"

"We've still got a few points to give away. I was thinking about half a point."

"How much is a point worth?"

"A lot of money, man. A lot of money."

"What's the half point from, Hugh, the gross?"

"The producers' share, after the Peace Foundation."

"After the what?" I hadn't heard of that before.

"The Peace Foundation. We're setting up a Peace Foundation with a board of trustees with people like Ted Kennedy and Pete Seeger and John Lennon administering the money for peace causes."

"I'll take cash. In front. And a contract for twenty thousand dollars."

"Whewww. That's awful high, Barry."

"Look, Hugh. I don't want to quibble or have to check your books to see that I got a fair share. And I didn't say twenty so you could say ten and we'd settle for fifteen. It's six months of a lot of hard work and a lot of traveling from New York and it's cheap labor at twenty anyway."

"Okay," said Hugh, "it's a deal."

"I want a contract."

"As soon as you talk to Brower we'll straighten out all the details and write up the contract."

"When do I talk to him?"

"As soon as he gets back from Denmark."

It was near the end of January when Hugh Curry called.

"Brower's back. Come on up."

"Did you talk about a contract?"

"It's all set."

"I'll be there Thursday, the fifth. Have a check for me when I get there."

"Okay, man."

In the middle of the night before I left, Bruce called from Toronto.

"John Lennon cut his hair. You're the first person besides Brower and me and Wesley to know."

"That's really wonderful, Bruce. I mean, so what? What's the big deal?"

"It's really heavy, Barry. It's Lennon's way of saying it's time for heavy changes. And you're part of it."

"Look, Bruce. I'll be in Toronto tomorrow and we'll talk about it then."

The two-hour flight took all day because of a snowstorm. When I arrived at the hotel, there was a message to call Mr. Curry. I did. He said he was sorry but John Brower had had to leave for California to book some talent and hold a press conference in Los Angeles.

I went to Karma Productions first thing Friday morning.

"What is it with you clowns?" I was yelling.

"Hey, man, I'm really sorry. He'll be back tonight." Hugh was defenseless. "We got real problems."

"Yeah? Well I don't want any part of your problems or anything else until I see a contract, a check and some sign of good faith."

"We'll draw up a contract after you talk with Brower and send it to you with a check. You're our creative director. I want you to know what's going on."

"What happened in Denmark?" I wanted to know.

"Listen to this," Curry began. "Brower gets to Denmark with Hamrick and Leonard. And they got to Tony's farm . . ."

"Who's Tony?" I interrupted.

"Yoko's ex-husband. And they go up to the door and some cat tells them to empty all their pockets before they come in."

"For what?"

"They didn't want any dope in their house. Anyway they go in and there's this big room and it smells weird like lots and lots of flowers and incense, but really heavy. John and Yoko and Allen Klein, the Beatles' manager, and Melinda and the baby and Tony are all sitting on the floor perfectly still. And Brower freaks out. I mean, Lennon and Yoko are almost completely bald."

"Yeah, I heard that. Bruce told me."

"Bruce? How did he know?"

"Telepathy, I guess. I don't know."

"Anyway," Hugh continued, "they're bald. Like a head of fuzz. Even Yoko's kid. John said the kid came up to him and said, 'I'm really a girl, I'm really a girl.' But nobody else said anything. They just sat there. Then Melinda started to pass this little dish around with some black sticky stuff. John said it smelled like medicine. And everybody ate some of it."

"What was it?"

"John doesn't know. It was something Melinda made and it got everybody really high. John said, *really* high. Like a completely nonphysical feeling. All of a sudden Lennon and Yoko start giggling to one another and Lennon whips out a piece of paper and it says:

> F R E E
> (for one dollar)
> JOHN LENNON
> PEACE FESTIVAL
> TORONTO, JULY 3, 4, 5
> TO CELEBRATE THE
> YEAR I A.P.
> WAR IS OVER IF YOU WANT IT

"Lennon said it was the only kind of a festival he'd have anything to do with and Brower should fly back to Toronto and draw up complete plans for the festival and submit them by March first for his approval. And he wanted Hamrick and Leonard to be part of the organization. Then Lennon leaned over to Allen Klein and started to pound his fist . . . and get this . . . he said: 'Hitler was right, Allen. Hitler was right. You've got to control the people.'

"Then Hamrick and Leonard start rapping about their invention. They invented a thing they call an air-car. A two-passenger car that looks like a plane that goes on the ground or flies in the air. And never needs fuel. They say it's powered by psychic energy. And they're going to get one ready for the festival and John and Yoko will arrive in one."

"Man, I want two seats up front," I said. "Right up front."

"No kidding, man. They're serious.

"Wait'll you hear it from Brower. It's really crazy. They're going to fly right down into the middle of Mosport Park in one of these psychic-energy planes, or cars, and freak out a million people."

"You don't believe a minute of it," I said.

"Of course not, man. But Brower does. It's like he's been hypnotized by these Harbinger cats . . ."

"Or drugged," I suggested.

"Brower says if these guys can pull off a cosmic stunt he's all for it. He's not making a move without them. And without them there's no Lennon and no Lennon means no festival."

"Woodstock didn't have a Lennon," I reminded him.

"Yeah, but we do, even though I sometimes wish we didn't."

"What about the free-for-one-dollar idea?" It seemed that was a reality we had better begin to deal with.

"That's bullshit," Curry said. "A million people at a dollar apiece is only a million dollars. It'll cost damn near that, or more, for toilets, lights, facilities and other crap. And get this. Now the Ontario police want us to post bonds. $875,000 for police and security. $425,000 for water. $377,000 for sewage. $50,000 for garbage. And $1,500,000 for medical care. Lennon doesn't know that. Once he knows what's happening he'll get over that *free* idea. When we show him the final proposal for the Peace Foundation he'll see that the festival can't be free if we want any kind of bread for the foundation."

The next morning I went to meet Brower at nine o'clock. I rang the doorbell of the townhouse repeatedly. I rapped the knocker.

Finally, there was some stumbling and coughing behind the door. It opened to reveal a puffy-eyed, puckish character, about twenty-three years old, wearing striped pajamas and a brand new short haircut. John Brower.

"Sorry, man. I was so wrecked I couldn't wake up. Want some coffee?"

"Sure."

I followed him into a kitchen filled up with a baby's playpen, tops and a stack of used-up pizza-pie delivery cartons.

"What happened with Lennon?" I asked. It seemed important to me to understand Lennon's role and attitude before we decided on what kind of advertising we would run.

Brower's story began with the call from Denmark to Lennon and Yoko in Toronto. He took us through the scene at the farmhouse door, the haircuts, the black sticky stuff, the little girl with no hair, the Hitler reference, the air-car and the free-for-one-dollar plan. And he amplified the cosmic-power theory.

"Hamrick and Leonard have been in contact with cosmic spirits. The Harbinger astrologers and numerologists have figured out the time and place for these cosmic forces to begin their work on planet earth. The time is early this summer and it will happen in North America, but not in the United States."

"Maybe they're talking about the solar eclipse," I suggested. "That's going to happen in North America, not in the United States and, with a little interpolation, March could easily mean early summer. And a solar eclipse is certainly cosmic activity."

"Leonard said it was Canada. And that's what the Toronto scene is all about. Trudeau is a peace person. Toronto is a haven for the draft resisters. It's part of the cosmic plan."

"How much do Hamrick and Leonard want for their part in this cosmic plan?" I asked.

"Lennon wants them to be part of the Peace Foundation."

"What about the car that flies?"

"All the profits from the sale of this car would go to the Peace Foundation."

"I have an idea," I said. "Why don't we take all the money your backers gave you and invest it in this flying car? We'd make a lot more money and we'd have a lot less hassles. The world wants flying machines a lot more than it wants peace anyway. Besides, you can still put the profits into the Peace Foundation. I'd sure buy a car that flies and doesn't need fuel."

"We're in the festival business, not the car business. If Leonard and Hamrick want to promote this thing, that's their business."

Three days later we lost Mosport. Curry related the news. "The New York State police were up here and they showed the Mosport people some films they say they shot at Woodstock. You know. The garbage, and the traffic, and all the nudie shots and people fucking. It really made the townspeople uptight and now the town council says the park can only be used for racing events. They don't want no festival."

I left for Mexico for a few weeks. The day I got home Hugh Curry called.

"Can you fly up here tonight? Hey, man, it's important."

"No. Not tonight. What's up?"

"We've got a new site. Seven hundred acres. Woods and streams and a whole series of natural-acoustic bowls. It's really outta sight." Hugh was very excited.

"Where?" I asked.

"About one hundred and twenty miles from here. Park Hill. We bought all the land."

"You *bought* all the land?"

"Yeah. Cost us twenty thousand dollars. Now we can do whatever we want. There's a big meeting with the mayor there tonight. Hey, man. We're ready to roll. When can you get here?"

"I'll take the first plane up in the morning. Have a round-trip ticket at the airport, get me a room and have my check when I get there."

"Will do, man. It's great to have you back."

My ticket was waiting, and a car was waiting at Toronto. We went directly to Karma Productions and spent the day on festival plans.

The following morning I showed for breakfast at Curry's house. Hugh's pretty girlfriend, Kathy, was making breakfast in a see-through when Curry came down. He was wrecked, shattered and twisted. "We lost Park Hill," he said instead of good morning.

"You *what?* What happened to the mayor and the twenty thousand dollars?"

"We found the mayor isn't where it's at. It's some guy they call the reeve. It's a town position or something. Anyway, the reeve hates us."

"Now what?"

"We'll just have to find another site," Curry said.

We finished breakfast and I went back to the hotel and checked out. Then I made one last visit to Karma Productions, Ltd.

"Hey, man. Read this," Curry caught me in the hall.

It was a copy of a telegram from Lennon to Brower in response to the festival plans that had been sent to London.

The telegram read: "Just read your report. You have done exactly what we told you not to. We said it was to be free. We want nothing to do with you or your festival. Please do not use our name or our ideas or symbols."

"Now read this," said Hugh, as he handed me a seven-page draft of a release to be sent out.

"John and Yoko Lennon are no longer involved with the Toronto Peace Festival, planned for July 3, 4 and 5 at Mosport Park. But the festival will proceed as planned, according to the producers."

"I thought you lost Mosport?" I said to Hugh.

"We're still working on it," he answered.

I read further: "John and Yoko now want the festival to be completely free, and while we agree with the intent, we are not prepared to accept the responsibility."

Brower pointed out that Lennon himself had initially wanted the festival to be run as a normal business enterprise, with artists and organizers being paid and patrons buying tickets. On December 17, 1969, at a press conference in Toronto, John Lennon made the following statement in reference to the Peace Festival: "People will be paid for their performance. We'll try to get some cream off the top to set up a peace fund, because I can just see all the performers thinking, 'Oh, no, he's going to hustle us to do something for nothing.' So we've got to give them something to get them interested and to pull them away from whatever work they're doing. We want to set up something that people will get wages and money for. Otherwise, it's another charity affair, so they will get paid. I think there's enough money to be made out of a show like this for everyone."

Brower's release continued:

"We don't understand this sudden switch, which renders the whole idea of a festival logistically impossible. There is no such thing as something for nothing . . . not even a Peace Festival."

I left for the airport. I had never wanted to believe what was so obvious. There never was going to be a Toronto Peace Festival.

I SAY GOODBYE

The following two pieces evoke the atmosphere of the last days of the Beatles. The tensions that marked their gradual breakup are in evidence as John and Yoko began increasingly to shape their lives as an independent couple.

ONE GUY STANDING THERE SHOUTING "I'M LEAVING"

By Jann S. Wenner/May 14, 1970

THERE is almost no attempt in this new set to be anything but what the Beatles actually are: John, Paul, George and Ringo. Four different people, each with songs and styles and abilities. They are no longer Sgt. Pepper's Lonely Hearts Club Band and it is possible that they are no longer the Beatles.

—From the review of the White Album (*The Beatles*)
Rolling Stone, December 21, 1968

The status of the Beatles hasn't changed much since then. Only now bitterness and mistrust have begun to set in. For if they have indeed "broken up," the break took place well before Paul McCartney released his new album and announced *he* was leaving.

In the words of John Lennon, "We were long gone, a long time ago."

What has happened in the last few weeks is the public result of the bitter fight over Beatle business manager Allen Klein and the formal end of the Lennon-McCartney songwriting team.

And underlying that is the passage of time, in which boys turn into men, in which they marry, in which they grow up, in which they grow apart.

"The Beatles haven't had a future, for me, for the last two years," John said after all this hit the papers. "All of us are laboring under this delusion about Beatles and McCartney and Lennon and Harrison and Starr. But, you know, we all have to get over it, us and the public. It's a joke. What we did was what we did, but what we are is something different."

If there is a "reason" the Beatles broke up, it goes back to a series of events that center around the formation of Apple. After Brian Epstein's death and the release of *Sgt. Pepper*, the Beatles were set adrift to find their own direction without guidance. They started Apple, set up to be "run" by the Beatles as a collective, and in it they installed their longtime friends and associates to take care of the business.

They found out, however, that four musicians and their road managers do not a successful record company make, no matter who they are. John, George and Ringo, bored with the daily meetings over minor business hassles, soon drifted away from it, and it quickly became Paul's trip.

Paul—who in the meantime had married Linda Eastman, whose father and brother are music-business lawyers—couldn't run it either. And it was a mess. Apple turned into a huge financial loss, draining like a sieve, under incompetent management replete with freeloaders, hangers-on, loyal and loving Beatle workers, and all of it bogged down by bickering, with the Beatles unable to resolve it.

John soon let it slip to the papers that the operation had bled the Beatles nearly dry. Then he brought in Allen Klein.

And the fight began. John and Yoko Lennon in one corner, Paul and Linda McCartney in the other. John, with his clothes off and other weird trips, drifting further and further away from Paul, the "nice Beatle" repulsed by John's carryings-on. And John, with George and Ringo, wanting Allen Klein in to bring order to the chaos, versus Paul, whose new in-laws wanted to take over the Beatles.

So it went. And so, they "broke up."

When did the Beatles break up?

John: "The Beatles' White Album. Listen—all you experts listen, none of you can hear. Every track is an individual track—there isn't any Beatle music on it. I just say, listen to the White Album. It was John and the Band, Paul and the Band, George and the Band, like that. Paul and the Band. What I did was sort of say, 'Fuck the Band. I'll make John—I'll do it with Yoko,' or whatever. I put four albums out last year and I didn't say a fucking word about quitting."

The current reports of the breakup were the result of a story released to wire services by McCartney's brother-in-law, New York attorney John Eastman, in which the new album was announced along with statements that Paul had formed his own production company and was planning to do more things on his own.

This was quickly followed by the release of a startling four-page question-and-answer interview in which Paul said he was not planning to make more records with the Beatles, disavowed Allen Klein, made a few "anti" remarks about John and Ringo, said he didn't foresee a time when he and John would

All together then: 1969.

write songs again and announced that he had broken with the Beatles.

"I'm telling you," said John, "that's what's going on. It's John, George and Ringo as individuals. We're not even communicating with or making plans about Paul. We're just reacting to everything he does. It's a simple fact that he can't have his own way so he's causing chaos. I don't care what you think of Klein—call Klein something else, call him *Epstein* for now—and just consider the fact that three of us chose Epstein. Paul was the same with Brian in the beginning, if you must know. He used to sulk and God knows what. Wouldn't turn up for the dates or the bookings. It's always been the same, only now it's bigger because we're all bigger. It's the same old game.

"You know, it's like this," John said, "when we read all this shit in the paper, Yoko and I were laughing because the cartoon is this: four guys on a stage with a spotlight on them; second picture, three guys onstage, breezing out of the spotlight; third picture, one guy standing there, shouting, 'I'm leaving.' We were all out of it."

DADDY HAS GONE AWAY NOW: LET IT BE

By Jonathan Cott and David Dalton / July 9, 1970

HE idea for a Beatles film came about toward the end of 1968, when Apple was still a kind of nucleus for the group. Some of the utopian schemes had already been abandoned. The film division was dispensed with as unnecessary, and the electronics division had dwindled to a little plastic apple with a transistor radio inside. Earlier in the year Apple Fashions, the projected spearhead of a Beatles retail empire, had folded and Paul had stopped talking about Apple as "a Western form of communism" or as a "huge commercial/creative complex along the lines of British Petroleum."

Apple's attempts to integrate the Beatles' own personal aspirations with the mechanics of business was proving a fruitless task. Even Apple stationery was being redesigned—from a peeling apple with the legend WORDS FROM APPLE to a peeling pear with the legend LIES FROM APPLE.

In this atmosphere, it is amazing that the film got together at all. But in January 1969, the Beatles spent over one hundred hours playing, arguing, rapping, rehearsing in the Twickenham Film Studios, the Apple studio and on the Apple roof. The film, like the long-awaited album, was first titled *Get Back*, but someone must have realized that after one year of getting back—the film still in the editing room—the best recourse, aside from going forward (which the

Beatles did with *Abbey Road*), was just to let it be. The film comes to us in its own good time. If *A Hard Day's Night* portrayed the Beatles' "real life" image as fiction, and if *Yellow Submarine* embodied that image mythically, *Let It Be* documents a few moments of the Beatles together "awake" and "for real." But we only get a few moments because with three hundred hours of footage, only the highlights, the more dramatic scenes and the funnier dialogue are shown.

Let It Be is not only a film about the Beatles deciding on the kind of film they wanted to appear in, it also shows them rehearsing for the imagined, debated possibility of their return to public performances after two and a half years: The House of Parliament, a Tunisian amphitheater, a Liverpool cathedral, a hospital and an ocean liner, "singing the middle-eight as the sun comes up."

With all the possibilities in the world, and after all the transformations and posturings, it is the desire to be seen, to communicate with an audience, to hear the screams that will bring them into the present and pump energy into the myth that drives them toward playing again in public. The roof concert is both the conclusion of the film and the solution to the debate about if and where to perform for an audience. The Beatles, wind-swept, as if on ship deck, the crowd of mildly surprised office workers and midday shoppers acknowledging the Beatles' first concert in two and a half years.

The unedited *Let It Be*, running to some eight hundred hours of film (including footage from all four cameras at Twickenham and on the roof) will perhaps someday be donated to the National Trust, where scholars will delve into its meaning. In its totality it is a revealing document, revealing, in the same sense as studies of scientists isolated in bathyspheres for months at a time are revealing, or like the slouch of a body cast in plaster that takes several hours to set. It manifests the idiosyncracies, blemishes, acts of vision and churlishness, the patterns and postures that the Beatles put themselves through while relating to one another and to their public images. The released version can reveal little of this.

Although the premise of the film at its inception was Warholian in the sense that you just turn the cameras on for two months and let it be, the end product is considerably more structured. For one thing, time will not allow what could have been a whole movie in itself, namely, the Beatles creating, working on, refining and finally distilling *one* song, with peripheral dialogue, old rock and general studio habits. Instead, we have a series of about twenty songs flashing by with occasional "representative" dialogue.

This is not to denigrate the quiet, unassuming, even magical moments *Let It Be* captures, as when the music always ends discussion, each Beatle submitting to it, John and George finally understanding each other in "Dig It" or "For You Blue." But it *is* a sleight of hand (as John says, "Bognor Regis is a tartan that covers Yorkshire") that presents to us this condensation of moments as an illusion of a day in the life. The structure of the film as we see it gives the impression of elation, partly by the very physical progression of scenes from Act I in the murky, sublunar atmosphere of Twickenham (rainbows on rainbows) through the intimacy of the Apple sessions and finally, to the four evangelists emerging onto the roof to air, light and the birth of spring. (The roof sequence was shot at the beginning of February.)

What dialogue there is in *Let It Be* suggests we could still be in some snug, day-to-day corner of Pepperland. The order of the day is cheerfulness (*Paul*: "Hi, lads." *John*: "Queen says no to pot-smoking FBI members"). Just the lads getting together for a bash. But, in the light of subsequent Beatle traumas, the illusion must seem somewhat false. The doubts about their being able to perform again in public, and the threatening clouds that were to break into open hostility with the release of Paul's album, are scarcely touched upon. In *Let It Be* we are given a glimpse of group friction (for the sake of realism), a dialogue between Paul and George that hits on one of the main contentions between them: None of them wants to be sessionmen for the others. *Paul*: I always seem to be annoying you. . . . *George*: All right, I'll play whatever you want me to play, or I won't play at all if you don't want me to play.

In another sequence, Paul talks earnestly to John ("now look, son") about how they *can* get it on, if they want to. But, because this is not *cinéma vérité* but a documentary made by the Beatles themselves, the emphasis is, quite naturally, not on the tensions. It is one of the paradoxes of reverence that we always wish to know the most intimate details of those we idolize, even when

At Apple offices with Paul (second from left), Allen Klein and Ringo.

the details are not flattering, and for this reason *Let It Be* is not a completely satisfying film. It presents an "as if" situation that any fairly observant Beatle fan knows does not exist. And, again, it is just this insatiable curiosity, like the probing eye of the camera, staring like a mirror at their every action, that has magnified their rifts and sealed their quarrels. (*Paul*: I get the horrors every morning about 9:00, when I get my toast and tea.)

One of the strangest phenomena in group situations is who will be "it," who will carry the weight; and here it is Paul, assuming the spectral role of Brian Epstein:

Paul: I mean, we've been very negative since Mr. Epstein passed away. We haven't been positive. That's why all of us in turn have been sick of the group, you know. There's nothing positive in it. It is a bit of a drag. It's like when you're growing up and then your daddy goes away at a certain point in your life and then you stand on your own feet. Daddy has gone away now, you know, and we are on our own little holiday camp. You know, I think we either go home or we do it. It's discipline we need. It's like everything you do, you never had discipline. Mr. Epstein, he said, sort of, "Get suits on" and we did. And so we were always fighting that discipline a bit. But now it's silly to fight that discipline if it's our own. It's self-imposed these days, so we do as little as possible. But I think we need a bit more if we are going to get on with it.

If Paul is elected to play "daddy" (and he has grown a beard to play the role), then George gets to play the "bad boy," and his answer to Paul is, "Well, if that's what doing it is, I don't want to do anything."

Paul comes across as desperately trying to pull the whole thing together, like the father of a family that has become divided ("It's silly for us at this point to crack up"), while George, with a mixture of apathy and mysticism, appears not to care one way or the other, business versus pleasure:

Paul: We should organize our career now. Like, the idea is to get us so we quite enjoy this . . . then what would you like to do next? Would you like to do a live show, lads?

George: It's, like, hard work really to do it. It's a drag 'cause I don't wanna work really . . . have to get up at eight o'clock and get into my guitar . . . "You've got to play your guitar now" and you're not ready for it. But we've got to do that in order to get the goods in . . .

Paul carries the weight and, like an overserious foster parent, occasionally trips over George's punky put-ons:

George: You dig, baby?

Paul: Yeah.

George: You're so full of shit, man.

Paul: What?

George: Before you can pry any secrets from me, first you must find the real me. Which one will you pursue . . . Did you see that?

Paul: What?

George: *The Beard* ⟦a play by Michael McClure⟧.

Paul: No.

George: It's Jean Harlow and Billy the Kid in eternity. It's just the idea of two people onstage and all this audience of different people overhearing what they're saying. Jean Harlow says: "Before you can pry any secrets from me, first you must find the real me. Which one will you pursue?" It ends where she just sits on his knee, and then she sits in the chair and spreads her legs.

In the flak between George and Paul, John, enigmatic, and profoundly humorous, traces out a cosmic antiworld of puns:

John: It's a feeling . . . it's enough to make a haggis grow legs; but tonight we'll celebrate on Irish whiskey, said Gene Pitney, the only Sassenach in the group.

Ringo, who is given a token appearance in *Let It Be* singing "Octopus's Garden" and a boogie duet with Paul, maintains his deadpan humor and dignity throughout. Derek Taylor once described Ringo as miscast in most of the films he has appeared in because "his genius is as a silent actor." And he bears this out beautifully in the sequence where Heather crashes down on his drum kit

At the "Let It Be" session, EMI studios, Twickenham, January 1969.

and his whole body jangles in a flip-flop mime of being-taken-unawares.

His long-suffering face allows him to play a straight man with quizzical intensity to John's ventriloquist:

John: Bognor Regis is a tartan that covers Yorkshire. Rutland is the smallest
county. Scarborough is a college scarf . . . And still the boon wasn't over, the
Queen of Sheba wore falsies.

Ringo: I didn't know that.

John: Didn't you know that? You weren't there at the time. Cleopatra was
a carpet manufacturer.

Ringo: I didn't know that.

John: John Lennon . . .

Ringo: A patriot.

John: I didn't know that.

George rephrases the universe in mystical homilies ("anywhere is paradise"),
and Paul, who's always "on" (a wink is as good as a nod) can never resist the
temptation to play himself. When his head fills the screen, singing the title
song on *Let It Be*, his face flashes between tramp and Old Testament prophet,
but it never quite sticks because he is always a little too sentimental to be
believable.

As the unedited tapes run on and on, fragments of their lives fill in a fraction.
They watch a lot of "telly": "Late Nite Line-Up" on BBC-2, "Spike Milligan,"
science fiction; "I Me Mine," in fact, is based on a tune played by an Austrian
marching band that George was watching late one night.

Visually, *Let It Be* is as beautiful as the sum of its accidents. Its unbelievable
grainy color (generated from 16-millimeter originals) washes about the screen
in the Twickenham sequences like video rainbows, giving each Beatle his own
aura: white for John, purple for Paul, mantra orange for George and red for
Ringo. At times it's like the Beatles in the land of Silver Surfer, especially in one
sequence where George, in yellow and brown (and grainy as Dakota), seems to
drift in and out of the rust background like a speckled trout.

The camera moves in and out as blindly and perceptively as coincidence
itself, picking up with insect eye: fuzz on a microphone while John intones
"Across the Universe"; Paul's fingers touching their reflection in the glazed
piano board; George's face, pale as wax with downcast eyes, as his guitar gently
weeps and John warbling shrilly as a sparrow on "Two of Us."

Outside, the oblique light reflects from Ringo's orange mac like molten lava
and everything looks as if it were shot on a set from *Mary Poppins*. Old men in
macs and sweaters gather around like out-of-work miners at the entrance of a
colliery. The moments are precious; they know they will soon have to move
and, in a gesture of devotion, Peter Asher kneels before John with lyrics on a
sheet of paper.

While, in the end, all we have to relate to are the soft, luminous images of *Let It Be*, the Beatles will insist, like the characters in Pirandello's *Six Characters in Search of an Author*, that "the play is in us, sir!" Their voices on magnetic tape, buried in some vault, will always be ready to reenact their drama, and only they know its true intensity:

Paul [in disembodied voice]: The awful tension of being locked in each other's

Filming and recording "Get Back" on the Apple building rooftop, London, January 30, 1969. This was the group's last performance.

arms snapped last night at TV rehearsal, and Beatles John, George and Harold
. . . A few vicious phrases took place.

John: He, the mystical one who lost so much of the Beatles' magic, she the
nudie . . .

Paul: It's only the suddenness of their decline from the status of boys next
door to the category of weirdies . . .

John [*singing drowns out words*]:

    Early in the morning

    I'm giving you the warning

    Don't you step on my blue suede shoes.

Paul: It would be about the middle of the 1960s [*next few words inaudible*]
began to have a few spots of rust. I would deliberately read Ringo out of it,
because he never developed any fetish toward the bizarre. Lennon was married
happily. McCartney was going steady and George Harrison was about to
marry. Everything in the Beatle garden was rosy. But that was a long time ago.
Having scaled every known peak of show business the Beatles quite deliberately
. . . never came home again. They went their own private way, found their
own friends and became less reliant on each other for guidance and comrade-
ship . . .

[*singing drowns out speech*]

John [*singing*]:

    Early in the evening

    I'm giving you the feeling

    Everybody's nothing

    And nothing to lose.

Paul: Today all of them find acute embarrassment at the stories of one another's adventures and conduct. Harrison's escapades with his favorite mystic
from India . . .

John [*singing*]:

    Hold my baby as tight as I can

    Tonight she's gonna be a big fat man

    Oh baby with your rhythm and blues

    Everybody's rockin tonight.

[*singer and speaker trying to drown each other out*]

Paul: Drugs, divorce and slipping image play desperately on their minds
and it appeared to them all that the public was being encouraged to hate them
. . . capacity to earn is largely tied up in their performances as a group and
until they are either rich enough . . .

[*music drowns out voice*]

. . . irrevocably doomed . . . all over . . . they will never be exactly the same
again.

LENNON REMEMBERS

By *Jann S.Wenner/January 7 & February 4, 1971*

In December of 1970, John Lennon and Yoko Ono spent several days with Jann Wenner, editor and publisher of Rolling Stone, to produce the now famous two-part interview "Working Class Hero." For the first time, Lennon presented an extraordinarily candid, intimate and sometimes angry view of the Beatles and his private life. It remains the definitive autobiographical account of Lennon's life.

When did you realize that what you were doing transcended . . .

People like me are aware of their so-called genius at ten, eight, nine. I always wondered, why has nobody discovered me? In school, didn't they see that I was cleverer than anybody in the school? That the teachers were stupid, too? That all they had was information I didn't need? I got fuckin' lost being in high school. I used to say to me auntie, "You throw my fuckin' poetry out and you'll regret it when I'm famous." And she threw the bastard stuff out.

Do you think you're a genius?

Yes, if there is such a thing, I am one.

When did you first realize that?

When I was about twelve. I used to think I must be a genius but nobody's noticed. I used to think, either I'm a genius or I'm mad—which is it? I used to think, well, I can't be mad, because nobody's put me away; therefore, I'm a genius. I mean, genius is a form of madness, and we're all that way. But I used to be a bit coy about it, you know, like me guitar playing. I didn't become something when the Beatles made it or when you heard about me; I've been like this all me life.

But it was obvious to me. Why didn't they put me in art school? Why didn't they train me? Why did they keep forcing me to be a fuckin' cowboy like the rest of them? I was different. I was always different. Why didn't anybody notice me?

A couple of teachers would encourage me to be something or other, to draw or to paint—to express myself. But most of the time they were trying to beat me into being a fuckin' dentist or a teacher. And then the fuckin' fans tried to beat me into being a fuckin' Beatle or an Engelbert Humperdinck, and the critics tried to beat me into being Paul McCartney.

The Beatles were always talked about—and the Beatles talked about themselves —as being part of the same person.

Well . . . yes.

What's happened to those four parts?

They remembered they were four individuals. You see, we believed the Beatles myth, too.

We were four guys. I met Paul and said, "You want to join me band?" Then George joined and then Ringo joined. We were a band that made it very, very big, that's all.

Why?

Because we were performers, and what we generated was fantastic. When we played straight rock there was nobody to touch us in Britain.

. . . I had a group, I was the singer and the leader; then I met Paul, and I had to make a decision—he had to make a decision, too—whether to have him in the group: Was it better to have a guy who was better than the people I had, or not? To make the group stronger, or to let me be stronger? The decision was to let Paul in and make the group stronger.

Then Paul introduced me to George, and Paul and I had to make the decision, or I had to make the decision, whether to let George in. I listened to George play and I said, "Play 'Raunchy,'" or whatever the old story is, and I let him in. I said, "Okay, you come in." Then the rest of the group was gradually thrown out. It just happened. Instead of going for the individual thing, we went for the strongest format, for equals.

George is ten years younger than me, or some shit like that. I couldn't be bothered with him when he first came around. He used to follow me around like a bloody kid, hanging around all the time; I couldn't be bothered. He was a kid who played guitar, and he was a friend of Paul's, which made it all easier. It took me years to come around to him, to start considering him as an equal or anything.

We had different drummers all the time, because people who owned drum kits were few and far between; it was an expensive item. They were usually idiots. Then we got Pete Best because we needed a drummer to go to Hamburg the next day. We had passed the audition on our own, using a stray drummer.

What did being from Liverpool have to do with your art?

It's the second biggest port in England. The North is where the money was made in the 1800s; that was where all the brass and the heavy people were, and that's where the despised people were. We were the ones who were looked down upon as animals by the Southerners, the Londoners. In the States, the Northerners think that down South, people are pigs, and the people in New York think West Coast is hick. So we were hicksville.

Liverpool is a very poor city, and tough. But people have a sense of humor because they are in so much pain. So they are always cracking jokes, and they are very witty. It's an Irish place, too; it is where the Irish came when they ran out of potatoes, and it's where black people were left or worked as slaves or whatever.

It is cosmopolitan, and it's where the sailors would come home with blues records from America. Liverpool has the biggest country & western following in England besides London—always besides London, because there is more of it there.

I heard country & western music in Liverpool before I heard rock & roll. The people take their country & western music very seriously. I remember the first guitar I ever saw. It belonged to a guy in a cowboy suit and a cowboy hat and a big dobro. They were real cowboys, and they took it seriously. There were cowboys long before there was rock & roll.

What was it like in the early days in London?

When we came down, we were treated like real provincials by the Londoners. We were, anyway.

What was it like, say, running around discotheques with the Stones?

Oh, that was a great period. We were like kings of the jungle then, and we were very close to the Stones. I spent a lot of time with Brian [Jones] and Mick [Jagger], and I admired them. I dug them the first time I saw them in whatever that place is they came from—the Crawdaddy in Richmond.

We were all just at the prime, and we all used to just go around London in our cars and meet each other and talk about music with the Animals and Eric [Burdon] and all that. It was really a good time. That was the best period, fame-wise; we didn't get mobbed so much. I don't know; it was like a men's smoking club, just a very good scene.

What about the tours?

The Beatles' tours were like Fellini's *Satyricon*. If you could get on our tours, you were in. Wherever we went there was a whole scene going. When we hit town, we hit it, we were not pissing about. You know, there's photographs of me groveling about, crawling about in Amsterdam on my knees, coming out of whorehouses and things like that, and people saying, "Good morning, John," and all of that. And the police escorted me to the places because they never wanted a big scandal. I don't really want to talk about it because it will hurt Yoko, and it's not fair. Suffice it to say, just put it like they were *Satyricon* on tour and that's it, because I don't want to hurt the other people's girls either, it's just not fair. I'm sorry.

YOKO: How did you manage to keep that clean image? It's amazing.

JOHN: Because everybody wants the image to carry on. The press around with you want you to carry on because they want the free drinks and the free whores and the fun. Everybody wants to keep on the bandwagon. It's *Satyricon*. We were the Caesars. Who was going to knock us when there's a million pounds to be made? All the handouts, the bribery, the police, all the fuckin' hype, you know. Everybody wanted in.

What accounted for your great popularity?

Because I fuckin' did it. I was like an artist who went off . . . Have you ever heard of, like, Dylan Thomas and all them who never fuckin' wrote but who just went up drinking—Brendan Behan and all of them—they died of drink, everybody who's done anything like that. I just got meself in a party. I was an emperor. I had millions of chicks, drinks, drugs, power and everybody saying how great I was. How could I get out of it? It was like being in a fuckin' train. I couldn't get out. I couldn't create, either. It came out, but I was in the party, and you don't come out of a thing like that.

It was fantastic! I came out of the sticks; I hadn't heard about anything— Van Gogh was the most far-out thing I had ever heard of. Even London was something we used to dream of, and London's nothing. I came out of the fuckin' sticks to take over the world, it seemed to me. I was enjoying it, but I was wrapped in it, too. I was hooked.

It just built up; the bigger we got, the more unreality we had to face and the more we were expected to do. They were always threatening what they would tell the press about us, to make bad publicity if we didn't see their bloody daughter with the braces on her teeth. And it was always the police chief's daughter or the lord mayor's daughter—all the most obnoxious kids, because they had the most obnoxious parents. We had these people thrust on us. Like being insulted by these junked-up middle-class bitches and bastards who would be commenting on our working-classness and our manners. I would go insane, swearing at them, whatever; I'd always do something. I couldn't take it, it was awful—and all that business was awful. It was a fuckin' humiliation. One has to completely humiliate oneself to be what the Beatles were, and that's what I resent. It just happens bit by bit, until this complete craziness surrounds you and you're doing exactly what you don't want to do with people you can't stand—the people you hated when you were ten.

You always said that the Beatles wanted to be bigger than Elvis.

Yes.

Why?

Because Elvis was the biggest. We wanted to be the biggest. Doesn't everybody?

When did you decide that?

Well, first of all, Paul and I wanted to be the Goffin and King of England, because Goffin and King were writing great stuff at that time. . . . We wanted to be this, we wanted to be the next thing, we wanted to be president or whatever. It goes on and on and on. But we always wanted to be bigger than Elvis because Elvis was the thing. No matter what people say, he was it.

When did you realize that you were bigger than Elvis?

I don't know. See, it's different once it happens. It's like, when you actually get to Number One, or whatever, it's different. It's the going for it that is fun.

Would you take it all back?

If I could be a fuckin' fisherman, I would, you know. If I had the capabilities of being something other than I am, I would. It's no fun being an artist. You know what it's like, writing, it isn't fun, it's torture. I read about Van Gogh, Beethoven, any of them—well, if they'd had psychiatrists, we wouldn't have had Gauguin's great pictures.

I resent performing for fucking idiots who don't know anything. They can't feel; I'm the one that's feeling because I'm the one expressing. They live vicariously through me and other artists. One of my big things is that I wish I was a fisherman. I know it sounds silly, and I'd sooner be rich than poor but ignorance is bliss or something. If you don't know, man, there's no pain. Probably there is, but that's how I express it.

How do you rate yourself as a guitarist?

I'm okay. I'm not very good technically, but I can make it fuckin' howl and move. I was rhythm guitarist. It's an important job. I can make a band drive.

What were the first devices and tricks that you used?

The first gimmick was the harmonica. There had been "Hey, Baby," and there was a terrible thing called "I Remember You" in England. We did those numbers, and so we started using it on "Love Me Do" just for arrangements, 'cause we used to work out arrangements. And then we stuck it on "Please Please Me," and then on "From Me to You," and then it went on and on. Then we dropped it—it got embarrassing.

Which songs really stick in your mind as being Lennon-McCartney songs?

"I Want to Hold Your Hand," "From Me to You," "She Loves You" . . . I'd have to have the list, there's so many—trillions of 'em.

In a rock band, you have to keep writing singles. We both had our fingers in each other's pies.

I remember the simplicity that was evident on the Beatles' [White Album]. It was evident in "She's So Heavy," which was about Yoko. In fact, a reviewer wrote of "She's So Heavy": "He seems to have lost his talent for lyrics, it's so simple and boring." But when it gets down to it, when you're drowning, you don't say, "I would be incredibly pleased if someone would have the foresight to notice me drowning and come and help me," you just *scream*. And in "She's So Heavy," I just sang, "I want you, I want you so bad, she's so heavy, I want you," like that. I started simplifying my lyrics then, on the double album.

What about on Rubber Soul—"*Norwegian Wood*"?

I was trying to write about an affair without letting me wife know I was writing about an affair, so it was very gobbledygook. I was sort of writing from my experiences—girls' flats, things like that.

You said to me that Sgt. Pepper *is the album* . . .

Well, it was a peak. Paul and I were definitely working together, especially on "A Day in the Life." That was the way we wrote a lot of the time: You'd write the good bit—the part that was easy—like, "I read the news today," or whatever it was; then, when you got stuck or whenever it got hard, instead of carrying on, you'd just drop it. Then we would meet each other, and I would sing half, and he would be inspired to write the next bit and vice versa. He was a bit shy about it because I think he thought it was already a good song. Sometimes we wouldn't let each other interfere with a song because you tend to be a bit lax with someone else's stuff; you experiment a bit. So we were doing it in his room with the piano. He would ask, "Should we do this?" "Yeah, let's do that."

I keep saying that I always preferred the double album [*The Beatles*], because *my* music is better on the double album; I don't care about the whole concept of *Pepper*; it may be better, but the music was better for me on the double album because I'm being myself on it; I don't like production so much. But *Pepper* was a peak, all right.

How did you get involved in LSD?

A dentist in London laid it on George, me and our wives at a dinner party at his house without telling us. He was a friend of George's and our dentist at the time, and he just put it in our coffee or something. He didn't know what it was; all the . . . middle-class London swingers, or whatever, had all heard about it, and they didn't know it was different from pot or pills. They gave it to us, and he was saying, "I advise you not to leave," and we thought he was trying to keep us for an orgy in his house. So we went out to the Ad Lib discotheque.

We didn't know what was going on, and we thought we were going crackers. It was insane, going around London on it. We thought when we went to the club that it was on fire, and then we thought it was a premiere and that it was just an ordinary light outside. We thought, shit, what's going on here? We were cackling in the streets, and then people were shouting, "Let's break a window." We were just insane. We were just out of our heads. . . .

We finally got on the lift. We all thought there was a fire on it; there was just a little red light, and we were all screaming *aaaagh*—like that—and we were all hot and hysterical. We all arrived on the floor—this was a discotheque that was up a building—and the lift stops, and the door opens and we were all *aaaagh*. We see that it's the club, and we walk in and sit down and the table's elongating.

I think we went to eat before that, and it was just like this thing I had read describing the effects of opium, and I thought, "Fuck! It's happening!"

Where did you go after the Ad Lib?

Well, it seemed to go on all night. I can't remember the details. George some-how or other managed to drive us home in his Mini, but we were going about ten miles per hour—it seemed like a thousand. And Patti [Boyd Harrison] was saying, "Let's jump out and play football." There were these big rugby poles and things like that. And I was getting all sorts of hysterical jokes, coming out like speed because I was always on that, too. George was going, "Don't make me laugh, oh, God!" It was just terrifying, but it was fantastic. I did some drawings of four faces saying, "We all agree with you!" You know, things like that. I gave the originals to Ringo. I did a lot of drawing that night. And then George's house seemed to be, you know, just like a big submarine. I was driving it; they all went to bed. I was carrying on in it; it seemed to float above his wall, which was eighteen feet, and I was driving it.

The second time we had acid, in L.A., was different.

What happened then?

Well, then we took it deliberately.

This portfolio is from Annie Leibovitz's first session with John and Yoko. The photos were taken in New York City in 1970 to accompany the "Lennon Remembers" interviews.

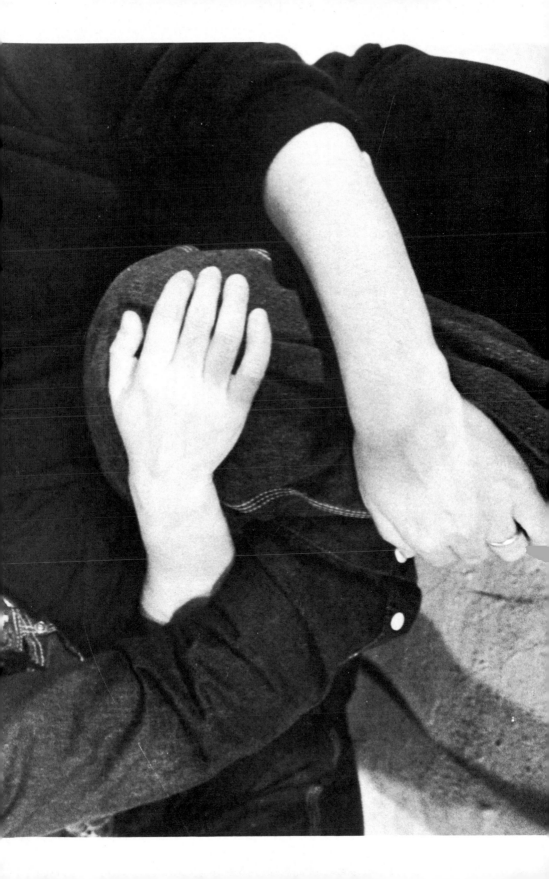

How do you think that affected your conception of the music, in general?

Well, it was only another mirror; it wasn't a miracle. It was more of a visual thing, and a therapy—that "looking at yourself" bit, you know. It did all that. But it didn't write the music. I write the music in the circumstances in which I'm in, whether it's on acid or in the water.

Whose idea was it to go to India?

Probably George's; I have no idea.

You wrote "Sexy Sadie" about the Maharishi?

That's about the Maharishi, yes. I copped out and I wouldn't write "Maharishi what have you done, you made a fool of everyone," but now it can be told, Fab Listeners.

When did you realize he was making a fool of you?

I don't know, I just sort of saw him.

While in India?

Yes, there was a big hullabaloo about him trying to rape Mia Farrow and trying to get off with Mia Farrow and a few other women and things like that. And we went down to him after we had stayed up all night discussing "was it true or not true?" When George started thinking it might be true, I thought, well, it must be true, because if George is doubting him, there must be something in it.

So we went to see Maharishi; the whole gang of us the next day charged down to his hut, his bungalow, his very rich-looking bungalow in the mountains. I was the spokesman and, as usual, when the dirty work came, I had to be leader —wherever the scene was, when it came to the nitty-gritty, I had to do the speaking. And I said, "We're leaving." He asked why and all that shit, and I said, "Well, if you're so cosmic, you'll know why," because he was always intimating, and there were all these right-hand men intimating, that he did miracles. And I said, "You know why." And he said, "I don't know why, you must tell me," and I just kept saying, "You ought to know." He gave me a look like, "I'll kill you, you bastard," and he gave me such a look. And I knew then, when he looked at me, you know, because I had called his bluff, because I said if you know all, you know. Cosmic consciousness, that's what we're all here for. I was a bit rough on him.

How would you trace the breakup of the Beatles?

After Brian [Epstein] died, we collapsed. Paul took over and supposedly led us. But what is leading us when we went round in circles? We broke up then. That was the disintegration.

When did you first feel that the Beatles had broken up? When did that idea first hit you?

I don't remember. I was in my own pain. I wasn't noticing, really. I just did it like a job. We made the double album, the set . . . it's like if you took each track off and gave it all mine and all George's . . . it was just me and a backing group, Paul and a backing group. I enjoyed it, but we broke up then.

I didn't really want to talk about all this . . . go on.

Do you mind?

Well, we're halfway through it now, so let's do it.

You said you quit the Beatles first.

Yes.

How?

Well, I said to Paul, "I'm leaving." I knew before we went to Toronto. I told Allen [Klein] I was leaving, I told Eric Clapton and Klaus [Voormann] that I was leaving and that I'd probably like to use them as a group. I hadn't decided how to do it—to have a permanent new group or what. Then later on I thought, fuck, I'm not going to get stuck with another set of people, you know, whoever they are. So I announced it to myself and to the people around me on the way to Toronto. Allen came with me, and I told Allen it was over. When I got back, there were a few meetings, and Allen had said, well, cool it, 'cause there was a lot to do business-wise, you know, and it would not have been suitable at the time. And then we were discussing something in the office with Paul, and I kept saying no, no, no to everything, you see. So it came to a point I had to say something, of course, and Paul asked, "What do you mean?" I said, "I mean the group is over, I'm leaving."

What was Paul's reaction?

Like anybody when you say divorce—you know, their face goes all sorts of colors. It's like he knew, really, that this was the final thing.

How did you meet Yoko?

There was a sort of underground clique in London; John Dunbar, who was married to Marianne Faithfull, had an art gallery in London called Indica, and I'd been going around to galleries a bit on me off days in between records, also to a few exhibitions in different galleries that showed sort of unknown artists or underground artists.

I got the word that this amazing woman was putting on a show the next week, something about people in bags, in black bags, and it was going to be a bit of a happening and all that. So I went to a preview the night before it opened. I went in—she didn't know who I was or anything—and I was wandering around. There were a couple of artsy-type students who had been helping, lying around there in the gallery, and I was looking at it and was astounded. There was an apple on sale there for two hundred quid; I thought it was fantastic—I got the humor in her work immediately. I didn't have to have much knowledge about avant-garde or underground art, but the humor got me straightaway. It was two hundred quid to watch the fresh apple decompose.

But it was another piece that really decided me for or against the artist: a ladder that led to a painting, which was hung on the ceiling. It looked like a black canvas with a chain with a spyglass hanging on the end of it. I climbed the ladder, looked through the spyglass, and in tiny little letters it said: YES.

So it was positive. I felt relieved. It's a great relief when you get up the ladder and you look through the spyglass and it doesn't say "no" or "fuck you" or something.

I was very impressed. John Dunbar introduced us—neither of us knew who the hell each other was. She didn't know who I was; she'd only heard of Ringo; I think it means apple in Japanese. And Dunbar had sort of been hustling her, saying, "That's a good patron; you must go and talk to him or do something." Dunbar insisted she say hello to the millionaire—you know what I mean. And she came up and handed me a card that said BREATHE on it—one of her instructions—so I just went [[pants]]. This was our meeting.

The second time I met her was at a gallery opening of Claes Oldenburg in London. We were very shy; we sort of nodded at each other—she was standing behind me. I sort of looked away because I'm very shy with people, especially chicks. We just sort of smiled and stood frozen together in this cocktail-party thing.

The next thing was, she came to me to get some backing—like all the bastard underground do—for a show she was doing. She gave me her *Grapefruit* book. I used to read it, and sometimes I'd get very annoyed by it; it would say things like "paint until you drop dead" or "bleed." Then sometimes I'd be very enlightened by it. I went through all the changes that people go through with her work—sometimes I'd have it by the bed and I'd open it and it would say something nice and it would be all right, and then it would say something heavy and I wouldn't like it.

So I gave her the money to back her show. For this whole thing, everything was in half: There was half a bed, half a room, half of everything, all beautifully cut in half and all painted white. And I said to her, "Why don't you sell the other half in bottles?" having caught on by then to what the game was. And she did that—this is still before we'd had any nuptials—and we still have the bottles from the show; it's my first. It was presented as "Yoko Plus Me"—

that was our first public appearance. I didn't even go to see the show; I was too uptight.

When did you realize that you were in love with her?

It was beginning to happen; I would start looking at her book, but I wasn't quite aware what was happening to me. Then she did a thing called "Dance Event," where different cards kept coming through the door every day saying BREATHE and DANCE and WATCH ALL THE LIGHTS UNTIL DAWN, and they upset me or made me happy, depending.

I'd get very upset about it being intellectual or all fucking avant-garde, then I'd like it, and then I wouldn't. Then I went to India with the Maharoonie and we corresponded. The letters were still formal, but they just had a little side to them. I nearly took her to India, but I still wasn't sure for what reason; I was still sort of kidding myself, with sort of artistic reasons and all that.

When we got back from India, we were talking to each other on the phone. I called her over; it was the middle of the night and Cynthia [Lennon's first wife] was away, and I thought, well, now's the time if I'm gonna get to know her any more. She came to the house and I didn't know what to do, so we went upstairs to my studio and I played her all the tapes that I'd made, all this far-out stuff, some comedy stuff, and some electronic music. She was suitably impressed, and then she said, "Well, let's make one ourselves." So we made *Two Virgins.* It was midnight when we started; it was dawn when we finished, and then we made love at dawn. It was very beautiful.

What was it like getting married?

It was very romantic. It's all in the song "The Ballad of John and Yoko," if you want to know how it happened. Gibraltar was like a little sunny dream. I couldn't find a white suit—I had sort of off-white corduroy trousers and a white jacket. Yoko had all white on.

What was your first peace event?

The first peace event was the Amsterdam Bed Peace, after we got married.

What was that like? That was your first re-exposure to the public.

It was a nice high. We were in the Hilton, looking over Amsterdam—it was very crazy; the press came, expecting to see us fuckin' in bed. They'd all heard John and Yoko were going to fuck in front of the press for peace. So when they all walked in—about fifty or sixty reporters flew over from London, all sort of very edgy, and we were just sitting in pajamas saying, "peace, brother." That was it.

There was a point at which you decided you and Yoko would give up your private life.

No, we never decided to give up our private life. We decided that if we were going to do anything like get married, or like this film we are going to make now, that we would dedicate it to peace. And during that period, because we are what we are, it evolved that somehow we ended up being responsible to produce peace.

Why can't you be alone without Yoko?

I can be, but I don't wish to be.

There is no reason on earth why I should be without her. There is nothing more important than our relationship, nothing. And we dig being together all the time. And both of us could survive apart, but what for? I'm not going to sacrifice love, real love, for any fuckin' whore, or any friend, or any business because, in the end, you're alone at night. Neither of us wants to be, and you can't fill the bed with groupies; that doesn't work. I don't want to be a swinger. Like I said in the song, I've been through it all, and nothing works better than to have somebody you love hold you.

What about Yoko's art?

We are both showing each other's experience to each other. I had to open up to hear it—I had to get out the concept of what I wanted to hear . . . I had to allow abstract art or music in. She had to do the same for rock & roll. It was an intellectual exercise, because we're all boxed in. We are all in little boxes, and somebody has to go in and rip your fuckin' head open for you to allow something else in.

What do you think of America?

America is where it's at. I should have been born in New York. I should have been born in the Village; that's where I belong. Why wasn't I born there? Paris was it in the eighteenth century; London, I don't think, has ever been it, except literary-wise, when Wilde and Shaw and all of them were there. New York is it.

I regret profoundly that I was not an American and not born in Greenwich Village. That's where I should have been. It never works that way. Everybody heads toward the center; that's why I'm here now.

Are you pleased with your new album (John Lennon / Plastic Ono Band)?

I think it's the best thing I've ever done. I think it's realistic and it's true to me. That has been developing over the years from "In My Life," "I'm a Loser," "Help," "Strawberry Fields." They're all personal records. I always wrote about me when I could. I didn't really enjoy writing third-person songs about people who live in concrete flats and things like that. I like first-person music. But because of my hang-ups and many other things, I would only write specifically about me now and then. Now I write all about me and that's why I like it. It's me! And nobody else.

You said at one point that you have to write songs that can justify your existence.

I said a lot of things. I write songs because that's the thing I choose to do, you know, and I can't help writing them; that's a fact. And sometimes I feel as though you work . . . I felt as though you work to justify your existence, but you don't. You work to exist and vice versa, and that's it, really.

What do you think are the best songs that you have written?

Ever?

Ever. What is the best song you have ever written?

The one best song?

Have you ever thought of that?

I don't know. If somebody asked me what is my favorite song, is it "Stardust" or something . . . I can't . . . that kind of decision making I can't do. I always liked "Walrus," "Strawberry Fields," "Help," "In My Life." Those are some favorites, you know.

Why "Help"?

Because I meant it; it's real. The lyric is as good now as it was then. It's no different, you know, and it makes me feel secure to know that I was that aware of myself then. It was just me singing "help," and I meant it. I don't like the recording that much; we did it too fast, trying to be commercial.

I like "I Want to Hold Your Hand"; we wrote that together, and it's a beautiful melody. I might do "I Want to Hold Your Hand" and "Help" again, because I like them.

Why "Strawberry Fields"? Did you think that was real?

Yeah, it was real for then, and it's . . . I think it's like talking, you know . . . it's like that Elton John one where he's singing, oh, I don't know—he talks to himself, sort of singing, which I thought was nice; it reminded me of that.

Songs like "Girl"?

Yeah, I liked that one.

"Run for Your Life"?

"Run for Your Life" I always hated.

Why?

I don't know, it was one of those I knocked off just to write a song, and it was phony. But "Girl" is real. There is no such thing as *the* girl; she was a dream, but the words are all right. It's about "was she taught when she was young that pain would lead to pleasure, did she understand it," and all that. They're sort of philosophy quotes. It was reasonable, and I was thinkin' about it when I wrote it; it wasn't just a song, and it was about that girl—which happened to turn out to be Yoko in the end—the one that a lot of us were looking for. There're many songs I forget that I do like. I like "Across the Universe," too.

Why?

Because it's one of the best lyrics I've written. In fact, it could be *the* best, I don't know. It's one of the best; it's good poetry, or whatever you call it, without chewin' it, it stands. See, the ones I like are the ones that stand as words without melody, that don't have to have any melody. It's a poem, you know; you could read 'em.

What do you think the future of rock & roll is?

Whatever we make it. If we want to go bullshitting off into intellectualism with rock & roll, we are going to get bullshitting rock intellectualism. If we want real rock & roll, it's up to all of us to create it and stop being hyped by, you know, revolutionary image and long hair. We've got to get over that bit. That's what cutting hair is about. Let's own up now and see who's who, who's doing something about what, and who's making music and who's laying down bullshit. Rock & roll will be whatever we make it.

Why do you think it means so much to people?

Because it is primitive enough and has no bullshit, really, the best stuff, and its beat gets through to you. Go to the jungle and they have the rhythm and it goes throughout the world—it's as simple as that. You get the rhythm going, everybody gets into it. I read that Eldridge Cleaver said that blacks gave middle-class whites back their bodies, you know, put their minds and bodies together through the music. It's something like that, it gets through—to me it got through. It was the only thing to get through to me after all the things that were happening when I was fifteen. Rock & roll was real. Everything else was unreal. And the thing about rock & roll—good rock & roll, whatever good means—is that it's real, and realism gets through to you despite yourself. You recognize something in it which is true, like all true art.

Do you see a time when you'll retire?

No, I couldn't, you know.
YOKO: He'll probably work until he's eighty or until he dies.

111

JOHN: I can't foresee it. Even when you're a cripple you carry on painting. I would paint if I couldn't move.

Do you have a picture of "when I'm sixty-four"?

No, no. I hope we're a nice old couple living off the coast of Ireland or something—looking at our scrapbook of madness.

YOKO ONO AND HER SIXTEEN-TRACK VOICE

By Jonathan Cott/March 18, 1971

In his song "One Day (at a Time)" John Lennon—referring to Yoko Ono, as he often did—sang: "I'm the fish and you're the sea . . . I'm the apple and you're the tree . . . I'm the door and you're the key." Who was this woman in whom he lived, from whom he grew and by whom he was opened up? The following article was the first piece in Rolling Stone *to explore these questions.*

N December 1970 John Lennon and Yoko Ono came to New York City for the first time as a couple. They visited some of Yoko's old friends; went out, as they rarely did in London, to films like *Diary of a Mad Housewife* and *Lovers and Other Strangers* and to the Muhammad Ali fight; made two new films of their own—*Up Your Legs Forever* and *Fly*—for inclusion in a three-night minifestival of John and Yoko films at the Elgin Theater; and did some publicity for their extraordinary twin albums, *John Lennon / Plastic Ono Band* and *Yoko Ono / Plastic Ono Band.*

The following scene takes place in a hotel room one Sunday evening: John is turning on the radio to hear Alex Bennett's WMCA phone-in program on which, tonight, he's playing tracks from Yoko's album—the first time her music has been featured on AM radio.

"There are people who are going to love it and people who are going to hate it," Bennett says enthusiastically. "I think that in 1980 music will probably sound like this. Here's a track called 'Why Not,' so phone in and tell us what you think of it."

"*It's today's 'Tutti-Frutti,*' " John writes on a note pad, so as not to interrupt the music.

"I'm forty-nine years old," a listener calls in to say, "forty-nine, and I dig it. I heard trains going through a tunnel, then rain—I'm just using my imagination —then what sounded like a bunch of Indians. I dig it, but I really like songs with a melody."

"It was truly disastrous," a nasal-voiced listener comments.

"It's music, you idiot!" John exclaims to the radio. "Because it's not got *da-da-da*, there's nothing for him to hook onto."

"You don't mind hearing the program?" Yoko asks.

"I want to," John says. "You see, with Yoko's and my album, we're both looking at the same thing from different sides of the table. Mine is literate, hers is revolutionary. She's got a sixteen-track voice!"

The radio program ends, and John and Yoko are relaxing on their bed, John half-watching the soundless television screen and reading an essay called "Concept Art" by violinist and composer Henry Flynt, whom John and Yoko have just visited.

"Before I met John," Yoko begins saying, "and when I had become sort of famous because of my film *Bottoms* [the 1967 film of 365 backsides for eighty minutes, a film John described as *Many Happy Endings*], that was the loneliest time in my life. Some people resented me because of my fame and made me feel isolated. Now, when my record is played on the radio, I've got someone who's pleased.

"And, concerning my notion of music, when I met John originally, he said it was okay for me to listen to the Beatles' sessions."

John: "I had to get permission!"

"And after one of the sessions I asked John, 'Why don't you use different rhythms instead of just going *ba-ba-ba-ba*?' It was a kind of avant-garde snobbery on my part, because my voice was going [*vibrating: uhghh . . . ghuhhh*], but there was no beat. So I thought to myself [*simpering tone*], 'Well, simple music!' You see, I was doing music of the mind—no sound at all, everybody sitting around, just imagining sounds. At my earlier New York City loft concerts I was throwing peas from a bag at the people and I had long hair and I was circling my hair and the movement was a sound. Even then, some people were saying that maybe it was too dramatic. Then there was my *Wall Piece*, which instructed you to hit the wall with your head, and that was called too dramatic as well. But I felt stifled even with that, I was dying to scream, to go back to my voice. And I came to a point where I believed that the idea of avant-garde purity was just as stifling as just doing a rock beat over and over."

"Dear," John interrupts, "one thing that's going to throw you. Henry Flynt is talking about 'Sweets for My Sweet' by the Drifters—he's been rocking for a long time. You know, he played us some fantastic stuff the other night when we saw him. 'Sweets for My Sweet' was a big rock & roll hit, so he's been aware of that for a long time. I don't think he got to that sound pissing about with mathematics. I had to interrupt since I was just reading something he wrote about concept art and it's bloody hard, but he gets to 'Sweets for My Sweet' and I understood him."

"Probably I was the only one who didn't," Yoko says.

"Right," responds John, singing: "Dun de dun dun! I'm not putting you down, I'm just very surprised to read this."

"I know you mean well," Yoko replies, "but I get sort of lost."

"You were talking about the 4/4 beat."

"I realized," Yoko continues, "that modern classical composers, when they went from 4/4 to 4/3, lost the heartbeat. It's as if they left the ground and lived on the fortieth floor. Schoenberg and Webern—Webern's on the top of the Empire State Building. But that's all right. Our conceptual rhythm got complex, but we still have the body and the beat. Conceptual rhythm I carry on with my voice, which has a very complicated rhythm even in 'Why,' but the bass and the drum is the heartbeat. So the body and the conceptual rhythms go together. These days I'm putting a beat under everything I do."

"Yoko and I have clashed artistically," John laughs. "Our egos have smashed once or twice. But if I know what I'm doing as an artist, then I can see if I'm being hypocritical in my reactions. I sometimes am overawed by her talent. I think, fuck, I better watch out, she is taking over, I better get meself in here. And I say, are you taking over? And then say all right, all right, and I relax again. I mean, she's going to haul three hundred and sixty-five legs and make a bloody film about a fly crawling over some woman's body, what is it? But it's all right, I know her."

"An artist couple is the most difficult thing," Yoko continues. "On the David Frost program, some guy was saying, 'I like to write music and my fiancée likes to write poetry.' The fact is that we both paint, compose and write poetry, and on that basis I think we're doing pretty well."

"If you do two LPs there might be a little change!" John laughs. "But until then I don't mind. When she wants the A side, that's when we start fighting. The reason the covers of our albums are similar is that I wanted us to be separate and to be together, too, not to have it appear that old John-and-Yoko is over, because they're dying for us to fall apart, for God knows what reason. It's just that everybody doesn't want anybody else to be happy, because nobody's happy."

"I think it's a miracle that we're doing all right. But we are doing all right, don't you think, John?"

"It's just handy to fuck your best friend. That's what it is. And once I resolved the fact that it was a woman as well, it's all right. We go through the trauma of life and death every day, so it's not so much of a worry about what sex we are anymore. I'm living with an artist who's inspiring me to work. And, you know, Yoko is the most famous unknown artist. Everybody knows her name, but nobody knows what she does."

Yoko stands five feet two and weighs ninety-five pounds, more or less. "It is nice to keep oneself small," she once wrote, "like a grain of rice, instead of expanding. Make yourself dispensable, like paper. See little, hear little, and think little."

An autobiography she once wrote states:
born: Bird Year
early childhood: collected skys
adolescence: collected sea-weeds

> late adolescence: gave birth to a
> grapefruit, collected snails,
> clouds, garbage cans etc.
> Have graduated many schools
> specializing in these subjects.

"I dropped out in my third year at Sarah Lawrence," Yoko explains, "and I started living in New York around Eighty-sixth and Amsterdam, where all the trucks go all the time. My new life was very exciting for me because I was living next to a meat market and I felt as if I had a house with a delicatessen in it. The only thing was that I couldn't figure out how to present my work because I didn't know how to communicate with people. And I didn't know how to explain to people how shy I was. When people visited I wanted to be in a big sort of box with little holes where nobody could see me but I could see through the holes. So, later, that developed into my *Bag Piece*, where you can be inside and see outside, but they can't see you.

"When I was going to Sarah Lawrence, I was mainly staying in the music library and listening to Schoenberg and Webern; they thrilled me, really. And I was writing some serial works at that time. But I was lazy writing out a whole score. And, further, I was doing the *Match Piece* in those days, just lighting a match and watching until it disappeared. And I even thought that maybe there was something in me that was going to go crazy, like a pyromaniac. See, I was writing poetry and music and painting, and none of that satisfied me. I knew that the medium was wrong. Whenever I wrote a poem, they said it was too long, it was like a short story; a novel was like a short story and a short story was like a poem. I felt that I was like a misfit in every medium.

"I just stayed in Scarsdale at my parents' home, and I was going crazy because I couldn't communicate with them very well. I was lighting matches, afraid of becoming a pyromaniac. But then I thought that there might be some people who needed something more than painting, poetry and music, something I called an 'additional act' that you needed in life. And I was doing all that just to prevent myself from going mad, really. And when I had this apartment in New York, what happened was that instead of drying my face with a towel, I used my best cocktail dress. And then I was imagining myself all the time as a kite, holding on to a kite, and when I was sleeping, I'd lose my string, go off floating. That's the time I thought: I'll go crazy. So I just imagined myself holding on to a kite, and the kite was me.

"People asked me what I was doing. I didn't know how to explain that actually I was just holding the string, making sure that I wouldn't let go. This was a trait I had when I was a little girl, too, when my mother asked me what I was doing all by myself, and I would say: 'I'm breathing,' and I was really counting my breathings, and thinking: 'My God, if I don't count them, would I not breathe?' That later became my *Breathing Piece*. And those events that I was doing in New York were very much connected with necessity."

This sense of disappearing, flying away, flames going out, suggests what the psychologist David Cooper writes about in *The Death of the Family*, the effort not to see oneself anymore, "to see through oneself as a person limited to relative being. . . . Few people can sustain this nonrelative self-regard for more than a minute or two without feeling that they are going mad, in the sense of disappearing. That is why people use mirrors in order not to see their selves with the possibility of seeing through, but to see fragmentary manifestations like their hair, eye make-up . . . and so on. If one did not effect this evasive fragmentation of the mirror image, one would be left with the experience of knowing that seeing oneself means seeing through oneself. There can be nothing more terrifying than that."

"Draw a line with yourself," Yoko writes in her *Line Piece*. "Go on drawing until you disappear." Many of these "pieces" are printed in *Grapefruit*—compositions of "music, painting, event, poetry and object"—in which the idea of dismembering and disrobing is seminal. Thus, in one of her events, Yoko asks each participant to cut off a piece of her dress until she is naked. And one remembers John and Yoko naked on the cover of *Two Virgins* and in their two *Self Portrait* films. Yoko once wrote: "People went on cutting the parts they do not like of me; finally there was only the stone remained of me that was in me but they were still not satisfied and wanted to know what it's like in the stone." The point is that the act of taking off one's clothes is merely a metaphor for the uncovering of the self.

And what does it mean to be "naked"? The American sociologist Erving Goffman writes: "The self . . . is not an organic thing that has a specific location, whose fundamental fate is to be born, to mature, and to die; it is a dramatic effect arising diffusely from a scene that is presented and the character issue, the crucial concern, is whether it will be credited or discredited." And Yoko finally existed in her "scene" by means of a fantastic humor, by transforming her obsessions, memories and ideas into her special art, and thus by realizing herself in her work. "*Grapefruit* was like a cure for myself without knowing it. It was like saying, 'Please accept me, I am mad.' Those instructions are like that—a real need to do something to act out your madness. As long as you are behaving properly, you don't realize your madness and you go crazy." She was accepted also by someone who once sang: "I am he as you are he as you are me and we are all together."

Yoko's "Music of the Mind"—e.g., "Peel. Peek. Take off." ("Pieces for Orchestra," 1962)—came to fruition in the winter of 1960. She rented a loft on Chambers Street in New York. "All the windows were smoked glass so that you couldn't really see outside, but there was the skylight, and when you were in the loft you almost felt more connected to the sky than to the city outside. It was a cold-water flat, $50.50 a month, and it was great. I didn't have chairs or beds, and so people downstairs gave me orange crates and I put all the crates together to make a large table, crates for the chairs, and at night I just collected them and made a bed out of them. And I started to live there.

"A friend of mine told me that there was a group of artists who were think-ing of putting on their works and would I mind if they joined me and did things together. And I said, no, I wouldn't mind, and perhaps they wouldn't mind painting my loft for free. Everyone was lazy and didn't get around to painting it white, but I got used to the gray."

The famous Chambers Street loft concerts featured artists, musicians, dancers and poets—a list of whose names reads like a roster of the avant-garde hall of fame: Walter De Maria, Joseph Byrd, La Monte Young, Jackson Mac Low, George Maciunas, Phillip Corner, George Brecht, Diane Wakoski, Yvonne Rainer, Henry Flynt, David Tudor and Richard Maxfield. "But there was no mention that I should have a concert there, and I wasn't going to be the one to mention it," Yoko says. "Somehow my work was still suffering. The idea had been to stop my suffering by getting a place to present my work and at last letting everybody know what I was doing. But it just went on like that. Many people thought that I was a very rich girl who was just 'playing avant-garde.' And some others thought that I was a mistress of some very rich man, which wasn't true either. I think that the reason that some people thought the whole thing was organized by some Chinese man was because La Monte's name is Young. And meanwhile I was just surviving by teaching Japanese folk art."

Within the next couple of years, Yoko had concerts featuring her own work at the Village Gate, The Bridge Theater and Carnegie Recital Hall. Her first art exhibition took place at the Agnus Gallery, owned by Fluxus originator George Maciunas. (Fluxus was the name of a group of Zen- and John Cage-influenced avant-garde artists who often worked in mixed media.) And among the instruction paintings there were: *Painting for the Wind*, which featured a bag full of seeds hanging in front of a blank canvas, and when the wind blew, seeds would fall out through the bag's small holes; *Smoke Painting*, where you lit a match and watched the smoke against the canvas; and *Painting to Be Stepped On*, where you stepped on the canvas and made a mark until many marks made up the painting. It was this element of participation, of adding things, of watching things grow and change, that enabled you to see Yoko's instructions as a way of "getting together, as in a chain letter." And, following this ex-hibition, Yoko's lecture-concert at Wesleyan College; events in Japan; exhibi-tions in London, like the one in 1966 at the Indica Gallery, where she met John, all created a growing interest in her work and an equal amount of incom-prehension.

And it was Yoko's and John's extensions of the idea of participating—the "additional act" that would suggest to others how reciprocally to involve them-selves—that led to the famous peace events, filmed and reported on many times —the bed-ins, the "War Is Over" poster, which appeared in hundreds of news-

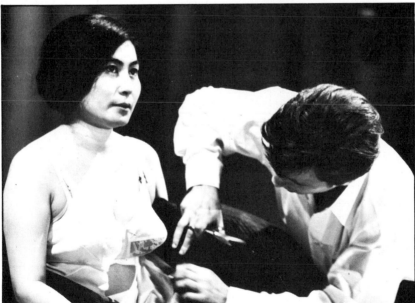

Top: Yoko performing Paper Music *by Benjamin Patterson. Third Annual Avant-Garde Festival, August 1965. Bottom:* Cut Piece, *the instructions call for members of the audience to cut off Yoko's clothes. Carnegie Recital Hall, New York City, March 1965.*

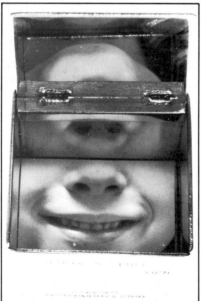

Top: Yoko's "This Is Not Here" show. Everson Museum of Art, Syracuse, New York, October 1971. Bottom right: Yoko's logo on plastic box, filled with rubber stamps of animal footprints and human handprints, 1971. Bottom left: "Box of Smile," reflecting box to smile in, dedicated to her daughter, Kyoko, 1971.

papers around the world and the sending of acorns to world leaders, who were invited by John and Yoko to plant them and watch them grow.

Yoko's first important concert took place at the end of 1961 at Carnegie Recital Hall. "It was a big moment for me," Yoko recalls. "George Brecht, Jonas Mekas, La Monte Young, Jackson Mac Low, just about everyone performed in it. And Richard Maxfield helped me on the electronic side. I set up everything and then made the stage very dim, so you had to strain your eyes—because life is like that. You always have to strain to read other people's minds. And then it went into complete darkness. The week before I had given instructions to everyone as to what they should do, so that there would be a feeling of togetherness based on alienation, since no one knew the other person's instructions.

"So everybody was moving without making any sounds onstage. There was a point where two men were tied up together with lots of empty cans and bottles around them, and they had to move from one end of the stage to the other very quietly and slowly without making any sounds. What I was trying to attain was a sound that almost doesn't come out. Before I speak I stutter in my mind, and then my cultured self tries to correct that stutter into a clean sentence. And then it comes out like 'Oh, and how are you today?' instead of 'O-O-Oh-h-how are you?' But before it comes out like that you have this stuttering in you. And I wanted to deal with those sounds of people's fears and stutterings.

"So I thought that if everything was set up in a lighted room and suddenly the light was turned off, you might start to see things beyond the shapes. Or hear the kind of sounds that you hear in silence. You would start to feel the environment and tension and people's vibrations. Those were the sounds that I wanted to deal with, the sound of fear and of darkness, like a child's fear that someone is behind him, but he can't speak and communicate this. And so I asked one guy to stand behind the audience for the duration of the concert.

"I wanted the sound of people perspiring to be in it, too, so I had all the dancers wear contact microphones, and the instructions were to bring out very heavy boxes and take them back across the stage, and while they were doing that they were perspiring a little. There was one guy who was asthmatic, and it was fantastic. And in the toilet there was somebody standing throughout the evening. Whenever I go to a toilet in a film theater, I always feel very scared. If nobody's there I'm scared, but if somebody is there it's even more scary. So I wanted people to have this experience of fear. There are unknown areas of sound and experience that people can't really mention in words. Like the stuttering in your mind. I was interested not in the noise you make but the noise that happens when you try not to make it, just that tension going back and forth.

"I think I would never want to go back again to where I was, doing things like that, even though few people have touched this area. Where I'd be so lonely and miserable that nobody understood. And the kind of thing I'm doing now is more understandable. I'm not saying it's better or worse. But now I just want to feel sort of playful sometimes. And when I feel playful, to do something. That's when people seem to understand more, or at least accept more."

She once wrote: "After unblocking one's mind, by dispensing with visual, auditory and kinetic perceptions, what will come out of us? Would there be anything? I wonder. And my events are mostly spent in wonderment." Before they are anything else, Yoko's poems, events, films and music exemplify a wonderment that suggests childlike awe, a way of seeing things as if you were entering a strange street, invisible until now, for the first time; or as if, for example, you were watching a Western—the sheriff, rustlers, corral fights—through the eyes of one of the horses. More than that, wonderment implies intensity of perception resulting in one's identification with what is seen, not as the "utterly other," but as the utterly same. Thus the everyday becomes the numinous. And eventually the perceived object or person disintegrates, for when you see something at this level of clarity, it disappears, and you find yourself asking, what really is there?

David Cooper writes: "To commence the unuse of the word 'neurosis,' let us regard it as a way of being that is made to seem childish by one's fear of the fear of others about one's becoming childlike. . . . The fear is the fear of madness, of being childlike or even being before-one's-origins, so that any act may cohere others against oneself to suppress any spontaneous gesture that has socially disruptive, archaic resonances." The childlike gestures and awarenesses reveal themselves in Yoko's ways of seeing everything: "An intensity of a wink is: two cars smashed head on. / A storm turned into a breeze. / A water drop from a loose faucet" (Wink Talk). And in her Touch Poem, Yoko writes: "Give birth to a child / See the world through its eye / Let it touch everything possible / and leave its fingermark there / in place of a signature."

"Sometimes," Yoko says, "I think that some of the things I've done could have been done by John, and vice versa." John, in fact, used Yoko's Imagine instructions (e.g., "Imagine the clouds dripping. Dig a hole in your garden to put them in") as the seminal idea for his song "Imagine." And together they collaborated on a number of films that, among other things, seem to be about seeing things as if for the first time—the "love that has no past."

Fly, John and Yoko's most recent film, made in New York in two days, shows a naked woman lying motionless on her back as one fly at a time settles on different parts of her body to go about its business—mainly leg-tasting-and-feeling. Some of the flies were stunned with CO_2, having failed to follow a trail of sugar water over the woman's body. The woman's catatonia remains a mystery.

Watching *Fly*, one might almost imagine that Walt Disney and the mini-malist director Jean-Marie Straub had collaborated, for the film's magnified focus on what a fly does if you don't brush it away is shot in long takes, with the camera obliquely observing the transformed landscape of a mountainous breast, a hillock nipple, or a desert of fingers on which the fly stands, legs investigating the scene. And at the film's conclusion, you see a long shot of the entire body with six flies standing here and there as if on a dead Christ—an amazing Bunuellian moment that makes the fly a metaphor for pain. The flies finally fly away, and we're left with a shot through the window of a New York Bowery roof, veiled in a diaphanous blue light like St. Elmo's fire, suggesting the beauty of seeing things anew.

"The idea of the film came to me," Yoko says, "when I thought about that joke where someone says to a man: 'Did you notice that woman's hat?' and he's looking at her bosom instead. I wondered how many people would look at the fly or at the body. I tried, when filming, to accept all the things that showed up, but at the same time tried not to make the film too dramatic. It would have been very easy for me to have made it become pornographic, and I didn't want that. Each shot had to project more than a pretty image of a body, so it was used more as an abstract line."

Yoko's voice on *Fly*'s soundtrack is a subtle rhythmic embodiment of the fly's excursions—intersected by John's forward and backward guitar track. And these amazing sounds reveal again those childlike gestures and archaic reso-nances. For it is most obviously in what John calls her "sixteen-track voice" that Yoko displays her extraordinary art. It is the true distillation of her *sens plus pur*, a kind of psychophysical instrument of amazing disparateness, rich-ness and range. Yoko's voice is a kind of vocal tachistoscope (the shuttered magic lantern that projects images for a thousandth of a second), immediately and almost subliminally communicating glittering movements of the smallest elements of sound, reminding you of the screams, wails, laughter, groans, cater-wauls of both a primordial, prebirth, premammalian past, as well as of the fogged-over, pained immediacy of childhood.

Musically, what happens is that nasals, fricatives, registral variants, pitch inflections and varying timbres all combine, interpolate and permute to convey the impression of anything from a Japanese shakuhachi to bantams in pine woods to swamp animals' madrigals to the feeling of being inside of one's own body cavities. Yoko's voice enters sound to reveal its most basic frequential characteristics and proposes to the listener that if he wants to hear, he might as well stop trying. "She becomes her voice," John says, "and you get touched." This vocal quality can be heard most powerfully on "Don't Worry Kyoko"; the soundtrack for *Fly*; and *Yoko Ono / The Plastic Ono Band* (with John on guitar, Klaus Voormann on bass, Ringo on drums and, on "AOS," by Charles Haden, David Izenzon, Ed Blackwell and Ornette Coleman).

"When I say things," Yoko comments, "I stutter a little bit. Most of us kill off our real emotions, and on top of them you have your smooth self. It's like the guy in the film *Diary of a Mad Housewife* with his singsong voice. There's that unreal tone. But when I want to say 'I'm sorry' in a song—because music to me is something so honest and so real—I don't feel like saying [*singsong*] 'I'm sorry, mother,' but rather as an emotion should be [*groaning, stuttering*] 'I'm so-or-orrrry.' A stutterer is someone who's feeling something genuine. So in 'Paper Shoes' I say: 'Pa-pa-pa-a-a-per sh-shooooes!'

"The older you get, the more frustrated you feel. And it gets to a point where you don't have time to utter a lot of intellectual bullshit. If you were drowning you wouldn't say: 'I'd like to be helped because I have just a moment to live.' You'd say, 'Help!' but if you were more desperate you'd say, '*Eioughhhh*,' or something like that. And the desperation of life is really life itself, the core of life, what's really driving us forth. When you're really desperate, it's phony to use descriptive and decorative adjectives to express yourself."

But isn't there another side, such as the seeming gentleness of "Who Has Seen the Wind?"—the quiet little song Yoko presented on the B side of John's "Instant Karma!"?

"On that song," Yoko says, "the voice is wavering a little, there are shrills and cracks, it's not professional pop singing; the background is going off a little. There was something of a lost little girl about it. What I was aiming at was the effect you get in Alban Berg's *Wozzeck*, where the drunkard sings—a slightly crazed voice, a bit of a broken toy. In that sense, it was a quiet desperation."

Religion, a philosopher once said, is what you do with your aloneness . . . or, one might add, with your pain and desperation. Yoko's music pushes pain into a kind of invigorating and liberated energy, just as a stutterer finally gives birth to a difficult word, since it existed originally at the fine edge between inaudibility and the sound waves of dreams. About her music for *Fly*, she comments: "It's nice to go into that very very fine, intricate mixture of sounds and rhythm. It's almost like going into a dream, getting something that doesn't exist in the physical world, unutterable sounds—a kind of metaphysical rhythm."

What Yoko calls "metaphysical sound" seems at first to be the true opposition to her unblocked music. Yet it is less an opposition than the idea of the dream of sound from which her new art emerges, a music which, the philosopher Max Picard tells us, is "silence, which in dreaming begins to sound . . ." and, as Picard—in a very Ono-esque manner—continues: "In silence the lines of the mouth are like the closed wings of a butterfly. When the word starts moving, the wings open, and the butterfly flies away."

"Around the time that I met John," Yoko tells me at the conclusion of our conversation, "I went to a palmist—John would probably laugh at this—and he said: 'You're like a very, very fast wind that goes speeding around the world.' And I had a line that signified astral projection. The only thing I didn't have was a root. But, the palmist said, you've met a person who's fixed like a mountain, and if you get connected with that mountain you might get materialized. And John is like a frail wind, too, so he understands all these aspects . . . I'm starting to think that maybe I can live. Before, it seemed impossible; I was just about at the vanishing point, and all my things were too conceptual. But John came in and said, 'All right, I understand you.' And just by saying that, all those things that were supposed to vanish stayed."

At the press conference for the publication of Yoko's Grapefruit in paperback. London, August 15, 1971.

SOME TIME IN NEW YORK CITY: JOHN & JERRY & DAVID & JOHN & LENI & YOKO

By Stuart Werbin/February 17, 1972

John and Yoko's political commitment did not die with the failure of the Toronto Peace Festival. They next concentrated their energies on the United States and became involved with several leaders and media stars of the radical American youth movement. That involvement was a fateful one, for it proved to be the key to the mystery of Lennon's harassment by the United States Immigration Service.

EW YORK. John sat propped up on the bed in his new West Village flat next to Yoko, who was wailing away on her tom-tom. At the foot of the bed sat Jerry Rubin; White Panthers leader John Sinclair and his wife, Leni; Charlie Manson biographer Ed Sanders and David Peel of the Lower East Side Ono Band (who calls his new album *The Pope Smokes Dope*). What deviltry could be afoot? It is a long story. We start in the middle, last May.

"Last year I was a very depressed and confused Jerry Rubin," said Jerry Rubin. "Everyone around me was depressed and confused, everyone in the Movement was condemning everything, condemning Mayday, condemning the Chicago conspiracy trial, condemning our whole history.

"Then a friend sat me down and played 'Working Class Hero' and 'Hold On John,' which could be 'Hold On Jerry' or 'Hold On Anybody,' for that matter.

"The Beatles had always been a distant myth. I never thought about meeting a Beatle. But 'Working Class Hero' was really a psychiatrist for me. I really mean that, it was a means for finding out who I was.

"So, when I saw in the *New York Daily News* that John and Yoko had come to New York, I decided I had to meet them. I called Apple, I said, 'This is Jerry Rubin and I'd like to talk with John and Yoko. Would you have them call me.' About two hours later I called again. The voice told me to hold a minute, and then the next voice was Yoko. She told me that John and her would love to meet me, and we made arrangements to meet the next Saturday afternoon in Washington Square Park. I told her I was going to bring Abbie [Hoffman] along, because at the time Abbie and I did everything together.

"So Saturday comes and Abbie and Anita and me are standing under the arch in Washington, and then we see them walking toward us. He's wearing American flag sneakers and she's dressed in all black. We run up to meet them. It's love at first sight. Great vibes. The greatest. We dug his sense of humor, we were knocked out by her sincerity, there was never a moment of anyone trying to protect any kind of image. At one time we're all talking in the back of their car and John says, 'I want to go to China,' but then he stops and he wonders if the Chinese know about the Beatle song 'Revolution.' So he says, 'That's all right, I'll just tell them that Paul wrote it.'

"We sat in Abbie's apartment for five hours and told each other at a high-speed rate what each of us had been doing. How the Yippies had been applying Beatle tactics to politics, trying to merge music and life. We talked about their bed-in as a Yippie action. All five of us were amazed at how we had been into the same kind of things all these years with no communication or contact.

"We talked about so many things at that first meeting. Yoko told me and Abbie that they considered us to be great artists. So Abbie said, 'That's funny, we always thought of you as the great politicians.' Yoko's art is waking people up to their own potentialities."

In the fall John and Yoko invited Jerry Rubin to the opening of Yoko's art show. "We hung out together up there and made arrangements to get together again in the city.

"So the next time we're having dinner together, in the Serendipity. They tell me that they've made a decision. It's an amazing decision. They say, 'Jerry, we're too young to retire. We'll retire when we're eighty. We don't want to live in Ascot, we want to do things.' Yoko says that they want to be part of the movement for change in America. John says he wants to put together a new band, he wants to play and he wants to give all the money back to the people. I was so ecstatic I embarrassed them. This was the most important conversation I could remember ever being involved in. I told them I wanted to work with them.

"This is when I got the title of 'political adviser.' It was only meant half seriously. My part was to be helping set things up and helping to determine where the money would go. Until you meet them it is impossible to explain the effect they have on people. They inspire tremendous loyalty from everyone they come in contact with. They've been through so much and they know so much.

"Then one day I came over to their apartment. They're not living in the St. Regis anymore, they're living in the Village, and they're on the bed doing

an interview for French TV. They invite me to come on the bed and be interviewed with them. One of the reporters asks me, 'Hey Jerry, when's your next
single coming out?' and John says, 'Right, you should be a member of the band.
If you're gonna work with us, you should play music with us.'

"Yoko says, 'We are all artists, we are all geniuses, but we are stilted and
blocked from birth by parents and schools.'"

While Jerry was in his highest hours in New York City, a Michigan man
who for seven years had been making statements which directly coincide with
Yoko's philosophy was caught in the downest of conditions.

John Sinclair was the manager of Detroit's most successful "avant rock"
group, the MC5, when he was sent to jail for marijuana possession in July 1969.
He was now into the third year of a nine-and-a-half- to ten-year sentence, and
his sixth appeal for bail bond had just been denied.

Sinclair's philosophy of rock group management is, in the words of one
writer, "to make the music totally real and human—a music that destroyed all
separation between the 'pop-star' musicians and the audience which sat at their
feet. No opportunity to play for the people was overlooked—every free concert, every benefit, every place where people wanted to hear the music and it
was possible to set up the amps and plug them in was a place we had to go to
kick out the jams as best we could.

*The rock liberation front: at a John Sinclair benefit concert. Chrysler Arena, Ann Arbor,
Michigan, December 1971.*

"All this flew in the face of the accepted policies of one of the honkiest, most uptight music scenes anywhere—a scene where promoters have called bands to tell them they would never get any other paying job if they continued playing free for the people."

Nonetheless, a record contract for the MC5 had been secured with Elektra and the first album had been recorded live, October 31, 1968, at the Grande Ballroom. The next day the White Panther Party had been formed with John Sinclair as minister of information. The White Panthers consider the MC5 their strongest weapon. The Panthers' purpose: "To put the cultural revolution into an explicitly political context by merging the total assault on the culture program of rock & roll and dope and fucking in the streets with armed self-defense and what Eldridge Cleaver and Huey P. Newton called 'the mother country radical movement.'"

At this point in history, the Michigan State Supreme Court was planning to hear the seventh appeal of John Sinclair, and the Rainbow People's Party (the since-transformed White Panthers) was planning a massive rally to culminate "Free John Sinclair Week," which would precede the hearing. This kind of thing had happened numerous times before during the twenty-seven months of John's incarceration.

Then one week before the rally, Leni Sinclair received a phone call at 3:00 a.m. Jerry Rubin wanted to read her words to a song.

> It ain't fair, John Sinclair
> In the stir for breathing air
> Let him be, set him free
> Let him be like you and me.
> —"John Sinclair" (John Lennon)

It was a new song that John Lennon had written—after learning about Sinclair's situation from Rubin.

At 3:30 a.m. Leni was on the phone again, talking to Yoko Ono. Plans for a special guest appearance were being finalized. Add John and Yoko to Bobby Seale, Rennie Davis, Ed Sanders, Stevie Wonder, Dave Dellinger, Father Groppi, Marge Tobankin of the National Student Association, Allen Ginsberg, Jonnie Lee Tillman of the National Welfare Rights Organization, Jim Fourant of the Gay Revolution Party, Jerry Rubin, Phil Ochs, Sheila Murphy of the Labor Defense Coalition, the Up, Archie Shepp, Commander Cody, Seger-Teegarden-van Winkle, Leni Sinclair, David Sinclair and David Peel.

The Chrysler Arena, where Big Ten basketball games are played, had been filled well over its fifteen-thousand-seat capacity for three and one half hours when the program finally opened with a recorded message from William Kunstler. Speaker after speaker then outlined a broad series of causes for Movement attention but noted the added power that rock music could bring. Jerry Rubin called the event "the first act of the Rock Liberation Front." Father James Groppi called it a "resurrection." Dave Dellinger said, "Like most of you, I came to see John and Yoko. But I came to see John and Yoko because they have a song to sing about John Sinclair."

At 2:30 a.m., surprise guest Stevie Wonder finished his "killer" nightclub act. Emcee Bob Rudnick informed the audience that there was but one act remaining. It took almost an hour to set up for the final act.

John and Yoko, dressed in identical black leather jackets over cannabis-flowered lavender FREE JOHN NOW T-shirts, took the stage, accompanied by three acoustic guitar players and a conga man. Dave Dellinger had gone to see John and Yoko in their dressing room during Stevie Wonder's set but had not joined the band. Leslie Bacon was one of the guitar players and Jerry Rubin was the conga man.

"The Pope Smokes Dope," John yelled into the microphone. They performed four numbers, "Attica State," "Sisters O Sisters," "Luck of the Irish" and finally "John Sinclair." At one point, when John was having trouble with his guitar strap a cry of "Free John Lennon" came from the audience . . . "I am," he replied without raising his head.

From the stage, just before doing their last number, John Lennon said, "We came here not only to help John and spotlight what's going on but also to show and to say to all of you that apathy isn't it, and that we can do something. Oh, so flower power didn't work, so what, we start again."

Three days after the concert, the Michigan Supreme Court, on the previously scheduled matter of John Sinclair, drew up a motion to grant Sinclair appeal bond in light of forthcoming changes in the state marijuana statutes. They passed the motion by a six-to-one vote and John Sinclair walked out of Jackson State Prison.

The Lennons were at the Record Plant in New York City when the news of Sinclair's release reached them. In a phone conversation between the two sets of "partners," Yoko said, "We hope that you're the first. We aren't going to stop until all brothers and sisters are freed from the prisons, inside and outside the walls."

But there was other, less positive, fallout from the rally. ". . . The whole evening was something of a misunderstanding between the politicos, who thought they were getting it on with fifteen thousand Sinclair followers, and the crowd, who put up with eight hours of rhetoric to see John and Yoko," wrote New York's *Village Voice* critic. "The long bill of musicians alternated with the political raps, making it hard to build up either political or musical momentum." She went on to describe the Lennons as "tired and uptight" and concluded: "The audience was slightly stunned. John and Yoko had performed for fifteen minutes, urged political activism and support for Sinclair and split. But the entire evening no one had offered or even hinted at any strategies. It was depressing."

The criticism disturbed Yoko and she later offered a meticulously thought-out defense of their performance. "Both in the West and the East, music was once separated into two forms. One was court music, to entertain the aristocrats. The other was folk songs, sung by the people to express their emotions and their political opinions.

"But lately, folk songs of this age, pop song, is becoming intellectualized and is starting to lose the original meaning and function. Aristocrats of our age, critics, reviewed the Ann Arbor Rally and criticized the musical quality for not coming up to their expectations. That was because they lost the ears to understand the type of music that was played there.

"That was not artsy-craftsy music. It was music alongside the idea of, message is the music. We went back to the original concept of folk song, like a newspaper, the function was to present the message accurately and quickly.

"And in that sense, it was funky music, just as newspaper layout could be called funky. Also it is supposed to stimulate people among the audience and to make them think, 'Oh, it's so simple, even I could do it.' It should not alienate the audience with its professionalism but to communicate to the audience the fact that they, the audience, can be just as creative as the performers on the stage, and encourage them to make their own music with the performers rather than to just sit back and applaud. . . ."

A few days later, in Greenwich Village, Jerry Rubin is on the telephone. "That's fantastic, John, I can't believe it. Man, you move so fast. A whole week. That's fantastic. Hold on, John." Rubin moves away from the receiver to talk to Stew Albert, who has the flu and is bundled up on Jerry's living-room mattress. "John and Yoko are going to do 'The Mike Douglas Show' for a week. They do five days and they can have five guests a day and the only stipulation is that they don't do anything that will embarrass Mike Douglas. They move so fast I can't keep up with them."

Rubin moves back to the receiver, "John? Yoko! Yeah, it's fantastic, I can't believe it. Yeah, I'll work on a list and you work on a list. What? Chuck Berry and Bo Diddley—that's fantastic. Okay. I'll work on a list of some political people and then I'll come over and we'll compare lists. Great. Oh, Yoko? John! Yeah, it's fantastic. You could have Dylan on. You could invite Kissinger. Yeah, if we have to have equal time we'll have some deaf and dumb right-wingers. Oh no? Okay. Yoko says only positive feelings, no right-wing lunatics.

"Okay, John, when do we want to see John and Leni Sinclair? Tonight? You're into doing the list now. Yeah, I just don't want them to think you're putting them off. Great. Wow, I can't believe it. It's fantastic."

Jerry begins making his list: "Bernadette Devlin, Ron Dellums, the Kent State mothers, fantastic. Huey Newton, Bobby Seale, fantastic. Jimmy Hoffa, Jennifer Dohrn, somebody from the Angela Davis trial—her sister—looks just like her, fantastic. Groucho Marx—no—maybe he gets enough air time, John and Leni Sinclair, Aretha Franklin . . ."

At nine o'clock, John Lennon, wearing white pants with stars on the back pockets and a black T-shirt that says FLY in white letters across the chest, jumps out of bed to embrace his guests.

"This is him, Yoko. He's a big one, isn't he!" John shouts as he holds on to John Sinclair around the Mao button.

Jerry Rubin is in ecstasy handling the introductions. Jerry is the catalyst in many of the "political" contacts that John and Yoko are making. Each new handshake that he produces is a euphoric joy-pop for him. He glows a burnt pink. (Conversely, situations when it is impossible to consummate a relationship drain Rubin. He turns a lifeless off-white.) But this is a good night. No, it's a *fantastic* night! Jerry is bordering between maximum tolerance and OD.

"Is this far out? Did I tell you it was going to be fantastic? Look at this group! Would you look at this group!"

After John Lennon exchanges running hugs and thumb-lock handshakes with John and Leni, Rubin catches Lennon to point out Ed Sanders. John is noticeably pleased by this second new guest.

Yoko puts aside an article called "The Feminization of Society" which she is writing for the *New York Times,* and invites this gathering of a new Plastic Ono Band to sit around the circular hard oak eating-meeting table off the kitchenette. At the left flank of the table is an overcrowded bookshelf jammed with titles by Bertrand Russell, Kate Millet, Mario Puzo, Herman Hesse, Jerry Rubin, Abbie Hoffman, Jerry Hopkins and Yoko Ono, among many.

The apartment has only two rooms. Take down the American Flag curtain that separates them and you have a typical basement loft.

Their papers, musical instruments, photographs, records, telephones, art objects, rotate in a disorderly but functional clutter throughout. There are more papers than things. The Oscar given for the *Let It Be* soundtrack is on a cabinet off to the side of the bed, waist deep in papers. A huge remote-control color TV is almost always running, but rarely with the sound on.

But a calm generates from the chaotic elements of this household and tensions vanish as John Lennon begins to talk. With Yoko's arm twined in his own, he begins to explain their plans, their schemes, their hopes and their dreams— all of which are still at a theoretical stage with a number of hard realities to be worked out.

"We've been planning to do a tour for some time. Your needs got us out earlier than we anticipated," he says to the Sinclairs.

The week before their visit, Jerry had been telling John, Leni and all the Rainbow People that a tour being planned by John and Yoko was going to be the biggest use of rock energy ever conceived. The Sinclairs were easily carried along with the vision. The idea seemed so akin to Sinclair's own blueprint for combatting "Rock & Roll Imperialism."

"Jerry was very persistent about the need for us to play in Ann Arbor," Yoko adds.

·"Yeah, if it wasn't for Jerry, we wouldn't have gone to Ann Arbor. But now we have the taste of playing again and we can't wait to do more. We want to go around from town to town, doing a concert every other night for a month, at least. We'll pick up local bands along the way in each town." The mention of local bands brings smiles to the faces of the Sinclairs. And when John Sinclair is happy, his lungs fill with air and he bloats like a huge, happy blowfish.

"If some of the bands have enough bread," Lennon continues, "they can tag along to the next town. We also want to have bands playing outside of the arenas on the streets, on the nights of the concerts. There will be people to take care of all these arrangements. I just want to be a musician and transmit some love back to the people. That's what excites me most, getting to play with a band again. It will be the regular scene, but without the capitalism. We'll play for the halls and the people will pay to get in but we'll leave our share of the money in the town where it can do the most good. We want it to be the regular scene except we also want to raise some consciousness."

"There's gonna be lots of resistance," Sinclair offers with the voice of experience.

"I don't really think so; Klein will take care of that," Lennon returns with the voice of a different experience, and knocks a bit of the wind out of Sinclair

With Jerry Rubin en route to Attica Prison benefit at the Apollo Theatre. New York City, November 1971.

with the dropping of this latest name. Allen Klein is a man whom Sinclair never considered as a brother or bedfellow in the crusade against "rock imperialism."

"We're trying to change the business," Jerry offers, noticing the sudden anxiety.

"What are we going to do when the rest of the business tries to trash us?"

"I think they'll all like us," Lennon picks up the ball again. "I think we'll replace ecology. We won't just be going around like Johnnie Ray, and we're not going to bring light shows either. The audience can supply light shows of their own."

"Right on," the Sinclairs answer, in unison.

Ed Sanders participated more as an observer and guest than as an active member in what the Sinclairs were already calling a "conspiracy." Occasionally he entered in the conversation with queries about the more pragmatic elements of this latest dream.

"Every show is going to have to run like clockwork. Precision. One-two-three," he says.

"I think we'll have Chip Monck to take care of that," Lennon replies.

"Do you have your band picked out yet?"

"I've been practicing with Elephant's Memory. Have you heard of them? They're a New York band, good musicians. I really like them. They understand everything that's going on, too. I'm going to play with them on 'The Mike Douglas Show.' Seems to keep changing, though. I'd like to have some of the people who played on the album, too. I'd like to have two drummers, like a lot of bands have now."

"This is gonna be a motherfucker to organize," Sinclair injects, "but if it works, we'll be developing strong relationships with youth cadres all over America."

"It'll work! It's gonna *happen!*" says Jerry Rubin.

When Sinclair fell into the role of the dominating revolutionary leader in charge of a strategy session — which he is in Michigan — the signs of strain that are common on the faces of youths participating in their first SDS meeting appeared on the face of the ex-Beatle now an enlistee in the Guitar Army. But Yoko remained calm and, while she was by his side, tensions would fly away.

Soon the politics of this first meeting gave way for another day and turned to record listening, TV watching, a guitar lesson for Peel and general socializing.

Just prior to leaving, John Sinclair stood in the American Flag zone between the two rooms. "It's nights like this," he told Leni, "that make it clear why they wanted to keep me in the penitentiary."

Afterward, John Lennon talked to his wife about their latest visitors, of whom they had known nothing until late in 1971. "Yoko, John Sinclair is really only a rock manager, but he got political after taking acid one day."

THE FIGHT TO STAY

*For more than four years John Lennon was harassed by U.S. Immi-
gration authorities who wanted him out of the country because of his
allegedly subversive political activities. The following three pieces are
taken from* Rolling Stone's *extensive coverage of the case. Ralph J.
Gleason's column of 1972—reprinted here—first drew national
attention to Lennon's plight and spurred an outpouring of letters to
congressional representatives around the country.*

FAIR PLAY FOR JOHN
AND YOKO
By Ralph J. Gleason/June 22, 1972

OHN LENNON and Charles Chaplin. There's a connection
between the two.

When Chaplin appeared at the Academy Awards broadcast for a special "tribute," I was saddened by it and filled
with pity and a kind of anger. That hall was at least half full
of people who were adults when Chaplin was Jim Crowed
out of the U.S., denied a permit to return and classified as
"undesirable." There was no question as to why. He had
been found guilty by association and was regarded as an
immoral communist agitator.

That half of the house old enough to have been adults
when he was declared an undesirable did precious little to
help him then and nothing at all to fight the vicious discrimination and prejudice of the U.S. government. When
Chaplin came back in his old age, I had hoped for one minute
he would look at them and tell it like it is. But he couldn't. Actors are all hams,
even the best of them, and they live for the applause and he went for it. Okay.
God knows, he deserved it, but it was a moment of supreme hypocrisy. All
that empty talk about his genius from people who should have, but did not,
fight when he was barred from the country. There's a lot of money to be made
out of him again and that's why there was the tribute.

The Chaplin night was full of how much everybody owed to Chaplin's
genius. Likewise, the airwaves are full of people who owe their very existence,
or at least the opportunity to do their thing, to John Lennon and to the Beatles.
Lennon's musical influence, as an individual and through the Beatles, is primary.
Only Dylan is his peer.

Right now the U.S. government is trying to throw Lennon out of the country as "undesirable" in the same fashion as it barred Chaplin.

As a fallout of the direct attack on Lennon for being outspoken about the immoral war in Vietnam, the lordly United States Immigration Service is asking Yoko to make a choice between her husband and her child, a heinous and immoral proposition if ever there was one.

Of course, we all know John Lennon represents considerably less of a threat to the United States than Richard Nixon does. But that's not quite the point. The point is that once again the Establishment is exercising selective enforcement of a special restrictive piece of legislation. John was busted once for grass. So was George. George is not having any trouble with the authorities over here but John is. What gives? Politics, is what. John is flagrantly and overtly anti-war—and embarrassingly so. George is not quite that hard-nosed about it. Diplomatic, even.

None of the issues has anything at all to do with whether or not John makes good records, whether Yoko can sing or whether John should or should not speak out. The point is that the government is being nastily legalistic (and maybe just a bit past that). John Lennon is a target of opportunity for the U.S. government, it seems.

The action of the Immigration Service is a public disgrace. If pressure from the government backed up by letters and phone calls from a lot of old biddies can allow them to throw John Lennon out, we're in worse shape than even I imagined we were in.

Tactically, I think a good publicist and some organization a couple of months

With Rolling Stone cofounder Ralph J. Gleason, after the Beatles' last performance. Candlestick Park, San Francisco, August 1966.

back would have aided the Lennons immeasurably. But I suspect they didn't want to do it that way. They wanted to be ordinary folks about it. Well, they are not ordinary and the U.S. is going to screw them if it can.

And what I want to know is: Where the hell is everybody? Where are all those who grew up and learned to make music and song turned on by the Beatles? There isn't an artist in the *Billboard* Top 200 albums who shouldn't be picketing the Immigration Office, writing letters in John's defense and campaigning actively to get him off this bum rap. Where is the new generation? Where are the members of the new community? Where, for instance, has *Rolling Stone* been? And the rest of the papers that concern themselves with and exist for this music?

So far, only Phil Spector has supported Lennon publicly. But if John Lindsay can make a gesture in this battle, where are all the other heavies from Lennon's own people? I mean all of you.

When Benjamin Franklin signed the Declaration of Independence, he said: "We must, indeed, all hang together, or most assuredly we shall all hang separately." It is just as true today as it was then.

Please come down out of your clouds and get up off your big fat rusty dusties (to mix a metaphor delightfully) and get with it. Write and wire your congressman and senator. Do it now. They want to divide us. Don't let them.

BACK IN THE U.S.S.A.
By Joel Siegel/October 10, 1974

LAST September, John Lennon acquired a document through a former New York City narcotics officer.

FROM: Supervisor, Intelligence Division, Unit 2.

To: Regional Director, Group 3.

SUBJECT: The Supervision of the Activities of Both John and Yoko Lennon

"It has come to the further attention of this office that John Ono Lennon, formerly of the Beatles, and Yoko Ono Lennon, wife of John Lennon, have intentions of remaining in this country and seeking permanent residence therein. This has been judged to be inadvisable and it was recommended that all applications are to be denied.

"Their relationships with one (6521) Jerry Rubin, and one John Sinclair (4536), also their many commitments which are judged to be highly political and unfavorable to the present administration. . . . Your office is to maintain a constant servaillence [*sic*] of their residence and a periodic report is to be sent this office. All cooperation is to [be] given to the INS and all reports are to be directed by this office."

The Board of Immigration Appeals ordered John Lennon to leave the United States voluntarily by September 8, 1974, or be deported. Of course Lennon chose the third alternative: His case is now at the Court of Appeals where it may stay a full year before going on to the Supreme Court. Meanwhile, Lennon has launched a counteroffensive: *John Lennon* vs. *the United States*. Still in its pretrial stages at the Federal District Court in New York City, Lennon's countersuit cries Watergate.

Late in February 1972, the scenario runs, South Carolina Republican Senator Strom Thurmond sent a note to then Attorney General John Mitchell. John Lennon, Mitchell was informed, was planning a massive peace demonstration at the 1972 Republican convention, then planned for San Diego. Columnist Jack Anderson has reported that Thurmond admitted the communication with Mitchell but denied suggesting any action. Regardless, Lennon's immigration problems began virtually within the week.

March 1, 1972, the Immigration and Naturalization Service granted Lennon a very standard fifteen-day extension on his visa, pending more very standard paperwork. Then, on March 6, and again on March 7, Lennon's attorney, Leon Wildes, explained, "They revoked it and labeled him an 'overstay' because he'd stayed past February 29. And they told him to get out."

Hearings and appeals followed, as did a series of petitions and protests. The latter took attorney Wildes to the office of New York Senator James Buckley. "I spoke with Tom Cole of Senator Buckley's office. He told me that my clients were considered to be security risks." (Yoko has been granted "Permanent Alien" status.)

The government's case against Lennon is based on a 1968 British marijuana conviction: Marijuana possession is specifically spelled out on the list of illnesses and illegalities that can keep a foreigner from becoming a United States resident, although Wildes is quick to point out the conviction was for hash—an illegality *not* listed—and that by U.S. definition (of possession) Lennon is guilty of no crime at all. "I was planted by a headhunting English cop who's now in jail for planting people." Why the guilty plea? "I was living with Yoko, who was pregnant. We weren't married. She was foreign and I thought they'd get her and they said they'd let her off if I pleaded guilty. I made a deal."

Wildes's research has netted 118 cases of aliens allowed resident status "even though they have convictions at least as serious as my client's," including one convicted murderer and one "with six convictions including rape, burglary and impairing the morals of children."

"There are narcotics dealers that've been allowed to stay," Lennon said. "Murderers, rapists, multiple convictions for dope, heroin, cocaine. What the hell. I'll fit right in."

"I've been doing deportation for fifteen years," Wildes said, "and no case has been handled by the government like this one." Why the government pressure?

Outside U.S. District Court, New York City, during immigration hearings, August 1974.

Lennon's countersuit is based on three major points: illegal government surveillance; prejudice on the part of INS officials who were "ordered" to get him out of the country; and Lennon's being denied constitutional rights guaranteed under the First, Fourth and Fifth amendments.

The Justice Department labeled Lennon's document "fraudulent and a counterfeit" and denied any illegal surveillance. INS has denied any prejudgment. And the government has asked the court to dismiss Lennon's countersuit on those statements.

Asked if he'd been singled out by the Nixon administration, Lennon replied, "I think somebody just thought, 'Oh, there's one of them, let's get him.' " His attorney is not so humble. He told the court, "The government has conspired to get him out under any circumstances . . . as a result of a communication from Strom Thurmond to his friend John Mitchell . . . this action was brought regardless of the circumstances and under orders from higher authorities."

Afterword: On December 5, 1974, a *Rolling Stone* reporter described the next unraveling of the "illegal plot to prosecute and oust John Lennon." It seems a high-ranking Immigration Service official had big plans for a political trial on the scale of the Chicago Seven. Lennon's own albums would be used to document his subversiveness—lyrics like "No short-haired, yellow-bellied son of Trickey Dicky / Is gonna Mother Hubbard soft-soap me."

IMAGINE: JOHN LENNON LEGAL
By Chet Flippo/September 9, 1976

EW YORK. It was just a formality, this little ceremony played out before reporters in a small hearing room on the fourteenth floor of the Immigration and Naturalization Service building here July 27. The United States government had long since—unofficially—backed down on its attempt to deport John Lennon.

But Lennon's attorney wasn't taking any chances. For the hearing he had brought along a coterie of character witnesses. Geraldo Rivera said that John and Yoko were great humanitarians. Isamu Noguchi, the Japanese sculptor, said the same. Norman Mailer lamented the loss of T. S. Eliot to England and hoped that America would not also lose Lennon.

The real star, though, was actress Gloria Swanson. She spoke softly but forcefully of her current work on behalf of physical fitness, especially of the young, and said that a decent celebrity like Lennon could do much for the same cause.

"It's great to be legal again," Lennon said as he held up his green card (which is actually blue). "And I want to thank the Immigration Service for finally seeing the light of day. I just feel overwhelmed." Was he, a TV reporter wondered, going to be an influence on American youth? "My influence is in the way they live and my life is an open book—I'm an artist." Why, another reporter asked, had he picked America for his home? "I have a love for this country," Lennon said. "If it were two thousand years ago, we'd all want to live in Rome. This is Rome now."

LENNONO

later that week in

75.

Dear R.S. AND readers,

A note to thank you all for your help in the immigration 'battle'...we couldnt have done it without you.Also many thanks to all the wellwishers who sent cards 'grammes, gifts,etc etc..for the great triple event.(judges decision/baby Sean/on J.L.s' birthday)!!!

What a week!

love and peace(still),

John and Yoko and Sean(three virgins).

John Lennon

Lennon wrote to Rolling Stone *after winning his immigration battle and after the birth of his son, Sean, two days later (on his thirty-fifth birthday).*

LONG NIGHT'S JOURNEY INTO DAY

▬▬▬▬▬▬▬▬▬▬▬▬▬▬▬

By Pete Hamill / June 5, 1975

By 1975 Pete Hamill had written extensively about Lennon's immigration problems in his syndicated column but wanted to do a longer in-depth interview. "I was really more interested in him as an artist," says Hamill. The following conversation was Lennon's last major interview before he went into a five-year seclusion.

▬▬▬▬▬▬▬▬▬▬▬▬▬▬▬▬▬▬▬▬▬▬▬▬▬▬▬▬▬▬

ERE is John Lennon: thin bare arms, a rumpled T-shirt; bare feet, delicate fingers curled around a brown-papered cigarette, reaching for a cup of steaming coffee. A pale winter sun streams into the seventh-floor apartment in the Dakota, an expensive apartment house that stands like a pile of nineteenth-century memories on the corner of Seventy-second Street and Central Park West. Earlier, the Irish doorman had expressed surprise when I asked for John, because this is where Yoko Ono had lived alone for a year and a half. The building, with its gargoyles and vaulted stone turrets, has seen a lot, and has housed everyone from Lauren Bacall and Rex Reed to Rosemary's baby. There is certainly room for Dr. Winston O'Boogie.

And now John Lennon is talking in a soft, becalmed voice, the old jagged angers gone for now, while the drilling jangle of the New York streets drifts into the room. He has been back with Yoko for three days, after a wild, painful year and a half away, and there is a gray morning feel of hangover in the clean, bright room. Against a wall, a white piano stands like an invitation to begin again; a tree is framed by one window, a plant by another, both in an attitude of Zen-like simplicity, full of spaces. I think of Harold Pinter's words: "When true silence falls we are still left with echo but are nearer nakedness." There is, of course, always echo when you are with John Lennon, an echo of the loudest, grandest, gaudiest noise made in our time. But John Lennon is more than simply a Beatle, retired or in exile, more than just an echo. At thirty-four, he is moving into full maturity as a man and an artist and seems less afraid than ever before of nakedness.

We talked only briefly about the Beatles. A few years ago, John told everybody how the Beatles were more popular than Jesus Christ and for a couple of weeks that summer most of the Western world seemed to go into an uproar. Was the

▬▬▬▬▬▬▬

world really that innocent so short a time ago? No. It was just that John Lennon was explaining that the world had changed and the newspapers had to catch up; we were not going to have any more aw-shucks heroes. So we could all run in the endless emptiness of the rugby field in *A Hard Day's Night*, rising and falling, in slow motion or fast, but sooner or later we would have to grow up. The Beatles were custodians of childhood. They could not last.

And yet . . . and yet, it seemed when it was finally over, when they had all gone their separate ways, when Brian Epstein lay dead and Apple was some terrible mess and the lawyers and the agents and the money men had come in to paw the remains, it often seemed that John was the only one whose heart was truly broken. Cynthia Lennon said it best, when all of them were still together: "They seem to need you less than you need them." From some corner of his broken heart, John gave the most bitter interviews, full of hurt and resentment, covered over with the language of violence.

We only know a small part of what really has happened to him in the years since he met Yoko Ono. The details belong to John Lennon alone. But we know how the other Beatles stood in judgment ("like a jury") on Yoko. We know how viciously the press in England sneered at them and attacked them. Yoko saw the artist in him: "John is like a frail wind . . ." But reviewers were already saying that Yoko had ruined his art. People started to write him off. His records were selling but it wasn't like the Beatles, it wasn't even like the other ex-Beatles. John was the one Who Had Gone Too Far.

A year and a half ago, he and Yoko split up and some people cheered. We live in strange times.

And then, as if from nowhere, came *Walls and Bridges*. John had a big hit single with "Whatever Gets You Thru the Night." And the music was wonderful: full of invention, tenderness, remorse, more personal than anything he had written before; the music clearly showing the effects of his time with Yoko. More than anything else, though, the songs were essays in autobiography, the words and music of a man trying to understand a huge part of his life. "I've been across to the other side / I've shown you everything, I've got nothing to hide . . ."

What follows is the result of two long talks with John Lennon at the end of a difficult year. As an interview, it is far from definitive, but nothing will ever be definitive in John Lennon's life: He is the sort of artist who is always in the process of becoming. I think of this as a kind of interim report from one of the bravest human beings I know. Oh, yes: He looked happy.

What's your life like right now?

Well . . . Life: It's '75 now, isn't it? Well, I've just settled the Beatles settlement. It must've happened in the last month, took three years. [*pause*] And on this day that you've come here, I seem to have moved back in here. In the last three days. By the time this goes out, I don't know . . . That's a big change. Maybe that's why I'm sleeping funny. As a friend says, I went out for coffee and some papers and I didn't come back [*chuckles*]. Or vice versa: It's always written *that* way, y'know. All of us. You know, the *guy* walked. It's never that simple.

What did happen with you and Yoko? Who broke it up and how did you end up back together again?

Well, it's not a matter of *who* broke it up. *It* broke up. And why did we end up back together? [*pompous voice*] We ended up together again because it was diplomatically viable . . . come on. We got back together because we *love* each other.

I loved your line: "The separation didn't work out."

That's it. It *didn't* work out. And the reaction to the breakup was all that madness. I was like a chicken without a head.

What was the final Beatles settlement?

In a nutshell, what was arranged was that everybody gets their own individual monies. Even up till this year—till the settlement was signed—all the monies were going into one pot. All individual records, mine, Ringo's, Paul's— all into one big pot. It had to go through this big machinery and then come out to us, eventually. So now, even on the old Beatle royalties, everything goes into four separate accounts instead of one big pot all the time. That's that. The rest of it was ground rules. Everybody said the Beatles've signed this paper, that means they're no longer tied in any way.

That's bullshit. We still own this thing called Apple. Which, you can explain, is a *bank*. A bank the money goes into. But there's still the entity itself known as Beatles. The product, the name, the likeness, the Apple thing itself, which still exists, and we still have to communicate on it and make decisions on it and decide who's to run Apple and who's to do what. It's not as cut and dried as the papers said.

Do the old Beatles records still go in a pot?

No one of us can say to EMI, "Here's a new package of Beatle material." We still have to okay everything together, you know, 'cause that's the way we want it anyway.

There's still a good feeling among the guys?

Yeah, yeah. I talked to Ringo and George yesterday. I didn't talk to Paul 'cause he was asleep. George and Paul are talkin' to each other in L.A. now. There's nothin' going down between us. It's all in people's heads.

You went to one of George's concerts; what are your thoughts on his tour?

It wasn't the greatest thing in history. The guy went through some kind of mill. It was probably his turn to get smacked. When we were all together there was periods when the Beatles were in, the Beatles were out, no matter what we were doing. Now it's always the Beatles were great or the Beatles weren't great, whatever opinion people hold. There's a sort of illusion about it. But the actual fact was the Beatles were in for eight months, the Beatles were out for eight months. The public, including the media, are sometimes a bit sheeplike and if the ball starts rolling, well, it's just that somebody's in, somebody's out. George is out for the moment. And I think it didn't matter what he did on tour.

George told Rolling Stone *that if you wanted the Beatles, go listen to Wings. It seemed a bit of a putdown.*

I didn't see what George said, so I really don't have any comment. [*pause*] *Band on the Run* is a great album. Wings is almost as conceptual a group as Plastic Ono Band. Plastic Ono was a conceptual group, meaning that whoever was playing was the band. And Wings keeps changing all the time. It's conceptual. I mean, they're backup men for Paul. It doesn't matter who's playing. You can call them Wings, but it's Paul McCartney music. And it's good stuff. It's good Paul music and I don't really see the connection.

What do you think of Richard Perry's work with Ringo?

I think it's great. Perry's great, Ringo's great, I think the combination was great and look how well they did together. There's no complaints if you're Number One.

George said at his press conference that he could play with you again but not with Paul. How do you feel?

I could play with all of them. George is entitled to say that, and he'll probably change his mind by Friday. You know, we're all human. We can all change our minds. So I don't take any of my statements or any of their statements as the last word on whether we will. And if we do, the newspapers will learn about it after the fact. If we're gonna play, we're just gonna *play*.

In retrospect, what do you think of the whole "Lennon Remembers" episode?

Well, the other guys, their reaction was public. Ringo made some sort of comment that was funny, which I can't remember, something like, "You've gone too far this time, Johnnie." Paul said [*stuffy voice*], "Well, that's *his* problem." I can't remember what George said. I mean, they don't care, they've been with me for fifteen or twenty years, they know damn well what I'm like. It just so happens it was in the press. I mean, they know what I'm like. I'm not ashamed of it at all. I don't really like hurting people, but Jann Wenner questioned me when I was almost still in therapy and you can't play games. You're opened up. It was like he got me on an acid trip. Things come out. I got both reactions from that article. A lot of people thought it was right on. My only upset was Jann insisted on making a book out of it.

Walls and Bridges *has an undertone of regret to it. Did you sit down consciously to make an album like that?*

No, well . . . Let's say this last year has been an extraordinary year for me personally. And I'm almost amazed that I could get *anything* out. But I enjoyed doing *Walls and Bridges* and it wasn't hard when I had the whole thing to go into the studio and do it. I'm surprised it wasn't just all *bluuuugggghhhh*. [*pause*] I had the most peculiar year. And . . . I'm just glad that *something* came out. It's describing the year, in a way, but it's not as sort of schizophrenic as the year really was. I think I got such a shock during that year that the impact hasn't come through. It isn't all on *Walls and Bridges* though. There's a hint of it there. It has to do with age and God knows what else. But only the surface has been touched on *Walls and Bridges*, you know?

What was it about the year? Do you want to try talking about it?

Well, you can't put your finger on it. It started, somehow, at the end of '73, goin' to do this *Rock 'n' Roll* album [with Phil Spector]. It had quite a lot to do with Yoko and I, whether I knew it or not, and then, suddenly, I was out on me own. Next thing I'd be waking up, drunk, in strange places or reading about meself in the paper, doin' extraordinary things, half of which I'd done and half of which I hadn't done. But you know the game anyway. And find meself sort of in a mad *dream* for a year. I'd been in many mad dreams, but this . . . It was pretty wild. And then I tried to recover from that. And [*long pause*] meanwhile life was going on, the Beatles settlement was going on, other things, life was still going on and it wouldn't let you sit with your hangover, in whatever form that took. It was like something—probably meself—kept hitting me while I was trying to do something. I was still trying to carry on a normal life and the whip never let up—for eight months. So . . . that's what was going on. Incidents: You can put it down to which night with which bottle or which night in which town. It was just sort of a mad year like that. . . . And it was just probably fear, and being out on me own, and gettin' old, and are ye gonna make it in the charts? Are ye not gonna make it? All that crap, y'know. All the garbage that y'really know is not the be-all and end-all of your life, but if other things are goin' funny, *that's* gonna hit you. If you're gonna feel sorry for yourself, you're gonna feel sorry for everything. What it's really to do with is probably the same thing that it's always been to do with all your life: whatever your own personal problems really are, you know? So it was a year that manifested itself [*switches to deep actor's voice*] *in most peculiar fashion*. But I'm through it and it's '75 now and I feel *better* and I'm sittin' *here* and not lyin' in some weird place with a hangover.

Why do you feel better?

Because I feel like I've been on Sinbad's voyage, you know, and I've battled all those monsters and I've got back *[long pause]* Weird.

Tell me about the Rock 'n' Roll *album.*

It started in '73 with Phil and fell apart. I ended up as part of mad, drunk scenes in Los Angeles and I finally finished it off on me own. And there was still problems with it up to the minute it came out. I can't begin to say, it's just *barmy*, there's a jinx on that album. And I've just started writing a new one. Got maybe half of it written . . .

What about the stories that Spector's working habits are a little odd? For example, that he either showed off or shot off guns in the studios?

I don't like to tell tales out of school, y'know. But I do know there was an awful loud noise in the toilet of the Record Plant West.

What actually did happen those nights at the Troubadour when you heckled the Smothers Brothers and went walking around with a Kotex on your head asking the waitress, "Do you know who I am"?

Ah, y'want the juice . . . If I'd said, "Do you know who I am?" I'd have said it in a joke. Because I know who I am, and I know *she* knew, because I musta been wearing a Kotex on me head, right? I picked up a Kotex in a restaurant, in the toilet, and it was clean and just for a gag I came back to the table with it on me head. And 'cause it stuck there with sweat, just *stayed* there, I didn't have to keep it on. It just stayed there till it fell off. And the waitress said, "Yeah, you're an asshole with a Kotex on," and I think it's a good remark and so what? Tommy Smothers was a completely different night and has been covered a million times. It was my first night on Brandy Alexanders and my last *[laughs]*. And I was with Harry Nilsson, who was no help at all *[laughs]*.

What's your relationship with Nilsson? Some critics say that he's been heavily influenced, maybe even badly screwed up by you.

Oh, that's bullshit.

. . . and that you've also been influenced by him.

That's bullshit, too. I haven't been influenced by Harry, only that I had a lot of hangovers whenever I was with him *[laughs]*. I love him. He's a great guy and I count him as one of me friends. He hasn't influenced me musically. And there's an illusion going around about my production of Harry's album. That he was trying to imitate me on his album.

You mean that he'd gone into his primal period . . .

That's it. They're so sheeplike—put this in—and childlike about trying to put a tag on what's going on. They use these expressions like "primal" for anything that's a scream. Brackets: Yoko was screaming before Janov was ever even heard of; that was her stint, usin' her voice like an instrument. She was screamin' when Janov was still jackin' off to Freud. But nowadays, everything that's got a scream in it is called *primal*. I know what they're talkin' about: The very powerful emotional pitch that Harry reaches at the end of "Many Rivers to Cross" on the album I produced for him [*Pussy Cats*]. It's there, simply enough, because when you get to a certain point with your vocals, there ain't nowhere else to go. Was Little Richard primaling before each sax solo? That's what I want to know. Was my imitation Little Richard screams I used to put on all the Beatles records before the solo—we all used to do it, we'd go *aaaarrrrgggghhhh*! Was that primaling? Right?

Richard Perry has described you as a superb producer but maybe in too much of a hurry.

That's true [*laughs*].

But supposedly, when making the Beatles records, you were painstaking and slow.

No, I was never painstaking and slow. I produced "I Am the Walrus" at the same speed I produced "Whatever Gets You Thru the Night." I would be painstaking on some things, as I am now. If there's a quality that occasionally gets in the way of my talent, it's that I get bored quick unless it's done quick. But "I Am the Walrus" sounds like a wonderful production. "Strawberry Fields" sounds like a big production. But I do them as quick as I possibly can, without losing (a) the feel and (b) where I'm going. The longest track I personally spent time on was "Revolution 9," which was an abstract track where I used a lot of tape loops and things like that. I still did it in one session. But I accept that criticism and I have it of myself. But I don't want to make myself so painstaking that it's boring. But I should [*pause*] maybe t'ink a little more. Maybe. But on the other hand I think my criticism of somebody like Richard Perry would be that he's great but he's *too* painstaking. It gets too slick and somewhere in between that is where I'd like to go. I keep finding out all the time—what I'm missing that I want to get out of it.

Is there anybody that you'd like to produce? For example, Dylan?

Dylan would be interesting because I think he made a great album in *Blood on the Tracks* but I'm still not keen on the backings. I think I could produce him great. And Presley. I'd like to resurrect Elvis. But I'd be so scared of him I don't know whether I could *do* it. But I'd *like* to do it. Dylan, I could do, but Presley would make me nervous. But Dylan or Presley, somebody up *there* . . . I know what I'd do with Presley. Make a *rock & roll* album. Dylan doesn't need material. I'd just make him some good backings. So if you're reading this, Bob, you know . . .

Elton John has revived "Lucy in the Sky with Diamonds." How do you feel about him as an artist?

Elton sort of popped in on the session for *Walls and Bridges* and sort of zapped in and played the piano and ended up singing "Whatever Gets You Thru the Night" with me. Which was a great shot in the arm. I'd done three quarters of it, and it was, "Now what do we do?" Should we put a camel on it or a xylophone? That sort of thing. And he came in and said, "Hey, ah'll play some piano!" Then I heard he was doing "Lucy" and I heard from a friend— 'cause he was shy—would I be there when he cut "Lucy"? Maybe not play on it but just be there? So I went along. And I sang in the chorus and contributed the reggae in the middle. And then, again through a mutual friend, he asked if it got to be Number One, would I appear onstage with him, and I said sure, not thinkin' in a million years it was gonna get to Number One. Al Coury or no Al Coury, the promotion man at Capitol. And there I was. Onstage.

With Elton John, Madison Square Garden, November 28, 1974. Lennon's last public concert appearance.

I read somewhere that you were very moved by the whole thing.

I was moved by it, but everybody else was in *tears*. I felt guilty 'cause I wasn't in tears. I just went up and did a few numbers. But the emotional thing was me and Elton together. Elton had been working in Dick James's office when we used to send our demos in and there's a long sort of relationship musically with Elton that people don't really know about. He has this sort of Beatle thing from way back. He'd take the demos home and play them and . . . well, it meant a lot to me and it meant a hell of a lot to Elton, and he was in tears. It was a great high night, a really high night and . . . Yoko and I met backstage. And somebody said, "Well, there's two people in love." That was before we got back together. But that's probably when we felt something. It was very weird. She came backstage and I didn't know she was there, 'cause if I'd known she was there I'd've been too nervous to go on, you know, I would have been terrified. She was backstage afterward, and there was just that moment when we saw each other and like, it's like in the movies, you know, when time stands still? And there was silence, everything went silent, y'know, and we were just sort of lookin' at each other and . . . oh, hello. I knew she'd sent Elton and I a flower each, and we were wearin' them onstage, but I didn't know she was there and then everybody was around us and flash flash flash. But there was that moment of silence. And somebody observed it and told me later on, after we were back together again, and said, "A friend of mine saw you backstage and thought if ever there was two in love, it's those two." And I thought, well, it's weird somebody noticed it . . . So it was a great night . . . .

There seems to be a lot of generosity among the artists now.

It was around before. It's harder when you're on the make, to be generous, 'cause you're all competing. But once you're sort of up there, wherever it is . . . The rock papers love to write about the jet-setting rock stars and they dig it and we dig it in a way. The fact is that, yeah, I see Mick, I see Paul, I see Elton, they're all my contemporaries and I've known the other Beatles, of course, for years, and Mick for ten years, and we've been hangin' around since *Rock Dreams*. And suddenly it's written up as they're-here-they're-there-they're-everywhere bit, and it looks like we're trying to form a club. But we always *were* a club. We always knew each other. It just so happens that it looks more dramatic in the paper.

How do you relate to what we might call the rock stars of the Seventies? Do you think of yourself as an uncle figure, a father figure, an old gunfighter?

It depends who they are. If it's Mick or the Old Guard, as I call them, yeah, they're the Old Guard. Elton, David are the newies. I don't feel like an old uncle, dear, 'cause I'm not that much older than half of 'em, heh heh. But . . .

yeah, I'm interested in the new people. I'm interested in new people in America but I get a kick out of the new Britons. I remember hearing Elton John's "Your Song," heard it in America—it was one of Elton's first big hits—and remember thinking, "Great, that's the first new thing that's happened since we happened." It was a step forward. There was something about his vocals that was an improvement on all of the English vocals until then. I was pleased with it. And I was pleased with Bowie's thing and I hadn't even *heard* him. I just got this feeling from the image and the projections that were coming out of England of him, well, you could feel it.

Do you think of New York as home now?

Yeah, this is the longest I've ever been away from England. I've almost lived here as long as I've lived in London. I was in London from, let's see, '64, '65, '66, '67, actually *in* London 'cause then it was your Beatlemania bit and we all ended up like a lot of rock & rollers end up, living an hour away from London in the country, the drivin'-in-from-the-big-estate bit. 'Cause you couldn't live *in* London, 'cause people just bugged the ass off you. So I've lived in New York *longer* than I actually lived in London.

In view of the immigration case, is one reason you've stayed here so long because if you left, they'd pull a Charlie Chaplin on you and not let you back in?

The Grammy Awards, March 1975. John and Yoko's first public appearance together after they reunited in 1975. With (left to right) David Bowie, Art Garfunkel and Paul Simon.

You bet. There's no way they would let me back. And . . . it's worth it to me. I can last out, without leaving here, another ten years, if that's the way they want to play it. I'll earn enough to keep paying them. I'm really getting black-mailed. I'm *paying* to stay. Paying takes, on one hand, about a half million dollars, and I've hardly worked very hard for that. I mean, that's with sittin' on me arse and I've paid a half million in *taxes*. So I'm paying *them* to attack me and keep me busy and harass me, on one hand, while on the other hand I've got to pay me own lawyers. Some people think I'm here just to make the American dollars. But I don't have to *be* here to make the dollars. I could earn American dollars just sittin' in a recording studio in Hong Kong. Wherever I am, the money follows *me*. It's gonna come out of America whether they like it or not.

Right. And the government doesn't choose that John Lennon makes money. The people who buy your music do that.

The implication is that John Lennon wants to come to the land of milk and honey 'cause it's easier to pick up the money, so I can pick it up directly instead of waiting for it to arrive in England. Or Brazil. Or wherever I decide to do it. I resent that implication, especially as I'm payin' through the nose. I don't mind paying taxes, either, which is strange. I never did. I don't like 'em using it for bombs and that. But I don't think I could do a Joan Baez. I don't have that kind of gut. I did never complain in England either, because, well, it's buying people teeth . . . I'm sick of gettin' sick about taxes. Taxes is what seems to be it, and there's nothin' to be done about it unless you choose to make a crusade about it. And I'm sick of being in crusades because I always get nailed up before I'm even in the crusade. They get me in the queue while I'm readin' the pages about it: "Oh, there's a crusade on, I wonder should I . . . " I mean, I get caught before I've ever even done anything about it.

You went through a period of really heavy involvement in radical causes. Lately you seem to have gone back to your art in a more direct way. What happened?

I'll tell you what happened *literally*. I got off the boat, only it was an air-plane, and landed in New York, and the first people who got in touch with me was Jerry Rubin and Abbie Hoffman. It's as simple as that. It's those two fa-mous guys from America who's callin': "Hey, yeah, what's happenin', what's goin' on? . . ." And the next thing you know, I'm doin' John Sinclair benefits and one thing and another. I'm pretty *movable*, as an artist, you know. They almost greeted me off the plane and the next minute I'm *involved*, you know.

How did all of this affect your work?

It almost *ruined* it, in a way. It became journalism and not poetry. And I basically feel that I'm a poet. Even if it does go ba-deedle, eedle, eedle, it, da-deedle, deedle, it. I'm not a formalized poet, I have no education so I have to write in the simplest forms usually. And I realized that over a period of time—and not just 'cause I met Jerry Rubin off the plane—but that was like a culmination. I realized that we were poets but we were really folk poets, and rock & roll was folk poetry—I've always felt that. Rock & roll *was* folk music. Then I began to take it seriously on another level, saying, "Well, I am reflecting what is going *on*, right?" And then I was making an *effort* to reflect what was going on. Well, it doesn't work like that. It doesn't work as pop music or what I want to do. It just doesn't make sense. You get into that bit where you can't talk about trees, 'cause, y'know, y'gotta talk about "Corruption on Fifty-fourth Street"! It's nothing to do with *that*. It's a bit *larger* than that. It's the usual lesson that I've learned in me little thirty-four years: As soon as you've clutched onto something, you think—you're always clutchin' at straws—*this is what life is all about*. I think artists are lucky because the straws are always blowin' out of their hands. But the unfortunate thing is that most people find the straw hat and hang on to it, like your best friend that got the job at the bank when he was fifteen and looked twenty-eight before he was twenty. "Oh, *this* is it! *Now* I know what I'm doing! Right? Down this road for the next hundred years" . . . and it ain't never *that*. Whether it's a religious hat or a political hat or a no-political hat: whatever hat it was, always looking for these straw hats. I think I found out it's a waste of time. There is no hat to wear. Just keep moving around and changing clothes is the best. That's all that goes on: *change*.

At one time I thought, well, I'm avoidin' that thing called the Age Thing, whether it hits you at twenty-one, when you take your first job—I always keep referrin' to that because it has nothing to do, virtually, with your physical age. I mean, we all know the guys who took the jobs when we left school, the straight jobs, they all look like old guys within six weeks. You'd meet them and they'd all be lookin' like Well, I've Settled Down Now. So I never want to settle down, in that respect. I always want to be immature in that respect. But then I felt that if I keep bangin' my head on the wall it'll stop me from gettin' that kind of age in the head. By keeping creating, consciously or unconsciously, extraordinary situations which in the end you'd write about. But maybe it has nothin' to do with it. I'm still mullin' that over. Still mullin' over last year now. Maybe that was it. I was still trying to avoid somethin' but doin' it the wrong way 'round. Whether it's called age or whatever.

Is it called growing up?

I don't want to grow up but I'm sick of not growing up—that way. I'll find a different way of not growing up. There's a better way of doing it than torturing your body. And then your mind. The guilt! It's just so *dumb*. And it makes me *furious* to be dumb because I don't like dumb people. And there I am, doing the dumbest things . . . I seem to do the things that I despise the most, almost. All of that to—what?—avoid being normal.

I have this great fear of this *normal* thing. You know, the ones that passed their exams, the ones that went to their jobs, the ones that didn't become rock & rollers, the ones that settled for it, settled for it, settled for the *deal!* That's what I'm trying to avoid. But I'm sick of avoiding it with violence, you know? I've gotta do it some other way. I think I will. I think just the fact that I've realized it is a good step forward. Alive in '75 is my new motto. I've just made it up. That's the one. I've decided I want to live. I'd decided I wanted to live *before,* but I didn't know what it meant, really. It's taken however many years and I want to have a go at it.

Do you think much of yourself as an artist at fifty or sixty?

I never see meself as not an artist. I never let meself believe that an artist can "run dry."

I've always had this vision of bein' sixty and writing children's books. I don't know why. It'd be a strange thing for a person who doesn't really have much to do with children. I've always had that feeling of *giving* what *Wind in the Willows* and *Alice in Wonderland* and *Treasure Island* gave to me at age seven and eight. The books that really opened my whole being.

Is there anything left to say about the immigration case?

People get *bored* with hearin' about Lennon's immigration case. *I'm* bored with hearin' about it. The only interesting thing is when I read these articles people write that were not instigated by me. I learn things I didn't know anything *about.* I didn't know about *Strom Thurmond.* I had no idea—I mean I knew *something* was going on, but I didn't have any names. I'm just left in the position of just what am I supposed to do? There doesn't seem to be anything I can do about it. It's just . . . bloody *crazy.* Terry Southern put it in a nice sort of way. He said, "Well, look, y'keep 'em all happy, ya see? The conservatives are happy 'cause they're doin' somethin' about ya and the liberals are happy 'cause they haven't thrown you out. So everybody's happy! [*pause*] Except you!" [*laughter*] I'm happy I'm still here. I must say that. And I ain't going. There's no *way* they're gonna get me out. No way. They're not gonna drag me in *chains,* right? So I'm just gonna have to keep *paying.* It's bloody ridiculous. It's just . . . beyond belief.

So nothing has changed with the departure of Nixon.

I'm even nervous about commenting on politics. They've got me that jumpy these days. But it's a bit of an illusion to think 'cause Old Nick went that it's all changed. If it's changed, prove it, show me the change.

Does the case get in the way of your work?

It did. It did. There's no denying it. In '72, it was really gettin' to me. Not only was I physically having to appear in court cases, it just seemed like a toothache that wouldn't go away. Now I just accept it. I just have a permanent toothache. But there was a period where I *just couldn't function*, you know? I was so paranoid from them tappin' the phone and followin' me. How could I prove that they were tappin' me phone?

There was a period when I was hangin' out with a group called Elephant's Memory. And I was ready to go on the road for pure *fun*. I didn't want to go on the road for money. That was the time when I was standing up in the Apollo with a guitar at the Attica relatives' benefit or ending up on the stage at the John Sinclair rally. I felt like going on the road and playing *music*. And whatever excuse—charity or whatever—would have done me. But they kept pullin' me back into court! I had the group hangin' 'round, but finally I had to say, "Hey, you better get on with your lives." Now, the last thing on earth I want to do is perform. That's a direct result of the immigration thing. In '71, '72, I wanted to go out and rock my balls off onstage and I just stopped.

Have you made any kind of flat decision not to ever go on the road again?

No. I've stopped making flat decisions. I change me mind a lot. My idea of heaven is *not* going on the road.

Will you ever be free of the fact that you were once a Beatle?

I've got used to the fact—just about—that whatever I do is going to be compared to the other Beatles. If I took up ballet dancing, my ballet dancing would be compared with Paul's bowling. So that I'll have to live with. But I've come to learn something big this past year. I cannot let the Top Ten dominate my art. If my worth is only to be judged by whether I'm in the Top Ten or not, then I'd better give up. Because if I let the Top Ten dominate my art, then the art will die. And then whether I'm in the Top Ten is a moot point. I do think now in terms of long term. I'm an artist. I have to express myself. I can't be dominated by gold records. As I said, I'm thirty-four going on sixty. The art is more important than the thing and sometimes I have to remind meself of it. Because there's a danger there, for all of us, for everyone who's involved in whatever art they're in, of *needing that love so badly* that. . . . In my business, that's manifested in the Top Ten.

So this last year, in some ways, was a year of deciding whether you wanted to be an artist or a pop star?

Yeah. What is it I'm doing? What am I *doing*? Meanwhile, I was still putting out the work. But in the back of me head it was that: What do you want to be? What are you lookin' for? And that's about it. I'm a freakin' artist, man, not a fuckin' racehorse.

1976-1980

THE PRIVATE YEARS

By Chet Flippo

HE tie was an obvious clue. Its design showed a butterfly caught in a spider's web. John Lennon was otherwise dressed conservatively: dark suit, white shirt, black cowboy boots. But the hand-painted tie had obviously been chosen for the occasion. "That's *me*," Lennon said in response to my question. "I'm caught in that web and I'm going to wear this tie to court every day until I'm *free*." He was not smiling when he said that.

It was January 12, 1976. Lennon was standing in a federal courtroom in Lower Manhattan, waiting for the latest trial against him to resume. This one involved a $42-million suit against Lennon by a man named Morris Levy. During the recess Lennon spoke haltingly with me about his decision to abandon rock & roll superstardom for an attempt at what he called "real life." He spoke of the awful prospect of spending months in this courtroom. He knew that he was the first and only major rock figure to quit the business voluntarily, and he was clearly uncomfortable as he talked about it. He toyed with the knot of the tie around his neck—not usual fashion for him.

Lennon had made no public announcement of this decision and I was not sure if he was serious. After all, rock & roll had been John Lennon's only real father and mother and if R&R wasn't good enough for Lennon, why, then, it might not hold much value for the rest of us. Lennon laughed at that suggestion. Even so, his healthy cynicism and earthy sense of humor could not hide the image of a man who felt his life had flown apart.

His every move seemed to stir lawyers into action. Only three months earlier, Lennon had won his four-and-a-half-year court battle to stay in this country. He had been alleging for years that the Nixon administration was seeking to throw him out of the United States because he was considered a radical influence on the youth of America, but he had not been believed. Then government documents came to light that revealed his paranoia had been justified.

Now he was involved in a suit that had begun during the Beatles years. Lennon told a friend that he felt that the Beatle fortune had turned into the Hope Diamond and that it carried a similar stigma. "It's *cursed*," he said more than once. He said that anyone who got caught up in the "Beatle Gold Mine" got swallowed and overwhelmed by it, by the public hysteria and the twenty-four-hour scrutiny by the media, and by the incredibly involved legal battles that never stopped.

On January 9, 1975, the Beatles had been formally dissolved as a legal entity and, as Lennon remarked to me in the courtroom a year and three days later, this was thus the first time in thirteen years that he had not been under written contract to at least *someone*. That fact he rather relished. (He had gotten so sick of the Beatles-reunion question that he'd developed a stock answer: "We'll get back together when you go back to high school.") His desire now was to exert that freedom by quitting rock & roll.

His current legal problems were proving to be the last straw: A $42-million lawsuit was being waged against him for allegedly not honoring an alleged verbal agreement to deliver an alleged TV album. How what John Lennon intended to be a tribute album to the beginnings of rock & roll as well as a collaboration with producer extraordinaire Phil Spector ended up also being a TV package on the order of *Boxcar Willie's Greatest Rides* is not an ordinary story.

It began in 1969, when the Beatles recorded Lennon's "Come Together" on *Abbey Road*. Morris Levy filed suit against him, charging copyright infringement on a Chuck Berry song, "You Can't Catch Me." Levy ran Big Seven Music, which had published "You Can't Catch Me."

The suit was finally settled in Levy's favor—although Lennon denied copying the Berry song—in October 1973. Under the terms of the settlement, Lennon was to record three Big Seven songs ("Angel Baby," "You Can't Catch Me" and "Ya Ya") on his next album. Additionally, he was to offer licensing rights to Big Seven to any three of these Apple Music songs: "Goodbye" and "Those Were the Days," by Mary Hopkin; "Carolina on My Mind" and "Something's Wrong," by James Taylor; and "Come and Get It," "Apple of My Eye" and "No Matter What," by Badfinger.

At the time of the settlement, Lennon was estranged from Yoko, living in a beach house in Santa Monica that had once belonged to Peter Lawford, and was recording an album of rock & roll oldies with Phil Spector. Nothing was going smoothly. Lennon was having trouble working and he was getting increasingly sucked into the L.A. coke-and-cognac cycle. By the time he and Phil Spector had put portions of nine songs on tape, things between them collapsed. So did the oldies album.

Lennon hadn't known that Spector had been taking the tapes home with him every night until one night when Spector (and the tapes) stayed home—and didn't call in or leave a forwarding number. Lennon tried, without success, to reach Spector: "It is very hard to get through to him if he doesn't want to— doesn't answer phones. For a period, I just kept trying to get people in touch with Phil. There was a rumor that he had this dreadful car accident, and with Phil one never knows if it really happened or if it didn't happen, if it just happened in his head. So I spent a lot of time trying to find out what actually had happened and I couldn't get any answer. So then I got bored and I started making an album with Harry Nilsson."

Recording costs on the Spector tapes had reached over $200,000 and Lennon later said, "I didn't feel like starting my own album again, because I was a bit disappointed or depressed that Phil had run away with the tapes. This was the first time I had never finished an album."

Soon he was in over his head with drugs and alcohol. He would go to Las Vegas and get drunk at Caesar's Palace and play number nine on the roulette wheel all night, usually losing. After producing Nilsson's *Pussy Cats* album (and recording, with the aid of gallons of warm sake, a number of X-rated songs), Lennon realized he was sinking, and looked back to New York City and Yoko. He began writing what would be the nucleus of the album *Walls and Bridges*. He wrote "Nobody Loves You (When You're Down and Out)," which accurately reflected his situation. He wrote "Scared," which admitted that he was. He wrote "#9 Dream" and "Whatever Gets You Thru the Night." He was a tired and lonely man.

He still had not been able to recover the Spector tapes, so he decided to go back to New York to cut *Walls and Bridges* (he took the title from a random scrap of conversation on a forgotten TV show but he liked the phrase because walls were protection and bridges were escape).

Lennon released *Walls and Bridges* in September 1974, and it consisted of all Lennon compositions, save for a version of Lee Dorsey (and coauthor Morris Levy's) "Ya Ya," a Big Seven song. Levy was not amused. He maintained that Lennon owed him three Big Seven songs on that album, since it was the "next" album as stipulated in the settlement. The fact that Phil Spector had kidnapped the tapes which would have allowed Lennon to fulfill his part of the bargain was irrelevant to Levy.

"I booked the time for *Walls and Bridges*," Lennon later said, "and I booked the musicians to come from L.A. [bassist Klaus Voormann, pianist Nicky Hopkins, drummer Jim Keltner] and it seems to me that three or four days before I went in to record *Walls and Bridges*, suddenly I had all these Spector tapes. There were ten boxes of Spector tapes. [Capitol president Al Coury had finally paid Spector $90,000 in cash to get the tapes.] So, I just thought, well, I am not going to cancel *Walls and Bridges* to go looking through all these tapes, I will do *Walls and Bridges* first and then I will deal with the Spector tapes."

During the next few months Lennon struggled to pull his life back together from his "lost weekend"—eighteen months spent on the seamier side of the Los Angeles rock-star demimonde. His first priority was to get back with Yoko. Even while he had been dissipating himself in L.A. he called her frequently, would sometimes get past the answering service and, if he were sober enough, would convince Yoko to talk to him. "I'm ready to come back," he began to tell her. She didn't think that he was. In the fall of 1974 he moved back to New York and stayed at the Hotel Pierre on Fifth Avenue, across Central Park from the Dakota.

John and Yoko's reunion was precipitated by a curious twist of fate—all because of a promise made to Elton John. Elton had sung backup on the single "Whatever Gets You Thru the Night" and had done "a damn good job," as Lennon later described it. "So I sort of halfheartedly promised that if 'Whatever Gets You Thru the Night' became Number One, which I had no reason to expect, I'd do Madison Square Garden with him." In late 1974 the unexpected happened, and Elton called in his chips. It was John Lennon's first Number One in the United States. So on November 28, 1974, about two thirds of the way through Elton's concert at Madison Square Garden, out walked a trim John Lennon. The audience reaction shook the rafters. John and Elton sang "Lucy in the Sky with Diamonds," "Whatever Gets You Thru the Night" and "I Saw Her Standing There."

It was a very emotional evening. Elton John later wept openly: He had worried about John's health and was happy to see him again. Yoko was in the audience and visibly touched by the sight of John. After the show she went backstage and she and John looked into each other's eyes. "Can we go out and have dinner?" he asked her. "Call me tomorrow and we'll talk about it," she replied.

He called her and asked, "Tea at the Plaza?" She took him back.

The reunion was so successful that Yoko soon became pregnant. Her pregnancy had come, at age forty-two, after three miscarriages with Lennon. When John learned the news, he made an immediate decision: to quit being a rock & roll star, quit recording at all and devote his life to his family. The prospect of a solid family life excited him. He had never known it himself as a child, his first marriage had been sacrificed to superstardom, and he scarcely knew his son, Julian, from that marriage.

He also made another important decision: to take an active, personal role to resolve the court cases against him. He knew he wouldn't be free until he'd resolved all his legal entanglements. He also believed those entanglements wouldn't stop unless he got out of rock & roll. The Morris Levy trial convinced him of that.

"All this trouble started," Lennon told me during another recess in federal court in Manhattan, "because I got bored after *Mind Games* and just wanted to play some good old rock & roll, what I played as a kid."

That innocent motivation landed him in court because when Lennon did record some "good old rock & roll," two different record companies believed they had the rights to it. In February 1975 two Lennon albums came out made up of almost the same material—one called *Rock 'n' Roll*, the authorized, Capitol Records version of the Phil Spector tapes, and one called *Roots*, the Morris Levy version (the latter had two extra cuts, "Angel Baby" and "Be My Baby"). Suits and countersuits started flying.

John said that when he was thinking about doing his "oldies" album, which he also referred to as "Old Hat," he had a typewritten list of rock & roll classics that he wanted to perform: "Be Bop a Lula (Gene Vincent), Peggy Sue (Buddy Holly), That'll Be the Day (Buddy Holly), Breathless (Jerry Lee Lewis), Slipping and a Sliding (Little Richard and Buddy Holly), Come on Everybody (Eddie Cochran), Rip it Up (Little Richard), Reddy Teddy (Little Richard), Do You Wanna Dance (Bobby Freeman), Bring it on Home to Me (Sam Cooke and Carla Thomas), Send Me Some Loving (Little Richard, Buddy Holly and Sam Cooke), Stand By Me (Ben E. King.)." Below that list he had typed and then crossed out with an ink pen the following: "(30) 40 Days (Chuck Berry and Ronnie Hawkins), Ain't that a Shame (Fats Domino), Summertime Blues (Eddie Cochran)."

At the bottom of the page, Lennon printed the following with an ink pen: "Bonie Maronie—Larry Williams, You Can't Catch Me—, Angel Baby—, Sweet Little 16—C. Berry, Just Because (Lloyd Price—Larry Williams), Be my Baby (Ronnettes/Spector), Since My Baby Left Me: (Arthur Crudup/ Elvis Presley), Ya-Ya." In the margin by these handwritten entries, Lennon had printed "this stuff in the 'can'."

Lennon also explained his song selection for the *Rock 'n' Roll* album thusly: " 'Be-Bop-A-Lula' was one of the first songs I ever learned, and I actually remember singing it the day I met Paul McCartney. I was singing at the church and McCartney was in the audience. 'Stand by Me' was one of my big songs in the dance halls in Liverpool. That was a Ben E. King number. And the same goes for 'Be-Bop-A-Lula' [in that] I knew these songs as a child.

" 'Reddy Teddy' was a sort of guitar-type song written by Little Richard and recorded by him. 'You Can't Catch Me' was the Morris Levy song but it was [by] Chuck Berry, so that was good enough reason to do it. 'Ain't That a Shame' was the first rock & roll song I ever learned. My mother taught it to me on the banjo before I learned the guitar. Nobody else knows these reasons except me. 'Do You Want to Dance' we had [done] at some jam sessions on the West Coast featuring numerous stars not worth mentioning the names of. I tried to get the reggae version. 'Sweet Little Sixteen,' I had been singing that, which is a Chuck Berry number that is also an old-time favorite of mine. 'Slippin' and Slidin' ' was the B side of 'Long Tall Sally,' which is the first Little Richard song I ever heard and was also recorded by Buddy Holly, so that covers a little of both. It was a song I knew. It was easier to do songs that I knew than trying to learn something from scratch, even if I was interested in the songs.

" 'Peggy Sue': I have been doing that since I started, and Buddy Holly did it and, in fact, I used to sing every song that Buddy Holly put out.

" 'Bring It On Home to Me' is one of my all-time favorite songs and, in fact, I have been quoted as saying I wish I had written it. I love it that much and I was glad to be able to do it.

" 'Send Me Some Lovin' ' is a similar kind of song and it was done originally by Little Richard—again, one of my favorites—and also by Buddy Holly.

" 'Bony Maronie' was one of the very earliest songs—along with 'Be-Bop-A-Lula'—and I remember singing it the only time my mother saw me perform before she died. So I was hot on 'Bony Maronie.' That is one of the reasons. Also, I liked Larry Williams, who recorded it.

" 'Ya Ya' I did because it was Morris's and it was a good song. It is an easy song.

" 'Just Because' I did because Phil Spector talked me into it."

The album cover for *Rock 'n' Roll* was an old photograph that Lennon picked out himself. It showed him back in Hamburg, circa 1961, and Lennon said he thought that it was "comic" that he was ending his career as he had started it, singing "straight rock & roll stuff."

At the end of "Just Because," you can just barely hear Lennon say, "And so we say farewell from Record Plant West." He later said that he was consciously saying farewell to the business.

The story of how Morris Levy got hold of the Spector tapes consumed much of the trial. It started with a call from Levy to Lennon's lawyer, Harold Seider, demanding a personal meeting with Lennon. Lennon described the beginning of his relationship with Levy: "Harold Seider told me that Morris wasn't too happy about the situation, about me not doing the songs or whatever I was supposed to do for that agreement we had made and he wasn't too happy about 'Ya Ya' on *Walls and Bridges*. And it would be sort of cool if I came along and explained what happened to the Spector tapes . . . explain what happened to the *Rock 'n' Roll* album." Seider later said that "default" would be a "nice word" to describe Levy's strong feeling that Lennon needed to answer to him.

Lennon and Levy developed a curious relationship. "I was intrigued by him [Levy] as a character," Lennon later said. "That's one way of putting it . . ." They had several meetings in late 1974—by Lennon's account, at Levy's insistence. The first one took place at the Club Cavallero on Fifty-eighth Street in Manhattan on October 8. Recalled Lennon: "All I was interested in saying was what I had to say about the tapes. I was very nervous, because I did not know the man. And I heard he was annoyed at me. So I told him as best I could all about the Phil Spector tapes and what had happened . . . 'I am sorry, you didn't get what you are supposed to get, but this is why.' I explained that for about three quarters of an hour or an hour. And he said something like, 'Well, that is all very well and good, but I am out of pocket.' And he started writing some figures down on a bit of paper. I don't know what they were, maybe $250,000 or something. I could not follow the reasoning, but if he thought he was out of pocket, he was out of pocket as far as I could see."

Levy was to later claim that Lennon then made a verbal agreement with him to allow Levy to market Lennon's oldies album via Levy's TV-mail-order company, Adam VIII. Lennon denied it, saying only that they had talked about the idea—and that he had found it appealing in principle: "I was thinking perhaps I could put it straight on TV and avoid the critics and avoid going through the usual channels. And Morris told me that is what he does . . . I said that is cool with me as long as it is all right with the record company. . . . My policy all the time is whenever they get into figures or business, I just tune out. . . ."

It was extremely rare for Lennon to get involved personally with business people. "I don't go to dinner with people much for fun," Lennon later said. "It is business. That's what you write to the taxman, business meeting." But Morris Levy was different. He managed to convince Lennon it was in his best interest to meet with him. He also managed to convince Lennon to give him a rough mix of the tapes of the Rock 'n' Roll album sessions, which Lennon was finishing at the Record Plant in late 1974. Since three of the songs on those tapes belonged to Big Seven, Lennon finally let Levy have them. Though they were not standard album quality sound, those tapes became the basis for the controversial Levy album.

Once Capitol Records—which distributed Apple Records—learned that Morris Levy was going to release a John Lennon album called Roots, Capitol scrambled to rush-release their version of the Spector tapes, Rock 'n' Roll. The latter was shipped February 7, 1975; the Roots ads appeared on TV February 8. Roots cost $4.98; R'n'R was a dollar more. Capitol wired TV and radio stations around the country that Roots was not an authorized album. It became a prime collector's item.

Ironically, the record that generated the $42-million lawsuit had a first pressing of only 2,444 albums, along with 500 8-track tapes. Only 1,270 of the albums and 175 tapes were sold. (Rock 'n' Roll itself did not sell all that well for Lennon: 342,000 copies. By comparison, John Lennon/Plastic Ono had sold 702,000; Imagine, 1,553,000; Some Time in New York City, 164,000; Mind Games, 376,000; Walls and Bridges, 425,000; and Shaved Fish, 456,000.)

Increasingly, as he sat on the hard courtroom benches, John Lennon became more restive and more cynical. He said one day that of the $4.98 charge for *Roots*, that Morris Levy wanted between one and two dollars profit for each LP, leaving Lennon and EMI twenty-three cents per album (after Adam VIII's pressing and advertising costs were deducted). Lennon said he had ordered a copy of *Roots* himself and had had to wait more than three weeks to get it.

The trial finally wound down February 5, and Judge Griesa said he would take a few days to render an opinion. When he did so fifteen days later, it was not an immediate victory for Lennon. Griesa held that Big Seven was not entitled to damages from Lennon, Capitol Records, Apple, *et al*. But that was only phase one of the three-tiered legal action. Lennon waited. On July 13, Judge Griesa ruled that Big Seven was entitled to $6,795 from Lennon for breach of contract. In phase three—counterclaims—Griesa awarded Lennon $109,700 in damages for lost royalties that *Rock 'n' Roll* might have earned had not *Roots* been issued and another $35,000 in compensatory damages for hurt to his reputation. Lennon gave a sigh of genuine relief: He knew the trial had been a close call. Still wearing his spider-web tie, he leaned forward in court to listen to Judge Griesa's final remarks.

"I wish to add on this point," the soft-spoken judge said, "that there has been a great deal of evidence produced in the record as to the exact status and movement of Lennon's career. I am convinced of the fact that Lennon perhaps has a career whose balance is somewhat more delicate than the career of other artists. Lennon has attempted a variety of ventures both in popular music and avant-garde music. Lennon's product tends to be somewhat more intellectual than the product of other artists. What this means in my view is that Lennon's reputation and his standing are a delicate matter and that any unlawful interference with Lennon in the way that Levy and the *Roots* album accomplished must be taken seriously. Consequently, I award the damages that I award."

Lennon smiled wryly at that, but he was happy that he had carried a court fight to victory. (The judicial process fascinated John: He and Yoko had attended the Watergate hearings as spectators.) "The reason I fought this," he said, "was to discourage ridiculous suits like this. They didn't think I'd show or that I'd fight it. They thought I'd just settle, but I *won't*."

John Lennon pursued his new career of being a non-performing ex-Beatle private person with the same intensity that he had always carried to his music. After Yoko took him back and—as important or more so—after Sean Ono Lennon was born on October 9 (John's birthday also), 1975, he did not so much become a different person as he became the adult man that he had always wanted to be. The reason was Yoko. She gave—nay, *imposed* upon him—the direction that he felt he needed. And she gave him Sean Ono, whom both viewed as a perfect child capable of being reared under ideal conditions to become an ideal human being: one free of sexism and racism and all the other -isms that John and Yoko felt were branded upon helpless children.

During the pregnancy, John and Yoko were fanatically health-conscious. They went to classes and studied natural childbirth. But Yoko had a difficult delivery. When labor began, she went into convulsions. John called for a doctor, but when the doctor entered the delivery room he allegedly ignored Yoko and raced over to John and said, "You know, I always loved your music as a Beatle and I always wanted to shake your hand!"

"Fuck *off!*" John screamed. "Save Yoko's *life!*"

They sedated Yoko and delivered Sean by Caesarian section.

While he was in the hospital nursery, John studied the behavior of the nurses and noticed that the black nurses turned on disco radio and that white nurses turned on country & western. John wanted Sean to be somewhere a bit freer, musically, and prepared his own collection for Sean at the Dakota. He stocked a jukebox for Sean's room with everything from Elvis Presley to Donna Summer: a musical Montessori School via 45 rpm.

Yoko, even while pregnant, had gradually assumed the role of running Lenono and being the business manager and assuming the role that rock managers Allen Klein and Brian Epstein had earlier played in John's career. John was happy to turn all of that over to someone he fully trusted; trusted to buy dairy cows or Florida real estate all day in Lenono's office on the ground floor of the Dakota, while he, John, on the seventh floor, raised Sean, with the aid of a large domestic staff.

John and Yoko had, for years, carried out what they called "secret out-of-the-country experiences"—sudden, unannounced trips abroad at the behest of Yoko's advisers, numerologists, astrologists, psychics and "direction people." During John's legal battles, John and Yoko made a swift trip to Egypt and spent a night in the Great Pyramid. Yoko, besides being a psychic, loves Egyptology and came back to New York City with a big collection of ancient Egyptian regalia. She had already confounded the many record-company attorneys at legal meetings by showing up as John's only representative (a non-attorney Japanese feminist artist). Now, she turned up for legal conferences garbed in ancient Egyptian robe and headdress. John said he loved that, as he sat at home and learned to bake bread in the wilds of Central Park West's most famous address.

Under other circumstances, John would have been described as "a kept man." Being John Lennon, he became a famous recluse whose wife was managing the family fortune into hundreds of millions of dollars. He seriously thought of himself as a "househusband." He agreed with Yoko's sentiment that carrying a child for nine months was an enormous obligation for a woman and that, after delivery, either the father or society ought to tend to the child for a while.

John not only did that, he gladly submerged his will to Yoko and turned his entire attention to his beloved son.

Elliot Mintz, an intimate of John and Yoko for years, recalls John saying, after he first saw Lenono staffers giving Sean a chocolate bar just to keep him quiet: "*Screw* these people. Sean is not gonna eat sugar and Sean is not gonna watch TV commercials and people shooting each other and he's not gonna have the TV as a baby-sitter and he's not gonna go to school and he's not gonna be ignored and he's not gonna have his questions unanswered."

Said Mintz: "He'd be bathed at night by John, with John in the same tub, and flesh would touch flesh and he'd be kissed goodnight and if he had a question, he'd be answered. And if John went out for a walk, Sean would go with him and he would not be put off onto someone. So, although they had all the money in the world, there were no baby-sitters.

"So he did that and prepared food and baked bread. Then, when Yoko came back from a day's work at night and talked about some big deal that she'd put together, John would say, 'I don't want to hear about that. Sean has a pimple — somebody must be slipping him sugar. So get twenty copies of *Sugar Blues* and distribute it to the staff and tell them that shouldn't happen.'"

John was quite serious; life with Sean and Yoko in the Dakota was all that mattered to him. One night, late, he called Mintz in Los Angeles. "He said, 'an incredible thing happened to me today, Elliot,'" recalls Mintz, "and he said it with such reverence that I thought he was going to divulge a really significant spiritual experience. I propped myself up and said 'Yes?'

"He said, 'I baked my first loaf of bread and you can't believe how perfectly it rose, and I've taken a Polaroid photo of it and I think I can get it out to you by messenger tonight.'"

They used a courier service instead of the mail because people collected souvenirs when they saw Yoko's or John's name on something. So someone would pick up the communication and get on an airplane and fly with the communication wherever it was going and then hand the communication to the person it was going to. "It's the same as the mail, except instead of an eighteen-cent stamp, it's a $430 plane ticket," explains Mintz.

John was a post-card fanatic and he liked to create his own cards. "He asked if I thought it would be a good idea if he turned that Polaroid of the loaf of bread into Christmas cards so he could send it to everyone so they could all see the loaf of bread," says Mintz. "I waited ten or fifteen seconds, just to make sure that this wasn't a little Lennon-ism over the phone; then I realized he was serious. A week or two later, when I got to New York and we were sitting around the kitchen one night—which was our second favorite place to sit— he brought out an object enclosed in silver foil. It was a piece of the bread that he had saved me from his first loaf. We broke bread together. By the way, it was never turned into a Christmas card."

John's abilities in the kitchen may have been self-exaggerated, Mintz said. "I must say, he did cook occasionally for us. The bread was great; the eggs were a little watery. Again, he approached everything with intensity, so when he was in his cooking period, he got a thing called a crockpot. For stews, steamed vegetables, all this rice and stuff. All day long. This was during the macrobiotic stage, where, when we ate together, the idea was that every time you put something in your mouth you had to chew it eighty-five times. You could chew but not speak. There were dinners with an incredible amount of chewing and very little speaking."

John's new life—and he *really* did intend it to be a new life after Yoko had taken him back—once he had renounced his coking and drinking and carousing in Los Angeles—became surprisingly ascetic. Except for a passion for multimegatar so-called cigarettes called Gitanes (which are to France as Luckies are to the U.S.) and a constant thirst for down-and-dirty black, *black* coffee, John was the most de-toxed of all rock stars. He and Yoko had been on heroin together (Yoko would later ill-advisedly say that they had done smack to celebrate their talents as artists) and had gotten off it together.

It was well known in certain circles that Yoko was very heavily into Magick and made no decisions without consulting one or several of the circle of astrologers, psychics, readers, spiritual consultants, numerologists, direction experts, interpreters of I Ching, seers and the like who made up an unofficial cabinet of advisers to Lenono.

John believed in Yoko and never questioned any decision or command that she made. He made many of what came to be called "rounds" or "direction trips" abroad without contesting the wisdom of her commands. He went around the world in two days. He went to South Africa; he went here, he went there. She told him it was something he needed to do.

When Elliot Mintz first asked Lennon about all that, Lennon told him, "She will say things you will not understand. Go with it. She's always right."

Years later, Mintz said that he felt that John/Yoko was a Don Juan/Carlos Castaneda sort of relationship. "John looked to her as a sorceress," Mintz said, "as a high priestess, as a magician. I'm a fairly pragmatic guy and consider myself to be a realist. But I am now a believer in her abilities. She *is* telepathic. I do know that. I do know she reads minds.

"I do know that she is extraordinarily psychic and has extraordinary premonitions. Whenever something would come up, John would look to her and say, 'I'd like you to check it out.' If she were to say, 'I think it's important for you to travel in a northwesterly direction for approximately eighteen thousand miles tomorrow morning,' that would be enough. She has said those things to me and I have done them. She would say, if you do this, it's going to dramatically alter the next six months of your life in a favorable way. There were direction moves that she gave me that did significantly alter the structure of my life.

"Sometimes, Yoko grew impatient with the necessity to explain it to us. At the same time, John was not a gullible man. He was basically a cynic. He had been burned by some of the best—like the Maharishi, for one. Yoko has been interacting with these people all of her life. You've got to run a pretty good scam to get past her for more than four or five readings. So if Yoko buys it, it's good enough."

(The unanswered question remains: With all the psychic and telepathic minds around John Lennon, why did none of them register at least a small alarm about the numbers that made up the day of December 8, 1980? Why was there no warning?)

The Dakota, a forbidding Gothic castle studded with gargoyles, is an appropriate setting for Magick. Its exterior is the one you saw in *Rosemary's Baby*—although the Dakota's ruling committee would not allow any filming inside the building. The Dakota has a long history of ghosts, the most famous being a little blond girl wearing silver shoes and bouncing her ball down the hallways. Her appearance supposedly signifies death. John apparently never saw her: The only Dakota ghost he acknowledged encountering was the "Crying Lady Ghost."

It often astonished cynics that John and Yoko's love affair was a romance of epic proportions. Their constant hand-holding and embracing after twelve years of marriage reflected genuine love (much to the chagrin of the legions of people who continued to blame Yoko for the breakup of the Beatles). They were totally self-contained. Other than the household and office staff, which ranged in number between ten and twenty, very few people ever gained admittance to the Lennons' apartments. There was Elliot Mintz; actor Peter Boyle and his wife, Loraine Alterman; Paul and Linda McCartney and a few Japanese friends of Yoko's. There were no more than ten names in John's address book, mostly lawyers. Mick Jagger lived a block north on Central Park West and he and John never saw each other. John and Yoko never had a party in the Dakota. John finally began turning away even Paul McCartney when he would show up with a guitar after John had had a rough day and just wanted to rest in his white bedroom and watch TV or simply study Central Park as the light changed in the evening. John never had to change his phone number, unlike most celebrities. There was no Beatle memorabilia at all in the main apartment; no gold albums on the wall. Restaurateur Warner LeRoy was a neighbor and it was in his apartment that Sean first learned that John had been famous as a Beatle: He happened to see *Yellow Submarine* on TV there and asked why Daddy was famous.

The one John-Yoko party was at LeRoy's Tavern on the Green, the opulent restaurant in Central Park. For Sean's fourth birthday, Yoko planned a party for him there and invited other children and their parents from the Dakota. It was a very low-key affair: no press leaks at all (since Sean's birthday is the same as John's). She let Sean off his health diet for once and had the party catered with ice cream and cake. She hired clowns and a magician, whom John loved, because every one of his tricks was askew just enough that even the kids could see behind them, and John loved that sort of humor. Finally, since Sean already had every toy in the world and got even more presents that day, Yoko had prepared a shopping bag full of expensive toys for each child there so that none of the children would go home envying Sean.

Elliot Mintz met John and Yoko when, in 1972, he did a phone interview with Yoko for ABC radio. How he physically met John and Yoko and became one of their few friends tells much about the way they lived. It is a story that Mintz himself tells best:

"Yoko was very pleased with the live interview. I called her back the next day to thank her. After we began talking, we found that both of us are telephone freaks. I average six hours a day on the phone; she averages eight. Yoko has a belief that one can achieve a greater level of intimacy over the phone than you can in person. The feeling is that through the veil of anonymity—of not looking into faces, not being conscious of clothing, hair, how you look—all you're dealing with is mouth-to-ear; it is highly personal. People say things over the phone, even to strangers, that they would never do in person. So, Yoko and I talked for a number of hours and we found that we had much in common—mainly the phone. She knew that I was an insomniac. Yoko herself does not sleep the way most people do: She takes catnaps, she practices auto-hypnosis, she counted John down to sleep.

"So we talk on the telephone. Three or four weeks after this dialogue has begun, John decides that he is kind of curious as to whom his wife is calling at four in the morning, leaving the bedroom and going to the kitchen and calling this radio announcer in Los Angeles. At about the same time, I started doing a syndicated television show, which turned up on channel five in New York at three in the morning. So, for the first time Yoko and John got to see what I look like. Then, Yoko said that I should do an interview with John. We did a live interview over the phone for an hour. After that, John became interested in what Yoko and I talked about, so he started calling me as well. You know how John had difficulty working the telephone and figuring out the numbers. But there was something about the freedom of calling me at all hours of the day or night. He knew that he would never wake me, since I'm an insomniac. So the three of us became phone pals.

"I would get home from my radio show at two in the morning and talk effortlessly to Yoko till 4:30 or 5:30, and then John would just be waking up and he would call. Neither of them had any friends because there was enough going on between them that they didn't need to see any other people.

"Some months after this, they decided to drive across the United States and found themselves in Santa Barbara. They called me. Yoko said, 'We've seen America; now we'd like to see you.' They gave me directions as to where to meet. I drove from L.A. to Santa Barbara; they ended up, for reasons I still don't understand, in Century City. So, after three hours of calls on pay phones, we laid eyes on each other for the first time. I had my white 1958 Jaguar and I pulled up beside a dusty station wagon in this field. I remember how excited John and Yoko looked, because they kept pointing at me and giggling to each other, having recognized me from television. This was a rather bizarre reversal of roles. I got inside their car and John said to Yoko, 'Well, there he is. Go over and give him a hug.' We were best friends before we met.

"They had rented a house in Ojai, near Santa Barbara. It was summertime and we went by the swimming pool. Yoko changed into a chartreuse one-piece bathing suit. She lay down on the diving board over the pool with her waist-length jet-black hair hanging perpendicular. I was struck by her extraordinary beauty. I kept hearing movement behind me: John was putting on a bathrobe to take off his pants so he could put on his bathing suit. He just smiled and said, 'I'm English, you know.'

"We talked politics for an hour. They said they had just made this album called *Some Time in New York City* and wanted me to hear it. We went inside and John took the record and did something that would characterize John for many years. When it came to anything mechanical—from a pair of binoculars to a hi-fi set to a tape recorder—he was thoroughly helpless. He couldn't get a stereo turned on for all the money in the world. He said, 'Wait'll you hear *this*,' and he put the arm down on the record and ran back to be between the two speakers where Yoko and I were sitting. *Nothing*. The machine was not plugged in. Yoko continued to stare at the ceiling. Finally, we got the thing playing. John referred to it as one of his 'lost' albums because it was about Angela Davis and John Sinclair and Black Panthers. They said, 'Hey, take this acetate back to your radio station and play it. You're the only guy who's got it.' I did. I was tired. I forgot that there were four-letter words and Black Panthers on it and ABC was not big on those at the time. I played the entire album and held all the commercials and opened the phones for the reaction. John and Yoko came to L.A. and I asked them if they'd heard the show. John said he'd tried to get it but the radio didn't work. Yoko looked at the ceiling. John had tried to get the show on AM, when it was on FM. John asked me how the show had been received.

"I said that it had been received very well, other than that I had been fired for playing the record and that my radio career had come to an end. 'That's fine,' John said, 'that's *fine*. You come with us. We're going to San Francisco tomorrow.' I came with them.

"We found ourselves in the Miyako Hotel in San Francisco for a month—a traditional Japanese hotel with tatami mats on the floor. The first three days, we conversed only by phone. It was more comfortable for me that way. I was still *overwhelmed* by their presence. One day, they invited me to their room. At the time, John and Yoko were in their 'incredibly skinny period,' and I knew that they had not been out of that room and had not eaten for two or three days. They said they wanted to talk to me about some stuff. I said, 'Fine.'

"They led me into the bathroom and turned on the water and the noise was deafening and the heat was overwhelming and they were talking about seeing Bobby Seale and Huey Newton for an appearance on an upcoming TV show which John and Yoko had been asked to host. I said, 'Excuse me, why are we sitting in the bathroom discussing this when you have a very nice room in there?' Yoko said the likelihood was that the room was bugged. John just looked at the ceiling. [It was later established that John and Yoko were under constant government surveillance.] The one time we left the Miyako, Yoko said, 'Let's try and eat, John.' He said, 'All right, let's try it.' We left the room, got into the car and started down the Pacific Coast Highway.

"About fifteen miles out, Yoko looked at John and said, 'It's too much, isn't it?' He said, '*Yeah*.' They turned the car around and went back to the hotel. It was too much for them to go out into the real world. When the two of them were together, they were insulated, isolated, protected and free. If that happened to mean starvation as well, you accept it as part of that."

Mintz became a confidant and traveled frequently with John and Yoko. A typical trip went like this: A courier hand-delivered to Mintz a one-way ticket to Japan with some accompanying instructions signed by John's distinctive line-drawing signature of himself with glasses and Yoko and Sean. The instructions said to fly to Tokyo, where a man would meet Mintz and take him to a train station and give him a card with Japanese markings to indicate which train to take. He should debark at the eleventh stop and wait for further instructions.

The day before Mintz left for Japan, Elvis Presley died. John Lennon's hero. Mintz called Lennon in Japan to give him the news. Said Lennon: "Elvis died in the army. The difference between him and us is that, with us, our manager died and we lived. With Elvis, he dies and his manager lives. Come to Japan."

Mintz: "So I fly to Tokyo and, of course, there is no one there to meet me and it's 110 degrees and I'm exhausted and have no idea where I'm going. This was characteristic of travel arrangements: Although John and Yoko always traveled first class, it was always bungled. Everywhere I went around the world with them, it was almost a joke. There was *never* anyone to meet them, never a VIP lounge, never a limousine. We'd be out there, looking for taxi cabs with everybody else, being shoved aside, baggage always lost. The primary reason for all this, we later learned, is that any reservation for John Lennon was taken as a joke! During those lost years, after 1975, the reason John quit using the phone was that any time he picked up a phone and said, 'Hi, this is John Lennon. I'd like a piece of chocolate cake,' the response would be 'Sure.' So he gave up trying.

"At the eleventh stop, at three in the morning, I get off the train and it looks like a ghost town. There's one very old man with a gray beard. I hope he's the guy. I smile at him and he bows. I say 'John Lennon' and he smiles. I say 'Yoko Ono' and his face lights up and he shakes my hand and says, 'Ah so.' He points at two broken-down bicycles and we peddle off into the night. It had to have been six miles. I thought I was gonna have a coronary. After seven light-years I see a lake and a Japanese inn and gardens and I hear the sound of flute music. I was looking to give the old man a tip, but he was long gone and I stood there alone, worn-out, in the rain, but dumbfounded by the smell of cherry blossoms. A shoji screen opens and a woman leads me in. I was given a mineral bath and a kimono gown and a room that was filled with incense and pounds of fresh fruit and in the center of the fruit is a grapefruit and on top of that was a little handwritten note saying, 'We are all together now, just like a family. We'll see you in the morning. John, Yoko and Sean.'

"I fell asleep. The next morning the screen opens and there they are. John had never looked as high and wonderful. He wore a beautiful antique kimono and Yoko was next to him in a white silk kimono—they both had hair down past their shoulders and washed it in magical water that just made it shine and come alive. It was just a *vision*—a sight to behold. We embraced and went down a little lane and had some sushi. Yoko left us. John said, 'Look, you're gonna see and hear a lot of stuff here that you're not gonna understand. Just trust her. Just *trust* her.' I asked, 'Well, what are we gonna do?' He said, 'We're just gonna be, we're just gonna *be*.' I said, 'Well, what do you do here all the time?' John said, 'Well, after you slow down a little you'll just see it.'

"They would wake up very early and then have a shiatsu massage. Yoko liked to take an ice bath, which she still does in the morning. She fills the bathtub with ice cubes and gets in it. Makes her alert. It's not my idea of how to start a day, but she likes it. Then, they would do yoga and go off with Sean for a walk, stop off somewhere for some noodles or something like that. Life just became more and more simple. Less and less input.

"We went out to Kyoto, the ancient city of shrines and temples, and John was into it. We sometimes joked about the paradox of him singing 'God' and 'I don't believe in I Ching and I don't believe in magic and I don't believe in Buddha and I don't believe in Krishna'—but, let me tell you, he believed in *all* of it. John basically read two types of books. His favorite subject was history. He entertained the idea briefly, he told me, of writing an historical text under a pseudonym. His second-favorite reading subject was occult-related material.

Even during the primal-scream period, he just went through the rituals. He did not describe himself as a religious guy and didn't go to church every Sunday, but he believed in the Spirit. Yoko was the same, only she was into it further. In many ways, John was a biblical scholar and could quote scripture at will. When we went to the shrines in Kyoto, and John worshiped in front of them, Yoko would get impatient because she had been through all of that before and she was less impressed with shrines and Buddhas and all that stuff. But John was deeply moved and deeply touched by all of it.

"I think we spent about four months in Japan that trip. They took over the presidential suite in the Hotel Okura. It was so large that there were nine or ten adjoining rooms for assistants. The living room was so big John and Sean played soccer in there, and we set up racing cars down the hallway. The Okura is the equivalent of the Plaza in New York or the Beverly Hills. The security was very tight.

"We always sang a lot. Yoko, John and I would spend at least two hours a day singing. It was always songs from the Forties or Fifties, because they never listened to the radio. Yoko had very little knowledge of Elvis or Bill Haley or the Shirelles except for what John had taught her. John had never learned how to read music and couldn't get the chords right and I couldn't sing. So the three of us in hotel rooms around the world would try to sing. Yoko would say, 'Let's do something that I know this time.' I'd say, 'Yeah, let's do "Silhouettes."' She would say, 'Hmm, "Silhouettes."' John would say, 'I think I've got the chords —let me see, passed your house . . .' I said, 'No, no, *no*, it's "took a walk and passed your house late last night."' Yoko said, 'I *can't* stand it!' John said, 'If you would just stop, I'll get the chords. . . .' Finally, Yoko would say, 'Do the one that I like—do my favorite one.' That was 'The Way We Were' from the Streisand-Redford movie. Gosh! Did they love that movie. John had his hair cut to Robert Redford-style.

"One night, John and I were sitting in the living room. He was a little bored, a little homesick. He said, 'I would just like to be in my own bed with my Scott amp next to me and my books.' I said, 'Yeah, I hope that the numbers will be right so we can leave soon.' He was playing acoustic guitar and started playing 'Jealous Guy.' Now, I can't tell you how huge this living room was. All of a sudden, the elevator doors opened and a Japanese couple walked in. They were obviously dressed for dinner. They walked around and looked out at the view of Tokyo and then sat down. John just kept playing.

"They lit cigarettes and talked. I suddenly realized that they thought they were in the lounge of the restaurant. They took a wrong turn, came into a huge, very dark room where there was a lounge musician playing guitar and singing in a foreign language, and there was one other guest, waiting. They had a cigarette or two and I guess it was because no waiter had arrived to take their order that they finally looked at John, exchanged some words and got up and left, obviously displeased. That was John Lennon's last public performance. It wasn't the Madison Square Garden show with Elton John in 1974; it was in the Hotel Okura in Tokyo in 1977. For an audience of three."

Whenever they flew—if there were John and Yoko and Sean and Mintz—they would buy four first-class seats. They would also buy all the seats on their right side or left side and in front of them and in back of them. Which would make it impossible for some stranger to turn to John and ask, 'When will the Beatles get back together?' on a twelve-hour flight. On a Lufthansa flight they once turned the dome or lounge of the 747 into a playroom for Sean, with electric race-car tracks.

John was an expert flier. One thing he loved was the gift catalogs on planes. He would ponder them very carefully. Yoko was less discriminating—she would just check every square and write down her American Express number and her address and that would be that. John loved buying attaché cases. He had dozens of them, literally dozens. He collected them. He was very proud of the fact that he could travel around the world with just one attaché case. He was a good traveler, in that sense. Yoko would take twenty-seven bags, with someone to pack and unpack them for her, and then do shopping in various cities, where she had to get more clothes. John believed he could get everything he needed to go around the world into an attaché case. In his case, one very lightweight suit, a couple of pairs of slacks, a couple of shirts, a toilet kit.

There was one time when John made a point of announcing who he was. It was in Frankfurt. They spent one night there between flights. There is a hotel in the airport complex and Mintz and Lennon figured that would do. John told Mintz, "Look, you make the arrangements. Just walk up to the desk and get two rooms—just regular rooms." Mintz walked up to the desk and the guy said, "No rooms." He walked back to John, who was staring at a wall, which was one of his disguises. He thought no one would recognize him. (He and Yoko frequently traveled as "The Reverend Fred and Ada Gerkin." On this trip, John was traveling as "Shingo Oyama.")

Mintz said, "Look, there's no rooms here." John said, "There've got to be rooms. We can't walk around in Germany." Mintz said, "Maybe if you walk up to the desk. . . ." "No, no," said John, "I can't say I'm a Beatle." Mintz said, "John, it's pouring rain outside. Please ask for two rooms." He walked up to the desk, he looked at the guy and said "I'd like to have two rooms for the night." The guy stared and asked, "Where's Paul?"

John pointed at Mintz and said, "That's him." The man said in very proper German, "Of course!" He took them to the two rooms. Mintz had a beautiful suite with a sauna, and the manager sent up food and wine. At about five in the morning there was a knock at Mintz's door. It was John in his pajamas and robe and scarf. "I can't sleep," he said. "This place is such a dive." Mintz said,

"What do you mean?" He said, "Follow me." They had put him in a broom closet—a cubicle with a pounding metal pipe. John went back to Mintz's suite and looked around at the luxury and asked, "What is all this?" and Mintz couldn't resist answering, "Well, I guess the clerk liked the fact that I wrote 'Yesterday.'"

Regarding his travels, John said, "All I am doing is changing bedrooms. The outside is not particularly relevant to me. I'm not gonna go sightseeing. It's not like I want to go see Disneyland and I'm not going to sign up for polo and volleyball." For John, a new hotel meant new room service and different foods and new TV programs, which he loved. In New York, he watched TV constantly. His favorite shows were Tom Snyder's "Tomorrow" and the Johnny Carson show.

When TV bored him, John would turn to radio and tapes. He liked "The Shadow." He would listen to old tapes by Hank Williams and Carl Perkins and Jerry Lee Lewis and everything Bing Crosby had ever done. He listened to Sir John Gielgud reading Shakespeare. He had one hundred taped hours of Alan Watts lecturing on Eastern wisdom.

Elliot Mintz gave John some books about Howard Hughes, and they started joking about how Hughes had lived his secret years in hotel rooms, watching movies. As a joke, Mintz started calling John "Mr. Hughes" and wore white gauze gloves and a white face mask when he entered John's bedroom. John loved it. John had already started to refuse to sign autographs and had quit answering the phone and was refusing to allow his picture to be taken; all apparently as part of his decision to retire from rock & roll.

Lennon's closest call with his public came one day in 1977, in Tokyo. John and Yoko enjoyed strong coffee and had sent an assistant out to find a suitable coffee shop in Tokyo.

After coffee, John and Yoko and Mintz decided to take a stroll on the Ginza. Some photographers gathered and John said, "No photos." One of them who spoke English pursued John, who threatened to break the camera. The subsequent argument attracted hundreds of onlookers and pushing turned into shoving. All of a sudden, John Lennon and Yoko Ono and Elliot Mintz found themselves being chased by a mob. They barely escaped—by finding a taxi—and John and Yoko did not venture out of the hotel after that.

John became a Polaroid addict. His vision was so poor that he had trouble focusing ordinary cameras, but when Polaroid introduced its auto-focus SX-70 Sonar, he became almost rabid. He ordered Polaroid film by the case loads, becoming such a good customer that Polaroid sent him a free copy of its instant-movie system.

With the SX-70 Sonar, John took thousands of pictures. Almost all of them were of Sean in different hotel rooms around the world. All that changed from picture to picture was the hotel room.

He would send dozens of them to Elliot Mintz. Sometimes there would be one hundred pictures of John trying to take his own picture in a mirror without getting the camera and his face in the picture. He took several hundred pictures of TV shows.

John and Mintz exchanged what John called "Zen koans." Mintz would receive a picture of a door and a note that read, "When is a door not a door?" Mintz would reply: "When it's ajar." John sent back a picture with Marilyn Monroe's face pasted over a goldfish bowl next to a door and a note reading, "with the face that she kept hidden by a door in a jar."

John and Elliot traded dozens of what John called "Mind Movies." They were audio cassettes of found sounds: John would lean out the window and record the voices and noises of Seventy-second Street and patch in radio and TV snatches and himself making up little bits of songs. John loved radio and kept WBAI-FM in New York on all the time. He appeared as a surprise DJ on Dennis Elsas's afternoon show on WNEW-FM in New York on September 28, 1974, and brought along several of his favorite 45s to play; such obscure singles as Bobby Parker's "Watch Your Step" and Derek Martin's "Daddy Rolling Stone."

As part of the return Mind Movies, Mintz would sing something like "As Time Goes By" badly and John would play it just as Yoko was trying to go to sleep and would covertly tape-record her moans and groans and protests and put them into another Mind Movie that he would send to Mintz.

The center of John Lennon's existence became his "white bedroom" in the Dakota, a room barely ten by twenty feet. Its walls were exposed white brick. The room is empty now: Yoko closed it off a few weeks after December 8, 1980, when she discovered that she could hear nothing but thousands of mourners seven floors beneath her window on Seventy-second Street, singing "Imagine."

When John Lennon inhabited the room, it was a quiet, dark sanctum. John had always loved bedrooms and sleep: His and Yoko's bed-ins for peace had been famous worldwide and his love for sleep showed up in such songs as "I'm So Tired."

The bed he loved was just box springs and a mattress resting on two dark wooden church pews. There was a white five-button phone on the white wall above the pew that served as a headboard. The phone never rang—its lights flashed, so John never answered it. There were dozens of other phones through-out the Lenono Dakota complex. This phone was for outgoing, rather than incoming, messages, as a rule. John liked to sit atop the white linen-covered bed with its rich brown quilts and read or write or play his red Stratocaster. Beside him on a white bookcase was his beloved old Scott receiver and his favorite earphones and his Manhattan Cable TV control box for the giant Sony at the foot of the bed. The fireplace in the room was seldom used; the TV always was. John referred to his TV as his "electronic fireplace."

It was not always even tuned to a channel. Without his thick-lensed glasses John was extremely nearsighted, and he liked the constantly changing warm hues of the TV screen. His Gitanes and ashtray were by his side. He liked to wear jeans and a cowboy shirt or one of his Japanese kimonos. Incense burned twenty-four hours a day.

The room was carpeted in deep white pile. Any visitors were expected to remove their shoes, Japanese-style, before entering the room. There was a single white wicker chair on the right side of the bed—Yoko's side—where a visitor might sit. If the visitor were male, he might also be asked to remove his jacket.

John's side of the bed was sacrosanct. It was the one territory he had reserved to himself. It was where he kept his writing and his reading and his music and his cigarettes. John said several times that when he was growing up in his Aunt Mimi's house, he had been confined; once he was grown and rich, he was determined to make up for that. Lenono assistants knew to hand John's tea tray to Yoko, who would then pass it to John. No one walked around John's side of the bed. It was his last retreat. John's attention span was relatively brief. He would run around the cable channels every few minutes. Yoko would agree or not. But John loved TV and usually picked the channels. Once, when a visitor from California was there and adjusted the TV, John started laughing and said, "The colors are all wrong. You're from Hollywood. All the people there wear makeup, so you're used to seeing people with pink faces and blue eyes and blue suits and the L.A. tan."

He said that he had learned that there were seven original directors and producers who came to Hollywood and that they were all of European ancestry and had had dark-haired mothers. He said they all had a sexual envy for light-skinned, light-haired women and that it was this handful—Sam Goldwyn, Louis B. Mayer, Irving Thalberg—who created the blond bombshells. And that's how we got Jean Harlow and Marilyn Monroe—all blond and white. John said that was what ultimately shaped the Western world's concept of color and race. It turned out that all he was talking about was the color mix on his Sony. *Maybe.*

What was probably John's last attempt to stand on his own was the Club Dakota.

John had heard about the Blues Bar—the little private club downtown that John Belushi and Dan Aykroyd kept for themselves and their friends. Even though John didn't go out, the idea of such an intimate boîte appealed to him: a good-time club where he would be ultimately protected from the three thousand fans who would ask "Where's Paul?" or "When will the Beatles get back together?"

It started when, for his thirty-eighth birthday, Yoko got John a beautiful old bubble-top Wurlitzer jukebox and Elton John sent him an electric Yamaha piano. John found an empty room in the Lenono complex and put both machines in there. He regarded them both and—for the first time in years—treated music seriously. With only Mintz present, John sat down at the Yamaha and played and sang for hours. He sang "In My Life" (Mintz's favorite song) and "As Time Goes By" and even Bobby Darin's old "Dream Lover" (another Mintz favorite) and some fragments of things he had been working on. He started spending more and more time in that room. The jukebox was full of Frankie Laine and Bing Crosby and Guy Mitchell and the like. The room was off limits to everyone but John and Yoko and Mintz.

On Mintz's next trip to New York, John told him, "What we should do with this room is turn it into a very chic, private club. Like an old English men's club. We'll just get some stuff and surprise Mother."

The two prowled Lower Manhattan and bought cheap overstuffed couches with crocheted doilies, dentist-office standing ashtrays, martini shakers, cheap watercolors of flamingos in flight and the like; a cheap cigarette machine so club members could buy smokes while waiting in the hallway to be seated. They got a bottle of aged brandy and sneaked brandy snifters out of the pantry. They went to Canal Street and bought moldy black-tie-and-tail outfits for themselves.

The Club Dakota opened on New Year's Eve, 1979. Lennon and Mintz were charter members and Yoko was an honorary member because John knew she would immediately try to integrate it sexually. They were the only three members. Mintz and Lennon put on their tails and white gloves and John sent a formal written invitation on a silver serving tray to Yoko to attend the opening.

She put on a simple but elegant black gown and came. She sat down and re-fused a drink and gaped at the flamingos. The room was candlelit. John was wearing a white T-shirt and his old Liverpool school tie with his tails. The Wurlitzer cast greens and purples and reds around the room. At midnight, the Wurlitzer played "Auld Lang Syne" and John and Yoko danced together. They and Mintz toasted each other and watched fireworks over Central Park. John never seemed happier.

A month later, Mintz returned to New York and found the Club Dakota nonexistent. The beautiful bubble-top Wurlitzer jukebox and the Yamaha piano had been put into storage. The rest of the club—the overstuffed couches and flamingo paintings and the like—had been thrown out. Mintz asked Lennon what had happened to the Club Dakota. John told him that the club had been getting a little too popular. That was all he said about it.

Yoko suggested that it was a good time for John to take the sailing trip that he always claimed he wanted to make. She thought Bermuda was a good direc-tion. He agreed. At this time, he had been hinting that he would not mind creating some rock & roll again but that he was not completely certain that he still had the spark within him to do so (even while watching Johnny Carson every night and admiring the show, he was not overly confident that he could go on such a show again).

When John reached Bermuda he called Yoko and thanked her: "It was *great!*" Life there proceeded placidly. Sean and his nanny flew to Bermuda to join John at John's request. Yoko had to take care of a few business deals so she stayed in New York. John and Sean enjoyed swimming and sailing and doing less. One day they toured the botanical garden and admired an orchid named "Double Fantasy." Every day at the beach they ran into a woman artist who finally summoned her nerve to ask John if she might be allowed to paint John and Sean as a family portrait. He agreed.

Every day the two of them, John and Sean, went to the artist's studio to pose for the portrait painting. When Yoko called them, the maid was instructed to tell Yoko that John and Sean were out swimming. John and Sean brought back the painting to the Dakota as a surprise gift for Mother. The painting—about four feet by three feet—now hangs above Yoko's desk in the Dakota.

Lenono assistant Fred Seaman, who was along on the trip, had long ago given John tapes of such new groups as the Pretenders, Madness, the B-52's and Lene Lovich (whom John referred to as Lenny Loveritch). John had laid them aside. He started listening to them in Bermuda and he said he snapped to the fact that what he and Yoko had been doing musically ten years earlier had finally caught on with new rock bands. He and Yoko had already been there and back, he said, with some satisfaction.

One night, he asked Fred to take him to a disco, to check out the latest musical developments (he had not been to one since going to the Ad Lib in London in the Sixties. He had studiously avoided all discos in New York City, especially Studio 54). John and Fred club-hopped and in one of the clubs, John heard the B-52's "Rock Lobster" and said immediately that they were doing Yoko's act from ten years before. He told Fred, "Jesus, get the axe [guitar] and call Mother. She's finally made it. They do her to a T."

He began writing songs at a furious pace: "Woman" took him perhaps fifteen minutes.

Simultaneously, in the Dakota, Yoko had started writing songs. One night, after John had had great difficulty reaching Yoko in New York, he got her on the phone and he said, "Listen, I just wrote this thing, let me sing it to you, it's 'Woman.'"

Yoko said, "That's good. I wrote a song too, it's called 'Beautiful Boys.' Let me sing it to you."

They sang songs to each other for days. John was excited and wanted to rush back to New York. When he finally got back, Yoko asked "Wanta do it?" John said "Yep."

They agreed to go into a studio and do an album and even a tour. At the Hit Factory in New York, Yoko forbade drugs and turned one room into an Egyptian temple—with palm trees, an antique white piano and white phones for her. Session musicians, who were used to coke and cognac, were served sushi and tea instead. John taped a huge photograph of Sean on the studio wall. Yoko put plates of sunflower seeds and raisins before each musician's microphone. Shiatsu masseuses were on call for them.

The evening of December 8, 1980, when they had recorded Yoko's "Walking on Thin Ice" for their next album, John was happy. He said several times that he was gratified to see that Yoko finally got the critical acclaim that he felt she should have already achieved, had she not been a Beatle wife. He was proud of that. In the limousine, on the way back to the Dakota, he told her that they had finally become a team and erased the old image of John and Paul.

The only thing John and Yoko ever differed about was the use of limousines. Yoko wanted them on call practically twenty-four hours a day whereas John often took taxi cabs. Both of them loved to walk the streets of New York City, the city they loved because they could walk its streets by themselves and the people were so cool that their coolness protected them more than any twelve bodyguards could. He had gotten used to the Dakota Groupies—just like the Elvis Presley Gate People—who were there all the time but respected his privacy.

Even when John and Yoko took a limo, they would often stop it out on West Seventy-second Street and then walk into the courtyard like ordinary citizens and say hello to the fans on the street instead of having the limo drive through the high iron gates to safety. On December 8, 1980, they stopped on the outside one too many times. When John fell, he was carrying in his right hand a tape of Yoko's song "Walking on Thin Ice."

STARTING OVER

A PORTFOLIO

By Annie Leibovitz

These are the last photographs of John Lennon.
They were taken by Annie Leibovitz
on Wednesday, December 3, and Monday, December 8,
in the Lennons' apartment on the seventh floor of the Dakota.
John and Yoko told Leibovitz that this was one of the few times
they had allowed a photographer to record them at home.

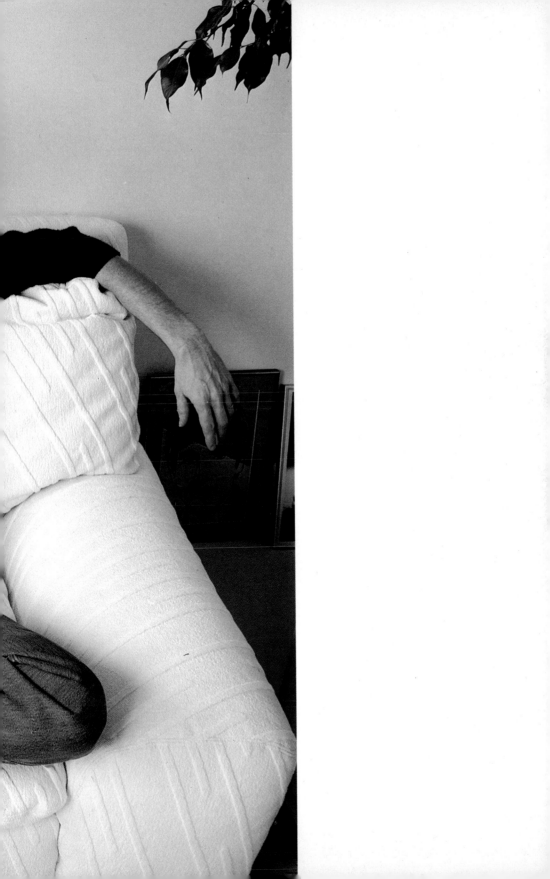

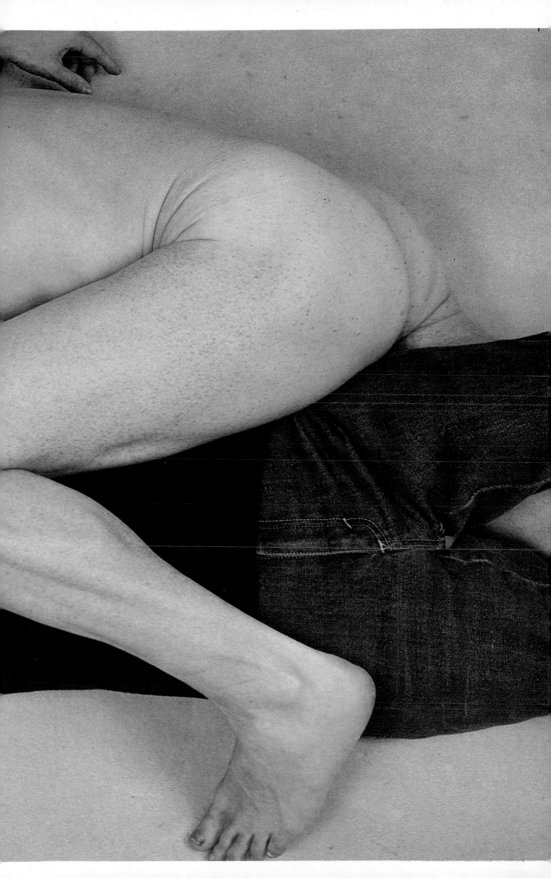

THE LAST
ROLLING STONE
INTERVIEW

By *Jonathan Cott/December 5, 1980*

ELCOME to the inner sanctum!" says John Lennon, greeting me with high-spirited, mock ceremoniousness in Yoko Ono's beautiful cloud-ceilinged office in their Dakota apartment. It's Friday evening, December 5, and Yoko has been telling me how their collaborative new album, *Double Fantasy*, came about: Last spring, John and their son, Sean, were vacationing in Bermuda while Yoko stayed home "sorting out business," as she puts it. She and John spoke on the phone every day and sang each other the songs they had composed in between calls.

"I was at a dance club one night in Bermuda," John interrupts as he sits down on a couch and Yoko gets up to bring coffee. "Upstairs, they were playing disco, and downstairs, I suddenly heard 'Rock Lobster' by the B-52's for the first time. Do you know it? It sounds just like Yoko's music, so I said to meself, 'It's time to get out the old axe and wake the wife up!' We wrote about twenty-five songs during those three weeks, and we've recorded enough for another album."

"I've been playing side two of *Double Fantasy* over and over," I say, getting ready to ply him with a question. John looks at me with a time- and interview-stopping smile. "How are you?" he asks. "It's been like a reunion for us these last few weeks. We've seen Ethan Russell, who's doing a videotape of a couple of the new songs, and Annie Leibovitz was here. She took my first *Rolling Stone* cover photo. It's been fun seeing everyone we used to know and doing it all again—we've all survived. When did *we* first meet?"

"I met you and Yoko on September 17, 1968," I say, remembering the first of our several meetings. I was just a lucky guy, at the right place at the right time. John had decided to become more "public" and to demystify his Beatles persona. He and Yoko, whom he'd met in November 1966, were preparing for the Amsterdam and Montreal bed-ins for peace and were soon to release *Two Virgins*, the first of their experimental record collaborations. The album cover —the infamous frontal nude portrait of them—was to grace the pages of *Rolling Stone*'s first anniversary issue. John had just discovered the then-impoverished, San Francisco-based magazine, and he'd agreed to give *Rolling Stone* the first of his "coming-out" interviews. As "European editor," I was asked to visit John and Yoko and to take along a photographer (Ethan Russell, who later took the photos for the *Let It Be* book that accompanied the album). So, nervous and excited, we met John and Yoko at their temporary basement flat in London.

First impressions are usually the most accurate, and John was graceful, gracious, charming, exuberant, direct, witty and playful; I remember noticing how he wrote little reminders to himself in the wonderfully absorbed way that a child paints the sun. He was due at a recording session in a half-hour to work on the White Album, so we agreed to meet the next day to do the interview, after which John and Yoko invited Ethan and me to attend the session for "Back in the U.S.S.R." at Abbey Road Studios. Only a performance of Shakespeare at the Globe Theatre might have made me feel as ecstatic and fortunate as I did at that moment.

Every new encounter with John brought a new perspective. Once, I ran into John and Yoko in 1971. A friend and I had gone to see *Carnal Knowledge*, and afterward we bumped into the Lennons in the lobby. Accompanied by Jerry Rubin and a friend of his, they invited us to drive down with them to Ratner's delicatessen in the East Village for blintzes, whereupon a beatific, long-haired young man approached our table and wordlessly handed John a card inscribed with a pithy saying of the inscrutable Meher Baba. Rubin drew a swastika on the back of the card, got up and gave it back to the man. When he returned, John admonished him gently, saying that that wasn't the way to change someone's consciousness. Acerbic and skeptical as he could often be, John Lennon never lost his sense of compassion.

Almost ten years later, I am again talking to John, and he is as gracious and witty as the first time I met him. "I guess I should describe to the readers what you're wearing, John," I say. "Let me help you out," he offers, then intones wryly: "You can see the glasses he's wearing. They're normal plastic blue-frame glasses. Nothing like the famous wire-rimmed Lennon glasses that he stopped using in 1973. He's wearing needle-cord pants, the same black cowboy boots he'd had made in Nudie's in 1973, a Calvin Klein sweater and a torn Mick Jagger T-shirt that he got when the Stones toured in 1970 or so. And around his neck is a small, three-part diamond heart necklace that he bought as a make-up present after an argument with Yoko many years ago and that she later gave back to him in a kind of ritual. Will that do?

"I know you've got a Monday deadline," he adds, "but Yoko and I have to go to the Record Plant now to remix a few of Yoko's songs for a possible disco record. So why don't you come along and we'll talk in the studio."

"You're not putting any of your songs on this record?" I ask as we get into the waiting car. "No, because I don't make that stuff." He laughs and we drive off. "I've heard that in England some people are appreciating Yoko's songs on the new album and are asking why I was doing that 'straight old Beatles stuff,' and didn't I know about punk and what's going on—'You were great then; "Walrus" was hip, but this *isn't* hip, John!' I'm really pleased for Yoko. She deserves the praise. It's been a long haul. I'd love her to have the A side of a hit record and me the B side. I'd settle for it any day."

"It's interesting," I say, "that no rock & roll star I can think of has made a record with his wife or whomever and given her fifty percent of the disc."

"It's the first time we've done it this way," John says. "It's a dialogue, and we have resurrected ourselves, in a way, as John and Yoko—not as John ex-Beatle and Yoko and the Plastic Ono Band. It's just the two of us, and our position was that, if the record didn't sell, it meant people didn't want to know about John and Yoko—either they didn't want John anymore or they didn't want John with Yoko or maybe they just wanted Yoko, whatever. But if they didn't want the two of us, we weren't interested. Throughout my career, I've selected to work with—for more than a one-night stand, say, with David Bowie or Elton John—only two people: Paul McCartney and Yoko Ono. I brought Paul into the original group, the Quarrymen; he brought George in and George brought Ringo in. And the second person who interested me as an artist and somebody I could work with was Yoko Ono. That ain't bad picking."

When we arrive at the studio, the engineers begin playing tapes of Yoko's "Kiss Kiss Kiss," "Every Man Has a Woman Who Loves Him" (both from *Double Fantasy*) and a powerful new disco song (not on the album) called "Walking on Thin Ice," which features a growling guitar lick by Lennon, based on Sanford Clark's 1956 song, "The Fool."

"Which way could I come back into this game?" John asks as we settle down. "I came back from the place I know best—as unpretentiously as possible— not to prove anything but just to enjoy it."

"I've heard that you've had a guitar on the wall behind your bed for the past five or six years, and that you've only taken it down and played it for *Double Fantasy*. Is that true?"

"I bought this beautiful electric guitar, round about the period I got back with Yoko and had the baby," John explains. "It's not a normal guitar; it doesn't have a body; it's just an arm and this tubelike, toboggan-looking thing, and you can lengthen the top for the balance of it if you're sitting or standing up. I played it a little, then just hung it up behind the bed, but I'd look at it every now and then, because it had never done a professional thing, it had never really been played. I didn't want to hide it the way one would hide an instru‑ment because it was too painful to look at—like, Artie Shaw went through a big thing and never played again. But I used to look at it and think, 'Will I ever pull it down?'

"Next to it on the wall I'd placed the number 9 and a dagger Yoko had given me—a dagger made out of a bread knife from the American Civil War to cut away the bad vibes, to cut away the past symbolically. It was just like a picture that hangs there but you never really see, and then recently I realized, 'Oh, goody! I can finally find out what this guitar is all about,' and I took it down and used it in making *Double Fantasy*.

"All through the taping of 'Starting Over,' I was calling what I was doing 'Elvis Orbison': 'I want you I need only the lonely.' I'm a born‑again rocker, I feel *that* refreshed, and I'm going right back to my roots. It's like Dylan doing *Nashville Skyline*, except I don't have any Nashville, you know, being from Liverpool. So I go back to the records I know—Elvis and Roy Orbison and Gene Vincent and Jerry Lee Lewis. I occasionally get tripped off into 'Walruses' or 'Revolution 9,' but my far‑out side has been completely encompassed by Yoko.

"The first show we did together was at Cambridge University in 1968 or '69, when she had been booked to do a concert with some jazz musicians. That was the first time I had appeared un‑Beatled. I just hung around and played feedback, and people got very upset because they recognized me: 'What's *he* doing here?' It's always: 'Stay in your bag.' So, when she tried to rock, they said, 'What's *she* doing here?' And when I went with her and tried to be the instrument and not project—to just be her band, like a sort of Ike Turner to her Tina, only her Tina was a different, avant‑garde Tina—well, even some of the jazz guys got upset.

"Everybody has pictures they want you to live up to. But that's the same as living up to your parents' expectations, or to society's expectations, or to so‑called critics who are just guys with a typewriter in a little room, smoking and drinking beer and having their dreams and nightmares, too, but somehow pretending that they're living in a different, separate world. That's all right. But there are people who break out of their bags."

"I remember years ago," I say, "when you and Yoko appeared in bags at a Vienna press conference."

"Right. We sang a Japanese folk song in the bags. 'Das ist really you, John? John Lennon in zee bag?' Yeah, it's me. 'But how do we know ist you?' Because I'm telling you. 'Vy don't you come out from this bag?' Because I don't want to come out of the bag. 'Don't you realize this is the Hapsburg palace?' I thought it was a hotel. 'Vell, it is now a hotel.' They had great chocolate cake in that Viennese hotel, I remember that. Anyway, who wants to be locked in a bag? You have to break out of your bag to keep alive."

. "In 'Beautiful Boys,' " I add, "Yoko sings: 'Please never be afraid to cry . . . / Don't ever be afraid to fly . . . / Don't be afraid to be afraid.' "

"Yes, it's beautiful. I'm often afraid, and I'm not afraid to be afraid, though it's always scary. But it's more painful to try *not* to be yourself. People spend a lot of time trying to be somebody else, and I think it leads to terrible diseases. Maybe you get cancer or something. A lot of tough guys die of cancer, have you noticed? Wayne, McQueen. I think it has something to do—I don't know, I'm not an expert—with constantly living or getting trapped in an image or an illusion of themselves, suppressing some part of themselves, whether it's the feminine side or the fearful side.

"I'm well aware of that, because I come from the macho school of pretense. I was never really a street kid or a tough guy. I used to dress like a Teddy boy and identify with Marlon Brando and Elvis Presley, but I was never really in any street fights or down-home gangs. I was just a suburban kid, imitating the rockers. But it was a big part of one's life to look tough. I spent the whole of my childhood with shoulders up around the top of me head and me glasses off because glasses were sissy, and walking in complete fear, but with the toughest-looking little face you've ever seen. I'd get into trouble just because of the way I looked; I wanted to be this tough James Dean all the time. It took a lot of wrestling to stop doing that. I still fall into it when I get insecure. I still drop into that I'm-a-street-kid stance, but I have to keep remembering that I never really was one."

"Carl Jung once suggested that people are made up of a thinking side, a feeling side, an intuitive side and a sensual side," I mention. "Most people never really develop their weaker sides and concentrate on the stronger ones, but you seem to have done the former."

"I think that's what feminism is all about," John replies. "That's what Yoko has taught me. I couldn't have done it alone; it had to be a female to teach me. That's it. Yoko has been telling me all the time, 'It's all right, it's all right.' I look at early pictures of meself, and I was torn between being Marlon Brando and being the sensitive poet—the Oscar Wilde part of me with the velvet, feminine side. I was always torn between the two, mainly opting for the macho side, because if you showed the other side, you were dead."

"On *Double Fantasy*," I say, "your song 'Woman' sounds a bit like a troubadour poem written to a medieval lady."

" 'Woman' came about because, one sunny afternoon in Bermuda, it suddenly hit me. I saw what women do for us. Not just what my Yoko does for me, although I was thinking in those personal terms. Any truth is universal. If we'd made our album in the third person and called it *Fred and Ada* or *Tommy* and had dressed up in clown suits with lipstick and created characters other than us, maybe a Ziggy Stardust, would it be more acceptable? It's not our style of art; our life is our art. . . . Anyway, in Bermuda, what suddenly dawned on me was everything I was taking for granted. Women really are the other half of the sky, as I whisper at the beginning of the song. And it just sort of hit me like a flood, and it came out like that. The song reminds me of a Beatles track, but I wasn't trying to make it sound like that. I did it as I did 'Girl' many years ago. So this is the grown-up version of 'Girl.'

"People are always judging you, or criticizing what you're trying to say on one little album, on one little song, but to me it's a lifetime's work. From the boyhood paintings and poetry to when I die—it's all part of one big production. And I don't have to announce that this album is part of a larger work; if it isn't obvious, then forget it. But I did put a little clue on the beginning of the record—the bells . . . the bells on 'Starting Over.' The head of the album, if anybody is interested, is a wishing bell of Yoko's. And it's like the beginning of 'Mother' on the Plastic Ono album, which had a very slow death bell. So it's taken a long time to get from a slow church death bell to this sweet little wishing bell. And that's the connection. To me, my work is one piece."

"All the way through your work, John, there's this incredibly strong notion about inspiring people to be themselves and to come together and try to change things. I'm thinking here, obviously, of songs like 'Give Peace a Chance,' 'Power to the People' and 'Happy Xmas (War Is Over).' "

"It's still there," John replies. "If you look on the vinyl around the new album's [the twelve-inch single "(Just Like) Starting Over"] logo—which all the kids have done already all over the world from Brazil to Australia to Poland, anywhere that gets the record—inside is written: ONE WORLD, ONE PEOPLE. So we continue.

"I get truly affected by letters from Brazil or Poland or Austria—places I'm not conscious of all the time—just to know somebody is there, listening. One kid living up in Yorkshire wrote this heartfelt letter about being both Oriental and English and identifying with John and Yoko. The odd kid in the class. There are a lot of those kids who identify with us. They don't need the history of rock & roll. They identify with us as a couple, a biracial couple, who stand for love, peace, feminism and the positive things of the world.

"You know, give peace a chance, not shoot people for peace. All we need is love. I believe it. It's damn hard, but I absolutely believe it. We're not the first to say, 'Imagine no countries' or 'Give peace a chance,' but we're carrying that torch, like the Olympic torch, passing it from hand to hand, to each other, to each country, to each generation. That's our job. We have to conceive of an idea before we can do it.

"I've never claimed divinity. I've never claimed purity of soul. I've never claimed to have the answer to life. I only put out songs and answer questions as honestly as I can, but *only* as honestly as I can—no more, no less. I cannot live up to other people's expectations of me because they're illusionary. And the people who want more than I am, or than Bob Dylan is, or than Mick Jagger is. . . .

"Take Mick, for instance. Mick's put out consistently good work for twenty years, and will they give him a break? Will they ever say, 'Look at him, he's Number One, he's thirty-six and he's put out a beautiful song, 'Emotional Rescue," it's up there.' I enjoyed it, lots of people enjoyed it. So it goes up and down, up and down. God help Bruce Springsteen when they decide he's no longer God. I haven't seen him—I'm not a great 'in'-person watcher—but I've heard such good things about him. Right now, his fans are happy. He's told them about being drunk and chasing girls and cars and everything, and that's about the level they enjoy. But when he gets down to facing his own success and growing older and having to produce it again and again, they'll turn on him, and I hope he survives it. All he has to do is look at me and Mick. . . . I cannot be a punk in Hamburg and Liverpool anymore. I'm older now. I see the world through different eyes. I still believe in love, peace and understanding, as Elvis Costello said, and what's so funny about love, peace and understanding?"

"There's another aspect of your work, which has to do with the way you continuously question what's real and what's illusory, such as in 'Look at Me,' your beautiful new 'Watching the Wheels'—what are those wheels, by the way?—and, of course, 'Strawberry Fields Forever,' in which you sing: 'Nothing is real.' "

"Watching the wheels?" John asks. "The whole universe is a wheel, right? Wheels go round and round. They're my own wheels, mainly. But, you know, watching meself is like watching everybody else. And I watch meself through my child, too. Then, in a way, *nothing* is real, if you break the word down. As the Hindus or Buddhists say, it's an illusion, meaning all matter is floating atoms, right? It's *Rashomon*. We all see it, but the agreed-upon illusion is what we live in. And the hardest thing is facing yourself. It's easier to shout 'Revolution' and 'Power to the people' than it is to look at yourself and try to find out what's real inside you and what isn't, when you're pulling the wool over your own eyes. That's the hardest one.

"I used to think that the world was doing it to me and that the world owed me something, and that either the conservatives or the socialists or the fascists or the communists or the Christians or the Jews were doing something to me; and when you're a teenybopper, that's what you think. I'm forty now. I don't think that anymore, 'cause I found out it doesn't fucking work! The thing goes on anyway, and all you're doing is jacking off, screaming about what your mommy or daddy or society did, but one has to go through that. For the people who even bother to go through that—most assholes just accept what is and get on with it, right?—but for the few of us who did question what was going on. . . . I have found out personally—not for the whole world!—that I am responsible for it, as well as them. I am part of them. There's no separation; we're all one, so in that respect, I look at it all and think, 'Ah, well, I have to deal with me again in that way. What is real? What is the illusion I'm living or not living?' And I have to deal with it every day. The layers of the onion. But that is what it's all about.

"The last album I did before *Double Fantasy* was *Rock 'n' Roll*, with a cover picture of me in Hamburg in a leather jacket. At the end of making that record, I was finishing up a track that Phil Spector had made me sing called 'Just Because,' which I really didn't know—all the rest I'd done as a teenager, so I knew them backward—and I couldn't get the hang of it. At the end of that record—I was mixing it just next door to this very studio—I started spieling and saying, 'And so we say farewell from the Record Plant,' and a little thing in the back of my mind said, 'Are you *really* saying farewell?' I hadn't thought of it then. I was still separated from Yoko and still hadn't had the baby, but somewhere in the back was a voice that was saying, 'Are you saying farewell to the whole game?'

"It just flashed by like that—like a premonition. I didn't think of it until a few years later, when I realized that I had actually stopped recording. I came across the cover photo—the original picture of me in my leather jacket, leaning against the wall in Hamburg in 1962—and I thought, 'Is this it? Do I start where I came in, with "Be-Bop-A-Lula"?' The day I met Paul I was singing that song for the first time onstage. There's a photo in all the Beatles books—a picture of me with a checked shirt on, holding a little acoustic guitar—and I am singing 'Be-Bop-A-Lula,' just as I did on that album, and there's the picture in Hamburg and I'm saying goodbye from the Record Plant.

"Sometimes you wonder, I mean really wonder. I know we make our own reality and we always have a choice, but how much is preordained? Is there always a fork in the road and are there two preordained paths that are equally preordained? There could be hundreds of paths where one could go this way or that way—there's a choice and it's very strange sometimes. . . . And that's a good ending for our interview."

Jack Douglas, coproducer of *Double Fantasy*, has arrived and is overseeing the mix of Yoko's songs. It's 2:30 in the morning, but John and I continue to talk until four as Yoko naps on a studio couch. John speaks of his plans for touring with Yoko and the band that plays on *Double Fantasy*; of his enthusiasm for making more albums; of his happiness about living in New York City, where, unlike England or Japan, he can raise his son without racial prejudice; of his memory of the first rock & roll song he ever wrote (a takeoff on the Dell Vikings' "Come Go with Me," in which he changed the lines to: "Come come come come / Come and go with me / To the peni-tentiary"); of the things he has learned on his many trips around the world during the past five years. As he walks me to the elevator, I tell him how exhilarating it is to see Yoko and him looking and sounding so well. "I love her, and we're together," he says. "Goodbye, till next time."

"After all is really said and done / The two of us are really one," John Lennon sings in "Dear Yoko," a song inspired by Buddy Holly, who himself knew something about true love's ways. "People asking questions lost in con-fusion / Well I tell them there's no problem, only solutions," sings John in "Watching the Wheels," a song about getting off the merry-go-round, about letting it go.

In the tarot, the Fool is distinguished from other cards because it is not numbered, suggesting that the Fool is outside movement and change. And as it has been written, the Fool and the clown play the part of scapegoats in the ritual sacrifice of humans. John and Yoko had never given up being Holy Fools. In a recent *Playboy* interview, Yoko, responding to a reference to other notables who had been interviewed in that magazine, said: "People like Carter represent only their country. John and I represent the world." I am sure many readers must have snickered. But three nights after our conversation, the death of John Lennon revealed Yoko's statement to be astonishingly true. "Come together over me," John had sung, and people everywhere in the world came together.

DECEMBER 8, 1980

FOR THE RECORD

INSIDE THE DAKOTA

By Gregory Katz

NSIDE the mahogany-paneled office of the Dakota apartment house in New York City, on one of the warmest December nights on record, Jay Hastings waited for John Lennon and Yoko Ono to come home. The burly, bearded twenty-seven-year-old doorman had worked at the Dakota for more than two years. He'd always said that the best part of his job was getting to know John and Yoko, who owned five apartments in the building. Hastings had been a Beatles fan since he was a kid; he'd even collected Fab Four picture cards. But now he was more than a fan. John Lennon knew him by name. Lennon would say, "*bon soir*, Jay," when he and Yoko came back from a night on the town or in the studio, and sometimes they'd joke around. Tonight, Hastings had a surprise: a red Plexiglas rain hat that an avant-garde clothes designer had dropped off for Yoko. He planned to ask them to guess what it was.

Hastings was reading a magazine shortly before 11:00 p.m., when he heard several shots outside the office, and then the sound of shattering glass. He stiffened. He heard someone coming up the office steps. John Lennon stumbled in, a horrible, confused look on his face. Yoko followed, screaming, "John's been shot. John's been shot." At first, Hastings thought it was a crazy joke. Lennon walked several steps, then collapsed on the floor, scattering the cassette tapes of his final session, which he'd been holding in his hands.

Hastings triggered an alarm that summoned the police and he rushed to John's side. The anguished doorman gently removed Lennon's glasses, which seemed to be pushing in on his contorted face. He struggled out of his blue Dakota jacket and placed it over Lennon. Then he stripped off his tie to use as a tourniquet, but there was no place to put it. Blood streamed from Lennon's chest and mouth. His eyes were open but unfocused. He gurgled once, vomiting blood and fleshy material.

Yoko, frantic, screamed for a doctor and an ambulance. Hastings dialed 911 and asked for help. Then he returned to Lennon's side and said, "It's okay, John. You'll be all right."

The doorman stationed outside ran in and told Hastings the attacker had dropped his gun on the sidewalk. Hastings went after the gunman. It wasn't necessary. The pudgy young man who had shot Lennon was standing calmly on West Seventy-second Street, reading *The Catcher in the Rye*.

Two squad cars screeched up and four cops jumped out, guns drawn. "Put up your hands!" they told Hastings, who was wild-eyed and covered with blood. "Not him," the other doorman shouted. "He works here." He pointed to the young man who had been reading. "He's the one." Two cops slammed the suspect against the Dakota's elegant stone facade. The other two policemen and Hastings ran into the building.

It was then, after seeing the splintered office window and the blood in the alley, that Hastings realized John Lennon had been dying in front of his eyes.

Against Yoko's wishes, police turned Lennon over to assess his wounds. They said they couldn't wait for an ambulance and gingerly hoisted him off the floor. Hastings, gripping Lennon's left arm and shoulder blade, heard shattered bones crack as they moved him out the door. Lennon's body was limp; his arms and legs akimbo. They put him into a police car for the trip to Roosevelt Hospital. Yoko climbed into a second cruiser. Hastings walked back to the building and waited in the office. Thirty minutes later, word reached the Dakota: John Winston Ono Lennon, forty-year-old husband and father, was gone.

The stately, gabled Dakota became a fortress under siege. Outside the tightly shut wrought-iron gates, hundreds of people who had heard the news were chanting, "All we are saying is give peace a chance." The Dakota courtyard—spacious and cheery by day—was a shadowy no man's land, patrolled by grim New York cops. Armed guards were posted at each entrance; the basement was secured. Yoko Ono, shielded by friend and record executive David Geffen, slipped in the back way.

Homicide-hardened sergeants commandeered the office, its gray stone floor stained by a dark pool of blood. Two stunned and red-eyed tenants, who had come down to find out what was going on, began preparing name tags for each Dakota resident, including those named Nureyev, Bacall, Bernstein and Radner. The phone kept ringing. No, a switchboard operator said, he did not know why John Lennon had been shot. No, he told another caller, he did not wish to contact a firm that freezes bodies until technology can bring back the dead.

For ninety minutes, more than a dozen anxious, well-dressed detectives grilled Jay Hastings. What time did it happen? Was Lennon in the office? Was he running? Did he speak? Did he fall? Then what? Hastings didn't know how to break down the events in his mind. The questions kept coming, over and over. His head ached. He smoked cigarette after cigarette. Dr. Elliot Gross, the city's dour medical examiner, arrived and made Hastings go through it one more time. When the questioning finally ended, he sat, dazed, near the ornate black gates, sipping Wild Turkey from a green paper cup. He stared blankly at the chanting mourners and at a dozen red roses that drooped from the gate. He did not change his white shirt, sullied with dried blood. "It's like a funeral dirge," he said of the Lennon music wafting through the warm night air.

At two in the morning, three hours after Lennon was shot, police called the Twentieth Precinct for reinforcements and ordered additional barricades. The crowd outside was growing. Richard J. Nicastro, deputy chief in charge of Manhattan detectives, set up a van equipped with telephone hookups, radios and other communications gear. About forty uniformed cops kept watch. But the thousand or so mourners were generally well behaved, struck dumb with grief.

Inside, Hastings lit another cigarette and peered at the crowd. The photographers, reporters and TV crews bothered him. Flashbulbs and floodlights cast a surreal glare. But he was glad so many had come to pay their respects. It was hard for him to comprehend why teenagers—who hadn't grown up with the Beatles, as he had—were so shaken by the assassination.

"It's like they're grabbing at straws to find their identity," he said in a soft, even voice. "I had Beatles cards and got *Meet the Beatles!* for my birthday; I saw *Help!* when it first came out. There was something there. I can understand their wanting to show something. The man is dead."

Cops shuttled back and forth to the nearby Twentieth Precinct house on West Eighty-second Street, where the suspected killer was under heavy guard. Police had identified him as Mark David Chapman, a Beatles fan and would-be suicide who had been hanging around outside the Dakota for three days. Lennon had autographed an album for Chapman that afternoon.

"He seemed like a nice guy," Hastings said of Chapman, still working on the bourbon. "Some bum came up and asked him for money, and the guy gave him a ten-dollar bill. The bum was ecstatic and kissed him and everything. He didn't bother anyone here; I hardly noticed him."

Hastings's voice trailed off as he pictured the killer, standing calmly on the curb after gunning down Lennon. The thought that something could have been done to keep Chapman away from the building flickered and passed. "People came to see John all the time; one more was just a drop in the bucket. You don't know who's who. Sometimes they're annoying, persistent veterans of the drug wars. Sometimes they're slightly psychotic. Usually you can tell right away if somebody's a little strange, and you can get fierce with him."

Lennon never complained about the situation, Hastings said, although sometimes, if strange people were hanging around, the doorman stationed outside the building would tell Lennon's driver to pull the limousine past them into the driveway. On December 8, the limo stayed outside, and Lennon walked from the curb to the Dakota's stone archway, where his killer waited in the shadows, ready to fire at point-blank range.

"At least he didn't suffer," Hastings said with a shudder. "He went in the blink of an eye. I knew he wouldn't make it unless a miracle happened."

Hastings sat still for a while, not talking. One of the Dakota night-shift workers urged him to go home and rest, but he kept his vigil. Hastings recalled his casual friendship with Lennon, who had once asked him how he trimmed his beard, and then sent an aide to buy the clippers Hastings recommended. A few months later, Lennon told Hastings he was shaving off his thick beard because it made him too recognizable on the streets.

"John seemed happier, now that he was making music again and going out in public more," Hastings said. "The new album with Yoko seemed like a profession of faith, like when people have their twenty-fifth wedding anniversary and go to church to renew their vows. He and Yoko had a lot of faith in each other."

At about 4:30, a Dakota spokesman walked outside and asked the mourners to turn down their radios because Yoko was having trouble sleeping.

Finally, Hastings decided to head for a friend's house to try to rest. He trudged into the bare employee locker room in the basement, still clutching the green paper cup and a cigarette. He slowly unbuttoned his bloody shirt, pulled it off and tucked it into a laundry bag. Then he put on his street clothes, went back upstairs and stopped for a moment to console the grieving entourage in the Lennons' ground-floor studio.

It was close to dawn when Hastings passed through the office a final time that morning. A janitor was now mopping up the blood. Outside, the gates of the archway were already covered with hundreds of flowers.

Outside the Dakota, December 9, 1980.

THE WORD SPREADS
By Chet Flippo

AN shot, One West Seventy-second" was the call on the police radio just before eleven p.m. Officers Jim Moran and Bill Gamble were in the third blue-and-white that screamed to a halt outside the Dakota apartment building. The man who had been shot couldn't wait for an ambulance. They stretched him out on the back seat of their car and raced to Roosevelt Hospital, at the corner of Fifty-ninth Street and Ninth Avenue. They lifted the bloody body onto a gurney and wheeled it into the emergency room. There was nothing the doctors could do. They pronounced John Lennon dead at 11:07 p.m.

Howard Cosell picked up a feed from WABC-TV News in New York and announced the shooting on "Monday Night Football." The news spread like a prairie fire. Within minutes, the small, brick-walled ambulance courtyard outside the emergency room was filled with at least two hundred people who were staring dumbly at the closed double doors.

Some of the cabdrivers, who were depositing reporters at the rate of two or three a minute, joined the throng. One of them volunteered loudly that he had it from a good source that John Lennon had been dead on arrival. One young woman stood alone in the middle of Ninth Avenue and wept.

The crowd continued to grow. At about midnight, a woman with a very crisp manner marched out. The black name tag on her white lab coat said that she was A. Burton, the hospital's director of public relations. The reporters hurled questions at her. "I'd rather have the doctor tell you," she said. "He is Stephan Lynn. He is director of the emergency-room service." She had to spell his name five or six times.

Dr. Lynn faced the press at about ten minutes after midnight. "A little closer, doc," a photographer yelled, and Nikon motordrives started whirring and strobe lights began zinging him like darts. The doctor, in his spotless white lab coat, was nervous. He said, "John Lennon," and then paused for at least twenty seconds. "John Lennon," he continued, finally, "was brought to the emergency room of the Roosevelt, the St. Luke's-Roosevelt Hospital, this evening, shortly before eleven p.m. He was dead on arrival." There were gasps from the press corps. "Extensive resuscitative efforts were made, but in spite of transfusions and many procedures, he could not be resuscitated."

"Where was he shot, doc, and how many times?" the corps demanded.

Yoko leaving Roosevelt Hospital with David Geffen, December 8, 1980, after Lennon was pronounced dead.

"He had multiple gunshot wounds in his chest, in his left arm and in his back," Lynn answered. "There were seven wounds in his body. I don't know exactly how many bullets there were. There was a significant injury of the major vessels inside the chest, which caused a massive amount of blood loss, which probably resulted in his death. I'm certain that he was dead at the moment that the first shots hit his body."

"What about his wife?"

"His wife was with him at the time of the injury and indeed accompanied him to the emergency department."

"Did you tell Yoko that Mr. Lennon was dead? What did she say?"

"I did tell his wife that he was dead. She was . . . *most* distraught at the time and found it quite hard to accept. She is no longer at the hospital."

"Is Mr. Lennon still in the hospital?"

"His body is in the hospital."

The press corps drifted back out to the emergency-room entrance, then raced off again on the trail of the assassin.

"There will be no Jack Ruby here," a hard-faced cop said almost matter-of-factly as the suspect was whisked into the Twentieth Precinct, on West Eighty-second Street. The alleged assassin was completely surrounded by cops, a pale moonface bobbing in a sea of blue uniforms. He disappeared into the elevator.

At two a.m., Chief of Detectives James T. Sullivan walked up to the podium in the briefing room to face the TV lights and the hundred or so members of the press. He was wearing an immaculate blue-serge suit and a pinstripe shirt and dark tie. The gold shield on his chest gleamed in the TV lights. He kept his left hand in his trouser pocket.

"We asked you to come here so we could give you a briefing on what we know at this point in the homicide of John Lennon," he said, a slight edge of nervousness in his voice. "We have arrested Mark David Chapman of 55 South Kukui—that's K-u-k-u-i—Street, Hawaii, for the homicide of John Lennon. He is a male Caucasian, tan complexion, five feet eleven, one hundred ninety-five pounds, brown hair, blue eyes, and he's twenty-five years of age. Born May tenth, 1955, has apparently been in New York City for about a week, was staying briefly at the YMCA—I'm not sure which one. He is most recently staying at the Sheraton Centre. He, Mr. Chapman, has been about at the Dakota for the last several days. He was able to obtain an autograph on an album from Mr. Lennon as he left for the recording studio. He remained at the Dakota all evening waiting for Mr. Lennon to come back. Some time shortly before eleven o'clock, John Lennon and his wife arrived back at the Dakota in a limousine. They parked the limousine outside the Dakota. There is a driveway into which they might have gone, but on this occasion did not. They got out and walked into the archway area of the Dakota. . . . This individual, Mr. Chapman, came up behind them and called to him, 'Mr. Lennon!' Then, in a combat stance, he fired. He emptied the Charter Arms .38-caliber gun that he had with him and shot John Lennon."

Sullivan, who had developed a solitary bead of sweat above his upper lip, went on to recount the arrest of Chapman, who "behaved very calmly." Sullivan answered a couple of dozen questions, ranging from "Has Chapman made a full confession?" ("I can't go into that") to "What did Mr. Lennon say?" ("He said, 'I'm shot,' as he went inside") to "Was he smoking?" which he didn't answer.

Sullivan answered the last question at 2:24 a.m.

It was over now, and yet it was just beginning. The death of John Lennon, and the arrest of his murderer, were on the record. The shock had been planted and the reaction was growing.

SHARING THE GRIEF

HEY stared as if they were expecting a show to begin; they seemed ready to lose themselves in music. But there was no band, no music to be heard outside the Dakota apartment house at Seventy-second Street and Central Park West in New York. Nonetheless, they crushed up against police barricades, knowing that John Lennon had been shot and killed in the courtyard just a few feet away. By midnight, hundreds of fans had gathered.

One young man passed out sticks of incense; another brought a case of beer and passed around bottles; a third gave away pictures of Lennon. One woman wept, and her face was hit with the blinding light of a TV camera prowling for tears. A drunk threw down the last of his flask and grabbed someone by the collar. "That sonovabitch had a sense of humor, ya know! We oughta party out!"

A woman approached a policeman, asking if she could leave a present, a stuffed octopus that had belonged to her son. "Please give it to Sean. Tell him I'm sorry I didn't have a stuffed walrus." Turning away, she talked quietly with a reporter: "I'm almost forty, and John was very important to me. How many other men do you know who would stay home for five years to raise a child?"

Mitch Weissman and Joe Pecorino, stars of the Broadway show *Beatlemania*, had walked over to the Dakota. They live just a few blocks away. "I keep thinking about all those years when the government tried to deport him," said Pecorino, who plays Lennon in the show. "Now it's too damn bad they didn't."

Weissman, who plays Paul McCartney, said he had met Lennon for the first time a couple of weeks before. "I told John how I was hoping to leave the show to do other things. 'I can feel for you,' John said. 'Once you're a Beatle, it's tough to get out.'"

Suddenly, there was music. A voice struck up "Give Peace a Chance," and others joined in, tentatively at first, finally full-throated. They sang the verses over and over for a solid thirty minutes. Then portable radios playing Lennon's songs were turned up, and the crowd sang along, on into the night.

About 4:30 a.m., the fans began to drift away. Trucks rattled down Central Park West, stopping here and there to deliver stacks of newspapers whose headlines screamed the bad news. In San Francisco, London, Tokyo, East Berlin and many other cities around the world, other trucks with other newspapers would soon be carrying the same news. Even in Warsaw, at least for one day, the newspapers would consider John Lennon's death more important than the Soviet troops massed on the Polish border.

"It was so sudden," Yoko told a friend who had come to her upstairs apartment at the Dakota. "We had planned to go out to eat after leaving the recording studio, but we decided to go straight home instead. We were walking to the entrance when I heard the shots. I didn't realize at first that John had been hit. He kept walking. Then he fell and I saw the blood."

That night, Yoko called Paul McCartney, who was at his farm in rural England, and Mimi Smith, the sixty-five-year-old aunt who had raised John from the age of three. Aunt Mimi was in Dorset, England, at the house John had bought for her. Yoko waited until the next day to tell Sean, the son born to her and John five years ago.

Yoko spent almost all of that first week inside the Dakota. Most of the time she stayed in the bedroom, with the shades drawn. Occasionally, she talked on the phone or saw a visitor.

Ringo Starr, who had been with the Lennons on Thanksgiving, cut short a Bahamian vacation to fly back to New York. He and his fiancée, Barbara Bach, arrived on Tuesday afternoon and went directly to Yoko's apartment. Ringo played with Sean for a while, and even got him to smile. After a few hours, Ringo slipped away and went into seclusion. "He's extremely shocked," a spokesman said. "He doesn't want to say any more than that."

About the same time Ringo left, seventeen-year-old Julian Lennon arrived at the Dakota from North Wales, England. The son of John and his first wife, Cynthia Twist, Julian had grown close to his stepmother and half-brother.

Paul McCartney, looking pale and drawn, emerged from his home at noon on Tuesday. "I can't take it in at the moment," he told reporters who had been waiting outside. "John was a great man who'll be remembered for his unique contributions to art, music and world peace." Paul then drove to AIR Studios in London; from there, he spoke to Yoko by transatlantic phone. He spent the rest of the afternoon working and talking with George Martin, the producer who had overseen the recording of almost every Beatles LP. Special bodyguards were brought in to keep at bay a mob of reporters and photographers, some of whom tried to enter by climbing up fire escapes.

On leaving the studio, Paul expressed the wish that everyone would "rally round Yoko." Paul had not always been on the best of terms with Yoko, and his friendship with John, which dated back to their boyhood, had fallen apart in the early Seventies. But a spokesman for Paul said that the two had talked and seen each other socially several times in the recent past. "The rift was years ago," he said. "John and Paul had gone through an awful lot together, and they respected each other's work." He said they were getting to be "great friends" again.

George Harrison's sister, Louisa, had phoned him in Oxford. George canceled a recording session and retreated inside his mansion. He refused even to contact his office, and for several hours, his business associates were not sure of his whereabouts. Much later in the day, he had this to say: "After all we went through together, I had—and still have—great love and respect for John. I'm stunned. To rob life is the ultimate robbery."

John's Aunt Mimi, interviewed in Dorset, said that "John looked upon me as his mum. . . . There was never the possibility that he would be just an ordinary person. He'd have been successful in anything he did. He was as happy as the day was long."

Ringo broke the news to his former wife, Maureen Cox, and to John's former wife, Cynthia, who happened to be staying in the Cox home. Cynthia said that despite their divorce, she had continued to hold John in the highest regard. "I would like to talk to you about John," she told reporters, "but I know if I tried, the words just would not come out. It's very, very painful. All I can do is stay here in England with my washing and ironing to keep my mind off it." Singer Harry Nilsson, a drinking buddy of John's during some tough times, was one of twelve people who took out an ad in *Daily Variety*. It called on "all people who loved him" to pledge to never again "vote for any political candidate who does not support federal control of handguns and ammunition."

The reaction of Elton John, who is Sean's godfather, was "real, real bad," according to an associate. "He was very saddened." He sent a telegram from Australia, where he was on tour. Eric Clapton, according to his manager, "was very, very angry. The first thing that hit him was this incredible anger. I've never seen Eric in such a state before—it affected him so badly." Bob Dylan went into seclusion in Los Angeles. Peter Townshend was also reportedly too overcome to say anything immediately, but Roger Daltrey, the Who's lead singer, said, "It's terrible. My heart goes out to his family." Mick Jagger, in Paris putting the finishing touches on an album, said, "I don't want to make a casual remark right now, at such an awful moment for his family." Both Jagger and Keith Richards sent telegrams to Yoko.

In London, people of all ages sat wet-eyed on subways and buses, shaking their heads in disbelief at the headline in the *News Standard*, the first paper to hit the streets with the story. In Liverpool, mourners headed over to Mathew Street, site of the Cavern, the dingy basement club where the Beatles established themselves as a local cult band.

In East Berlin, radio station DDR-1 broke its usual ban against Western rock music and aired an hour and a half's worth of Beatles songs. The official East German news agency praised Lennon for his stand against the Vietnam War. Hamburg's best-known jazz club, Onkel Po, played Lennon's "(Just Like) Starting Over" before a show—the first time a rock & roll song ever preceded a jazz performance there. The audience stood.

Sales of Lennon's records, old and new, increased dramatically. In West Germany, orders for *Double Fantasy* reportedly rose from 10,000 a week to 50,000 a day. Memorials were held in dozens of cities all over the world. In Toronto, a crowd of 35,000 gathered on Tuesday night in snow and freezing wind for a candlelight vigil.

By Wednesday, the story was front-page news almost everywhere, including Britain's eight major dailies. The *Daily Mirror* headlined its coverage DEATH OF A HERO. The staid *Times* described Lennon as a "poet," and said of the Beatles, "They were not the first working-class youths with provincial accents to make an impact on British life, but their example enabled millions more to crack the barriers that existed between classes. . . . Their example was the most influential."

The official Soviet press agency, Tass, took a dim view of all the media attention. Interest in Beatles records is being "artificially whipped up to incredible heights," a Tass dispatch said. *Komsomolskaya Pravda*, organ of the Communist Youth League, said it was "a bitter irony that a man who devoted his songs and music to the struggle against violence should become a victim of violence."

Other reactions ranged from that of an elderly Liverpool housewife—"He should never have left Liverpool"—to Jerry Lee Lewis's comment: "I don't believe it. I don't fucking believe it."

By Thursday, two persons—a sixteen-year-old Florida girl who took an overdose of pills and a thirty-year-old Utah man who shot himself—were dead by their own hand because they couldn't cope with Lennon's assassination. Yoko phoned the *New York Daily News* with a statement she hoped would prevent other suicides. "People are sending me telegrams saying 'This is the end of an era and everything,' " she said, in what was described as an "emotion-choked" voice. "I'm really so concerned. This is not the end of an era. 'Starting Over' still goes. The Eighties are still going to be a beautiful time. . . . It's hard. I wish I could tell you how hard it is. I've told Sean and he's crying. I'm afraid he'll be crying more. . . . But when something like this happens, each one of us must go on."

Yoko made arrangements for John's body to be moved secretly to Hartsdale, New York, where it was cremated. In lieu of a funeral, she asked for John's fans to remember him with ten minutes of silent prayer at 2:00 p.m. on Sunday, December 14. "John loved and prayed for the human race," she said. "Please pray the same for him. Please remember that he had deep faith and concern for life and, though he has now joined the greater force, he is still with us here."

Inside her seventh-floor apartment, neither the radio nor the TV set had been turned on. No newspapers had been allowed in, and no music was played. Even many of John's closest friends were kept away. "In a situation like this," a spokesman said by way of apology, "these decisions of who gets in and who doesn't are not made democratically." One or two reporters who were friends of the couple were allowed to speak with Yoko for a few minutes. She told Robert Hilburn of the *Los Angeles Times*: "People say there is something wrong with New York, that it's sick. But John loved New York. He'd be the

A few hours after Lennon's death.

first to say it wasn't New York's fault. There can be one crank anywhere."

Down below, on the sidewalk, a hundred or so fans had set up what amounted to an around-the-clock vigil. Many others stopped by briefly, to look for a few minutes or to add a memento or wreath to the others at the front gate.

That Sunday, a crowd of more than 30,000 listened to prayers and sang "Give Peace a Chance" in front of St. George's Hall on Lime Street in Liverpool. About 5,000 of them had waited there the previous night in grim, rainy weather. By late afternoon, the crowd had swollen past capacity and some people fainted. At one point, several hundred young toughs trashed the makeshift stage where a local band had been playing, and there were minor injuries. Things quieted down when taped Beatles music and prerecorded messages from Yoko Ono, former Prime Minister Sir Harold Wilson and Muhammad Ali were played. At 7:00 p.m. (2:00 p.m. in New York) they fell into silence as Yoko had asked. Other fans gathered peacefully at London's Hyde Park and Trafalgar Square.

Formal and informal vigils were held across America: in Seattle, Chicago, Boston, Los Angeles, Philadelphia and numerous smaller communities. But the largest gathering took place in New York's Central Park, where a crowd of 100,000 fell silent as they said goodbye to John on this gray afternoon. Yoko remained inside her apartment, which overlooks the park.

The band shell was empty except for some garlands of evergreen, a wreath and a picture of Lennon. Two stacks of speakers were playing some of his quieter music: "In My Life," "You've Got to Hide Your Love Away," "Norwegian Wood." The sun broke through during "All You Need Is Love," and most of the crowd responded by singing along and flashing the V sign—a reminder of an era that suddenly seemed long ago. The clouds reappeared at the end of "Give Peace a Chance," the final song before the ten-minute silence.

At two sharp, every radio shut off, every hot-dog vendor shut down, every button peddler shut up. As a body, the crowd seemed to freeze. The meditation ended with the playing of "Imagine," leaving the crowd with "I hope someday you'll join us / And the world will live as one" as Lennon's last words of the afternoon. Bach's "Jesu, Joy of Man's Desiring" accompanied the people out of the park, as clouds grew more threatening. And then, for a few minutes on an otherwise dry afternoon, snow fell on New York City.

HEARING THE NEWS

By Scott Spencer

T doesn't work. If I were writing a story about a man of his magnitude, and all I could come up with was a horrid little ending like that, I would have to say I didn't deserve to write it at all. How would it read? Once upon a time there was a man who heard music and poetry, and he told us what he heard and people everywhere, in all the kingdoms of the earth, fell in love with what he made of himself and he lived in a castle with his wife and child and had untold riches laid at his feet, and then one day a little man hid in the dark and with four jerks of the finger killed the man who made the music. What a pathetic conclusion. How utterly unworthy of the complexities, the possibilities. No one would publish such a thing. No one would represent it. You should throw it away. Quickly. Before someone reads it.

This is so difficult to write about. So dispiriting. I have a cigarette in my hand and another one is smoking in the ashtray. There's loose change on my desk, a lucky stone from Massachusetts, a coffee cup, unopened mail, a bank deposit slip. Everything I want to say is receding from me. Everything these past twenty-four hours reminds me of death. It seems, whether we know it or not, we are in constant rehearsal for death: by forgetting, by sleeping, by looking away, by failing to hold the precious warm bodies we are meant to hold.

As a child, I would wait for my mother to come home. I'd peer out the window and see her walking down the street. And then I'd overturn a table, scatter magazines over the floor and fall in some dexterous approximation of a murdered corpse, waiting happily for her to discover me. Rehearsing, rehearsing. Half the games we played as children were about killing one another, choking one another, clobbering one another, shooting one another, lunging out from hiding places to frighten one another: We were trying to learn the art of dying while we were still rightfully stupid enough to bear it.

Because he allowed us to know him, to love him, John Lennon gave us the

209

chance to share his death, to resume the preparations for our own. Because we were so used to the way he thought, the habits, the turns, the surprises of his mind, we can enter him as we remember his last moments, to let it be us in the car, pulling up to the curb, opening the door, stepping out, breathing the night. Someone said he was happy that night, and we somehow know what his happiness felt like, and we can imagine ourselves resurgent, electric with energy.

Most of those who pass for heroes are not real heroes at all. They are hidden from us, uncommunicative, of no final use. But because he was an artist, and a brave one, we *knew* him. We felt the rhythm of his thoughts. We knew what he meant, no matter what he said, no matter if we disagreed. He had the great moral transparency of genius, and so we could enter him at will. (This power he gave us surely must have terrified him.) And so we are there, feeling what he felt, having this sordid education in death forced upon us, rubbed in our faces. As far as I can tell from the daily papers, his last word was "Yeah." In the police car that took him to the emergency room, someone asked him if he was John Lennon, and he said "Yeah." There are compilations of the last words of the great and the famous, and some of them are real rousers. Yet John Lennon's simple syllable allows me to lean closer to the true and absolute reality of life running out, death hurtling forward, because with John Lennon, we somehow knew everything he meant, everything he implied: the sudden thrusts of meaning, the cast of his eye, the silences.

His death is everywhere. Like his life and his art, it is a unifying force. The astonishing—and, for me, unduplicated—characteristic of his art was that it brought together people who may have had no other single thing in common. It was the only true mass phenomenon that's ever touched me. Through the Beatles—and, I think, primarily through John—I was able to share with millions my thoughts and their thoughts—*our thoughts*—about growing old, falling in love, seizing happiness, transcendence. A genius is a connector of theretofore disparate elements. A genius can take an orange and a chunk of coal and create a unity. A genius like John Lennon can create a community of hearts and minds from ten million separate appetites. Part of the grief we feel about his murder is our longing to once more belong to something larger than ourselves, to feel our hearts beat in absolute synchrony with hearts everywhere. Passionate love can lift us out of our skins, can join us with one another in a realm outside of time. Art can do the same, and when millions are lifted by an artist, he allows us to see one another in that moment as we never have before, never will again.

It was, of course, like the Sixties again, waking up, hearing of his death. There's no use injecting paranoia into something already so terrible, but it felt like the beginning of our new reactionary decade: History, as it fingers us in the chest, somehow able to reach back into the Sixties and renew the cycle of hideous assassinations. It's like a hurricane suddenly returning after it was supposedly spent at sea.

I am consoling myself now: He had a magnificent life. He fell deeply in love and knew enough about the heart and its lazy habits never to allow his essential connections to go stale. Like other great artists, he was a teacher. He taught us something about integrity. And risk. He taught us about speaking up against injustice. And he is an integral part of my most extravagant, farflung dreams about the potential power of art. It is no inspiring feat to capture the attention of millions—"Dallas" can do that. But to capture the *imagination* of millions is an accomplishment on a wholly different scale. It is mythic. His life and our view of him were, of course, mucked up by all the by-products of success, image-making, celebrity and high finance. But his achievements always rose above the cheapness· of publicity, the empty craziness of stardom. He proved that you can follow your vision, explore your talents, speak your mind—take any leap you dare. In a cautious age, John Lennon was uninterested in existing on any but his own terms. He sang and wrote what he believed, and he trusted us to listen. And he was right: We listened. Taking his lesson to heart, embracing his radiant example, ennobles the work *we* do. John's success, his awesome ability to communicate with millions—to say difficult things to people whom others felt were fit only to hear the emptiest words, to say emotionally vulnerable things to the most cynical and say them so well they could not be denied— remains a towering standard. He teaches us faith in ourselves, and confidence in and affection for the human community.

I am left with the one thing I wanted not to say, because it's so old and so fucking funereal: We are better people because of John Lennon. And now, when we need to be better still, and braver, with a deeper, more encompassing vision, losing him is terrifying. It just cuts so deeply. It's hard to believe our luck has gotten this bad.

REMEMBERING
JOHN

There are places I remember all my life,
Though some have changed,
Some forever, not for better,
Some have gone and some remain.

All these places had their moments
With lovers and friends I still can recall.
Some are dead and some are living.
In my life I've loved them all.

—"In My Life"
(John Lennon and Paul McCartney)

An Oral
Appreciation

*What follows are tributes and reminiscences from friends, acquaint-
ances and peers who knew John Lennon from his earliest days as a
Quarryman and who spoke to* Rolling Stone *during the week following his death. Editor Jonathan Cott spoke to Mick Jagger and
Harry Nilsson several months later.*

Gerry Marsden

I met John about twenty-three years ago, when we were both playing places
around Liverpool. He was in the Quarrymen, a skiffle group. We used to have
competitions between his band and mine, and we'd tour together. He was a
great, great friend—just about the funniest guy I ever met.

The Beatles and Gerry and the Pacemakers played together for one show at
the Liverpool Town Hall. We had eight people onstage and called ourselves the
Beatmakers. John played piano, so our regular piano player had to play sax. I
guess that was *the* original rock & roll big band.

What I remember most about those days is how much *fun* it all was—and
how loud the fans screamed. There were no hassles, no animosities, no hard
feelings when the Beatles got so big. There couldn't be, because all of us who
saw them when they started out in Liverpool knew that's where they were
headed. The talent those guys had was obvious to everybody, and to stop them
would have been like stopping a freight train going 150 miles an hour.

Ray Charles

I met the Beatles around 1962, when I was touring Germany; those boys
were my intermission band in Hamburg and Stuttgart. They'd hurry in during
intermission and play a few songs to keep things warmed up. There was no
way of knowing that in a year they were gonna change the world, but they
sounded good and were nice guys. Backstage afterward, we would sit and
bullshit and say we loved each other's music—the typical thing that people
in our musical brotherhood all do. See, we were just common people, working
together.

As for John Lennon, I was spellbound and hurt and upset when he died,
because he was a brilliant musician, and I respected what the man stood for.
John Lennon was one of our own, and losing him just makes me mad as shit.
We've got to have some damned gun-control laws, and psychiatrists should

examine the people who buy them. Hell, anything that can kill people should be controlled; it's easier to get a gun in this country than a driver's license.

I loved the Beatles music enough to record it, and I scrutinize something *very* carefully before I do. Each song was a beauty; "The Long and Winding Road" made me cry the first time I heard it. People ask me, "Ray, what's your favorite Beatles song? How do you compare 'Yesterday' and 'Eleanor Rigby' to 'Georgia' and 'What'd I Say'?" Hell, that's like asking, "Which tastes better, red beans or cabbage?" Don't you know, they *all* taste good.

Yes, I'm gonna miss that man and his wonderful talent.

BILL WYMAN

I first met John in March 1963, when the Beatles came down to see the Stones play in this dingy club called the Station Hotel in Richmond, England. They stood in line in their little leather coats and later came back to the flat; we stayed up all night talking about music, and we became good friends.

John knew where he was going, and he was very strong; he really got it together. Very determined.

TOMMY ROE

Chris Montez and I were headlining a tour of England and Scotland in 1963, and the Beatles were at the bottom of the bill, but they soon became the stars. It was a thirty-day bus tour, all one-nighters. My first record, "Sheila," was a hit in '62 in England, but I had no real experience as a performer, while the Beatles had a lot of stage experience but no hit. It was their first big tour.

When I met John, he told me the group used to sing "Sheila" at the Star Club in Hamburg, and I thought he was kidding until the *Live* album came out years later and "Sheila" was on it. He was always inquisitive about the States, asking about my hometown, Atlanta, and everywhere else. He was a bundle of energy, always talking, always clowning. I have a photo I took of him backstage during the tour, and he's coming at me with his hand up like a claw, his glasses on crooked.

MURRAY "THE K" KAUFMAN

I was ticked off about having to come off of my vacation in Florida to cover the arrival of the Beatles in 1964. I said, "Get an exterminator." But my program director said that we were gonna be the only station at the airport to cover their press conference live, so I came back. I was pissed at the station, so I said, "Okay, I'm gonna put the mike on and let everybody ask the questions and I'll get the answers"—until George looked down at me and said, "I love your hat." I said, "Well, here, you can have it." Then I said—I'm *live*, right?—I said, "You came over on the plane with some friends of mine." He said, "Who's that?" I said, "Phil Spector and the Ronettes." He said, "Who're *you*?" I said, "I'm Murray the K." He said, "You're kiddin'," and he turned to the other guys and said, "Hey, fellas, this is Murray the K." They had heard of me. So all of a sudden, they started talkin' to *me*. One guy from CBS hollered, "Hey, tell Murray the K to cut that crap out." So Ringo said, "Murray, cut the crap out, the guy says."

I spent the next few days in the Plaza Hotel; I never left, and I did my show from their suite that night. Then I took 'em around to the Peppermint Lounge, and to the Playboy Club to eat. After the Ed Sullivan rehearsal, we went to Washington to do the first concert. Then they invited me to Miami, and then I went to England for four weeks and hung out with them there. And in '65, I traveled with them to Austria, England and Nassau, where they filmed *Help!* One day, I threw up a microphone and said, "I can't do this anymore." John said, "What're you talkin' about?" I said, "I can't put a microphone in front of you and ask you all these dumb questions." I was having an identity conflict —all of a sudden, my destiny seemed to be hangin' onto my friendship with them. I had a lot of problems bein' called the "Fifth Beatle."

Of all of them, John was probably the most compassionate and kindest. When I was in England, John asked me, as a favor, to look after the Rolling Stones, and he introduced me to Mick Jagger. Lennon went out of his way to make sure they were taken care of.

The last time I saw him was in New York, about seven months ago, walking along Seventy-second Street. There was something in the expression on his face I hadn't seen there before. There had always been a tightness, a grimness— maybe because he was nearsighted and would squint. But this was a new expression; he looked *great*. We talked about the fact that, for the first time in his life, he had lost his anger. He felt whole; he had a single purpose. And he said, "Now I'm ready." I said, "Wait a minute; that means you're ready to start doin' music again, aren't you?" He said, "Right." That was a great rush to me. And that was it.

WALTER SHENSON

John was about twenty-three years old when I produced *A Hard Day's Night* and *Help!* Back then, the Beatles were totally fresh to moviemaking; they brought their own personalities to the project, but they were also tractable and cooperative. That was a lovely time for them, because they suddenly had lots of money and were having fun and being creative.

John and his wife at the time, Cynthia, always used to come over to my house for dinner. He called me Uncle Walter, because I reminded him of Paul's uncle. He and Cynthia went to the Cannes Film Festival one year with my wife and me. He was really curious about the whole thing, because when he toured with the Beatles, all he saw were hotel rooms, airports and concert halls, and it was the first time in a long while that he'd been able to get a little un- sophisticated. I remember him turning to me at a formal dinner and whispering,

"Tell me if I'm using the wrong fork." It was all a very pleasant experience; little French kids would run up to him on the beach yelling, "Ringo, Ringo," because that was the only English name they knew. He thought it was great, and he signed autographs using Ringo's name.

Even then, it was obvious that John had so many talents that he could have gone any way he wanted. But he wasn't as cynical as lots of people thought; he was just honest and straightforward, and he wouldn't stand for phoniness. He used to get the biggest kick out of some of the reviews for *A Hard Day's Night*. Writers would scrutinize the movie, find all kinds of symbolism and deep significance. John thought it was hilarious, because he knew the movie was just a comedy.

PETER NOONE

I saw the Beatles about fifty times before they made it, and twice afterward. But I never really knew John; after all, the Beatles were the *Beatles*. I was too awed by him to know what to say, even before they made it big, because he was so cool. For any English kid, he was the rebel, the fighter, the rock & roller. We all looked up to Gene Vincent, Buddy Holly, Eddie Cochran, and then the Beatles came along and did it all themselves.

John had this reputation for being cynical, but he was exactly the opposite to me. You could always go into his dressing room. John was the one who tried to make me feel at home when I was just the new kid looking up to him. Herman's Hermits were on "Thank Your Lucky Stars" once with the Beatles, the Stones and the Animals. That week, we had the Number Two record in America with "Can't You Hear My Heartbeat." I didn't think the Beatles even knew who I was, much less knew about my record, but John came up to me and said, "Well, Herman, I see you're Number Two in America." I was so shocked that I said the stupidest thing possible, which was, "Thank you very much."

PETER FONDA

I first met the Beatles in 1966, while they were renting a house in Benedict Canyon, near Los Angeles. I went over there with some of the best of whatever I had on me at the time, and as I approached the house, I could see that the entire canyon was *filled* with kids. They mobbed my Jaguar—they didn't know who the hell I was beyond a longhair in a Jaguar—and they dented that sucker pretty good.

I finally made my way past the kids and the guards. Paul and George were on the back patio, and helicopters were patrolling overhead. They were sitting at a table under an umbrella in a rather comical attempt at privacy. Soon afterward, we dropped acid and began tripping for what would prove to be all night and most of the next day; all of us, including the original Byrds, eventually ended up inside a huge, empty sunken tub in the bathroom, babbling our minds away.

I had the privilege of listening to the four of them sing, play around and scheme about what they would compose and achieve. They were so enthusiastic, so full of fun. John was the wittiest and most astute. I enjoyed just hearing him speak, and there were no pretensions in his manner. He just sat around, laying out lines of poetry and thinking—an amazing mind. He talked a lot, yet he still seemed so private.

It was a thoroughly tripped-out atmosphere, because they kept finding girls hiding under tables and so forth; one snuck into the poolroom through a window while an acid-fried Ringo was shooting pool with the wrong end of the cue. "Wrong end?" he'd say. "So what fuckin' difference does it make?"

At one point, Paul, George and I were talking about death, and I was explaining that I had once died on the operating table. "I know what it's like to be dead," I said, and just then John walked past and said, "Who put all that *shit* in your head?"

That exchange turned into the song "She Said She Said."

JOAN BAEZ

I was doing a show in Denver in 1966 and the Beatles were coming through the next day, so I stayed on to see them. I spoke with them after the show and they talked me into traveling with them for a few dates.

They were prisoners of their own stardom in the truest sense of the word, unable to go anywhere in safety or even part a window curtain without causing pandemonium. They were living in danger even then, and there was a sense of fear that made them want to take along any friendly spirits.

In concert, they had a habit of lunging to the edge of the stage and then retreating, bringing a rolling, wailing heap of hysterical fans with them. At the Oakland show, I was standing on the side of the stage with this policeman, and I volunteered to help him drag away, escort or otherwise assist the overwrought fans, most of them girls, who would be sobbing uncontrollably about having touched or not touched one of the Beatles. I was doing the best I could when the policeman finally laid down onstage, having either fainted or simply given up, and I helped him off.

Later, John—who was *constantly* teasing me—began joking that I was "the eternal Florence Nightingale, always helping out the downtrodden."

TONY KING

I worked for George Martin and later as general manager of the American Apple label, so I went to some of the *Abbey Road*, *Sgt. Pepper* and White Album sessions. One night, they were doing "Lovely Rita." You know those funny noises on the song? Well, they were done with combs and paper. George said to me, "Would you mind going into some of the other recording sessions to see if you can find anybody who's got a metal comb?" Then we were all in the bathroom, tearing up toilet tissue to make the right sound through the comb. The Beatles had the luxury of being able to spend an hour of their recording time getting the right combs and the right strength of toilet tissue.

I first got involved with John on a one-to-one basis in 1973, when I was sent by Apple to Los Angeles. I found him to be the most stimulating person I've ever worked for, because he was so fast and so bright and so on the ball. We had some great times together. John was crazy about America—that was liberation to him. I remember taking him to Vegas to see Fats Domino at the Flamingo Hotel. Fats came over to John and said, "Oh, I'm really honored to meet you." John said, "No. You're the man I've come to see. You shouldn't be honored to meet me. I should be honored to meet you."

NAT WEISS

John and Paul came to stay at my apartment while they were setting up Apple in New York. I was in partnership with Brian Epstein at the time; I had first met John in 1965, when Brian and I had made our initial deal.

I was startled at how witty, sensitive, extraordinarily well organized and considerate John was. Fans were frequently calling the apartment; once, John picked up the phone and it was some kid wanting to speak to Paul. "He's not here right now," John said. "Anything I can do for you?" The kid, having no idea who he was speaking with, just hung up.

When they were preparing to leave for L.A., I watched John pack his suit-case, and in all my years in rock & roll, I have never seen anybody so neat; he folded all his clothes with unbelievable meticulousness. Yet he could be so loose about things. I was having trouble locating a place for them to stay in L.A., and John laughed and said, "Aw, if you can't find us a house, see if you can get us a *large car*."

I'd worked with Brian on preparing John's statement during the Jesus Christ controversy. John was very upset that people had misunderstood his statement, and he wanted people to know how truly sorry he was that he'd hurt their feelings. He took great pains to try to communicate that. He liked integrity and honesty; he could not abide fools, and he was most perceptive about people who were striving to be groovy and false. He was a thoughtful, often tender man.

In April 1967, I was with Brian in his hospital room—he had been ill—when an enormous bouquet of flowers arrived. There was a note with the flowers, and in one of the few times I've ever seen him get emotional, Brian broke down and cried. The note said: "I hope you get well soon, because I love you, and you know I mean it, John."

BILL OAKES

In 1969, John decided to return his M.B.E. medal to the queen, and he wrote a letter that read: "Your majesty, I am returning this M.B.E. in protest against Britain's involvement in the Nigeria-Biafra thing, against our support of America in Vietnam and against 'Cold Turkey' slipping down the charts. With Love, John Lennon of Bag."

I was an employee of Apple Corps at the time, and I had to type this letter for John; when I tried to talk him out of the third point, he would have nothing of it. He really *was* pissed off that his record wasn't a hit. I think that illustrates the crazy paradox about him, especially during that period when he was heavily into causes.

I remember another time, on a Friday afternoon, when he came back to the London Apple office from Denmark and he had cut off all his hair. He decided to donate it to Michael X, an activist in the Nottinghill Gate area who was one of his causes, and he thought that the idea was "instant karma." That afternoon, he sat down at the piano and began banging out "Instant Karma!" Then he had me round up a bunch of guys, like Alan White and Eric Clapton, and they went into the studio that night. It was mixed and mastered over the weekend, and the record was in the stores by Tuesday or Wednesday. He wanted to have the idea in his head one day and have the record available in stores in less than a week.

RITCHIE YORKE

During the "War Is Over! If You Want It" campaign in 1969, which I covered for the *Toronto Globe & Mail*, John totally believed that love could save us. He thought that if one person really stood up, things could be changed. I've never seen anyone so committed to a cause, regardless of the cost. If he thought his actions would serve a purpose, he didn't give a damn if they cost a lot of money or if they offended anyone's sensibilities.

The guy was amazingly open-minded; we used to sit around thinking of things to do in the peace campaign, and he never ruled out *anything*. At one point, somebody decided that the way dates were broken up into B.C. and A.D. was ridiculous, that we should start all over with Year One A.P., which was After Peace. John didn't think that was too farfetched; he threw himself into the campaign.

Many people thought John was naive, but I think he was just determined to be truthful, whatever the cost. I remember him asking me to find out what top music-industry people thought about Allen Klein, because that's when everyone was making allegations against Allen. So I talked to lots of people and compiled a dossier of charges. Then John asked me to come to Denmark, where he was staying in a little cottage. When I got there, John read the whole report to Allen and gave him a chance to reply. I'm sure nobody would've talked if they'd known Allen was going to hear what they'd said, but John was so concerned with honesty that he read it all to him.

A Canadian commission was once investigating drug abuse in youngsters, and John must have sat down with that commission for a good six hours, patiently explaining what he thought was happening, how he thought drug abuse could be curtailed.

John's presence always overwhelmed people. I was at Ronnie Hawkins's house once when John and Yoko were staying there, and they'd gone upstairs to take a bath. I guess they'd forgotten to turn the faucet off, because pretty soon water started dripping through the ceiling. Everyone was so intimidated that no one had the nerve to go up and tell him. Finally, we talked Ronnie's wife into going up and asking him to shut off the water.

I took John and Yoko to meet Prime Minister Pierre Trudeau, and it was the only time I ever saw John Lennon nervous. He hadn't had much contact with state leaders, even in England, and he was really worried for the half-hour or so before they met. It was strange to see him unnerved at anything. But the meeting turned out wonderfully, and when John and Yoko sent out their acorns for peace to thousands of world leaders, Trudeau was one of the few people who responded and planted the seeds.

John took a lot of heat for the things he did in that movement. People forget that the English press ridiculed him for what he was doing. But he never worried; he was ready to do whatever he felt was right. It's just the ultimate horror that this happened to an amazingly peaceful, nonviolent guy who was prepared to live that to the nth degree. I guess John's a martyr now, and that's the last thing he ever wanted to be.

NICKY HOPKINS

The first time I worked with John was in 1968, when I played electric piano on "Revolution." He was real pleased with the way things went and told me there'd be a lot more sessions he'd be inviting me to. But I didn't see him again until 1971, at his home in Ascot, where he was recording *Imagine*. I reminded him of his comment and asked him why I hadn't been invited to any more sessions. "Well, Nicky," he said, "we thought you were too involved with the Stones, and we were afraid to ask." If only I'd known *that* was the reason!

Later that year, John and Yoko invited my wife and me to his birthday party. It was in Syracuse, New York, where Yoko's "This Is Not Here" art exhibition was being held, and John flew us there and back from California. He gave everybody silver zodiac necklaces, even though it was *his* birthday.

John was never one to mince words, but he never offended you. Like, at the first session for *Imagine*, one of the horn players started to roll some joints. John said, "I'd rather you'd wait until the end of the session. That way you won't forget where you are and mess up your parts. After the session, we can all sit down, listen to the playback and relax."

I played keyboards throughout much of *Imagine*, but on the title track I only played a bit of electric piano, which sounded like a synthesizer and wasn't prominent. Yoko had wanted me to play the piano on it, but John was adamant about doing it himself.

John had a real high energy level, and he liked to get things done fast. We recorded all of *Imagine* in about nine days. Soon after he moved to New York, I asked John what it was about the city that he liked. He said, "It's the only place I've found that can keep up with me."

JIM KELTNER

John and Yoko invited me to play drums and percussion on *Imagine*. The thing I remember about meeting them was that they were both very chubby; they had this kitchen for the musicians and crew with a long oak table filled with all kinds of puddings and rich English food. I remember going back to my hotel room and calling my wife and telling her about all this food.

When we started to work on the album, John would always be messing with the sound board. Most producers play with EQ and that kind of stuff, but whatever John did was simple, which I think was part of his genius.

Coming home from one of those sessions, John and I saw a girl on the street-corner playing guitar and singing, and I told John that someday I'd like to produce a record with somebody like that. John told me that all you have to do to produce is act like you know what you're doing.

The next time John and Yoko sent for me was for *Some Time in New York City*. They were living in the Village then, and their apartment had two rooms: a front room for secretaries and a bedroom. They had a huge bed, and that's where they did everything. They lived the same way they worked—very simply—and I was always impressed by that.

JOHN SINCLAIR

I'm grateful to John Lennon for playing at the John Sinclair Freedom Rally on December 10, 1971. I had been locked up for giving two joints to an under-cover policewoman.

John didn't even know me. He was introduced to my plight by a mutual friend, Jerry Rubin, and he came out and performed, and in so doing took this two-year effort over the top, playing a huge role in getting me out of prison.

I was always struck by the depth of his commitment to doing things that were socially useful—uncommon for a pop star. He was *not* too deeply impressed with being John Lennon, and he would have kept on if the government had not come down on him with the immigration harassment.

The first time I met him, to express my appreciation for his help, we sat around and smoked quite a bit of herb, and made the fact that the stuff was illegal the object of much laughter and ridicule.

He was one beautiful cat.

Wayne "Tex" Barrett

I came to New York from Detroit when I was nineteen and auditioned as guitarist for Elephant's Memory. A month after that, an opportunity came along to back up Lennon on *Some Time in New York City*. It came through Jerry Rubin. He'd played our tape for John Lennon, who was looking for a New York-based rock band. We set up a meeting at a studio in the Village. He walked in and said, "Are you they?" We asked, "Are you him?" It was like getting together with any guy to start a band. He was more nervous than we.

My mother had just died, and John had had a bad experience with his mother's death, so he helped me through a bad period and gave me a lot of encouragement. And I remember his words exactly: "Death is only a dream." You could see the depression in his face when he talked about her. You know, sometimes you can talk to someone else and help them, but you can't help yourself. That was the impression I got of him. I felt he was in a lot of pain all the time.

Richard Perry

I first met John while I was producing the *Ringo* album in 1973. John had written a song for Ringo called "I'm the Greatest," which was a kind of chrono-logical outline of their careers together. The night we were going to record it, Ringo, John, Klaus Voormann and myself grouped around a piano in the studio to put the finishing touches on the song. Then someone called me out of the studio to say that George was on the phone. "I hear there's some recording going on," George said. "Can I come down?" So I said to John, "George is on the phone and wants to come down to record with us. Is it okay?" "Hell, yes," John said. "Tell him to get down here right away and help me finish this bridge."

George arrived, and without saying a word, he joined in on the same wave-length we were on. He played guitar and John played piano, and they comple-mented each other perfectly. There was the Beatles magic unfolding right before my eyes!

I can remember very distinctly every minute I spent in the studio with John; it was probably the greatest thrill of my career. He had amazing energy and electricity. He worked at a fast pace, and it spread to everyone else. He loved the recordmaking process as much as anyone in the business, and whenever he was in the studio, he was smiling.

But one of the other things about John was that he was a great fan. One time there was a big Hollywood benefit party being thrown—Barbra Streisand was singing—and the sponsors wanted me to get the Beatles to come. Well, I didn't want to endanger my relationship with them over some party, so I didn't do anything about it. Then, on the morning of the party, the sponsors called and begged me to get them to come. So I decided to call Ringo and just mention it to him, and he said he'd mention it to John. Well, when John found out that people like Burt Lancaster and Kirk Douglas were going to be there, he said, "Are you kidding? I'm coming!" And he was there with bells on.

ROY CICALA

John used to joke around a lot. The funniest incident I remember occurred when I was engineer on *Mind Games* at the Record Plant. John had taken the finished tapes of the album into the cutting room. When I walked in, loose tape was piled all over the place; John was just sitting there with this sad face. I went out to the elevator—I guess to count to 100 or something—and John came running out. It had been a joke, and the tape all over the room was blank.

BOBBY KEYES

I really got to know John in Los Angeles, when we were hanging out with Harry Nilsson, Keith Moon, Ringo and those guys. Of course, there are stories about how wild that period was, and we did have a lot of fun. But I always felt that the place one got to know the real John Lennon was in the studio, where he was really a special person. He always set everybody at ease. You never got the feeling that he was a Beatle; he was just like any other guy. And he always treated you first-class, whether it was flying your whole family to the East Coast, where he was recording, or putting everyone up in the Waldorf. He really made music a pleasure.

He had some peculiar ways in the studio. Like, he never used horn charts. He'd just write down the lyrics and pass them around. He had contracted some horn players for *Walls and Bridges*, and he didn't give us any charts. I think he knew that would have embarrassed me, because I can't read music. He used to bring out the best in everybody. I can't really describe it; it was more of a feeling. For me to verbalize it is very difficult. I just had more respect and feeling for that man than for just about anyone I've ever known.

JAY BERGEN

John was never at a loss for wit, and it served him well.

John gave entrepreneur Morris Levy a tape of a rough mix of *Rock 'n' Roll* to listen to. In 1975, Levy put it out without permission, under the name *Roots*, with this garish cover—an old photo of John with long hair. When John went ahead and put out *Rock 'n' Roll* on Capitol, Levy sued for breach of oral agreement, John filed a counterclaim under the New York civil-rights statute that states that you cannot use a prominent person's image for any commercial purpose without written permission, and he claimed that *Roots* damaged his reputation because it was so shoddy.

By the time of the trial, in January 1976, John had cut his hair short. During cross-examination, Levy's lawyer was trying to build a case that the *Roots* photo was not a bad picture, and he was trying to get tough with John.

The lawyer said, "Now, you also testified under direct examination that this is an old picture of you."

"Yes," said John.

"Isn't it a fact, Mr. Lennon, that this is pretty much as you looked in the winter of 1974 and 1975, before you cut your hair?"

"I wish I did."

"When did you cut your hair, by the way?"

"I tried to do it on New Year's, but I believe it was the day after."

"Isn't it a fact that you cut your hair for the purpose of this trial?"

"Rubbish. I cut it every eighteen months."

The whole courtroom *exploded* in laughter, including the judge. John sat there smirking, knowing he'd really bombed this guy. He was the best witness I've ever had.

John was awarded $35,000 for damages.

When Levy appealed this decision, we won, although the damages were reduced. The second judge's opinion began with a quote from Lennon's "Nobody Loves You (When You're Down and Out)": "Everybody's hustlin' for a buck and a dime / I'll scratch your back and you scratch mine. . . / All I can tell you is it's all show biz."

"The words of John Lennon," said the judge, "are an appropriate introduction to this case, which involves alleged broken promises and acrimony between supposed friends in the record industry."

Boy, John got a big kick out of that summation.

TOM PANUNZIO

I had been at the Record Plant only a few weeks when I did my first session as an assistant engineer—an assistant's assistant, really. It was with Jimmy Iovine and Roy Cicala for *Rock 'n' Roll*. One night, I stretched a finished tape and ruined one of the tracks, "Boney Maronie." I was freaked.

The next day, I told John what had happened; he laughed and said, "Didn't like that one, huh?" Then he and Roy took my picture, and they said, "We'll show you this picture someday when you're a great producer, you dumb fuck." John laughed again, and we went back to work and finished the record. I'll never forget John for that kindness and vote of confidence. He was a great guy.

ROY CARR

John liked to collect Beatles memorabilia, and he rang me up in 1975 for some copies of *The Beatles: An Illustrated Record*, by myself and Tony Tyler. He then sent me a correction about the Silver Beatles, which we later put in the 1978 revised edition. He wrote a note, accompanied by a clipping about an early Beatles show at Neston Institute: "I was *never* . . . repeat *never* known as

Johnny Silver. Preferred my own name. See enclosed rare item from the files (possibly the first review of Beatles ever). Set the (illustrated) record straight . . . or forever hold your penis! There was *one* occasion when a guy introduced me as Long John and the Silvermen . . . in the days of old when they didn't like the *word* Beatle! I'm actually *serious* about this . . . it gets on my TIT!"

And he signed it "Bonnie Jock Lennon."

I was in New York once, trying to get hold of him, and he left me a little note, signed "Johnny Rhythm," telling me he was at the Americana Hotel. I went over there and sat with Yoko and him, and we drank beer and talked and talked. He said he hadn't had the childhood he'd wanted, but that Auntie Mimi had been good for him. He said he wanted to be there for Sean. And then he smiled and said, "You know, I still get a blast out of watching the Beatles cartoons on TV."

CARLY SIMON

James and I spent New Year's Eve with John and Yoko and ten other people at the Shun Lee Dynasty restaurant in Manhattan, and I happened to sit next to John. It was the first chance I ever had to sit close to him and study his face and have a good talk. At midnight, everybody put on goofy hats and blew noisemakers, and John had on this little pointed hat that brought all his features, including his nose, into a kind of pointed focus.

I was pregnant with Ben at the time, and John began to give me the compelling, potentially grim story of Yoko's problematic delivery of Sean. It took twenty minutes to tell, and all the while he wore that silly hat—it would have been difficult to take anyone else but John seriously. I was very moved by the loving, ultimately happy story.

On the day Ben was born, when he had barely been brought back to my room to be placed in my arms, a Tiffany porringer was delivered, and it was inscribed: To BENJAMIN 1-22-77 LOVE, JOHN, YOKO AND SEAN. I was amazed at how rapidly and thoughtfully they had reacted to the birth, because it takes two to three weeks to get anything engraved at Tiffany's, and to this day, I cannot imagine how they found out what my son's name was.

I prefer to think that they got the information through some mystical process, because I believe that's something they were both capable of.

ETHAN RUSSELL

I first encountered John in England during the *Let It Be* period, when I took a bunch of pictures of him and Yoko in a basement. Being only twenty-one and an amateur, I overexposed the photos, but I got great pictures of Yoko. They liked 'em so much they asked me to take more, and I was surprised that someone of his stature would overlook my mistakes and give me another chance.

Years later, I sent John some videotapes to show him what I had been up to, and he and Yoko asked me to shoot a promotion film for "(Just Like) Starting Over" that Yoko would direct and produce.

Once, while we were shooting in Central Park, he laughed and said, "This reminds me of *Rubber Soul*—only my face has fallen."

DAVID GEFFEN

It was very easy to become intimate with John. He was immediately himself, laughing and telling stories, just being ingenuous and extremely lovable. When Yoko's alone, she's Yoko Ono and she takes care of everything. But when she was with John, she deferred to him. She had an incredible respect for what he thought and what he wanted and what he aspired to. She influenced him a great deal and he influenced her a great deal. They are one of the great love stories of this century.

When we first met, they took me to the studio and played the new record for me and it was so good, you know. I told John I thought it was going to be a big hit. "I hope so," he said. "But you must remember, I haven't picked up a guitar in six years. I forgot how heavy they are. The last time I was in the studio, they didn't have all of this equipment." He wanted to show me what it could do, and he was so thrilled.

As I was leaving, John pulled me aside. "You know, we have to take care of Yoko," he said. "You and I have what we set out to have, but Yoko never got what she deserves. And that has to be our goal with this record."

I used to think that Yoko was this ambitious woman who was pushing out her music through John's success. What I came to learn was quite different. She kept saying, "Oh, John, you don't want me on this record. People really want to hear you." And he would say that he wouldn't *make* records without her, and he was going to see that she got the recognition she deserved. This was a constant theme in my conversations with John.

John was very anxious to have a Number One hit in England. That would have been a real kick for him and it had nothing to do with money. They had left England because people there had been so disrespectful to Yoko. John had once said to me, "How could *anyone* think we could be friends when they treat Yoko, who I love so much, this way?" So he wanted this record to be a hit in England for Yoko—and for himself.

He was really excited about what a good record he was gonna make after this. In fact, they were in the studio already. They weren't gonna wait six months. They weren't gonna wait five days.

The last time we talked was that Monday afternoon. I told John his record was gonna be Number One in England, and Yoko gave me this real funny look, like it *better* be Number One in England. That was the thing she was interested in, not for herself but because John wanted it so badly. Then we talked about a record they wanted to make that would be called *Yoko Only*.

I said I was going to go. But I added, "Maybe we'll have dinner tomorrow." He said, "Great, where do you want to eat?" I said, "We don't have to make that decision now." He said, "Yeah, that's right." And we said goodbye.

HOWARD COSELL

Near the end of the "Monday Night Football" broadcast, my producer, Bob Goodrich, said, "Roone Arledge just called and told me that John Lennon has been shot and rushed to the hospital. We're waiting for details from ABC News." I couldn't believe it. Goodrich then told me that he was dead on arrival. I was devastated. We were in the midst of a tied football game that was about to go into overtime, and I was wrestling with the problem of breaking the news on TV, thinking that, even in this sick, sports-obsessed country, *this* is far more important than any goddamned football game will ever be. I went on the air and said that it was just a game, and I felt compelled to tell this story.

John and I became friends in 1975, when he did a one-hour interview with me for an ABC talk show, and I found him to be candid, engaging, a man who understood himself. We kept in touch and, ironically, I even had him on "Monday Night Football" as a guest.

This man meant a great deal to me. My own daughters came of age in the era of the Beatles, and I saw a lot of the magic and excitement of that time through their eyes and experiences; they truly touched us all.

I'll tell you something that no one should forget about John Lennon: He was *never, ever* a hypocrite about anything he ever did or said or believed. With his family, his music, his ideals and his opinions, he was a man of conviction and commitment. I am proud to have known him.

NORMAN MAILER

We have lost a genius of the spirit.

FRANK SINATRA

It was a staggering moment when I heard the news. Lennon was a most talented man and, above all, a gentle soul.

CHUCK BERRY

Since the time they had one of their first hits with "Roll over Beethoven," I've always felt very close to the Beatles. I feel as if I lost a little part of myself when John died.

MICK JAGGER
REMEMBERS

y first encounter with John Lennon gave me a sense of humility, which is funny in a way. I didn't know what to say to him. The Beatles were such a big deal then—this was in 1963, before we had made a record—and we weren't really anyone. We were just that one step away from being successful when they came to see us play. I mean, they were so huge. They weren't just musicians, they were like teen idols and larger than life. And they had *leather clothes*, which we couldn't afford yet.

One night when we were playing at a club in Richmond—we were only playing rhythm & blues and some Chuck Berry songs in those days —they came and stood in the audience on one side (wearing leather trench coats!), and I didn't want to look at them. I was too embarrassed. But John was really nice afterward. I said, "You play the harmonica, don't you?"—he'd played harmonica on "Love Me Do"—and he said, "But I can't really play like you guys. I just blow and suck. We can't really play the blues."

That was the first time I saw them. And they came to hear us play a number of times at the Crawdaddy and in the West End, and John came more often than the others. They used to hang around discos like the Ad Lib—this was around a year later (John used to like the nightclubs)—and I remember that one time, when we were all hanging out at one of the clubs, George was giving me a big spiel about how many records the Beatles had sold more than us. Which wasn't in dispute! He was so anxious to make the point. And after he'd heard all of this John said, "Well, don't worry about George. He just hasn't got over the fact that he can sell records." He was nice about it. He wasn't always the caustic person he sometimes could be.

I liked him a lot. He was the one I really got on with the most. We weren't buddy-buddies but we were always friendly. But after the Beatles and the Stones stopped playing clubs, we didn't see each other that much: We were on tour and they were on tour. And, in a way, we were in competition in those days. Brian Jones, more than any of us, felt we were in competition—*everyone* was in *dire* competition then—and, if they were in America, we'd make a lot of capital about their not playing in England and all that. But we were friendly with them, I must say.

I didn't see John that much after that until he separated from Yoko, around 1974. We got really friendly again, more friendly than we'd ever been, in fact. We saw each other in L.A. a bit, but mostly in New York City and also out in Montauk, Long Island, where he came out to stay with me. We had some funny times. We got really drunk, and we went out on sailboats and just sat around with guitars and played. This was the time when John was preparing to record his rock & roll album, and he was quite openly trying to pick my brains, to decide what to record. We'd run through all the oldies and he'd pick out ones that he liked.

And when he went back with Yoko, he went into hibernation. He was living close to where I was living in New York City, but I was probably considered one of the "bad influences," so I was never allowed to see him after that. On one or two occasions when I went to visit someone in the Dakota, I'd leave him a note saying: "I live next door. I know you don't want to see anyone, but if you do, please call." He never did.

With Mick Jagger, March 1974.

I have in my passport a notation stating that the ineligibility of my visa is withdrawn "because of the Lennon precedent." He fought the court case concerning his visa problems because of his marijuana conviction in England—we were busted around the same time, actually—and he won it after five years and $250,000 worth of legal bills. So I have him in my memory every time I enter this country.

There was one thing, though, about John: You were always a bit aware that he was "on." You felt relaxed, but on the other hand you weren't, 'cause if you let your guard down, if you said anything stupid, he'd jump right on it and take the piss out of you. I think all that fame and money made him a bit overguarded, first of all mentally and, at a later date, physically. But the Beatles had always had the feeling that they couldn't go out. They led a sheltered life; they never went out to the corner to buy their cigarette papers, for instance, and they used to comment on the fact that I did. At that period, of course, there were queues of girls outside one's door, and you couldn't go out. You had to send someone out to buy ice cream. But after a while that went away and one could live the life one normally leads, except that people would stop you on the street to say hello. But John was still living a sheltered life until he and Yoko moved to New York. And he thought he was much freer here. He walked out on the street and people would say: Hello, John, and that was it. He liked that, but I think—and this is the ironic and awful part of it—that he still felt that he wanted to stay protected from the outside world.

HARRY NILSSON
REMEMBERS

ARLY in 1968, even after I'd made my first album (*Pandemonium Shadow Show*), I was working in a computer center of a bank ... but I also had a small office at RCA Records. And one day I was sitting in the office when I got a phone call from someone who told me that there had been a Beatles press conference in London to announce the formation of Apple—the second biggest press conference since World War II!—and that, when asked to say who their favorite singer was, they said me, and when asked who their favorite group was, they said me.

What had happened was that Derek Taylor (head of press relations for the Beatles)—who is a very forceful and persuasive person, the most intelligent man I've ever met, Ronald Coleman on acid!—had taken my album to England and played it for John. The story I got was that they listened to it for thirty-four hours on acid by a lake. And sometime later, one Monday morning at seven, I got a telephone call:

"Is this Harry? This is John."

"John who?"

"John Lennon."

"Huh?"

"This record is fuckin' fantastic, man. I just wanted to say you're great."

"Wow, is this really John Lennon?"

"Yeah, is this really Harry Nilsson? You're great."

"Well, you're not so bad yourself. I don't know what to say."

"That's it. I just called to say hi."

The following Monday at seven, *Paul* called.

"Harry? This is Paul."

"McCartney?"

"Yeah. I just wanted to say you're fuckin' great, man. I loved that one tune (whatever it was)."

"Thank you, man."

So, the following Monday morning, expecting *Ringo* to call, I got up, got washed, put on my English clothing . . . and, of course, there was no telephone call. I was very disappointed! But all of a sudden I was the fab blond Beatle from the U.S.A., and a man of mystique, and people started calling to manage me and sign me up.

Then Derek called me and asked if I wanted to fly over to London to attend some of the Beatles' recording sessions. "Go to England? London, England?" And the first night I arrived I was met by Ringo's white Mercedes 600, and I said "Wow!" Not only that, there was a carton of Larks in the back seat, which brand I happened to smoke, so I thought, "These guys really *are* magic. They even know the cigarettes I smoke!" (It turned out that Ringo smoked Larks himself.) So, first I stopped off at the Apple boutique and bought an Apple jacket just to be in the swing of things, then was escorted to Apple, where people were wearing buttons and badges saying NILSSON IS HERE. (Part of my paranoia told me that this was all a joke.) And there was all this madness going on—the Hell's Angels were there, and then people started flushing hash down the toilet ("Cops outside, don't sweat!").

And after that I was taken to Tittenhurst, where Ringo now resides, but which was John's place at the time. And that day was the same day Cynthia had moved out and Yoko had moved in. So we spent all night on the floor, talking about what it was like to be divorced, since I had recently been divorced. And Yoko fell asleep from boredom. I don't blame her. At the time I didn't understand what John was doing with her—I didn't then know about her sense of humor (later on she used to call me Milkman and I called her Bag of Laughs)—but it was really that I just wanted to know John.

Then at dawn the next day—we were still up and Yoko was still asleep next to the couch, crumpled up by John's feet—we went to fix breakfast in the kitchen, and there wasn't really much to say. John played me his slow or fast version of "Revolution"—I don't remember which—and I played him my new album, *Aerial Ballet*. John liked "Mr. Richland's Favorite Song" best. And then I noticed his gold-and-lambskin Indian "I Am the Walrus" jacket hanging on the coat rack. I admired it, and he said, "Here, take it."

"No, no, no, it's too short."

"Nah, take it."

So I did, and later gave it to my sister, who put it in a vault.

Eventually, I went to a session for the White Album—George was doing "Piggies"—and I was hanging out and looking and listening. And then John came up to me and with a straight face said, "Here's my new album." He showed me the cover of *Two Virgins*, and I just cracked up. I practically fell on the floor, thinking, "And you know what, he's going to get away with it!" The first thing I did was to see if he'd shined his dong a little bit, to make it look harder, and then looked at the largesse of her mams. "Wow, he's out there!"

At the same time John was laughing at the same jokes I was laughing at, with the attitude of "Yeah, why not?" So then I really fell in love with him. I knew he was all those things that you wanted somebody to be. That was my intro-duction to John.

At that time I was convinced that the Beatles were about as big as it ever gets. And I thought, "Ah, it's a part of history I'd like to be associated with." Derek was always the link. Ringo and I became very dear friends—we did the movie *Son of Dracula* together and we're still the closest pals in life forever. And George played on the *Son of Schmilsson* album. Then there was a period missing, and another when John and I hung out for a while, then again in 1974 when we were reunited in Los Angeles after he'd separated from Yoko.

I was hanging out one night with nothing to do, no one around, when I happened to walk into the Gold Star recording studio and asked a guy I saw there what he was doing. "Working for Phil."

"Spector?" I asked (I had worked with him years before).

"They're doing a session with John Lennon in there."

"What!" (I was really lonely that night.) And I walked into the session (John was recording his *Rock 'n' Roll* album), and Phil and I just started danc-ing, and then John started dancing: "Yay, my man!" And we began hanging out together. Phil is one of those guys, like John—to know him is to love him. I always stand by Phil. But Phil was taking his toll on John. One night, for instance, he had someone tie John to a chair—John told me about it. He man-aged to squeeze out of the chair and dialed a friend who came to get him through a window.

And this was a time when we drank a lot. One night a reporter caught us pissing in the bottle opener of a Coke machine! Those were the days when we used to pee on everything. And it was during this period that, on another night, John said, "I'm going to produce a Harry Nilsson record." I didn't want to push it. But when he committed himself to something he'd follow through. And a few weeks later we were hanging out at the Beverly Wilshire Hotel— Keith Moon, Mick Jagger, Ringo were there—and nobody knew what anyone was going to do next. And then the next thing I knew, John and I were sitting in a room and picking out tunes for an album (*Pussy Cats*). We also each had half a song and we put them together ("Mucho Mungo/Mr. Elga") and it worked. Later we wrote "Old Dirt Road" together, which John sang on *Walls and Bridges*.

Anyway, we did *Pussy Cats*, and my voice went during the sessions. Some say it was nerves, some say it was drugs, some say it was alcohol. In fact, I had ruptured a vocal cord and it was bleeding. But we actually had a great time doing the album, which we recorded in New York City and L.A. We lived part of the time in the Hotel Pierre in New York, and before that for a month and a half in a beach house that used to belong to the Kennedys with Ringo and

Keith Moon and Klaus Voormann and my wife-to-be, Una.

"It was the first commune I ever lived in," Ringo said. And me, too. It started off great. In the morning it was always: "Morning." "Morning." "Morning." "Would you mind passing the tea or butter?" "Oh, thank you."

By the night we'd be under the table. We'd get a convoy of limos and go to Burbank and record the album, take the tapes home and get bombed out of our nut, listen to them, pass out or do whatever we did, and the next day we'd go off on our different ways.

And sometimes John and I used to have these arguments late at night about who was more blues—Una or Yoko. I used to say Una, he said Yoko. "Don't you know she fucking went to Sarah Lawrence and knew Ferlinghetti before his name was spelled differently?"

And I'd say, "That's my point. Una's from Dublin and she doesn't know anything about those people. She's the street. *She's* the blues." And he'd yell back at me, and one night we ended up arguing all night at the piano where we were trying to write something.

There was a lot of crazy stuff going on at that time. It all ran together, and it was a year or two of just getting it out there: Everyone expected that that was what it was supposed to be like. But in his *Playboy* interview John blamed everybody but himself. He was over twenty-one, he got drunk, he couldn't

Shooting pool with Harry Nilsson during the "lost weekend."

handle it and he got a little crazier than most. (I was used to drinking because I'm a better "alcoholic.") In *Playboy* he spoke of me, saying: The poor bugger, he's probably out there, killing himself.

But the funny thing is that I've lost fifty-five pounds, don't drink and here I am. And John's dead from a handgun, which I'm trying to get rid of. (The disarming of America, if and when it happens, might very well be singularly credited to John Lennon.) I was building a house, raising three children and carrying on with what was left of a recording career—all of which John didn't know about. But at least he did say, God bless him wherever he is, the bugger . . . which I thought was okay.

There was that infamous incident at the Troubadour when John and I went to see Tommy Smothers, who was reuniting with his brother. Waiting for them to come on, we started drinking Brandy Alexanders. Now, at that time, our favorite song was Melvin Van Peebles's "Can't Stand the Rain"—so John and I started clapping and singing the song, and soon everyone around us was clapping along, but then someone started to *shhh* us, and we argued back.

Meanwhile, the Smothers Brothers were about to come onstage, and the next thing we knew some husky people ejected us bodily from the place, and some woman said John had hit her on the head with a camera, which wasn't true. But that incident ruined my reputation for ten years. Get one Beatle drunk and look what happens! John's line was, "I get all the headlines and you get all the bad stuff." So I said, "I'm Peck's bad boy getting *you* drunk. What about you? You're the guy who got drunk. You're the one who got us ejected from the Troubadour." "Yeah, yeah, a fine excuse," he said.

He didn't like vulnerability, yet he was one of the most vulnerable men in the world. It took a lot for him to trust, and when he did you had it from him. But he was very concerned—almost obsessed—with *mine, mine*: I wrote this word, Paul wrote that word. Who cares? In coauthorship one shouldn't remember who wrote what. People who know will know.

I don't think John liked to take the responsibility for failure or making a mistake. He didn't like to admit he was wrong, and it was hard for him to cop. And even if he did, he could hurt people—I've seen him do it—and if he realized he was hurting someone too much, he'd say, "Come on, man, I'm only kidding."

One night he was crying on Mal Evans's (a friend of and ex-roadie for the Beatles) shoulder, saying, "I was always a good boy. I was always a good boy," and Mal said, "Right, brother, you were always a good boy." And I told him, "What is this horseshit? Stop being a baby. You're being a baby."

"Well, if you don't like it, you can get the fuck out!" John yelled.

"Well, all right," and I slammed the door, and I was crying . . . "rejected by John," and I was so pissed off I took a bottle of whiskey and threw it through what I thought was his little window but which turned out to be a seventeen-foot-high window in the Beverly Wilshire Hotel—*crrrrash!* So there was this total overlapping madness, but, Jesus, it was a good time.

And when it came time to get straight, John was the only one to sober up and straighten out. Someone had to produce the album. And I dug him for that, always will. After he went back to Yoko, we wrote letters back and forth to each other—postcards when Sean was born, and I sent pictures when my kids were born. My wife and I would say, "They'll never last." And he'd say, "They'll never last." It was back to that. But I was always his friend, I think.

And I always dug his humor. He was one of the great comedians. There are only two or three people who can make me laugh involuntarily—Ringo, Albert Brooks and John. I remember one night when we were on our backs at 50,000 on acid, and some guy with a foreign accent called. And John just picked up the phone and said, "Yah . . . yah . . . uumm . . . yah sure, cheese cheese." It was his way of saying *sayonara* or *arivederci*, and I just cracked up. (You had to be there, folks.) Or he used to say to the violin players, "More linguini, more linguini!" He spoke the way James Joyce wrote. And to me he was the Beatles. He was always the spark. In a late wee-hours-of-the-morning talk, he once told me: "I'm just like everybody else, Harry. I fell for Paul's looks. George knew more chords, so he was in. And Ringo, he's just Ringo."

Someone once said that art is something that you throw up in the air and you let people attack it and then you defend it: It's the buffer between you and other people. So John used his art and his humor that way. But inside he always had a laugh, he liked the publicity, he liked the fun of being a star, he enjoyed living, he enjoyed being alive, he enjoyed doing anything. Some mornings I'd see him, hung-over, just enjoying polishing his shoes ("Polishing my shoes, who can beat that? I haven't done that in years!").

John and I were once going down the tram in Palm Springs—I actually witnessed this: A carload of maybe forty or fifty people in the dark, last tram down, everybody drunk—they turned out the lights so we could see the lights of the city. And there was this very sexual atmosphere in the car . . . I think it was because John was there, and people knew it. They didn't know what to expect and they were ready for anything. And by the time we got to the bottom, strangers who had never met before were feeling each other up—perfect middle-aged strangers! And I remember one woman grabbing my hand and putting it to her breast, saying, "Twist it harder, harder!" It's hard to explain. It was like the Twilight Zone. There was this vibe in the tram. And when we got to the bottom, people all of a sudden straightened their ties, put their breasts back in their dresses. And John, I and two friends of ours ran to our car, jumped in it and took off, saying, "Do you believe what just happened? What the hell was *that*?" I've never heard of it, or seen it, before or since.

What kind of effect did he have? Enough to change the world. He was the most amazing man ever, I'm very glad to have known John, I'm glad I decided to get on board that one.

A LOOK BACK

PORTRAIT OF THE ARTIST AS A ROCK & ROLL STAR

By Robert Christgau and John Piccarella

OHN LENNON's greatest work—greater than his persona, his marriage, even his music—was the Beatles. Obviously, though, he didn't create the Beatles alone. It's arbitrary to separate John Lennon the artist—the lyricist, composer, singer, guitarist, tape tinkerer, bandleader, author, actor, cartoonist, filmmaker, politico, publicity hound, comedian and sage—from the culture of the Sixties. It's conjecture to separate his Beatle image from the efforts of Brian Epstein, Derek Taylor, Richard Lester or the thousands of journalists who turned him into copy. But it's just about impossible to separate his Beatle music from that of Paul McCartney, George Harrison, Ringo Starr or George Martin.

Yet it was John Lennon who created the Beatles if anyone did. John's skiffle band, the Quarrymen, absorbed first Paul, then George and finally Ringo, changing name and style along the way. Brian Epstein fell for John and then taught the world that, as Greil Marcus put it, "you did not have to love them all to love the group, but you could not love one without loving the group." John was the Beatles' chief composer and singer, edging Paul out statistically (by about fifteen percent) and thrashing him aesthetically. The most outspoken of the Quotable Quartet, he was perceived as the leader by everyone including his three mates until acid went to his head. Years later, John talked as if the Beatles had already sold (him?) out when they walked into EMI; certainly, Brian Epstein's insistence that they trade in their leather for ties and smiles and George Martin's preference for Paul's tuneful tonsils went against John's more primal urges. But John did Brian's bidding because he also had a primal urge for money—and when money talked, Martin released Paul and John's "Love Me Do" (respectable debut) and then topped it with John's "Please Please Me" (Beatlemania!). Anyway, this was a *group*, and to have a group was John's most primal urge of all. A loner he wasn't.

That the Beach Boys and the Beatles each evolved a format in which four or five coequals shared vocals and played their own instruments is proof enough that the rock group was inevitable. Teenage fans of such leaders-with-backup as Bill Haley & His Comets or Buddy Holly & the Crickets were sure to create their own guitar-playing equivalents of the Ink Spots and the Ames Brothers eventually. Had simple lads like Elvis or Buddy come along a little later, they might have set all that community, compromise and reciprocal self-fulfillment into motion themselves. But as it was we have the Beach Boys and the Beatles, the former led by a borderline catatonic who turned "In My Room" into the story of his life, the latter by a jealous guy whose chronic acute separation anxiety began when his mother turned him over to his aunt at age three. Lots of ordinary boy geniuses are natural leaders, but you can see how having his own group might have been a special comfort to John Lennon.

What he got from the music was something else. Like most young skiffle groups, the Quarrymen picked up on the fad because it was easy and there. As soon as they could afford amplifiers they graduated from ersatz acoustic jug blues to ersatz electric hillbilly blues—rock & roll. And this too was John's need. Paul was even more intense about fancy pop chords and corny pop tunes

Their first publicity photo.

241

than he was about Little Richard. George's look was all rockabilly flash, but his music began with skiffle king Lonnie Donegan and proved even vaguer than that of most lead guitarists when he finally got out from under John's thumb. And while Ringo wouldn't have traded his back seat on the magic bus for any better drummer's solo spotlight, he recorded albums of country tunes and sentimental standards as soon as he had the chance.

None of this is to imply that Paul, George or Ringo was an opportunist— these guys were real and probably born rock & rollers. No one who played rock & roll professionally back then (back before the Beatles, that is) chose the music casually, and stardom was a fantasy of the crazed. But John didn't merely love rock & roll. For him it was a passion, a calling, a way of life. Yoko Ono was the only artist who ever challenged the preeminence of Chuck Berry, Jerry Lee Lewis and idol and predecessor Elvis Presley in John's pantheon, and this arty exception was in a sense inevitable; if it hadn't been his one-and-only, then some other prophet of total communication would sooner or later have captured his imagination, however temporarily. For John's sole reservation about rock & roll was that it couldn't say everything. He fought this reservation all his life and rejected it in the end as he had in the beginning. And that was just what attracted Paul, George and Ringo to his leadership. Most of the time, John Lennon believed that rock & roll *could* say everything.

In retrospect, the upsurge of rock & roll seems like the most natural thing in the world. It was sexy, it was lively, it was popular, it was real—who wouldn't love it, especially in the Fatuous Fifties? The answer is lots of people, including a good many fond but finally uncommitted teenage fans. And even when a kid did fall in love with rock & roll, it would rarely be forever—as a focus of romantic fantasy or peer-group macho, the music tended to vanish into a nostalgic limbo once the job of growing up was done. But that wasn't how it was for the Beatles. Sure, they became entertainers for the same general reasons that egomaniacs everywhere go into show business (and the arts) (and journalism, too). But they became rock & rollers so they wouldn't have to grow up—like a lot of war babies, these lads wanted to be sexy and lively (and maybe even popular) until they died, and good for them.

In John, though, the love of rock & roll went even deeper, and so the question of why he put so much more of himself into it must go deeper too. One answer— simple, impolite and almost certainly true—is that he had more self to put: more energy, more conviction, more emotion, more humor, more ideas and probably more sheer talent (note to McCartneyites: We said talent, not facility and/or technique). But that answer implies yet another question: Where'd he get all the self? Well, it's silly to pursue such inquiries too far, and what we're going to suggest is obvious if not redundant; under the sway of Arthur Janov, John once based a whole album on it. But there's no way to understand John Lennon without understanding how he felt about pain, and for John pain meant his mother, Julia, so here's the story. When he's an infant his ne'er-do-well father deserts Julia, who meets another man and farms the baby out to her sister Mimi; when he's five or so his father claims him for a few weeks, then accedes to Julia, who again passes him on to Mimi; seven years later Mimi's husband dies and then, five years after that, Julia, who has always visited Mimi's frequently and whose home is now a haven of flaky permissiveness in his teen psychodrama, is run down not far from Mimi's house by an off-duty cop. She had John, but he never had her.

On balance, this is far from a horror story. John always emphasized that he enjoyed his childhood. He was working-class but not poor, a healthy combination, with a surrogate father or two and two mothers most of the time. And if reliable Mimi was less fun than Julia, the sisters shared three virtues: affection, animation and good sense. But all those separations were just the thing to give somebody who didn't repress the whole business an uncommon taste for realism. Granted, realism might be too generous a term. Dead certain by the time he was five that life wasn't just a bowl of cherries, he threw up a barrier of precociously bitter wit, specializing in cripples almost as soon as he learned to draw cartoons. But he was just as quick to develop a healthy aversion to hypocrisy. So it's fair to say that if he was attracted to rock & roll because it was sexy (affection) and lively (animation) and popular (affection, animation and good working-class sense), he loved it because it was real—because it had soul and grit, a common touch and a tough lip. What would have happened if John had been exposed to real blues we'll never know. Given the underlying stability and habitual high jinks of his family life, he might well have preferred the ersatz electric hillbilly kind anyway—white blues aficionados tend to have the kind of self-conscious commitment to alienation that John only developed as he approached thirty.

John was a natural musician, just as he was a natural artist and a natural writer, an original in all three media without half trying. In a way, though, this ease of self-expression was a limitation, because it made him impatient with technique and formal discipline: One reason John ended up in music was that while he might (and did) fail his exams in English composition and even art, there were no O-levels in rock & roll, no adult authority figures dictating standards. And then there was another convolution: Rock & roll transmutes less into more as only a mass-produced, internationally distributed, electronically amplified folk art can, which means it makes the most of limited means as "higher" art cannot. And then the final one: His rock & roll would never have said as much as it did if John hadn't been crazy to make it say everything.

John was the undisputed leader of the Quarrymen when he first met Paul McCartney, who immediately intimidated the older boy with his technical accomplishments—this snot-nosed tyro knew *lyrics*, he knew *chords*, he could *tune a guitar*. In short, he was a real threat to John's preeminence, and John wasn't sure he liked it. But a week later Paul was in the band, and for the next decade-plus his unreconstructed boyishness, snazzy melodic ideas, transcendent harmonies and insufferable pop treacle would clutter and inestimably enrich John's passion, calling and way of life. Though it seems safe to rely on the old rule of thumb that John was chiefly responsible for the songs he sang lead on (with additional hints from Harry Castleman and Walter J. Podrazik's Beatle discography, *All Together Now*), it's the fecund if often theoretical Lennon-McCartney songwriting partnership that makes it especially hard to sort John out from the band. That's why it's important to remember that John *chose* Paul, deliberately encouraging this alien alter ego to modify and distort his music.

And though John was definitely the leader, he would never have led as fast or as far afield without Paul pushing from behind. By 1959, with George on second or third guitar and John's art-school confrere Stu Sutcliffe on bass, before the band had a drummer or a name they liked, the ever-hustling Paul was describing their wares to a journalist he'd met in a pub without resorting to the dread words "rock & roll" at all—"modern music" was what he called it. And in 1961, with Pete Best providing the heavy off-beat Liverpool's beat boom required, the now-Beatles brought their hodgepodge to Hamburg and whipped it into modern music—the music John would later say they sold out to become the biggest act in show business. The only extant recordings are some backups for one Tony Sheridan (after McCartney replaced Sutcliffe on bass) and the ragged, listless, all but inaudible *Live! At the Star Club* tapes, cut during their sullen Christmas '62 farewell to the Reeperbahn, with "Love Me Do" on the charts and the moptops dreaming of world conquest. So we can't test John's contention that the Beatles in Hamburg were at once tighter and more anarchic than they'd ever be again. But no one doubts that Ringo was a stronger drummer than Best, bumped in August 1962. And it's clear that it was only by choosing diverse material from their stage repertoire—including Paul's sappy "Taste of Honey," John's mad "Twist and Shout" and originals that were by no means pure rock & roll songs in the three-chord Fifties sense, though we now regard them as classic rock—that George Martin defined what the world perceived as the Beatles' "sound" on *Introducing the Beatles*.

The Beatles grew up on rock & roll in Anglo-Irish Liverpool, with no racial, regional or cultural stake in the American rockabilly and R&B and girl-group and show-tune records they recombined. Their music arose from the odd circumstance of Lennon and McCartney, pop composers by virtue of the advanced chords Paul taught John, leading their own guitar band—a band that made its living hurtling top-volume barrages at sailors, teenage rowdies, women of the night and other port-town lumpenbohos. Thus they evolved their own completely synthetic, completely organic version of the music—wilder than Little Richard, more civilized than Pat Boone, and immensely more complex and spirited than the Beach Boys. Where Brian Wilson begins his song of solitude with a gently ascending "There's a world where I can go / And tell my secrets to," gathering strength to tumble back down "In my room / In my room," the John Lennon song that kicks off from the same conceit is faster, more confident: "There, there's a place / Where I can go." The melody begins high and stays there until it drops a step to the seventh of "When I feel low / When I feel blue." But John has better places to go but his room, and better ways to get there than Brian Wilson. Instead of continuing his descent, he modulates, taking the melody with him to cloud nine: "And it's my mind / And there's no time / When I'm alone."

Or so he claims. In its avowal of self-sufficiency—of the singer's ability to transcend the isolation he dreads (not to mention time itself) by retreating dreamlike into that part of the Beatle being he calls home—this early song typifies his urge to say a great deal (though not everything) within the conventions of the rock & roll love song. For the first time John makes a primitive style serve the ironic complexities of his own half-schooled modernism. John himself often dismissed his early lyrics as off-the-cuff made-to-order, and it would be silly to read too much into them, but it would also be silly to think that any pre-Beatle rocker (not counting Robert Johnson) would have written a line as

From the movie, A Hard Day's Night, *1964.*

metaphysical as "And there's no time," awkward and slightly ambiguous though it may be. An artist obsessed with separation can do a lot worse than write love songs, and as a young husband John was already exploring the nuances of the one-on-one.

Sure he has his euphoric-to-cutesy moments, usually in his collaborations with Paul, though "I Feel Fine" and "Do You Want to Know a Secret" (which he had George sing) are John's alone. But he never allowed himself a love-at-first-sight goody like "I Saw Her Standing There" or "I've Just Seen a Face," and even such blithe moments as "I'm Happy Just to Dance with You" and "Ask Me Why" are touched with fear. Relatively complex themes—homecoming ("A Hard Day's Night," "When I Get Home"), reconciliation and betrayal ("No Reply," "Not a Second Time"), pain concealed ("I Call Your Name," "You've Got to Hide Your Love Away")—are dealt with in relatively complex ways. Early on he's writing "If I Fell," in which the yearning for tenderness and the yearning for revenge become almost inextricable, and "Please Please Me," an oral-sex song that precedes "Chewy Chewy" by half a decade. In "Tell Me Why" he seeks dialogue, and in "I'll Be Back" he volunteers (with apologies) for the second time he once rejected. And before Beatlemania has crossed the line into psychedelia he's come up with "Help!" an outcry of raw polysyllabic need, and "Ticket to Ride," a female-autonomy song that precedes *The Redstockings Manifesto* by half a decade.

Musically, too, John is an ironic primitive. He's the Beatles' most committed rock & roller, but he never just lets go like Paul on "Long Tall Sally" because both his realism and his belief that rock & roll can say everything impel him to undercut/overreach himself—he can never settle for just one meaning. So what is basically a very foursquare time sense is tempered by his nervously aggressive rhythm guitar signatures, many of them variations on the slightly syncopated rest-one-two-and-rest figures that define the beat of "I Saw Her Standing There." Sometimes he tampers with a song's thrust just for the hell of it—listen to the vaguely Latin swing of "Ask Me Why" and "No Reply" or the broken-up intro to the reverberating "I Want to Hold Your Hand." Elsewhere, as with the stop-and-start verse that sets up the straight-ahead acceleration of "All I've Got to Do," he'll play up a song's drive with tension-and-release. Similar contrasts are implicit in his mixtures of blues and pop chords and in the way his harmonies sour Paul's ebullience (as well as the way Paul's boundless enthusiasm leaps over his feelingful leads). And they're present as well in the wicked, joyful pop-art jokes that are this band's birthright: the "Little Darlin' " la-la-las that he tacks onto "Misery," the bacchanalian fade-out of "Please Mr. Postman" or the "Mr. Moonlight" travesty, with Paul on lounge-lizard organ, George on African drum, and John ripping up the vocal like it's rock & roll or something.

Needless to say, John did a lot more with vocals than rip them up—it was as a lead singer that he made the most of his greatest musical gift, his voice. It would be a mistake to attribute solely to one man a collective spirit in which the three little words "yeah yeah yeah" became a truth known only to young gods and the biggest giggle in the world simultaneously. But it would be dog-matic to pretend that John's voice couldn't have created a somewhat narrower version of this magic antithesis all by itself. Physically, his instrument didn't approach Paul's; it was rather nasal, with average range, strong but rarely rich. Technically, he lacked the rhythmic finesse and timbral liquidity of Jagger, the innuendo of Dylan, the surging purity of the American rock & roll originators. And we hesitate to just say he had soul, because one of his charms was that he never tried to "sound black." Yet soul is something like it. Maybe sincerity would be closer, but that's a strange term to apply to the class clown. So call it substance. However difficult it was to distinguish John from his mates in the early days of image saturation, it was the conviction and playfulness of his singing—the way it combined a passionate, decent emotional solidity with an extrovert's array of pranks, tricks, moves and nuances—that made us feel there were real human beings in the grooves rather than cuddly toys.

Lennon found more vocal inspiration in rockabilly—Buddy Holly, Jerry Lee Lewis and (once he hooked up with Paul) the Everly Brothers—than in the black rock & rollers he loved, and he certainly sounded white, partly because he was unashamed of his Scouse accent (not that he didn't drawl more when he sang than when he spoke) and partly because there was almost no swing to his natural rhythm. But his basic attack has something of Kansas City and the territory bands in it; it's flatter and more classic than that of any of the singers he covered, black or white. Although he definitely isn't above novelty effects, he's a shouter rather than a screamer, sweaty rather than hysterical and forceful rather than piercing, especially on his own straightforward rockers. His robust, unexpectedly steady assurance simply doesn't have much to do with Little Richard or Rockin' Jerry Lee; during "Please Please Me" and "When I Get Home" you can hear him shiver the timbre and beat the beat at crucial mo-ments, like Joe Williams adding a decisive touch of urgency to a phrase. But there's something combustible just beneath the surface, and other times he goes to a scream instead, especially on remakes—in contained yelps for Larry Wil-liams, all over the place on Barrett Strong's "Money" or the Isley Brothers' "Twist and Shout." And while most white people singing black music overdo it —whether as stupidly as Pat Boone or as passionately as Janis Joplin—the in-tensity of John's covers rarely seems forced, because despite Ringo's earnest dynamics he owns these tunes before he cuts loose. When the Beatles outrock their exemplars, John is usually why.

But from a shout to a scream isn't the only way to go, especially for magicians and extroverts, and John proves it every time he camps up (or feminizes) a backup with a coy, lemonsugary purse of the lips. Although he can barely approximate the breathy vulnerability of a Smokey Robinson or Shirley Alston, his delicacy at ballad tempos is irresistible whether the underlying mood is purely plaintive ("This Boy") or lull-before-the-hullabaloo ("No Reply"). The hammered vowels on a simple word like I-I-I-I augment "All I've Got to Do" 's aura of longing, a trademark device, as is the scratchy moan that points up the pain of the third set of "Hold me, love me" s in "Eight Days a Week." Even the silly coda to the silly "Misery" turns from heartsick groan into sublime falsetto into comic sendup.

By absorbing such vocal contradictions and playing them off Paul's more one-dimensional hard-rock and sweet-pop modes, John dramatized the confusions of adolescence in a singing style emulated by fans everywhere, none of whom would have gotten the spirit if his uneasy rhythms hadn't exorcised the confusions almost as soon as they were out. Of course, the fans didn't think John was singing about adolescence in any case. They thought he was singing about life. And for the next five or ten years it appeared that they were right.

It is coming on Christmas 1965. In England, the Beatles have been more popular than the Christ child since early 1963; in the U.S., where the craze started later, the group has released at least seven legitimate (if sub-thirty-minute) LPs—plus a few odd singles, one redundant soundtrack, an interview album and the Tony Sheridan tapes—within about a year and a half. They have also starred in two fast, heady Richard Lester comedies, A Hard Day's Night and Help!, the first of which established them as the new Marx Brothers with a postcollege audience that in 1963 had been too old for rock & roll. They've said a lot of cheeky things to interviewers (Journalist: "What will you do when Beatlemania subsides?" John: "Count the money"). And John has published two funny, nasty little books of stories, drawings, and verse, In His Own Write and A Spaniard in the Works, both replete with cripples, fantasy mayhem, solecistic spellings, and imagery that reminds critics of Edward Lear and suggests untapped lyrical possibilities. Enter Rubber Soul, with Our Boys tieless in suede and fisheye effect on the cover, and suddenly—not that there've been no portents—the world is about to change again. Rubber Soul is the Beatles' most unqualified triumph, the record claimed by their Sgt. Pepper faction and their Hamburg faction both. It is also the beginning of the end, if only because it carries the seeds of such factionalism.

The young John Lennon really was singing about life, but he was also really singing about adolescence. That is, he was making like an artist, trying to universalize his unique experience into a coherent rakka-rakka-rakka. A war baby in his early twenties, class-conscious but not classbound, beset since age three with an identity crisis less who-am-I? than where-do-I-fit-in?, and determined by nature and nurture to come out a winner, he found his form (and how) in rock & roll. This was the language of John's generation, a language and a generation that his history destined him to blast open. Because he knew the difference between alienation and growing pains, he could infuse his deeper hurt with the giddy poignancy of teen trauma and vice versa. Because he also knew the difference between personal alienation and general anomie, he didn't content himself with assigning social significance to his problems; that was often essential to what he did, but only when he got pretentious did it take over. Finally, what made him special—what made him a youth gadfly as well as a youth symbol, and what made him such a precocious adult—was his confidence that he could smash alienation altogether.

This confidence—which was intermittent, of course—in part reflected John's rise from a secure but never comfortable economic base; when he yelled out "I want to be free!" at the end of "Money," he added another level of spiritual ambition to the original. Such upward mobility was common in the boom years before the mid-Sixties, but less so in England than elsewhere in the industrialized world; a working-class Liverpudlian with a sharp aversion to hypocrisy was well suited to put its exuberance across with a little bite. And by 1963, something even more confidence-inspiring had entered his life: success. We're not talking about money, which has made many stars even more unhappy than they were before; we're talking about success at smashing alienation. Having projected his longings onto the early heroes of rock & roll, whom he first emulated and then assimilated, he was able to invent an emphatically unalienated identity for himself, as leader/member of the Beatles. And then, with Beatlemania rampant, he found that the protective circles had grown even wider—adored by an enormous audience, he was also at the heart of a nascent subculture, which in England was temporarily dubbed Swinging London.

Even if this whole configuration had been frozen in a time capsule at its peak of perfection, though, John's confidence would still have been intermittent. And peaks of perfection were all too rare. For starters, he still wanted rock & roll to say everything, and up till mid-'65 or so he'd pretty much limited himself to happy love songs, sad love songs, assertive love songs, hurt love songs, idyllic love songs, enraged love songs, married love songs, away-from-home love songs and so forth. What's more, like Elvis (and Valentino) before him, he had made the alarming discovery that there's nothing more alienating than stardom. He had no way to make human contact with his fans and not much reason to want it—by definition they were all but incapable of understanding his dilemma, which was them. John was beleaguered by well-wishers and mendicants, on the job whenever he walked out his front doors; forced into an intimacy with his fellow Fabs he simply hadn't bargained for, he found that the creative tension essential to any fruitful collaboration could get pretty irritating. And Swinging London—the cronies, business associates, starfuckers and fellow celebs who were one portent of the hippiedom just over the horizon—proved hectic and disorienting. Marijuana, some say, entered the life of this long-time pill-taker via a 1964 house guest who got his dander up in lots of ways—Bob Dylan. LSD was slipped into his coffee at a posh dinner party in 1965.

Convinced by mind expansion, rival songpoets and his own insatiable muse to really start *writing* songs, John (with equal input from Paul and some from George) set about expanding the Beatles' music as well. In 1965, they were no longer the great bar band of 1962, but their playing had never been more assured and, although studiocraft was encroaching on their spontaneity, their records retained a bar band's spark. On *Rubber Soul*, the bar was definitely tonier—some cross between a cocktail lounge and a folkie rathskeller, with the Byrds, Dionne Warwick and Dobie Gray's "The 'In' Crowd" on the jukebox. There was plenty of folk-rockish guitar, quiet when not actually acoustic, with George's sitar a stab at exoticism and Paul's limp "Michelle" proof that he believed in "Yesterday." But at a mean length of 2:29, every other one of the fourteen songs (on the original English version, the one the Beatles designed) had some snap. And the lyrics did nothing less than consolidate the conventional expectations of the Beatles' audience with the ambitious tastes of the Beatles' subculture.

Only three of them tackled new subjects. The double-reversed rock-star fantasy, "Drive My Car," and John's first aural caricature, "Nowhere Man," in which he hints at dreamsongs to come by gently chiding a woolgatherer who's "a bit like you and me," were openly satiric. "The Word," in which John notes that the message of his first love sermon can be found in bad books as well as good, is subliminally satiric. But on the rest of the album such grown-up romantic advisories as George's "Think for Yourself" and Paul's "I'm Looking Through You" augment three of the most mature songs John ever wrote. "Norwegian Wood" is a comedy of manners in which John doesn't get the girl, although he may end up torching her furniture next morning. "In My Life" pledges lifelong loyalty and more with a simple, elegant melody that's built to last. And in "Girl," the poor boy's put-down (cf. "Like a Rolling Stone") is sweetened with a lovesick vocal—in the line "She's coo-ool oo-ool oo-oo oo-ooh girl" he sinks from censure to swoon in midword—and deepened by one of the most politically suggestive stanzas in the music: "Was she told when she was young that pain would lead to pleasure? / Did she understand it when they said / That a man must break his back to earn his day of leisure / Will she still believe it when he's dead?"

Rubber Soul smashed a lot of alienation. Without reneging on the group's mass cult appeal, it reached into private lives and made hundreds of thousands of secretly lonely people feel as if someone out there shared their brightest insights and most depressing discoveries. These honest, sharp and resonant songs helped older admirers—the ones who would soon comprise a counterculture—feel connected to the world, and encouraged teenyboppers to mistrust comforting love-dove-above propaganda. But to John they were still genre pieces—rock & roll could say more, as he set about to prove on the B side of Paul's Lennon-esque "Paperback Writer." Transmuting fatalism ("Rain, I don't mind / Shine, the weather's fine") into mysticism ("I can show you that when it starts to rain / Everything's the same") into idealism ("Can you hear me that when it rains and shines / It's just a state of mind"), or else confusing the three, "Rain" unveils the druggy, vinyl-tower, war-is-over-if-you-want-it tautology that would keep John's natural working-class materialism at bay for the rest of his life. He complements this circular thinking with a sinuous, whining, Byrds-derived guitar texture and tops it off by playing a snippet of the vocal track in reverse. Psychedelia starts here.

And then, nine months after *Rubber Soul*, came *Revolver*, and psychedelia was in flower. Even in the U.S., where its impact was dulled somewhat by the inclusion of three of John's *Revolver* songs on *The Beatles*—"*Yesterday*" and *Today* two months before, it seemed, well, revolutionary at the time. With its string octet and French-horn solo and soul brass, its electronics and tabla-and-sitar, its kiddie sound effects and savage guitar breaks, its backward tapes and backward rhythms, its air of untrammeled eclecticism, mystic wandering and arty civility, this was really where the Beatles stopped being a bar band. More than any specific song, what's most remarkable about John's presence is his vocals, because he's just about stopped shouting—his campy, kissy-lipped back-up harmonies have turned into the sometimes almost prissy lead voice of a yea-and-nay-saying oracle, lyrical one moment and bummed out the next. On the nowhere man's victory cry "I'm Only Sleeping" he achieves this effect solely with mouth and larynx, but on "And Your Bird Can Sing," a two-minute "Queen Jane Approximately" and "Dr. Robert," which caricatures a pill-scripting jet-setter, he's added his own double-tracking to Paul's. And on "She Said She Said" and "Tomorrow Never Knows," the climactic side-closers that are John's only showcases on the U.S. release, a filter makes him sound, as one of us wrote at the time, "like God singing through a foghorn."

This is not the voice of a lover because John is leaving what few love songs the Beatles are singing to his mates. From a man who'd snuck the word "trivial-ities" into "When I Get Home" two years before, "She Said She Said" is even more strikingly basic English than "She Loves You," but with a big difference: This time the simple diction is about impoverishment rather than outgoing charity, satirizing mind-damaged bad-tripping pretension and positing a tran-quil if illusory childhood certainty against it. And "Tomorrow Never Knows" dispenses with pop song altogether. Incorporating violin snatches, mock war whoops, barrelhouse piano and lots of run-it-backward-George into a rhythmic layout rooted in Ringo's off-center pattering and a static bass-and-tamboura drone, the song ignores ordinary verse-chorus-break structure. There's only the continuous downstream unfolding of the same melody going nowhere, like time, or consciousness, until it circles around to a conclusion that is also a rebirth:

"Or play the game existence to the end / Of the beginning / Of the beginning."

In early 1967, the broken epistemology and childhood memories of "She Said She Said" meet the hallucinogen rock of "Tomorrow Never Knows," achieved this time with orchestral instrumentation and standard song form. "Strawberry Fields Forever" takes us down to the depths of John's psychedelic pessimism where even the innocence of ignorance recalled offers no respite. In "Strawberry Fields," nothing (but nothing) seemed real—John's inner circle of security was. beginning to fall apart. On the A side, "Penny Lane," Paul recalls similar dislocations in his own boyhood, but for him they're only "very strange," quaintly picturesque in the unthreatening rain, because for Paul, with his hustler's self-assurance, psychedelia was costume, spectacle and art-deco nostalgia—vaudeville for the mind. For George it was liberating, its exotic dangers neutralized by mystic formulas that offered autonomy of a sort and for Ringo it just meant longer card games between drum tracks. But for John it was experimental, synesthetic, deconstructive, chaotic and ultimately frightening, not least because his group shared almost none of these perceptions. At the heart of the new subculture, alienation was the craze but John was the only Beatle who went with the flow down into the flood. Testing his ever-more-fragile ego boundaries, he had already begun to surrender musical control to random juxtaposition and the aesthetic of collage. His primary instrument had become the recording studio, and in some essential sense the Beatles had ceased to be any kind of a band at all. But you'd never have known it. *Sgt. Pepper's Lonely Hearts Club Band* was about to turn them into artists for the world.

Depending on who you ask, *Sgt. Pepper* is either the greatest album of all time or Paul McCartney's folly—cute, contrived, dinky except for "A Day in the Life." Certainly its vague-to-phony "concept" did originate with Paul, who wrote the bulk of the material. But Paul had been doing wonderful work—"For No One" is probably the Beatles' finest heartbreak song, and even if it's sacrilege to say so, "Penny Lane" holds up as well as "Strawberry Fields Forever." Though *Sgt. Pepper* is a little stiff for rock & roll, Paul's whimsy reaches some kind of peak on "Lovely Rita" and "When I'm Sixty-four," and John's brief contributions to two of Paul's songs catapult them into a complexity of lyrical tone that neither Beatle ordinarily approached on his own. The "I used to be cruel to my woman" section of "Getting Better" (like the "Life is very short" bridge John added to "We Can Work It Out") illuminate Paul's aphoristic moralism with a flash of brutality, and in "With a Little Help from My Friends" John sums up pop psychedelia's balmy, life-is-ours-for-the-digging equanimity with a surprisingly warm, characteristically witty couplet: "What do you see when you turn out the light / I can't tell you, but I know it's mine."

And in fact the mood John projects on *Sgt. Pepper* partakes of the same life-affirming passivity. Turning the disjoint collages of his recent music into an all-encompassing lyrical embrace, he "finds" the content of his songs in a drawing by his son Julian ("Lucy in the Sky with Diamonds"), a circus poster ("Being for the Benefit of Mr. Kite") and the newspapers ("Good Morning, Good Morning" and "A Day in the Life"). The first two come out as McCartney-esque conceits, despite "Lucy" 's supposedly surreal imagery, and while the hectic "Good Morning, Good Morning" begins with a death, it ends with one of John's gnostic truisms: "I've got nothing to say but it's okay." Only the five-minute minisymphony "A Day in the Life," with Paul's woke-up-got-out-of-bed routine imparting tragicomic import to the disconnected leads of John's dream journalism, fully expresses his personal turmoil. By saying "holes" where he should say "people" in the final verse (typical Freudian dreamwork), John names the emptiness at his center. Yet it was the last line of this popular master-piece that people quoted: "I'd love to turn you on."

This was nothing new. Since "Help!" and probably before, Beatle fans had been reluctant to take their heroes' dark side seriously. They didn't know, and they didn't want to know—if separating John's art from his group, his image, and the culture of the Sixties is problematic now, it was out of the question then. When the biographical facts were available at all, they were obscured by an overarching presentation that was optimistic as a matter of policy, and this wasn't all Paul's (or Brian's) doing: John was happy to play the stand-up guru. The Beatles' image was so powerful that it subsumed not only their life stories but their art itself; their tragic/absurdist ("heavy") tendencies were rarely taken at face value, serving instead to make the group's collective positivism seem more substantial. Sure there were rumors of internal friction, but the Beatles were the Beatles, our great symbol of the communal, and even the simple notion that John and Paul wrote many of their songs separately scarcely creased our consciousness. Sure many of us got off on John's irreligious skepticism and mor-dant quips, but for most of his fans the transition from irrepressible cutie pie to the owl-rimmed hippie who beamed out benignly from the double-fold of *Sgt. Pepper* was wrenching enough. Sure "All You Need Is Love" was another pop-art joke, parodying its own simplistic message from the *La Marseillaise* at the intro to the laughing horn phrase that follows the hook down the three-blind-mice coda. But it was also what all those entranced by the Summer of Love wanted to believe—quite possibly including John Lennon himself.

Six months later came Paul's real folly—*Magical Mystery Tour*, saved from its own preciosity only by the singles that made it an album, especially "Hello Goodbye," Paul's delightfully simple-minded play on the "She Said She Said" idea, and John's psychedelic nightmare, "I Am the Walrus," in which his dream-scapes and rhetorical confusions give way to a dadaistic poetry *concrète*. John begins "Walrus" in a state of egoless universality—"I am he as you are he as you are me and we are all together"—but by the end his heavily filtered voice has disappeared altogether. When he sings the words "I'm crying," echoed at one point by an anonymous crowd, there's no sadness, just the matter-of-fact expression of an ego coming apart. Love was what John needed after all, not egolessness, and Sixties cant to the contrary the two were anything but identical. Enter Yoko Ono. Enter and exit the Maharishi Mahesh Yogi.

At the time, John's ego-breakdown songs seemed to prove that he'd learned to sing about life rather than adolescence—they explored an existential dilemma, and what makes dilemmas existential is their, harrumph, general human relevance. But existentialism has always been a philosophy popular among college students because its central insight is available to anyone who knows what it's like to be dead (as they say). And ego breakdown enjoyed a major generational vogue in the Sixties. For reasons having more to do with the rise of students as a leisure market than with justice or the bomb, a fairly large, mostly young audience began trying to smash alienation chemically—to achieve connectedness by dissolving the ego's petty subjective prison. You were supposed to find yourself (and your brothers and sisters) by losing yourself. Whether this was discipline or abandon, search or escape no longer matters— it didn't work. Although acid took courage for John, who'd spent years building up an identity that would fend off painful truths about isolation to which his psychohistory had sensitized him, his thousand trips were also a surrender to his desperate need to expand his self as far as it would go. In the end, the psyche-delic life was nearly a disaster for him personally. Artistically, his ingrained pop craftsmanship (perhaps reinforced by his ingrained awareness of how scary true ego loss can be) put him off the pulsating formlessness of San Francisco, so that the epochal "Tomorrow Never Knows" clocks in at three minutes. But that doesn't give it any big edge in the Great Art Sweepstakes. Like all rock & rollers, John was a lyric artist, better at evocation than analysis, and though his depiction of ego breakdown is vivid enough, its real subject is adolescence-three-years-after. This is important work, especially because his case is an interesting one, but no more so than "There's a Place."

Yet by putting him out on his own, ego breakdown drove John to surpass himself. Bereft not only of his group but of all his defenses, John was compelled to start over. By the time of the White Album, much of which was written on their all-together-now jaunt to India, he had abdicated, though not without a push from the young tyro: The group had turned into a solo project of Paul's that the others personalized with friends, family and sidemen. John's boldest, most perverse negation was "Revolution 9," an anti-masterpiece that took the collage-chaos of "I Am the Walrus" 's finale to unpopular extremes. There were no chords, no melody, no lyrics; there were no instruments, no vocals; in fact, for eight minutes of an album officially titled The Beatles, there were no Beatles. Elsewhere, with a few exceptions—most notably the baton-passing "Glass Onion" ("The Walrus was Paul") and the pacifist pastiche "Happiness Is a Warm Gun" ("Down to the bits that I left uptown")—John signals that he's rebuilding from the ground up with a formally self-conscious return to basics.

The tenderness and sweet simplicity of "Dear Prudence" and "Julia" are all but unprecedented in his work; the dream-song-as-insomniac-mumble "I'm So Tired" is pointedly unadorned; "Everybody's Got Something to Hide Except Me and My Monkey" says just that. But the watersheds are "Revolution," which isn't what it says it is, and "Yer Blues," which is and a half. In its very rejection of left-wing rhetoric (the line about Maoists not getting laid is a stupidity John would later regret), "Revolution" implies that for him public (or at least sub-cultural) prominence carries with it political responsibilities. And "Yer Blues" announces the third phase of John's struggle to make rock & roll say everything —first Paul's received pop wisdom, then psychedelia's techno-wizardry and avant-decoration, now Yoko's anti-artifice. Reasserting his ego in a spectacular (though not unironic) renunciation, he returns to the passion the Walrus re-pressed: "Feel so suicidal / Even hate my rock & roll."

This may have felt like a truth when he wrote it, contemplating Yoko (whose terse, provocatively simplistic art directives had been bugging him for over a year) and rock & roll (permanent obsession) in his ashram fastness, but all it really proved was how much he cared. A year later Yoko and rock & roll were his life and his ego was doing as well as could be expected. After the White Album, the Beatles started dissolving in public, played by cartoons in their third feature film while the fourth, Paul's own (get-) back-to-basics move, stalled in production. Their 1969 record-release schedule was a mishmash. "The Ballad of John and Yoko"—a Beatle song most assuredly, featuring Paul on bass, piano, drums and backup vocals—competed with "Get Back" for Top Ten space in June; "Give Peace a Chance"—composition still credited Lennon-McCartney, but artist listed as "Plastic Ono Band," the first official acknowl-edgment of what was going on—came out six weeks after that. In September, John played Toronto with one Plastic Ono Band, cut "Cold Turkey" with a slightly different one and decided he wanted out for real, though Allen Klein persuaded him to keep it to himself until more m-o-n-e-y could be squeezed out of attendant corporations.

Throughout this rich if confusing period, which ended with the release of McCartney and Let It Be in April and May of 1970, John divided his major work between political statements like "Come Together," "Instant Karma!" and "Give Peace a Chance" (far more rousing on Live Peace in Toronto than in its original bed-in production) and personal outcries like "Don't Let Me Down," "The Ballad of John and Yoko," "Cold Turkey" and "I Want You (She's So Heavy)." Either way the music is the most direct he's yet recorded, based on blues structures of irreducible harmonic and rhythmic simplicity. Yet, if any-thing its expressiveness has intensified, and this certainly isn't because he's jazzing up the lyrics. Even when he wants a satiric tone, as in the sexually political "Come Together" or the plastic "Polythene Pam" or the Lennon-McCartney swan song "I've Got a Feeling," the wordplay is mostly play, with no nightmare surrealism lurking down below. And in his outcries, John says what he means as baldly as he can manage: "Get me out of this hell," "Christ, you know it ain't easy," "She done me good," "She's so heavy."

Physically, in measurable aural reality, you could say that what put flesh on these bones was John's voice, which hadn't returned to basics. John (after Paul) was rediscovering the chord changes he'd lived and breathed as a teenager (before Paul), but he was no longer a teenager and he wasn't ashamed of it— he held on to his vocal technique no matter what happened to his chords. So every nuance and timbre he's mastered over the years is still on call—every taste of honey and spit of sand, every rasp and scream and coo. Nor is he suddenly shy of the studio's instant virtuosity, except that now he exploits it to underline and accent rather than obscure and/or show off: The harmony of "Don't Let Me Down" is either Paul in a fit of genius mimicry or one of the most gorgeous, tormented double-tracks ever recorded, and there are even hints of the filtered oracle in "Come Together" and "Instant Karma!" (which also puts John's Jerry Lee Lewis lessons to good use). It's obvious, though, that what enabled John to produce these sounds wasn't merely physical—plenty of sleep and a crack voice coach, or lotsa dope and some shredded nodes. Given his hard-earned skills, his margin was spiritual and conceptual. He glimpsed into the abyss of no-self and with his old come-out-a-winner confidence concluded that, as Greil Marcus might say, singing *mattered*—even an occasional piece like "The Ballad of John and Yoko" sounds as if his life depends on it. But he would never have achieved this conviction without Yoko Ono—not just to prop him up and ease his isolation but to provide artistic direction.

Since the time he was in art school, John had been acutely aware of what cultural arbiters defined as his left flank—in art and politics both, he felt threatened or at least challenged by self-declared vanguardists. Were they heroes making way for deeper communication and fulfillment than he and his rock & roll could offer, as they claimed, or just pretentious twits? Yoko's theories were a way out of this quandary. Her minimalist psychodrama and self-conscious just-do-it primitivism offended the craftsman in John, who was, after all, the more accomplished artist of the two technically. But at the same time Yoko's work gave him a clue as to how rock & roll might say more—say everything important there was to be said—and at the same time reassert his eroded identity. Yer blues indeed—*his* blues was what they were, real and ersatz hillbilly both. Less was more.

Of course, almost as soon as he made his commitment to Yoko he started doing pretentious things himself. But no matter how fatuous his various bagisms got, only the love-is-all-you-need moralism of John, Wisest of the Hippies was actually twitty. The rest—some of it at least educational (the return of the M.B.E. more than the bed-ins) or groundbreaking (the guitar solos more than the tape trips), some of it great rock & roll—was part of a demystification program. Nakedness was the metaphor—as Lou Reed would describe it a decade later, "growing up in public with your pants down." Having rashly dismantled some of his own anti-alienation devices and then watched the rest of the structure fall apart, the man who had once hidden his love (and pain) away did his best to take it all off—to divest his life of its ultimately crippling defenses/dependencies and his stardom of its aura. If at the same time he had the presumption to play the political leader, that was part of the process. Fans had to become ex-fans, or something more than fans. They had to understand that smashing alienation meant affirming one's own energy, conviction, emotion, humor and ideas—and suffering, because coming to terms with suffering is the only sure way to be strong. And once they'd achieved this kind of strength, then the project of liberation—for that was certainly the prescription—would naturally continue. As he put it all together in "Instant Karma!": "Who on earth d'you think you are, a superstar / Well, alright you are."

John released his solo debut just in time for Christmas 1970. From the funeral bell that kicked off "Mother" it was a shock—an austere, agonized catharsis. Yet it was also the natural culmination of two years of growth, and it was also rock & roll. Less was more. In the wake of primal therapy, John wanted to make another stab at everything by ignoring sex, liveliness and popularity in an undeviating realism. *John Lennon / Plastic Ono Band* is hardly his richest music—on "Mother," Hamburg buddy Klaus Voormann plays less than one bass note per beat while Ringo is reduced to a metronome, and it goes on from there. But it's certainly his most powerful. With their three- and four-piece accompaniment, these monodic, pentatonic, preharmonic blues melodies fit the fundamental human afflictions at the album's root not just adequately but with a poetic justice that more civilized music couldn't match. And the album's starkness isn't always what it seems—without transgressing against form, John exploits our reduced expectations to enormous dramatic effect. Alien rhythms (12/8 in "Mother," 3/8 and 5/8 in "I Found Out") make the pain more jarring, and John has never sung more virtuosically. At first his voice seems to veer between just-the-facts recitation and primal ululation with no stops in between, but in fact all that's missing from his performance is fun. "My Mummy's Dead" employs a familiar-sounding filter to decidedly anti-oracular effect, while on the two love songs, "Look at Me" and "Hold On John," Lennon duets with himself. And after beginning "God" with a round of grit, he climaxes in a transported high dream-is-over croon that's the most exalted, plainly beautiful singing of his career.

Superficially, *John Lennon/Plastic Ono Band* came across like an ad for primalist Arthur Janov, something on the order of "Know your pain and conquer the world." But it only reached six on the charts, because it doesn't make salvation sound so easy. John emphasizes that the awareness of loss is ongoing. Throughout the album he presents himself as both parent and child—literally (between Julia and Julian) and figuratively (to an audience whose disloyalties hurt him). In "Working Class Hero" he's both messiah and victim. And in "Well Well Well" his love for Yoko turns mysteriously sour for an evening. This working-class hero identified so tellingly with the fucked-up generation of fans that followed him through teen trauma to psychedelic heaven to bring-down (even junkie) hell to married-adult-in-love-in-a-troubled-world purgatory that not all of them wanted to know the details.

Whether applying kitsch sophistication to a crude guitar band (with Paul) or exploring a trippy technology that enabled everyrocker to come on like a highbrow (with acid), John had made aesthetic connections available only to a born artist with no patience for discipline. *John Lennon / Plastic Ono Band* was his pinnacle, the kind of primitivism that only a natural formalist (with avant-garde advice) could have gotten to. But like most minimalism, it left only one way out. John's next album, *Imagine*, was a pop move and a populist bid—an attempt to turn on a larger (and Paul- and George-sized) audience to his psycho-political program. Artistically and commercially, it was a major success. An even stronger record compositionally than *John Lennon / Plastic Ono Band*, exquisitely sung, with Phil Spector's naive yet grand studio work constrained by Lennon's lingering reductionist tendencies, it went Number One on the strength of its Top Five title single. But as the satirical ricky-tick of "Crippled Inside" proved, this was the end of the bare-boned form-is-content purism announced by "Yer Blues."

Soon John's struggle for identity began to falter both politically and personally. By early 1971 his working-class and artistic identifications had drawn him into the radical movement he'd once dismissed so smugly. But soon he wearied of the Movement's strategic and ideological failures, not the least of them his and Yoko's back-to-basics agitprop album, *Some Time in New York City*, and by late 1972 his working-class attraction to money and his art-making disinclination for analysis had put his politics out on their own again. Though John's name is permanently linked to hopes for peace, his confusion about political means was chronic. Between his upward mobility and his distrust of intellectualism, he would always have been susceptible to the paradoxical fatalism-as-stability voiced most poignantly by this lifelong count-me-in-out-in activist in "Across the Universe": "Nothing's gonna change my world / Nothing's gonna change my world." And, of course, stability was as elusive as ever—primal therapy had betrayed its limitations as well. You can only know your own pain for so long before familiarity begins to breed contempt; therapeutic insights may well be permanent, but the thrilling intensity of the break-through always fades. After all, John's belief in himself had a codicil, something about "Yoko and me." No victim of separation anxiety can ever just believe in himself and be done with it. When his marriage got into deep trouble, so did he.

It was 1980 before he made another good album, though it's not as if there were no good songs between *Imagine* and *Double Fantasy*. "Woman Is the Nigger of the World" actually gained acuity over the years ("Take a look at the one you're with"), as did several Yoko remembrances (especially dreamsong number nine), and the versions of "Be-Bop-A-Lula" and "Stand by Me" that open *Rock 'n' Roll* showed where he was coming from. But most of that album was busy and spiritless, and his Number One single from the period, "Whatever

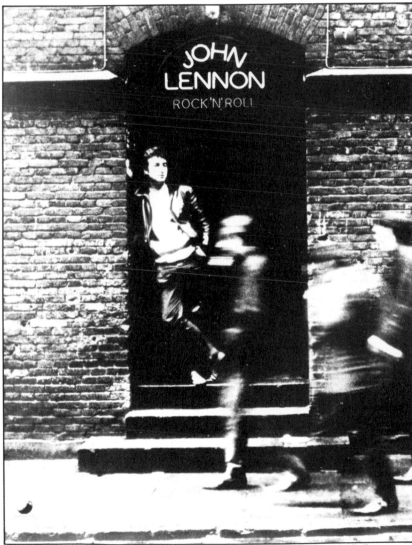

Lennon in Hamburg, 1962. This was the cover art for his 1975 album, Rock 'n' Roll.

Gets You Thru the Night," is almost as self-pitying as its title. What got him through the night was his L.A. boozing buddies, but he knew his pain anyway, and it didn't do him a bit of good. Neither did art—self-expression, as it's called. When the marriage was finally patched up, Beatlemania hadn't subsided— Broadway packagers were proving that—but John said the hell with it. He didn't even bother counting the money—left that to Yoko. He just cooked and played with his new son and watched TV, content to be part of a home he was sure of. Had he conquered alienation? It seems unlikely. But love was all he needed, or almost all.

Like *John Lennon / Plastic Ono Band*, *Double Fantasy* began with bells, only these were smaller, brighter, like dinner bells. On this defiantly civilized (even tame) marriage album, John again recast a classic form—the studio rock he'd hacked his way through in 1973 and 1974—to new expressive needs. The sound was rich and precise, the command of ready-mades—from New Orleans R&B to James Brown funk, from magical mystery dynamics to detonating synthe-sizers—almost uncanny. Reinventing himself, he again reinvented rock & roll, and after five years off his voice sounded better than ever—sweet, tough, pained, reflective, calm and above all soulful. It's possible, of course, that *Double Fantasy* would have been John's hello goodbye—that he would simply have returned to silence after hitting Number One. But it's also possible that he would have continued translating contentment into clear, deeply felt albums, and his guitar solo on Yoko's "Walking on Thin Ice" hints that more daring music might also have been in store. Whatever, as long as he was done with turning out product on someone else's schedule. We'd like to think that for however long he might have lived John Lennon would have made rock & roll say everything—everything he had to say, and nothing more.

THE FILMS OF JOHN AND YOKO

By J. Hoberman

OWARD the end of the Sixties, a flirtation brokered by the counterculture developed between rock music and avant-garde film. As early as 1966 Andy Warhol was featuring the Velvet Underground in his 1966 discotheque environment, "The Exploding Plastic Inevitable"; not long after, San Francisco filmmakers Bruce Conner and Robert Nelson were staging light shows at the Avalon and Fillmore auditoriums. In 1967 Nelson made two short movies with the Grateful Dead. In 1968 John Lennon and Yoko Ono released their first films, while the Rolling Stones were featured in Jean-Luc Godard's *One Plus One*. The next year Mick Jagger composed the Moog music for Kenneth Anger's *Invocation of My Demon Brother*. Meanwhile, following the example set by Conner's *Cosmic Ray* (1961) and Anger's *Scorpio Rising* (1963), underground movies all over the world were using rock & roll soundtracks. If it was a time when many avant-garde filmmakers fantasized of being pop stars, John Lennon was the only pop star who became an avant-garde filmmaker.

The films John and Yoko produced were of two basic sorts. The first were the promo shorts—*Instant Karma!, Give Peace a Chance, The Ballad of John and Yoko, Cold Turkey*—half lifestyle documentaries, half rhythmic montages, which were made in 1969 and 1970 for British TV to introduce various songs. As film, these are far less interesting than those of the second sort—the score or so "concept" movies the Lennons made in London and New York between 1968 and 1971. The impetus for these may have initially come from Yoko, but they quickly turned into collaborative efforts. In many respects, the gulf between Yoko's sensibility and John's was somewhat exaggerated. He, after all, was an art-school dropout and she'd begun her career as a composer. The Beatles' *Sgt. Pepper* was quite consciously a work of pop-music avant-gardism and at least since the early Sixties, Yoko had been an avant-garde populist. Both were given to whimsy and provocative public gestures. Nevertheless, Yoko was already a filmmaker when she met John, and the concept films grew out of her aesthetic, which had far less to do with self-expression than it did with the playful subversion of habitual perception. "I don't consider myself a director but a filmmaker who makes instructions," she once said; and of her notorious *Number 4*, remarked, "This film proves that anybody can be a director."

Yoko's notion of art is inseparable from her association with Fluxus—a group of avant-garde poets, painters and musicians who were active in New York during the early Sixties and shared a common interest in chance operations, "monostructural" forms and depersonalized expression. Cutting across several different media, Fluxus products were variously known as "object music," "concept art" and "neo-haiku events." George Maciunas, the group's main organizer, defined its aesthetic as "the fusion of Spike Jones, vaudeville, gag, children's games, and Duchamp." The ideas of John Cage were a major influence, and so was Zen. (Many Fluxus artists were Japanese or Korean expatriates, including the video pioneer Nam June Paik.) From the onset, Yoko was a key Fluxus personality. The 1961 series of concerts held at her Chambers Street loft were a crucial event in the group's formation. Even after she left New York for London, she maintained her ties. When she and John paid their first conjugal visit to New York in the spring of 1970 Maciunas arranged a two-month "Fluxfest" in their honor.

In 1964 Yoko had privately published six paragraph-long "film scripts" that humorously questioned the nature of the film medium from the standpoints both of production and consumption. One script simply gave instructions to document all the reactions of a group of people watching and listening to the filmmaker; another was to distribute scissors to a movie audience so they could cut their favorite parts of the film out from the screen. A year later, Yoko made her first actual movies as part of a specific Fluxus event: "George Maciunas called me up one day and said, 'There's going to be a film festival and there's a deadline. Do you have any ideas?'"

The 1965 Fluxfilm Program was a harbinger of the reductivist tendency in the American avant-garde—featuring short works by future "structural" filmmakers George Landow and Paul Sharits (as well as *Police Car*, one underexposed minute of the blinking light atop a New York City patrol car, shot by the pre-Velvet Underground John Cale). Most of the movies employed aggressively minimal or repetitive forms, and a number of them were made with a high-speed scientific camera Maciunas borrowed from underground filmmaker Ed Emshwiller. By shooting several hundred frames per second, the machine was capable of extending fleeting gestures into monumental events. Yoko made two five-minute contributions to Fluxfilm—*Number 1*, a superslow-motion shot of a match striking, and *Number 4*, a close-up succession of twelve naked buttocks. In addition, she was the subject of Chieko Shiomi's twelve-minute

Disappearing Music for Face, a superslow-motion close-up of a mouth relaxing out of smile, and she later claimed authorship of the anonymous *Eye Blink*, which used the Emshwiller camera to distend the wink of an eye into three minutes of screen time.

In September 1966 Yoko moved to London. Quickly, she established herself as one of the city's most visible avant-garde artists, organizing several flamboy-ant performances and a one-woman show within a few months of her arrival. Although the latter gallery exhibit (at which she first met John Lennon) startled the London press by inviting spectators to complete her paintings and offering an ordinary apple for the price of 200 pounds, by far the most sensa-tional of her London art works was a feature-length version of *Number 4*. Popularly known as *Bottoms*, it was filmed during the spring of 1967 and pub-licized as a peace petition that 365 people had "signed" with their bare rumps. This deadpan work, austerely shot in black and white from a fixed camera angle, presents each subject on a treadmill and framed from lower waist to upper thighs so that the screen is divided into four rippling, fleshy quarters. The soundtrack is a montage of remarks made during the film's production: Some participants compare Yoko to Samuel Beckett, others wonder how tedious the finished film will be and one wag suggests that the spectators' seats should be wired to grow increasingly hotter as the eighty-minute film progresses.

During the filming of Bottoms (Number 4), *spring 1967.*

Underground movies had only recently surfaced in London and so, with its provocative combination of nudity and boredom, *Bottoms* repeated, in milder form, the scandals that Jack Smith's *Flaming Creatures* and Andy Warhol's *Sleep* had caused three years before in New York. Despite the fact that Yoko wooed the British Board of Film Censors with thirty boxes of flowers, the film was denied a certificate. However, after several months of escalating publicity, it was finally cleared by another government bureau, opening at a commercial theater to extensive, if negative, reviews. Later in the year, *Bottoms* was shown out-of-competition at the Knokke-Le-Zoute avant-garde film festival in Belgium. (The grand-prize winner that year was Michael Snow's 45-minute zoom, *Wavelength*; Robert Nelson's *Grateful Dead* also won a cash award.) In that context, the film attracted less attention than did its maker's ploy of lying inside a large black bag on the floor of the casino foyer for eight hours flanked by signs proclaiming YOKO ONO IS NOT HERE.

Although John and Yoko met shortly after her arrival in London, each was married to someone else and their relationship was slow to blossom. Once it did, in the spring of 1968, they collaborated on two celebratory films: *Number 5*, a.k.a. *Smile*, and *Two Virgins* were shot in super 8 on the same afternoon in John's Kenwood garden. "They were done in a spirit of home movies," Yoko later wrote. "We were mainly concerned about the vibrations the films send out and the kind that was between us."

Both films are portraits. *Number 5* is a 52-minute superslow-motion close-up of John sticking out his tongue, raising his eyebrows, pursing his lips and smiling twice. (Most likely, it approximated the glacial pacing of Yoko's Fluxfilms by step-printing each frame of the three-minute super 8 original eighteen times.) In her notes, Yoko mentions she had considered making the film last four hours but decided to stick to a "more commercial" length, offering super 8 prints "for people who'd like to have the film on their wall as a light portrait." In any format, *Number 5* was designed as an environmental work: The film had its world premiere at the Chicago Film Festival in November 1968 and the audience was invited to bring their own musical instruments to augment the soundtrack of ambient Kenwood garden noises. "By the time 30 minutes had passed," *Variety* reported, "some 50% of the house had ankled. Those who remained played their flutes, tambourines, made vocal sounds and frolicked under the ever-present face of John Lennon, who by then was displaying a broad, winning smile."

Number 5 clearly grows out of Yoko's previous interests—not only the Fluxfilm *Disappearing Music for Face*, in which she appeared, but also her unrealized project, announced in the press release for *Bottoms*, to make a film that included "a smiling face snap of every single human being in the world." The lyricism of *Two Virgins*, on the other hand, was a departure that may reflect John's unreleased super 8 experiments with slow motion and multiple superimposition. For most of its nineteen minutes, the film superimposes John and Yoko's faces, shifting focus so their features alternate and ultimately merge. A final shot silhouettes the couple against the sky as they kiss and embrace each other in slow motion. The soundtrack, a *musique concrète* mix of bird calls and piano chords from the album *Two Virgins*, gives way to muffled snatches of dialogue.

With these portrait films, John and Yoko embarked on their first period of intensive moviemaking, lasting through 1969. "They devoted hundreds of hours to filming, editing and re-editing," according to former associate Anthony Fawcett. "It was a creative experience they could share, it was fun and it took their minds off more depressing problems." At the same time that *Two Virgins* and *Number 5* were being screened in Chicago, John and Yoko were preparing their first feature, taken from one of Yoko's *Thirteen Film Scores* published that year: "The cameraman will chase a girl on a street with a camera persistently until he corners her in an alley, and, if possible, until she is in a falling position." The film was called *Rape*, and it is among the most brilliant and disturbing pieces in their œuvre.

Rape begins without titles. The camera spies an attractive long-haired woman wandering through a rustic London cemetery and sets off in pursuit. The prey, twenty-one-year-old Eva Majlata, doesn't speak any English. But she's basically amiable and makes many attempts to establish contact with the filmmakers in German and Italian. They are totally noncommunicative, ignoring even her re-quest for a match to light her cigarette, while shifting the camera to keep her always in the frame. The movie approximates real time. Whenever a roll of film ends, the crew falls behind the woman so that each new sequence begins with them catching up to, and startling, her again. After the third roll, her initial poise has given way to annoyance and, by the time the crew has followed her out of the park and onto the street, she's angry and frightened—so spooked at one point that she nearly dodges in front of a truck. When, ultimately, she hails a cab, the camera promptly climbs into another and the first reel ends with the crew still dogging her tracks as she walks morosely by the Thames.

The second, even more frantic and oppressive, half of the film finds the woman and crew cooped up together in a small apartment. As she paces like a caged animal, babbling hysterically in German with tears of frustration streak-ing her elaborate eye makeup, the camera's tight, violently hand-held close-ups mirror her agitated movements. The woman sometimes hides her face or half-heartedly blocks the lens while repeatedly trying to open the apartment's apparently locked front door. At the very end, she makes a phone call and starts yelling about her passport. The sound of her distress continues over the credits. *Rape* was shot by Nick Knowland and one sound assistant in November 1968 while Yoko (and John) were in the hospital recuperating from Yoko's mis-carriage. "Nick is a gentleman, who prefers eating clouds and floating pies to shooting *Rape*. Nevertheless, it was shot," wrote Yoko in a statement prepared for the film's world premiere in March 1969 over Austrian TV.

Although Yoko's score for *Rape* indicates that the film's subject should be chosen at random, in practice this was not the case. *Rape* is clearly some sort of set-up, though it is difficult to ascertain exactly how much of it was pre-planned. Eva Majlata was obviously selected for her good looks, lack of English and unfamiliarity with London. The filmmakers are never shown entering her apartment; according to various accounts, the key was obtained from either her sister or the owner of the building and was then used to lock her in. Majlata never completely panics or appears to think herself in physical danger, but her anger and confusion are absolutely convincing. This, of course, is part of the film's fascination. In one sense, *Rape* is a particularly brutal dramatization of Andy Warhol's aesthetic discovery that the camera's implacable stare could disrupt ordinary behavior and enforce its own response. In another sense, the

During the filming of Rape, *starring Eva Majlata.*

film is a graphic metaphor for the ruthless surveillance that can theoretically attach itself to any citizen of the modern world.

Indeed, it is hard not to see the film as a reaction to the media coverage John and Yoko had alternately courted and been victimized by at various stages in their careers. *Rape* was shot following a period of maximum, mostly adverse publicity. John's hashish bust had occurred on October 18, his divorce proceedings began on November 8 and Yoko entered the hospital on November 21. A week later, the album *Two Virgins*, with its scandalous nude cover, was released. But *Rape* is more than just a hyperbolic representation of blanket media coverage. As a film, it radically challenges the normally privileged position of the movie viewer. Basically, *Rape* presents a beautiful woman in peril, her plight overtly sexualized by the very title. Although this spectacle is a movie staple, the absence of a distancing narrative strongly invites the audience to identify the camera's controlling gaze with their own; the sadistic aspect of "secretly" watching another person on the screen becomes a self-conscious complicity. In other words, *Rape*'s behaviorism cuts two ways. As Jonas Mekas observed, "Two things are interesting to watch as the film progresses — one is the girl . . . and the other is the audience."

The first of John and Yoko's films to be primarily credited to John was *Apotheosis* (1969–70), an unbroken eighteen-minute shot taken from an unseen helium balloon as it floats upward over the snowy countryside. Continuous, real-time movement is crucial to the film; an earlier, edited version using both balloon and helicopter footage was scrapped as insufficiently seamless. *Apotheosis* opens with the camera passing vertically over a bundled-up John and Yoko as it ascends rapidly from the town square of Laveham, Sussex, into the sky. ("We are left on the ground in this film, and suddenly *you* are the God," Lennon told critic Amos Vogel.) The sounds of voices and barking dogs grow fainter as the camera drifts high over the brown and white fields, then the landscape gradually fades away. Two thirds of the way through the film, the balloon enters a cloud, resulting in five minutes of a blank, white screen. Suddenly the image turns pink, then a brilliant white. The camera rises above the cloud bank, the sun bursts into a corner of the frame and, on this heady note, the film ends.

Lovely as it is, *Apotheosis* was the worst received of John and Yoko's films. Booed at the 1971 Cannes Film Festival — where the *New York Times* correspondent erroneously described it as silent, and estimated the cloud sequence at three times its actual length — *Apotheosis* provoked a small riot at the Elgin Theater during its New York premiere as well. ("The peace-and-love generation couldn't face the peace of the white screen," wrote Mekas acerbically of the incident.) However, its concern for a continuous upward motion — as well as the acceptance of whatever happens within its perimeters as integral to the work — is shared by Lennon's other two London films, *Self Portrait* (1969) and *Erection* (1970–71). The former is a fifteen-minute close-up of his semierect penis: "My prick, that's all you saw for a long time. No movement, but it dribbled at the end. That was accidental. The idea was for it to slowly rise and fall—but it didn't." The latter film, which was not premiered until 1972, depicts a more substantial "erection," compressing the construction of the London International Hotel into eighteen minutes.

Like its predecessors, *Erection* was a film that John "set in motion," rather than directed. It was filmed over an eighteen-month period by a still camera, at a fixed point of view, taking intermittent slides of a massive, square-block construction site. The slides were then filmed in sequence, each dissolving quickly into the next to create a kind of stutter-step pixillation. Contrapuntal to the steady progress of the building are various shifts in color and light as well as the droning sirens, electronic squawks and stylized jungle noises of Yoko's soundtrack, composed with her Fluxus crony Joe Jones. It is tempting to see *Erection* as a playful response to P. Adams Sitney's influential essay on "structural film," which had been published in *Film Culture* shortly before the movie went into production. A number of Fluxus artists were annoyed that Sitney had ignored their contributions, and John and Yoko would certainly have been aware of this controversy. *Erection* both fulfills Sitney's definition ("the structural film insists on its shape and what content it has is minimal and subsidiary to the outline") and literally depicts the evolution of a structure while ironically suggesting the sublimation of the sexual drive underscoring the "advance" of civilization.

When the Lennons visited New York in December 1970, Jonas Mekas arranged for a three-evening festival of their films at the Elgin Theater. John and Yoko spontaneously decided to add some new movies to the program and, working under tremendous deadline pressure, they executed two more of Yoko's film scores—*Up Your Legs Forever* and *Fly*—the movies that inaugurated the second, New York phase of their film production.

The eighty-minute *Up Your Legs Forever* is in many ways a sequel to *Bottoms*. John and Yoko recruited 331 performers and filmed them all, from toes to upper thighs, using a small crane with a vertical lift. This upward movement was repeated continually and the film's cameraman, Steve Gebhardt, remembers consuming three bottles of Harvey's Bristol Cream during the two-day shoot. "We asked everybody to donate their legs for peace," Yoko explained. "The thing I liked about it was that everybody who performed in it became a star. There wasn't one prima donna that just everybody focused on." *Legs*'s anonymous subjects included art-world luminaries (Larry Rivers, George Segal, Henry Geldzahler), local filmmakers (D. A. Pennebaker, Shirley Clarke, Jack Smith), underground personalities (Paul Krassner, Taylor Mead, David Johansen), a small army of journalists and a soupçon of society swells. Mekas—himself in the movie—would later observe that "the thing that shocked me when I saw the film was how ugly, abnormal, distorted, crooked, uneven, sickly most of the legs were. Now the world can see on what legs the whole New York art, intellect and culture rest. What a document for future historians!"

As soon as Legs was in the can, the Lennons moved downtown to the Bowery loft that was the set of Fly. Probably the best remembered of their films, Fly consists of huge close-ups of an unconscious nude woman as she is explored by the Vasco da Gama of the insect world. The macro lens employed allows for considerable individuated behavior on the fly's part—one reviewer singled out the eponymous creature's performance for its "hammy histrionic exuberance"— while depicting the woman's body as a terrain of Brobdingnagian proportions. This conversion of the human form into a vast, almost abstract landscape follows the tradition established by Willard Maas's 1943 Geography of the Body, an early avant-garde film, which used a magnifying glass in concert with the camera. Maas's visual trope was revived in a number of later underground movies including Taka Iimura's 1963 Love (for which Yoko composed the soundtrack), Barbara Rubin's 1964 Christmas on Earth and Warhol flicks like Shoulder or Taylor Mead's Ass, both 1964. What distinguishes Fly from its predecessors is the visceral, beauty-and-the-beast alienation effect, which, as in Rape, complicates the audience's voyeuristic enjoyment of the spectacle on the screen: "I wondered how many people would look at the fly or at the body?" Yoko explained. Or who would identify with what, she might have added.

Fly begins its expedition on the woman's toes, crawls up to her crotch, settles into the pubic hair and investigates her vagina. Later, it tours her nipples, perches upon her fingertips and scuttles around her face. Meanwhile, the insistent soundtrack of Yoko's scratchy caterwauling, accompanied by a reverse recording of John's guitar, suggests an amplified insect love call (if not a soprano machine gun or the death throes of a violin). The film's original version ran three quarters of an hour; after its Elgin premiere, the film was cut nearly in half. At the end, two flies converge on the woman's abdomen and four more are shown grouped on her hand. Finally, there's a long shot of her unmoving body covered with half a dozen flies; the camera then shifts focus out the window behind her, pans over a building and into the sky as though to suggest an aerial escape.

Yoko's instructions for the film were simply to "let a fly walk on a woman's body from toe to head and fly out the window." In practice, these did not prove so easy to follow. The original plan was to "direct" the fly's path with a trail of sugar water. When this proved ineffective, it was necessary to stun the insect with CO_2 gas, place it on the desired location and hope that it would wake up. Obviously, a cast of hundreds was required—at least one fly for every take. The situation was further complicated by the fact that the macro lens creates a depth of field so shallow that the cameraman is obliged to refocus every time its subject moves more than a few inches. These difficulties not withstanding, Fly was shot in a single marathon session lasting a day and a half. The film's human star, Virginia Lust, was apparently sedated. "Everyone is that female, just lying down, just taking it," Yoko remarked at the 1971 Cannes Film Festival, where *Fly* proved a far greater crowd-pleaser than *Apotheosis*.

The Lennons' move to New York in August 1971 precipitated another round of intense film production. "We filmed everything you can think of and more," remembers Steve Gebhardt, their chief cameraman at the time. John and Yoko were primarily interested in fancifully documenting their lifestyle for the feature *Imagine*, but other projects came frequently to the fore. *Clock* (1971)—an hour-long fixed-camera meditation on an old French timepiece and a mirrored mantle in the lobby of the St. Regis Hotel—was made by John for Yoko's retrospective at the Everson Museum in Syracuse. Two one-minute *Freedom Films* were done for the 1971 Chicago Film Festival (Yoko's had a woman throwing off her brassiere in superslow motion, John's scratched the word *freedom* into thirty-five feet of black leader so that it jumped and quivered like one of Stan Brakhage's titles).

There were longer films as well, including an unfinished documentary on Yoko's Everson show, and the unreleased feature, *Ten for Two*. The latter, shot in December 1971, documents the John Sinclair Freedom Rally held in Ann Arbor, Michigan. Among the participants were four of the original Chicago Eight—Rennie Davis, Dave Dellinger, Jerry Rubin and Bobby Seale. Although screened in Europe, the film was never publicly shown in the U.S. because of John's continuing immigration problems. The Lennons supported other filmmakers as well. They underwrote John Reilly and Stefan Moore's pro-IRA video documentary, *The Irish Tapes* (for which John also supplied some music), and persuaded John's agent, Allen Klein, to ante up half a million dollars for the rights to *El Topo*, the Alejandro Jodorowsky cult film which had been running midnights for six months at the Elgin Theater.

But, as far as filmmaking went, the couple were spreading themselves paper thin and it is unfortunate that *Imagine*, which in some ways was their most ambitious film, should have also been their weakest. An epic version of the promo movies, it was originally conceived as a TV plug for John's album and its images were mainly cut to that pre-existing soundtrack. The footage was filmed during the summer and fall of 1971 in New York, London and Japan, including scenes of John and Yoko solemnly exploring their all-white country mansion, leading a London peace march and capering about Lower Manhattan. A few sequences—notably the outdoor party shot by Jonas Mekas—have an unpretentious charm, but the film's literal illustrations of John's songs are as heavyhanded and embarrassing as the black leather miniskirt-cum-urban guerrilla ensemble that Yoko frequently wears. A perfunctory Vietnam/Kent State/A-Bomb montage only serves to highlight *Imagine*'s underlying frivolity. None of John and Yoko's portraits seem nearly this narcissistic and, as compared to the concept films, *Imagine* is hopelessly disorganized and indulgent. Not surprisingly, much of it was shot spontaneously. "We just wanted to do what came into our heads that day," Yoko said. Gebhardt estimates the film's shooting ratio at a minimum of 100:1 and possibly twice that amount. *Imagine* took John and Yoko nearly a year to edit, then had to be shortened by about twenty minutes for its televised world premiere on December 23, 1972—the last of their films to be released.

Given its duration, John and Yoko's filmmaking career was quite productive —not least, in an intellectual sense. *Rape* and *Fly*, particularly, are unjustly obscure films that, released in advance of the revival of Freudian film theory (à la française) and the rise of feminist filmmaking, seem now even more impressive than they did a dozen years ago. The less radical *Apotheosis* and *Erection* are both eminently respectable examples of the structural/reductivist/minimal mode that reached its own apotheosis in the early 1970s. (*Clock*, which was never put in distribution, sounds like a conceptually valid and visually interesting single-shot film as well.) The fact that none of these works has been claimed by either the British or feminist avant-gardes is a form of inverted snobbery complicated by cultural amnesia.

This paradoxical marginalization is an aspect of John and Yoko's œuvre which has nothing to do with its intrinsic worth. After the 1968 "retirement" of Andy Warhol, the Lennons inherited his position as the world's most notorious "underground" filmmakers. Although their work has had little influence on other artists, *Smile*, *Self Portrait*, *Rape*, *Apotheosis* and *Fly* were virtually the only avant-garde films of their period that received sufficient media coverage to impinge upon popular consciousness. This, of course, was a factor of the Lennons' prior celebrity and it is precisely this celebrity that has complicated their films' subsequent reputation: Dismissed as inexplicable put-ons by an offended public, their work was mistaken for idle pretension and dilettantism by the avant-garde as well.

ROCK AND AVANT-GARDE: JOHN AND YOKO'S RECORD COLLABORATIONS

By John Rockwell

HEN the Beatles were breaking up, in the late Sixties, and Yoko Ono seemed to their fans like an alien intrusion into a heretofore blissful band of innocents, the avant-garde collaborations of John and Yoko were widely regarded as proof of her evil nuttiness and his helpless infatuation.

A small group prized these discs and the events they document, but mostly the records were ignored, reviled or forgotten. Mostly forgotten: These records are collectors' items in their original pressings, and even reissues here and in Japan are extremely hard to find. Other than for diehard Beatlemaniacs, who have to own such things even if they don't listen to them, these records are gone.

The records in question are, essentially, three: *Unfinished Music No. 1: Two Virgins*, recorded in May 1968; *Unfinished Music No. 2: Life with the Lions*, recorded in November 1968 and on March 2, 1969; and the *Wedding Album*, recorded in March and April 1969.

There were, of course, many more collaborations between the two; just as for legal and personal reasons all of John's songs up through the Sixties are credited jointly with Paul, so much of his work from then to his death is credited to him and Yoko, or as having been coproduced by them. There are some Beatles cuts that are really John and Yoko avant-garde collaborations in the same sense as the central trilogy of albums listed above—notably "Revolution 9" on the White Album, which was made between *Two Virgins* and *Life with the Lions*. But most of the rest of the John-Yoko collaborations, from the Plastic Ono Band and Yoko's own albums through *Double Fantasy*, are in a pop-rock idiom, however weird, and are dealt with elsewhere in this book.

Neither John nor Yoko came to their avant-gardism naively; both had had prior experience with avant-garde ideas, Yoko especially. The world of post-Dada, post-Cage avant-garde experimentation in the Sixties was a determinedly fluid one, questioning the very notions of "standards" and "expertise." But if anyone could claim solid credentials in this milieu, it was Yoko. She did not stumble amateurishly and exploitively into happenings and concept art only after her association with Lennon gave her a worldwide platform; she was deeply involved in such work years before she met him.

At the same time, John was no simple pop star, albeit an impossibly famous one, before he met Yoko. He had already explored avant-garde ideas himself, and it was her artistic influence that clarified his own aspirations and attracted him to her in the first place. Lennon's artistic strivings are well known, in his pun-ridden prose above all. In the recording studio, he had led the Beatles in sonic experimentations and extensions of their basic pop-rock sound, learning the range of tricky alterations that one could work with tape recordings, slowing things down and speeding them up, playing songs backward, turning simple tunes into audio-*vérité* sound collages.

Both John and Yoko were operating within the general spirit of the Sixties, which seemed to make almost anything possible; more than that: *likely*. A wide range of rockers indulged in such experiments, sometimes to conform to what seemed to be the fashion of the moment (cf. *Their Satanic Majesties Request*) but more often out of some kind of earnest, slightly addled determination to create a new world. Such work was not even unique to Lennon within the Beatles: At the same time that John and Yoko were making their avant-garde albums, George Harrison came forth with his *Electronic Sound* LP.

Part of the reason for all this experimenting, to be sure, was that it seemed a logical extension of the drug trips that were fashionable in those days. In the sour aftermath of the Sixties, it is too tempting to think of drug trips in light of the sad burnouts and early deaths that trailed in their wake. But drug-taking was, for many, a genuinely enlightening experience: People had their ears, eyes and minds opened up in ways they hadn't previously imagined.

For all their eagerness, however, rock experimenters lacked roots, in that they weren't always aware of the spiritually similar experiments that had taken place in earlier decades among the literary, and even musical, avant-gardes of Europe and America. And they often lacked the craft to shape their newly liberated imaginations. Too much art rock became clumsy imitation of the classics or shallow vulgarization of real avant-gardists or cynical exploitation of teenagers' seemingly endless capacity to be blown away by the obvious. John Lennon was too clever to be that crude. But it took Yoko to bring out his tendencies fully for both liberated expression and primal self-indulgence.

Avant-garde artists tend not to come from the streets; it's a rich man's—or at least a rich man's child's—game. Yoko fulfilled that specification. She came from what an early résumé called one of "Japan's finest families" and attended an "elite school." She studied music at Sarah Lawrence College and creative writing at Harvard, all in the mid-Fifties.

By the late Fifties, she had already made a name for herself in downtown Manhattan avant-garde circles. She gave concerts, made films, read poetry, painted, sculpted and staged ever more elaborate "events." She was a name.

It is not surprising that she was attracted to rock & roll, quite apart from her personal fascination with John. The connections between avant-gardism and hip popular music go back at least as far as the Beatniks reading to jazz. The connections between serious artists and venturesome rockers were common in London and New York in the late Sixties—the Velvet Underground—and have flowered since: One need only think of Patti Smith, Brian Eno and the Talking Heads. Avant-gardists have been attracted to rock in part as a way of purging themselves of isolation and pretension, and Yoko was no exception. "I suddenly realized that my Music of the Mind was getting too Zen, too finished, and I was suffocating, as if I were in an ivory tower and there was nowhere to go," Yoko told Jonathan Cott soon after she met John. "People were silent. I felt the lack of a sense of humor. John was doing this healthy beat music, and I got stimulated with that."

It is difficult to explain or excuse vanguard art to those who don't know it or can't stand it. To them, it can seem like deliberate provocation, with its apparently tedious length, deafening volume, aggressive behavior toward an innocent audience and other unpleasantries. There are such artists and such pieces—literal-minded extensions of Brecht's alienation theory into the realm of actual assault. But more frequently a hostile audience will mistake entirely benign intentions for provocation.

Post-Cagean artists, in many mediums, many still active in the Eighties, are hard to describe in simple, all-purpose terms, but a few generalizations can be ventured. The influence of Far Eastern meditative ideas was common and clearly contributed to Ono's cachet in this circle. There was a widespread belief that techniques and traditions in the Western arts had grown too complex and constraining: Artists wanted to strip technique down to the basics and if they later built it back up again, it was on their own terms. As part of their flouting of received traditions, they often experimented from medium to medium, enlivening one art form with ideas from another. As a result, for instance, musicians in Lower Manhattan often have more in common with downtown dancers and painters than with uptown composers. There is less of an emphasis downtown on the making of masterpieces than on the discovery of an interesting, suggestive process; audiences are willing to accept good intentions even if those intentions are not realized in some final, finished form.

In the Sixties, all of this was allied with religious, political and social idealism that made, for a brief time, the most extravagant utopianism seem perfectly plausible. Romantic artists have often been political idealists, however naive; they honestly believe that if they can make good, fresh, healthy art, society will be transformed. Today, this same sort of art still exists, but in a less optimistic and outward-looking way. The transcendence of avant-gardists now is almost all inward, in the arena of mystical enlightenment.

The experience for an audience at such an event, for those who are sympathetic to the presuppositions of this art, can be deeply moving. The very lack of busily crafted detail can be a relief; once one gets attuned to "minimalism," normal art can seem overstuffed and rhetorical. Part of what Cage, who still counts as the father figure of contemporary American avant-gardism, tries to say in his many books is that it is up to the audience to create along with the artist. The artist offers up a part of the experience; the sympathetic observer, his sensibility heightened and tuned, completes the bargain.

That is what John and Yoko meant by the term "unfinished music," which they applied to the first two of their album collaborations. As Yoko put it to Cott at the time: "If you listen to it, maybe you can add to it or change it or edit or add something in your mind. The unfinished part that's not in the record —what's in you, not what's in the record—is what's important. The record is just there to stimulate what's in you, to make it come out."

The three John and Yoko albums must be perceived as part of a larger process of avant-garde collaboration and documentation by the two. At the time of her *Season of Glass* LP in 1981, Yoko said, "Everything I've done has always been directly autobiographical," and that certainly applies to these discs from the late Sixties. They are all aural home movies, in a more or less direct way, of happenings and events that stretched over longer periods of time and involved theatrics, visuals and political statements that go far beyond the conventional idea of "a record"; most of them were also accompanied by films shot at the time of their recording. As such, they don't make for easy listening; they are, instead, catalysts for thought.

The first, *Two Virgins*, is the most complex and appealing. It is best known because of its nude cover art and its brown-bag outer jacket. For John and Yoko, nudity was a challenge to a stuffy and overserious society, a statement about innocence and openness and a talisman of trust between them. The record itself was a pure improvisation made at dawn in a studio, with John providing the nonvocal sounds, Yoko singing and yowling in her brittle way, and both offering up occasional snatches of conversation and dialogue. There is a coherent flow to side one lacking on the more fragmentary side two, but both are of a piece in terms of mood—a bucolic, gentle time, a bit of nostalgia, perhaps, for John's parents and past, a "good trip."

The instrumentals that John provides blend rhythmically lulling tape-looped bird calls; filtered guitar and piano sounds; snatches of records—mostly trad jazz and Victorian ballads—and consoling church-organ effects. The filtering, distortion and looping come from the manipulation of two tape recorders. Yoko's vocalizing sounds a bit intrusive here and there but generally contributes to the childlike mood.

The first side of *Life with the Lions* is another matter: This "bad trip" is a deliberate evocation and exorcism of their own darkness and violence. Innocently entitled "Cambridge 1969," it offers Yoko and John at their most grating, Yoko in particular. After a typical girlish spoken introduction, Yoko sets to howling in her most abrasive manner. Some interesting timbral effects emerge. But unlike, say, Meredith Monk's more recent vocal experiments, the effect is more emotionally cathartic for her than aesthetically engrossing for us. John accompanies with guitar feedback that is nearly as hard to take. But then, almost at the end, the music suddenly sweetens into fragments from another generation, played on the saxophone. It is another remembrance of things sadly dead and gone, and the effect is unexpected and moving.

The other side is more varied. The most curious bit is two minutes of silence, broken only by whatever imperfections fleck a given record's surface; the intention and results seem the same as Cage's "4′ 33″," although a record is less likely to compel attention than a formal concert. The rest consists of a stream-of-conscious a cappella song by Yoko, a recording of the heartbeat of the child she subsequently miscarried, and some staticky fussing with a radio. It is not all that riveting.

The *Wedding Album* has another unbroken first side: alternating cries and whispers of "John" and "Yoko" over a thudding heartbeat. The idea may sound like self-indulgence at its most extreme and, of course, it is that. It is also fascinating for the range of emotion it encompasses and curiously touching. Side two is nearly all documentation of bed-ins for peace: John and Yoko explaining why they're doing what they're doing to bemused members of the press; John ordering breakfast from room service; life going on; snatches of song.

Just how one should rank these records next to the more conventionally pop-rocking John-and-Yoko collaborations is hard to say, just as it is difficult to compare them to other, less world-famous avant-gardists. To this taste, too many of Yoko's own pop experiments, while often unusual and forward-looking, are undercut by a singing voice that is just horrendous on any but novelty terms. In the ambience of the avant-garde, that peculiarity is less of a problem, although still a limitation. And there can be no denying the fecundity of her imagination.

John, in turn, was, at heart, a rock & roller until the moment he died. His avant-gardism never quite rings true; there's too much anger and passionate practicality right below the artsy affectations. Yet some of the Beatles collages in which he had a guiding hand, and especially the gentle dream world of *Two Virgins*, suggest that he had a deep and genuine gift for affectionate aural evocation rooted in precise, concrete detail. Whether this was quite so avant-garde as Yoko had in mind doesn't matter so much as that it was she who inspired him in the first place. But before he could realize that gift, they had moved on to other collaborations, and now it is too late.

All three of their avant-garde collaborations that remain have moments of magic. And on perhaps the deepest level at which they were meant to be taken —as aural records of two people's lives together—they are beyond challenge. If you care for John and Yoko, if, through their lives or art they *made* you care, then you must hear this work.

GIMME SOME TRUTH:
THE SONGS OF JOHN LENNON

By Stephen Holden

HE night after John Lennon was murdered, I happened to attend the Broadway musical *Evita*. At the curtain call, the show's star, Patti LuPone, asked for a moment of silence for the slain ex-Beatle. Other than as a simple gesture of respect, it surprised me at first. While I couldn't think of a single rock & roll genre —from the most conservative crooning to the most radical punk rock—that hadn't drawn a good deal of inspiration from Lennon, I didn't quite understand this tribute from the Great White Way. Bruce Springsteen, launching into a turbulent "Twist and Shout" from a Philadelphia stage that same night, made perfect sense. But *Evita*? As I stood there, I began to realize the extent of John Lennon's artistic influence—that, even on Broadway (whose aesthetics are, for the most part, diametrically opposed to everything Lennon stood for), he'd made some kind of mark that would not or could not be forgotten. Indeed, without Lennon's early and bold fusion of politics and pop, a play like *Evita*, in which Ché Guevara is a major character, probably wouldn't exist. Truly, the man's stamp was everywhere.

More than any other rock musician (with the possible exception of Bob Dylan), John Lennon personalized the political and politicized the personal, often making the two stances interchangeable but sometimes ripping out the seams altogether. Both Lennon and Dylan manipulated the style and form of popular music as it suited them, challenging bourgeois notions about the place and purpose of art, by making pop culture intellectually respectable. Both were torn between the traditional idea of art as an artifact and the modernist notion of art as event. But, whereas Dylan expressed his personal and political iconoclasm mainly by expanding and exploding the narrative line (thus forcing the melody to accommodate a torrent of language and imagery), Lennon assaulted pop music from a dozen different directions.

John Lennon believed passionately that popular music could and should do more than merely entertain and, by acting out this conviction, he changed the face of rock & roll forever. By taking such huge risks he sometimes failed or seemed silly. Yet, in retrospect, even his failures take on the glow of nobility: The fact that he *cared* so much shines through his occasional shortcomings.

For Lennon popular music was an intellectual and moral platform for discussing the large questions that troubled his generation—the Vietnam War and the capitalist system, personal freedom and sexual equality and, ultimately, the future of humanity. He accepted the responsibilities the counterculture handed him and set about making the world a gentler, more peaceable place. Even though his commitment to radical causes had all but evaporated by the end of the Seventies, what Lennon stood for, both as a Beatle and an ex-Beatle, ultimately transcended issues. Inspired and encouraged by his wife, Yoko Ono, he was rock music's supreme solipsist—someone whose art and life were so inextricably bound that they were practically indistinguishable. The public response to his assassination in December 1980 was overwhelming testimony to the fact that Lennon still had the power to influence masses of people by simply being who he was—a utopian dreamer with extraordinary artistic gifts who believed in giving power to the people, in giving peace a chance.

From the first, it was apparent to anyone with ears that both Lennon and the Beatles were originals. The full force of Lennon's solo artistry first emerged in December 1970, with the release of *John Lennon / Plastic Ono Band*, the landmark album in which he repudiates the Beatles' mystique and bares his soul with a shattering honesty. This primal shocker didn't come out of the blue. In November 1968, the same month that saw the release of the Beatles' White Album, John Lennon and his new love, Yoko Ono, had put out the first of three experimental LPs, *Unfinished Music No. 1: Two Virgins*. This aural-vérité collage of random noise, conversation and experimental music is a record of their courtship and is best known for the cover art—a photo of the couple naked, which was deemed scandalous by many. A second experimental album, *Unfinished Music No. 2: Life with the Lions*, which deals in part with Ono's miscarriage, was released the following May and, in October 1969, *Wedding Album*, in which the newlyweds repeat each other's names against a background of amplified heartbeats, was released.

Even though this trilogy of experimental works alienated many, it stands as a significant prologue to Lennon's solo career, for it demonstrates the profound artistic influence of Ono.

Her influence would be lasting, but at the same time Lennon's solo artistry reasserted his allegiance to rock & roll, perhaps in reaction to the flowery psychedelia of the Beatles' late period. On *The Plastic Ono Band—Live Peace in Toronto 1969*, in which he was backed by a pickup band that included guitarist Eric Clapton, Lennon delivered blistering renditions of "Blue Suede Shoes,"

"Money" and "Dizzy Miss Lizzie" as well as powerful versions of two singles from the period—"Cold Turkey," a bleak, scary evocation of heroin addiction, and "Give Peace a Chance," his first and most stirring piece of street music. "Give Peace a Chance" was a perfect marriage of conceptual art and pop politics, a collective mantra, a pop hit and a slogan that cajoled rather than demanded. In early 1970, "Instant Karma! (We All Shine On)," a pounding Phil Spector-produced single, featured Lennon at his aphoristic best. This triumphant hit turned the pop cliché that everyone's a star into a stomping rock hymn and spiced it with a double-edged spiritual zinger—"Instant Karma's gonna get you."

Later that year came *John Lennon / Plastic Ono Band*, the artist's greatest album. Lennon the acolyte, the hard rocker and the crafty sloganeer finally blended to create one of the greatest, most prophetic rock albums of the decade —despite, or maybe because of, its monumental self-centeredness and the fact that it confronted a specific moment of pop cultural history. The stark, formal production, which features Lennon on guitars and piano, Ringo Starr on drums and Klaus Voormann on bass, enhances the dark eloquence of Lennon's graffiti-like songs. While the album has its moments of tenderness—the aphoristic "Love," the wavering "Hold On John" and "Look at Me"—its dominant mood is one of frustrated rage, as Lennon, catalyzed by primal-scream therapy, confronts the terrors of his past and relives the traumas of parental absence and childhood pain. It's an album that had no precedent in rock & roll.

In "Mother," a toweringly gloomy reminiscence of his love-starved child-hood, Lennon howls the final refrain—"Mama don't go / Daddy come home"— in a devastatingly powerful, pseudo-infantile squall. And in "Well Well Well," the other primal-screamer, he daringly equates his childhood agony with the adult dilemma of being both a political radical and a rich rock star. The sneaky blues song, "I Found Out," the vengefully atheistic "God" and the Dylan-styled acoustic ballad, "Working Class Hero," balance these stylized tantrums with rationalized anger. Though Lennon had already mocked the counter-culture while still a Beatle (the White Album's "Glass Onion" and "Sexy Sadie" had criticized the hippie dream world and the Maharishi Mahesh Yogi) he had never used such stinging vitriol. "I Found Out" sneers at hippies and gurus. "God" sermonizes against all creeds with its shouted-out list of "don't believes"—culminating with "Elvis, Zimmerman and Beatles"—and the shat-tering admission, "The dream is over." "Working Class Hero," the album's subtlest and most melodic song, drew a bleak picture of English working-class life. This relentless excoriation of the socialization process portrays individuals as systematically degraded and terrorized by institutions until they become self-deluded cogs, numbed by fear, "doped with religion and sex and TV," in a death-dealing social machine run by the rich. If the song seems even more pertinent today than it did a decade ago, it also transcends the issues of class with which it so fervently deals. There is tenderness, sadness and maybe envy here: One gets the feeling that John Lennon wanted to be a working-class hero but that his money and celebrity had made it impossible.

While *John Lennon / Plastic Ono Band* was an anomaly it set off shock waves that are still being felt. Unprecedented in its soul-baring candor, it paved the way for Paul Simon's and Joni Mitchell's dour confessional masterpieces, *Paul Simon* and *Blue* and, eventually, for Bob Dylan's *Blood on the Tracks*. The atheism of "God" found a powerful reprise in Randy Newman's cynical and sophisticated "God's Song (That's Why I Love Mankind)," while the child-like riddles of "Love" were echoed years later in Stevie Wonder's passionate pop-soul ballad, "Love's in Need of Love Today." The album's musical stark-ness and mood of sustained rage also anticipated the punk-rock blast of the late Seventies, although Lennon's despair never came close to outright nihilism.

Imagine (1971) didn't cut to the bone like its predecessor did, but it is an excellent record that restored some of the hope the first album had stripped. Yoko Ono's warming influence is much more evident and producer Phil Spec-tor's famous "wall of sound" gives *Imagine* a plush aural glow in keeping with its more generous spirit. Though there are bitter moments (the punning, anti-Nixon diatribe, "Gimme Some Truth" and the notorious attack on Paul McCartney, "How Do You Sleep?"), Lennon's petulance is outweighed by his sweetness. In two wrenching ballads, "Jealous Guy" and "Oh Yoko!" he touchingly exposes his need for an all-embracing maternal love.

But the album's masterpiece is "Imagine," the most complete artistic and philosophical statement Lennon made as a solo artist. Like "Instant Karma!" and "Love," "Imagine" is a perfect blend of aphorism and pop as well as a masterful exercise of conceptual artistic strategy. By asking people to envisage a utopian world with no religious, political or material strife, Lennon entices the listener into joining him in a communal prayer. This dreamlike invitation floats on Lennon's most seductive tune, an ethereal lullaby that the production draws out with strings and rippling keyboard figures. But, ultimately, the song's underlying sadness implies Lennon's doubt that this age-old dream might ever be realized.

Having dredged the past in *John Lennon / Plastic Ono Band* and the present in *Imagine*, Lennon boldly turned his attention to street politics with *Some Time in New York City* (1972). Made with the leftist bar band, Elephant's Memory, this was John and Yoko's first nonexperimental album. (It was a direct attempt to reach the people; but the simplicity of its music and lyrics was something of an experiment.) *Some Time in New York City* was a paean to their adopted city. It imitated the form and style of a radical newspaper, with the couple sharing songwriting credits and editorializing for a slate of politically correct causes, including Irish independence, women's liberation and Angela Davis. Unfortunately, the verses are pure agitprop, with Lennon's anti-male-chauvinist anthem "Woman Is the Nigger of the World" a typical example of the album's forced rhetoric.

After this well-meaning failure, Lennon's music turned less overtly political once again. While neither *Mind Games* (1973) nor *Walls and Bridges* (1974), his last two LPs of original material before his five-year withdrawal from the pop life, broke new ground, each contains its share of tunefulness and humor. *Mind Games*, which came out the same month the Lennons began a year-and-a-half-long separation, is an uneven work, whose title cut is its strongest track. Restating the aesthetic principles behind the song "Imagine," this time more didactically, *Mind Games* says simply that imagining something—like peace on earth—is the first and essential step toward making it happen. It was, to quote Lennon, "playing the mind guerrilla." The album's other highlight, the rockabilly novelty, "Tight A$," echoes the cheeky, strutting style of Lennon's mid-Sixties Beatles songs.

Walls and Bridges is melodically stronger and emotionally bleaker. Separated from Yoko, Lennon's anguish welled up again in the abjectly remorseful "Going Down on Love," and also in "Nobody Loves You (When You're Down and Out)" and "Scared." The album spawned two hits, "Whatever Gets You Thru the Night" (a catchy duet with Elton John) and "#9 Dream," a hauntingly surreal evocation of eternity that echoes Lennon's late Beatles masterpiece, "Across the Universe."

The basic tracks for *Rock 'n' Roll* (1975), Lennon's last album before his five-year retreat, were laid down in 1973, a year and a half before he completed the record. Here, Lennon reasserts his rock & roll roots with fierce performances of classic hard rockers like "Be-Bop-A-Lula," "Ain't That a Shame," "Do You Want to Dance" and "Sweet Little Sixteen," as well as touching renditions of the ballads "Just Because" and "Stand by Me." The album's major flaw is Phil Spector's turgid production; this time his "wall of sound" blunts the incisiveness of Lennon's vocals and drags down the material.

Shaved Fish, a compilation of the Plastic Ono Band's "greatest hits," also appeared in 1975. In addition to several hit album tracks, it collected the singles "Cold Turkey," "Power to the People" (the Black Panther slogan done as a street chant à la "Give Peace a Chance"), "Instant Karma!" and "Happy Xmas (War Is Over)."

Through all his ups and downs, John Lennon never abandoned two basic assumptions about pop music and his relation to it, assumptions that others began to question as the decade wore on. In the wake of *John Lennon / Plastic Ono Band*, the deluge of confessional singer/songwriters harping on their personal problems began to give pop solipsism a bad reputation. And as the individual ex-Beatles released an uneven succession of solo projects, the group's mystique tarnished somewhat. The mythic heroism the counterculture had invested in rock stars was beginning to seem quaintly naive. None of this seemed to faze Lennon, however. On his return to recording in 1980, he appeared fully confident that his five years out of the limelight hadn't significantly diminished his audience or altered his status as the symbolic spokesman for the rock culture's lingering utopian yearnings. For in denouncing the Beatles' mystique so vociferously a decade earlier, Lennon had shrewdly appropriated most of that mystique for himself. In "God," the only thing Lennon hadn't denounced was his own world. "I just believe in me / Yoko and me / And that's reality," he had proclaimed.

Double Fantasy, an equal collaboration with Yoko Ono, presents the Lennons' marriage as an exemplary pop fairy tale with fourteen songs, seven each by John and Yoko, sequenced as a his-and-hers dialogue. Lennon's contributions to *Double Fantasy*—easily his strongest songs since *Imagine*—were recorded with a fine aural clarity by producer Jack Douglas, working with top New York sessionmen.

In one sense, *Double Fantasy* literally fulfills the dream of "Imagine" by describing a real utopia. If it wasn't the angelic global village Lennon had originally envisaged, the blissfully cocoonlike existence Lennon's songs evoke represents a compelling microcosm of that utopia. Lennon's music maintained its characteristic balance between lean rock & roll—"(Just Like) Starting Over," "I'm Losing You," "Cleanup Time"—and childlike postpsychedelic ballads—"Beautiful Boy," "Woman." And his voice never sounded stronger. The same twisting, corkscrew guitar lines that nailed down his proclamations in "I Found Out" and "Well Well Well" snarled through "I'm Losing You," a howl of primal dread.

In the conventional political sense, *Double Fantasy* seems monumentally (and, to its detractors, monstrously) irrelevant. But within its own frame, *Double Fantasy* is as intransigently passionate and potentially subversive as Lennon's best earlier work. For Lennon sang and wrote about domestic life with the same intensity as he had once addressed social issues. What was maddening to some but inspiring to many more was the gleeful relish he took in his personal happiness and the almost triumphant tone with which he dismissed his past selves in order to live more fully in the present. In the album's reflective masterpiece, "Watching the Wheels," he almost boasts of having lost touch with issues: "I'm just sitting here watching the wheels go round and round / I really love to watch them roll / No longer riding on the merry-go-round / I just had to let it go."

Because John Lennon had built his career on being his own best example, *Double Fantasy* presents an exemplary portrait of perfect heterosexual union. Earlier in the decade, perhaps, this portrait might have spurred controversy, for the ideal marriage the Lennons flaunted was certainly unconventional, with the happy househusband "aboard the magic ship of perfect harmony," content to sing the joys of housework and fathering while "the queen is in the counting house." And in "Woman," "Dear Yoko" and "I'm Losing You," Lennon also expresses a dependence on his wife that, in its vulnerable, childlike worshipfulness, is the antithesis of traditional machismo. Such reverence involves a mutual submergence of ego within a profoundly matriarchal setting. In this environment, Lennon could finally have the idyllic childhood he'd always wanted.

The ideal of true love hadn't been on the agenda of the rock counterculture. Ending the war and the pursuit of all sorts of "liberation" had seemed far more urgent. But by 1980, with second-generation rock idols like Bruce Springsteen and Jackson Browne exalting monogamy in songs like "Two Hearts" and "Hold Out," the ideal loomed as more than a revived pop-music panacea. As the sexual revolution's failure to make people's lives demonstrably happier became increasingly apparent, monogamy became a legitimate subject for serious rock music. But the trouble with Springsteen's and Browne's exhortations was their vagueness. And Bob Dylan, rock music's only other mythically heroic prophet figure, had chosen Jesus. It was John Lennon who had the most convincing answers about love, for he had the happy family to hold up as evidence. But, true to form, his vision of marriage remained iconoclastic, even revolutionary, in its style.

"All you need is love," Lennon had once proclaimed and in 1980 he was living by that slogan. But as it turned out, he was only half right. Love didn't stop the bullet that killed him but it did keep him happy while he was alive. And after his death, the dreams, and the double fantasies lived on in some of the most powerful and moving rock music ever created.

THE OTHER HALF
OF THE SKY:
THE SONGS OF YOKO ONO

By Robert Palmer

т would be a gross understatement to say that until recently few people understood Yoko Ono's music. Few people wanted to. In the aftermath of the Beatles' breakup, she was an easy target, and her records probably stirred up more animosity and drew more critical barbs than the work of any other (nominally) popular artist. How many listeners knew, or cared, that Ono was combining vocal techniques derived from such disparate sources as Japan's traditional kabuki music and Alban Berg's operas? How many knew or cared that this fusion was a logical by-product of her upbringing, which combined traditional Japanese and modern Western elements, or that she had nurtured her art during a performing career of almost ten years' duration before John Lennon brought her to the attention of a wider public? Yoko Ono's records sounded like a woman screaming, and that, as far as most pop listeners were concerned, was that. "It's easier for people to listen to mechanical sounds," Ono commented recently, "than to listen to a woman cry out."

Yoko Ono's five solo albums—*Yoko Ono/Plastic Ono Band* (1970), *Fly* (1971), *Approximately Infinite Universe* (1973), *Feeling the Space* (1973) and *Season of Glass* (1981)—seem to document an avant-garde artist's gradual education in pop music. There are no pop songs on *Yoko Ono/Plastic Ono Band*; each piece is an improvisation, using a variety of extreme vocal techniques, with rock band and (on one selection) free jazz backing. For the most part, *Fly* offers more of the same, but there are a few more or less conventionally structured pop songs— "Midsummer New York," "Mrs. Lennon." *Approximately Infinite Universe* is all songs, but Ono frequently sounds unsure of herself, especially when the music is closest to melodic mainstream pop. On *Feeling the Space*, another album of songs, she sounds much more confident. And *Season of Glass* is the work of a mature pop craftsman.

In a sense, this is an accurate analysis. The conceptual and performance art

Ono was heavily involved in when she met John Lennon and began recording for Apple existed in a rarefied world of art galleries and museums and was the apparent antithesis of popular art. Once she began to concentrate on pop song-writing and to let her avant-garde involvements lapse, Ono did develop a pop sensibility—not all at once but over a period of years. However, there's more to the story of Yoko Ono, avant-gardist-turned-pop-musician, than is immediately apparent. She was a shrieker and a screamer until she met John Lennon and began writing songs, right? Wrong. Some of the more extreme aspects of her vocals on the Apple albums were the result of her choosing to sing against superamplified electric instruments for the first time in her career. When she met John Lennon, she had been writing songs for years; in fact, she was trying to sell some of her songs and was negotiating with Island Records before she decided on Apple. The first single Lennon and Ono made together, "Give Peace a Chance," had an Ono song, "Remember Love," on its flip side.

Nevertheless, most listeners failed to hear the melodic elements in Ono's music and remembered the "crying out." In part, Ono was "crying out" in order to try to make sense of a profound cultural schizophrenia she had been grappling with since she was a child. Her father was Westernized, including his taste in music. Though the career as a concert pianist he had dreamed of never materialized, his musical tastes remained firmly Western; for him, the three Bs —Bach, Beethoven and Brahms—were the be-all and end-all of music, and when Yoko began piano lessons at an early age, the three Bs were prominent in the curriculum. But Ono's mother played "seven or eight" traditional Japanese instruments, she recalls, and was well versed in the courtly traditions of Japan's very different classical music. The cultural schism within the family extended to religion; Yoko's father was Christian, her mother, Buddhist.

In 1953, Yoko and her family moved to Scarsdale, an affluent New York suburb and Yoko enrolled in Sarah Lawrence, where she studied composition. By this time she had long since given up on piano lessons. Her father had told her she might as well, and she recalls the lessons as sheer torture. But she had learned enough about harmony and melody and learned her way around the keyboard sufficiently to be able to write songs easily later in life. After the piano lessons came voice lessons with a German instructor who intended to prepare her for singing lieder and opera, but by this time she was beginning to rebel against these stern artistic disciplines. Her father's reaction to her desire to study composition was that women would never make first-rate composers; becoming fine pianists or singers was the best they could hope for. Yoko thought differently.

At Sarah Lawrence, Yoko met a young Japanese musician and budding composer, Toshi Ichiyanagi. She dropped out of school and they decamped to Lower Manhattan to live in artistic squalor. Yoko found a loft at 112 Chambers Street, where she could compose on a piano, and by the early Sixties she was one of a group of artists who were up to something radically different. Some, like father-figure John Cage and gifted organizer La Monte Young, were primarily composers. Others, like Dick Higgins and Jackson Mac Low, had a particular interest in the written word. Walter De Maria was a sculptor who doubled as drummer with the original Velvet Underground. All of them accepted John Cage's dictum that art could be just about anything one wanted it to be, and most of them ended up giving performances of one sort or another. Some involved music, some body movement, some live-action painting or sculpture, some lights and other visual effects, some mixtures of any or all of the above. In later years, this activity would become known as performance art. In the early Sixties, those performances were generally referred to as "happenings." The artists themselves were loosely banded together as Fluxus, a name thought up by the gallery owner who was their principal patron and catalyst, George Maciunas.

Fluxus was never much more than a conceptual umbrella, a way for George Maciunas to befriend and encourage a select group of artists. One of his favorites was Yoko. He mounted shows of her paintings and other art objects at his gallery. After Yoko presented the initial Fluxus concert series (directed by La Monte Young) at her own loft, Maciunas began presenting Fluxus concerts and events as well. Gradually some of the artists associated with Fluxus began to make names for themselves—Young and Terry Riley as pioneers of musical minimalism, Simone Forti as a dancer, Nam June Paik as a pioneering video artist. And Ono's shows began to move out of smaller, less established galleries and into locations as prestigious as New York's Museum of Modern Art.

Her work was mercurial and could never be pinned down. For one piece she wired her body so that the creaking of her limbs, heavily amplified, made a kind of music. John was first attracted to her work because it seemed to have a positive message and was fun, but Ono was also giving musical performances that were extreme and abrasive. "A lot of my work was about using the human body," she said recently. "The piece with contact microphones on the body, for example, and the singing. There are so many ways of using the throat and the vocal cords; you can use different areas, different parts of the body to express different emotions. As far as influences in my singing, I got a lot of influence from Berg's operas, like his *Lulu*. I think you can hear that very strongly on some of *Approximately Infinite Universe*, and I think I'm still influenced by it. There's also a lot of Japanese kabuki influence, from the old Japanese way of singing. There's one particular kabuki singing style called *hetai*, a kind of storytelling form that's almost like chanting and requires you to strain your voice a bit. I also listened to tapes of my voice playing backward and tried to make sounds like that. And I listened to Indian singing, Tibetan singing . . . all that mixed."

The earliest of Ono's vocal performances on record is "AOS," on *Yoko Ono/*

Plastic Ono Band. It's actually an excerpt from a longer performance that was a collaboration with jazz saxophonist Ornette Coleman (who is heard on trumpet) and his group of the period—Charlie Haden and David Izenson on basses, Charles Moffett on drums. Because of her free-flowing style, Ono had gravitated toward free-style jazz musicians, and "AOS" finds her in a comfortable milieu. She begins with rising slides, reiterated moans and, finally, as the drums come crashing in behind thick bowed basses, some all-out screaming, or "energy playing," as jazz saxophonists like John Coltrane and Albert Ayler used to call such soul-rinsings in those days.

The rest of *Plastic Ono Band* finds Ono backed by Lennon, bassist Klaus Voormann and drummer Ringo Starr. When they fail, they fail with a dull thud. "Why Not" begins with some exotic glottal stops from Yoko and sounds like an obvious inspiration for Kate Pierson and Cindy Wilson of the B-52's, but the rhythm section holds it down with an inappropriate "heavy" shuffle— British blooze with fudged chord changes. On the other hand, "Why" is a staggering success. The driving rhythm sounds like 1980s dance rock, and Lennon outdoes himself with some of the most shattering, abrasive guitar playing of his career. The rest of the record falls somewhere between these two extremes.

Fly featured an inside cover designed by George Maciunas and some home-made instruments courtesy of a Fluxus fellow traveler, Joe Jones. There was also "Toilet Piece," thirty seconds of a toilet flushing—but was it art? The meat of the album is its first side. "Midsummer New York" is a frightening and remarkably adept fusion of Fifties rockabilly and Yoko's vocal extremism, a kind of cross between "Cold Turkey" (with its addiction-withdrawal imagery) and "Heartbreak Hotel." "Mind Train" is a long free-association piece that builds up an impressive head of steam, and on "O'Wind" Lennon unleashes bursts of brittle, dissonant guitar that sound momentarily like free-jazz guitarist Sonny Sharrock or contemporary No Wave guitarist Arto Lindsay. One of the most exciting things about these early albums is the performances they draw from an audibly liberated Lennon—years later he would talk about them with a great deal of pride. But as albums they are uneven. All-out vocal assaults do get wearing, even if one is cognizant of their cultural context. And, as many Fluxus artists have proved over the years, the line between artistic freedom and self-indulgence is a fine one, and easily crossed.

Still, there is plenty of gripping, well-made music on these discs, and Lennon and Ono were taken aback when they met with virtually unanimous disdain. They sound much fresher and make more comfortable listening today, alongside, say, Lydia Lunch and James Chance and DNA. But since the world was very evidently not eager for another album of vocal brinksmanship, and since Ono was beginning to write more songs anyway, her next album, *Approximately Infinite Universe*, was an album of songs. They were a grim lot of songs, on the

whole, full of childhood terrors, rebuffs from lovers, loneliness, suicidal tendencies and the pains of being a woman. On some of them, one can hear Ono
straining to make her voice glide gracefully through the studio-smooth instrumental background. But some performances, particularly the closing "Looking
Over from My Hotel Window," are utterly effective and touching. On *Feeling
the Space*, too, the tone is not always quite right. It's as if Ono had trouble
getting the phrasing and "feel" of all the instruments to contribute to the mood
she was striving for—listen to "Woman of Salem" and "Run, Run, Run" for
example. There are more gripping lyrics here, despite some intrusive didacti-
cism, and the music is finely wrought. But things only come alive when Lennon,
transparently disguised as John O'Cean, contributes some of his stinging guitar
leads, or when Ono's imagery is so nightmarish ("Coffin Car," "Run, Run,
Run") it overcomes the relative blandness and occasional lapses in tone of the
studio band.

When Lennon and Ono reemerged in 1980 with *Double Fantasy*, they expected reactions similar to those that had greeted their earlier collaborations.
Their one previous attempt at contributing songs to the same album had been
the stridently political and much-maligned *Some Time in New York City*, and
when the contents of *Double Fantasy* were first announced in the press, music-
industry cynics joked that record-buyers would probably rerecord the album,
omitting Ono's material.

When reviews began coming in that praised her contributions for being
more up to date and more emotionally compelling than Lennon's, everyone was
surprised, including Lennon and Ono. But there had been a shift in the public's
perception of Ono's vocal mannerisms. The B-52's and other New Wave groups
had popularized some of her more extravagant effects by placing them in a more
alluring pop-song context. Ono had changed, too. She had learned to say what
she had to say in songs that were telegraphically urgent but also finely crafted,
with instrumental riffs, lead lines and solos that sported an attractive lyricism
and were well suited to her more conventional but still distinctive singing. In
effect, Ono and the popular audience had met each other halfway. Songs like
"Give Me Something," "I'm Moving On" and especially "Kiss Kiss Kiss" did
not sound dramatically different from much of the music that was popular in
rock discos, and these songs were heard frequently in the discos, while Lennon's
songs conquered AM and FM radio, as expected.

Tragically, Yoko Ono's pop masterpiece is the single she had finished the
night John Lennon was murdered. "Walking on Thin Ice" begins as a pounding
dance track and a statement of uncertainty and danger, and somehow these
apparently disparate elements dramatically reinforce each other. Yoko's nursery
tale of the girl walking across a frozen lake is chilling, and Lennon's guitar solo
—he sat in the studio, hammering on the instrument as hard as he could and
gesturing to coproducer Jack Douglas to brutally pull its tremolo bar every four

beats—is a masterpiece. Lennon was saying before he died that "Walking on Thin Ice" represented the beginning of a new phase in Lennon-Ono music, but it was not to be.

"She Gets Down on Her Knees," on *Season of Glass*, approaches the power of "Walking on Thin Ice." The rest of the record is a report from grief and delirium, though most of the songs were written some years before the tragedy. What emerges is a pop songwriter who has finally learned to channel her anxieties and frustrations—her cultural schizophrenia, the strictness of her father, her years as an artistic rebel—through finely modulated pop-song forms. Parts of the album are positively brilliant—the sweet cooing of "Nobody Sees Me Like You Do," the dirty edge of "Dogtown," the forthright treatment of sexual revulsion in "No, No, No"—and it is never less than gripping. But one remembers "Walking on Thin Ice" and longs for something more, for that final edge of greatness. That is undoubtedly asking too much, especially now. In time, it may come. It seems strange, but Yoko Ono is a forty-eight-year-old pop singer and songwriter who may be just beginning to realize her full potential.

DOUBLE FANTASY:
PORTRAIT OF
A RELATIONSHIP

By Robert Christgau

N late 1966 John Lennon attended a preview by New York avant-gardist Yoko Ono at a chic new London gallery run by Marianne Faith-full's ex-husband. Lennon, who spent a lot of time back then guessing which of the red lights in his "nothing box" would flash next, was intrigued by what he saw, especially the £200 apple (watch it de-compose) and the ladder-and-telescope (pointed at the one-word message YES). When he was introduced to the artist, who had never heard of him, she handed him a card that said BREATHE. They next ran into each other at a Claes Oldenburg exhibit. Soon John had received a copy of *Grapefruit*, Yoko's book of conceptual-art koans, and agreed to contribute work to a John Cage project. The following June he backed the artist's new show, a roomful of furniture cut precisely in half, which she entitled "Yoko Plus Me." John was too shy (para-noid? ambivalent? skeptical? smitten?) to attend.

At this point I should acknowledge my dependence on secondary sources that aren't entirely reliable, even (or especially) when the primary source is the principals. It's bad enough that the only people who can be sure of what goes on in a marriage are the wife and husband; what's worse is that all too often the spouses don't really know either and, if they do, they may prefer to keep it to themselves. So it's quite possible that Ringo was the only Beatle name Yoko knew—that's how it was for many basically indifferent Americans in late 1966. But since couples do tend to mythologize their own beginnings, the tale would be tempting even if it stretched the facts a little. There is in any case a different version of the First Meeting—Yoko's, in which John refuses to pay five shillings to hammer a nail into a board, electing instead to pay nothing and work with an imaginary one. As Yoko told an interviewer: "It's so symbolic you see; the virginal board, for a man to hammer a nail in." So symbolic. It was eighteen months before John hammered a real symbolic nail in, at the dawning of a day that followed a night of tape-collaging in John's

Weybridge mansion. The tape was eventually released as an album whose jacket, nude self-photographs of the couple front and back, caused quite a stir. The title, as you may recall, was *Two Virgins*. So symbolic.

Thus began a marriage in which two compulsive artists took all the therapeutic bromides about creative relationships further than any therapist ever intended them to go. Other couples have been as deeply involved, though, after they'd been together only a year, Derek Taylor estimated (somewhat hyperbolically) that they'd already spent as much time together in one year as most husbands and wives do in fifty. But John and Yoko did more than expend unimaginable amounts of psychic energy on each other—they also took it upon themselves to present their mutual effort to the world. The marriage was Yoko's overarching concept, the masterwork of John's maturity as surely as the group was of his youth.

In a way, this revived an old role for John, who in 1963 and 1964 was known as "the married Beatle." His wife Cynthia was one of those reassuringly out-of-synch details that made the Beatles such a powerful idea—a pretty blond art student, she may have put one Beatle off limits (yeah, sure), but she also gave the girls something to strive for. Who knew that John had only tied the knot because he'd knocked up this very model of the hip young modern mom? And who knew that she was only a transitional symbol, soon to be outflanked by the liberated chick and the hippie earth mother? Needless to say, she also proved transitional for John, who always went with the zeitgeist or vice versa. Nor did this surprise anyone familiar with the facts. John was married to the Beatles; on his wife he fucked around. Not flagrantly, to be sure; he even kept "Norwegian Wood" inconclusive so Cyn wouldn't figure it out. Yet though she never caught on until the verse of their bitter breakup, she knew her dreams had not come true: "I didn't blame John or Yoko. I understood their love. I knew I couldn't fight the unity of mind and body that they had with each other. I had after all subconsciously prepared myself for what happened. But the implementation of their love for each other was without feeling for anyone else at the time. Their all-consuming love had no time for pain or unhappiness."

John's fans, even those who thought of themselves as far out, were astonished and dismayed when the most famous group member in the world merged with the obscure avant-gardist. But such single-minded involvement was just as surprising in Yoko. She'd been married twice—first to a Japanese pianist, then to an American filmmaker, both of whom had it at least as hard as Cynthia Lennon—and she identified with various New York art cliques. But the Fluxus Group, say, obviously didn't swallow up personal identity the way the Beatles did. Like so many of those drawn to the artistic life, Yoko had always felt "alone," and with her enigmatic manner, "John Rennon's Excrusive Gloupie" (to cite a charming *Esquire* title of the period) came across inscrutable at best and aloofly manipulative at worst. Her cool self-sufficiency, her apparent confidence that she was as worthy of the spotlight as the hero she'd bewitched, made all her other shortcomings—her age, her race, her gender, the wide-eyed stranger-than-fiction impassivity of her work, and her failure to resemble Jean Shrimpton—doubly distressing.

Yoko resented the pop world's suspicions keenly, but she didn't let them faze her. Her "inordinate flair for self-publicity"—to quote Philip Norman, one of the many suspicious middlebrows who've been overimpressed with it— didn't equal that of Warhol, or Charlotte Moorman, or her Japanese-born contemporary Kusama, also adherents of the Duchampian avant-garde creed in which provocation becomes the *sine qua non* of the artistic act; for the most part, Yoko's stunts never reached outside the modest ambit of New York's loft bohemia. But in London she'd been a hit, and when she found the Beatles' more expansive pallette at her disposal she didn't hesitate to put it to work. John was trying to harness his inchoate fame well before he got involved with Yoko —hence the "All You Need Is Love" telecast, hence Apple itself—but it was only after their hookup that he began to exploit himself as an art star. Because the pair were inseparable, Yoko became a professional celebrity along with him, and inevitably their devotion became the subtext of everything they did. Beneath the acorn plantings, the bag events, the erection movies, the three "unfinished" album collaborations and the naive rhetoric of the bed-ins—not to mention John's erotic lithographs and such putative Beatle songs as "I Want You (She's So Heavy)" and "The Ballad of John and Yoko"—was the image of a couple in love replacing that of a group in magical cooperative union.

Even at best, however, the public image is an elusive aesthetic mode, and its vagueness was compounded in the case of John-and-Yoko by the stylistic habits of the principals, who—despite surface appearances—resembled each other as artists. Without doubt, certain polarities—East vs. West, Duchamp vs. Berry —did enrich their synthesis. But the magnetism of opposites-attract wasn't the only force that pulled the Japanese avant-dilettante and the Liverpool super-bloke into the first passionate monogamous attachment of their lives. They shared a rather naive, self-absorbed fecundity, undercut with sly humor, artless play elements and a tendency to erupt in anger and pain. Like so many Sixties heroes, they were attracted to direct expression and enjoyed outrage for its own sake. They were unsophisticated ideologically. And neither had much interest in the concrete—compare Yoko's gnomic *Grapefruit* to John Cage's paradoxically eloquent *Silence*, or John's allusive "Strawberry Fields Forever" to the nostalgic detail of Paul McCartney's "Penny Lane." All of which means that they weren't especially inclined to let us know exactly what the relationship they'd created was like day to day. At around the time *Grapefruit* was republished in 1970—with a new "Introduction": "Hi! My name is John Lennon / I'd like you to meet Yoko Ono"—*John Lennon's Diary* also appeared. Most of its entries read like this: "Got up. Fucked wife. Watched telly. Went to bed."

Bagism in New York City, 1969.

Yet the image of John-and-Yoko proved prophetic and long-lasting. When they went public in mid-1968, the only visible pop-music couple was Billy Vera & Judy Clay, who'd scored a doomed interracial one-shot early that year. By the time of *Imagine* and *Fly*, barely three years later, Delaney & Bonnie were already on the brink of d-i-v-o-r-c-e, Ike & Tina Turner's sexy hassled-pimp and triumphant-whore routine had peaked pop, Sonny & Cher were readying their terrifying parody of suburban bliss for the TV-rock market, and Paul Mc-Cartney, of all people, had formed a new group around the amateur keyboard player who wore his ring. In short, John Lennon had once again gone with the zeitgeist or vice versa, only this time he didn't end up staring at a nothing box. There was something there. John-and-Yoko may have been short on texture and filigree—Delaney & Bonnie offered a fuller sense of what married life is actually like, while Ike & Tina and Sonny & Cher drew very educational cartoons, and let us not forget George Jones & Tammy Wynette. But, as was so often true of Lennon, the work made up in feeling, and with luck durability, what it lacked in technical finesse, and after three years it had recognizable contours.

First of all, John and Yoko were absolutes in each other's lives—their love subsumed even art, even peace. Happily-ever-after mythology notwithstanding, this sort of mutual obsession is very uncommon. Most people don't want it or can't do it—a rare synthesis of childlike neediness and the strength of character we mislabel autonomy is required. Only a couple who share work are likely to bring it off and, while wealth isn't a prerequisite, money certainly can help dispel the drudgery and distraction that wither so many great romances. So there was no way for John-and-Yoko to aim for the verisimilitude of Delaney & Bonnie—they didn't *know* what married life was actually like. And it really was Yoko who broke up the Beatles—or rather, the unwillingness of the other three to welcome her aboard as the fifth. When it was over, John summed up his new world view quite succinctly: "I just believe in me / Yoko and me / And that's reality."

As co-absolutes—especially given Yoko's will to independence and our old friend the zeitgeist—John and Yoko were theoretical equals. But up against the theory went eons of male chauvinism and tons of fame, all concentrated in one very bright no-longer-a-lad from Liverpool who towered over his diminutive wife at five-foot-eleven and couldn't stop himself from interrupting her in interviews. John meant it when he claimed Yoko as an equal—as much as anything, he fell in love with her because she was like a bloke, and out of reach of cameras and microphones it's likely that he deferred to his wife a lot more than most husbands do. But he didn't defer enough, in public or in private. Nothing in John's cultural conditioning or star privilege had prepared him to put an equal marriage into practice, and as millions of men learned in the Seventies, there's a big difference between meaning it and living it, between disavowing power and actually doing without. Anyway, even if living it had come easy, the world was going to take a lot of convincing. He and Yoko could have collaborated until they were sixty-four, released albums on simultaneous schedule in perpetuity, and she still would have been perceived as his appendage.

Yet the marriage changed him more drastically than her. Granted, it may only seem so because Yoko's previous identity remains cloudy; certainly no one noticed at the time, so accustomed were we to the mutations of rock stars and so much faith did we place in this one. But where in 1967 John had been the avant-garde Beatle by default—the others just didn't have the stuff—by the end of 1968 he'd earned the title. This wasn't just a matter of a lot of confusing "experimental" work, either—Yoko had opened him up, so that he began to move away from the sidelong punning and aggressive wit that had become his trademark toward the naked rock & roll emotionality that was the other half of his gift. And unlike so many other prophets of pretentiousness, he never retreated into simple-minded hippie positivism. Next to George Harrison's doltish gurumania, for instance, John's Yoko-derived post-Maharishi Oriental-ism, complete with a vegetarian-to-macrobiotic regime that included lots of caviar once the rigors of Diet No. 7 were past, seemed quite intellectual. Veteran of a thousand acid trips, John could come on like a psychedelic asshole, but once he'd rejected the Maharishi he was never ashamed to act the working-class hero as well—principled and combative at best, with a serious mean streak when he got riled.

At Tittenhurst Park, early 1970.

Most important, John's politics, always half a function of his big mouth, took a turn to the left when he and Yoko (hardly a rad herself) dedicated their celebrity, which is to say their lives, to "peace." Never mind that their ideas were in a real sense reactionary, impossibly idealistic philosophically and tactically; never mind that by giving peace a chance they also gave legions of fuzzy-wuzzies a permanent copout. Simply by politicizing their fame, they changed the way their audience and colleagues thought about conscience. And if it seems arbitrary to credit Yoko with a propaganda campaign waged entirely in the first-person plural, remember that information dispersal was her specialty. There was, after all, a difference between her art and John's even more fundamental than Berry-vs.-Duchamp—she had to get it out there herself. John was hardly naive about marketing, but Yoko—who in 1959 had conceived some of Manhattan's first loft concerts—was an organizer by inclination, habit, and necessity. On every front, it was her vision and energy that transformed John's restless dabbling into the febrile work-as-play-as-work that filled their idyll at its most inspired.

So, what did Yoko get out of all this—beyond the money, fame and power that some begrudge her to this day? Although she's given contradictory signals on this issue, the answer seems to be that she found somebody she could trust and that thus she learned to nurture. Although his enthusiasms were often short-lived, John never had trouble trusting—if anything, he was an easy mark. But Yoko, as a woman who wanted to be herself, maintained a safe distance. Both of her previous marriages had been to men who liked to take care of her. By her own testimony, the first was riddled with destructive infidelities that acted out her envy of her husband's success; the second began when (on the advice of spouse number one, who thought abortions were driving her crazy) she agreed to bear the child of filmmaker Tony Cox, a decision she apparently regretted for years. But when she conceived with John (almost immediately), she elected to go ahead and, after the pregnancy ended in a traumatic miscarriage, sought to gain custody of her daughter, Kyoko, from Cox. This is certainly not to suggest that the desire for motherhood equals health—the story would be depressing if Yoko hadn't remained productive in so many other ways. The point is her emotional transformation, her sudden embrace of capacities she'd always found threatening before.

This was a great romance because it opened up two great romantics. And if equality, deeply felt no matter how frustrating to put into practice, was the key, then sex was the door. This is hardly to suggest that together the couple completely transcended their sexual hangups—that's a rare and perhaps not entirely desirable achievement. But it seems quite possible that these two non-virgins found the meaning of their lives in bed. As it happens, this sexual consciousness seems to have been Yoko's doing as well. Where the Beatles' sexiness had been automatic and hence almost subliminal, John-and-Yoko had the mock-

Erotic drawing from Lennon's Bag One lithograph series, 1970.

one-dimensional, épater-les-bourgeois, do-it-in-the-road aura of a woman who turned the sound of orgasm into a vocal style and flaunted hot pants in an era of pastoral nostalgia. Think of the nude photos and movies, or the pseudo-titillating bed-ins or *John Lennon's Diary*. Nor was this quasi-porn an advertisement for free love—John, fanatically jealous himself, refused to describe Beatle orgies in *Lennon Remembers* for fear of hurting Yoko. Among his erotic lithographs, there's one paradigmatic image of monogamous lust: *Two John Lennons* do Yoko simultaneously, one at her pussy and one at her right nipple, while Yoko tongues the left nipple herself. A decade later they were still at it: Yoko's "Kiss Kiss Kiss" was a more convincing come song than Donna Summer's, and the "Walking on Thin Ice" video moved from the torsos of the two lovers to Yoko's face, rippling in sexual transport.

They were in love for the first time, and they knew it was going to last—their passion constituted an eternal present. But in the less blissful moments that afflict any passionate relationship and were numerous with these two, who could never go cold turkey on their manic (hence depressive) tendencies, they wondered how their love was going to persist through real time; after a while John began to worry about "mad couples" like Scott-and-Zelda. From Arthur Janov they learned that their future hinged on the traumatic separations in their respective pasts, including John's from his mother, Julia, who turned him over to her sister as a three-year-old and died when he was seventeen, and Yoko's from her parents during World War II. And from the future they learned that Arthur Janov hadn't taught them enough.

Part of the push for John's *Imagine* and Yoko's *Fly* was a ninety-minute feature called *Imagine* (heavier title than *Fly*, right?) that never got theatrical distribution. A leisurely succession of silent scenes accompanied by songs from the albums, *Imagine* can be pretty dumb. Yet if a chess game played entirely with white pieces makes for a tolerable shot and a tedious sequence, John and Yoko's eye and body contact throughout the film generate an almost euphoric intimacy that's heightened by the relaxed pace—the most seductive connubial image they ever created. But beginning with "The Ballad of John and Yoko" (the second time John compared himself publicly to Christ, though by 1969 no one cared) it was apparent that they also felt embattled, and on *Imagine* the domestic epiphany of "Oh Yoko!" was balanced off and then some by the doubt and struggle of "How?" and "It's So Hard" and "Jealous Guy." Nor did "Mrs. Lennon," "Oh Yoko!"'s sardonic companion piece on *Fly*, radiate contentment. Soon the fight for Kyoko, the strain of childlessness, John's battle with U.S. Immigration, and the failure of *Some Time in New York City* to move up the charts were all taking a discernible toll. Ignored as an artist in John's world, Yoko felt her identity slipping away, and John's moody support didn't compensate. His "Aisumasen (I'm Sorry)," on 1973's *Mind Games*, was written entirely in the eternal present: "And when I hurt you and cause you pain /

Darlin' I promise I won't do it again." In late 1973 they separated, apparently at Yoko's insistence—though it's equally apparent that John had been asking for it.

"I don't know what marriage is. I have no idea. Marriage has nothing to do with a man/woman relationship," John told Loraine Alterman in late 1974. "Yoko and I are sort of separated but equal and together. I don't know what else to say except that Yoko is probably the first and only woman I've ever been with who'll remain a real friend, no matter what goes down with our marriage." This was a typical statement for John—direct, insightful and commonplace, the sort of thing spouses often say before they admit to themselves that the bond has somehow been broken. Yet for these two it was different: Their separation turned their great romance into a great marriage.

Initially, of course, it just looked like another dream-is-over. John and Yoko had exposed themselves as two more creative egomaniacs who couldn't make room for each other, characters as familiar in bohemia as they are in show biz. Yoko remained in New York while John drank himself stupid in L.A., where he was once spotted with a Kotex on his head. Yoko tended to her work and John tended to his, neither with as much success as had been hoped, though John did get the Number One "Whatever Gets You Thru the Night" out of his misery. But *Walls and Bridges*, his 1974 album, also included a benediction to Yoko in someone else's arms and the crazed "What You Got," which brought to life the ancient line "Oh baby, baby, baby gimme one more chance." And eventually, baby—usually known as mother—did. They'd never stopped talking on the phone, and after John returned to New York they started "dating" again. Soon the marriage was back on.

This time, however, it was going to be different, and it was, though since one big change was that they no longer conceived their union as any kind of public art event, few facts are clear. On October 9, 1975, Yoko bore John a son in an arduous delivery. When his contract with EMI expired in 1976, John signed with nobody, freeing himself to care for Sean as neither of his parents had ever cared for him. Yoko, meanwhile, devoted her time to the family fortune, diversifying into real estate and dairy cattle. In May 1979, full-page ads in major dailies and music trades announced the Lennons' continuing tranquillity and advised those awaiting John-and-Yoko's return to music and/or political action to free their minds instead. Nevertheless, by August of 1980 they were recording a, yes, concept album about their, yes, relationship. And that relationship, as it emerged, from *Double Fantasy* and the surrounding interviews, seemed quite remarkable—and also quite credible.

Since John is sometimes cited as a pioneering househusband, I'll mention that a househusband with full-time servants (nanny included) is not the same thing as a househusband who vacuums while making sure that the cake and the baby don't burn—in short, works like a mother. And it's worth pointing out not only that John sacrificed art to marriage at least partly because he didn't want to turn into a hack (cf. Paul, George, Ringo), but also that Yoko made a not dissimilar sacrifice. Of course, Yoko's foray into finance had an arty aura—to conduct business "just as a chess game" is almost an homage to Duchamp, who quit art to play chess himself. But those who believe that Yoko pussy-whipped John into handing over the money forget that after Brian Epstein (who as it happens was in love with him) John never met a businessperson worthy of his trust, including his inefficient self. It may seem odd for Yoko to have left the rearing of their child to her spouse, but fathers impose the opposite division of labor all the time. And to assume that wheeling and dealing does more for the soul than playing patty cake is to be deceived by conventional notions of status, not a common failing among superstars, all of whom know the secret terrors of the obeisance jones and some of whom even manage to kick.

With baby Sean: *Three Virgins.*

None of which is to rationalize away the striking peculiarities of this rela-tionship. My feminist assumption that John oppressed Yoko is based on the evidence—their own testimony, John's history of male chauvinism and head-strong bullshit, and our knowledge of how marriage works. But Yoko is ob-viously hell on wheels as a matter of habit—driven, demanding, temperamental, impossibly egocentric. Her feminist credentials are compromised by her general unsisterliness—like most blokes, Yoko has always preferred the company of men. Her stated disinclination to mother her infant son is connected to a notion of status only marginally more forgivable in a woman than in a man. Also, as both of them were happy to make clear to Annie Leibovitz's camera, Yoko encouraged in her husband an infantile or even fetal dependency. She needed him, but one reason they split up—and reorganized their marriage the way they did—was that she also needed her independence. He needed her, period.

But even if we conjecture (falsely, I believe) that Yoko re-entered the mar-riage coolly, calculating the power balances in her own favor because she knew John would be unable to resist after a year and a half of acute separation anxiety, how does that change things? If Yoko consciously chose an intimacy that was sheer compulsion for John, does that make her commitment any less impressive? Marriage doesn't match models of sanity; it accommodates two human beings with the usual quota of quirks and worse. This may have been an unusually neurotic relationship. But why do we always assume that neurosis must be defeated, transcended, escaped? John Lennon learned not merely to make do with his compulsions but to make something fairly miraculous out of them. After a traumatic breach, he managed to collaborate in a marriage that con-founded traditional sex roles, and thus to achieve some of the loving wisdom he'd always hoped to find on the other side of his mean streak. And this is in keeping with everything we love about him, for as an artist his indelible value was the way he transmuted abrasive anger into joy and hope—something that only happened when first his group, then his wife shielded him from the alone-ness he dreaded before anything else on earth.

For John Lennon to replace a cooperative with a couple was to give up on the best hopes of the Sixties, but I blame that on the zeitgeist; the best hopes of the Sixties were hopes only, and their failure left each of us free only to scramble. After enormous anguish, he and Yoko figured out a structure in which their passion could persist through real time. Personally, I find this structure short on dialectics and long on yin-and-yang. But since it's up to each of us who sees marriage as a potentially exalting compromise to discover what the terms of our own particular compromise—and exaltation—might be, my only real regret is that for a long time there was no way for John and Yoko to make their own particulars public, as art. That changed with *Double Fantasy*, which offered a sharp sense not just of the obvious stuff, the tenderness and struggle and rage and delight, but of a few emotional specifics, not all of them universally appealing: game-playing, occult quietism and mystagogy, hints of subordination and condescension. I like to fantasize that in future albums we would have gotten an idea of what day-to-day proportions of intimacy and solitude, work and goofing off, ecstasy and boredom went into the mix—not so we could copy the formula but so that our belief in their union could become more vivid. For by the time the best hopes of the Sixties had made a martyr out of John Lennon, he did know—his wife had taught him—what marriage was, or might be. Equality without stasis, tranquillity without stagnation, and let your face be the last I see.

"It helps people who mourn to be able
to do something for the cause of the fallen,
not to have let them die in vain.
Even though you may feel a deep weariness and
despair, you mustn't abdicate a leadership
that has meant a great deal to mankind."

"Think globally and act locally."

ABOUT THE
CONTRIBUTORS

BARRY BALLISTER was formerly creative director of Ted Bates and Company Advertising in New York City and a one-time contributor to *Rolling Stone*.

ROBERT CHRISTGAU is the music editor of the *Village Voice* where his Consumer Guide column has appeared for over ten years. He has written for numerous publications including the *New York Times* and *Esquire*. His 1973 collection of writings, *Any Old Way You Choose It*, was one of the first books of rock criticism published, and he is the author of *Christgau's Record Guide: Rock Albums of the '70s*.

JONATHAN COTT has been a contributing and associate editor of *Rolling Stone* since its inception in 1967. He was *Rolling Stone*'s first European correspondent, and as such, interviewed John Lennon for the first interview Lennon granted the magazine. Cott's *Rolling Stone* interviews with Henry Miller, Oriana Fallaci and Werner Herzog were collected, with others, in *Forever Young*. He has published a volume of poetry, *City of Earthly Love*. He is the author of *He Dreams What Is Going On Inside His Head; Stockhausen: Conversations with the Composer;* and the editor of *Beyond the Looking Glass: Victorian Fairy Tales, Novels, Stories and Poems;* and *Wonders*.

DAVID DALTON began writing for *Rolling Stone* in 1967 and from 1968 to 1971, he served as contributing editor. In 1970, he and Jonathan Cott collaborated on *Get Back*, a booklet about the *Let It Be* sessions that was packaged with the British edition of that LP. His other books include *Janis; James Dean, the Mutant King;* and *The Rolling Stones—The First Twenty Years*. His work has also appeared in *Esquire, Penthouse, Oui* and *High Times*.

CHRISTINE DOUDNA was an associate editor of *Rolling Stone* from 1973 to 1978. She currently writes for and edits a variety of publications including *The New York Times Magazine, Savvy* and *Channels*.

CHET FLIPPO is a native of Texas who began writing for *Rolling Stone* in 1970. In 1974, he moved to New York to found *Rolling Stone*'s New York office, and over the years, has served as senior and contributing editor. His articles have appeared in *Playboy* and *New York*. His first book, a biography of country singer Hank Williams, *Your Cheatin' Heart* was published in 1981.

BEN FONG-TORRES was an editor of *Rolling Stone* from 1969 to 1980. During that time, he served as senior and music editor; his interview with Ray Charles won the ASCAP-Deems Taylor Award in 1973. He has edited several books for *Rolling Stone*, including *The Rolling Stone Rock 'n' Roll Reader* and *What's That Sound? Readings in Contemporary Music.*

RALPH J. GLEASON (1917–1975) was a cofounder of and steady contributor to *Rolling Stone*. A columnist for the *San Francisco Chronicle* for twenty-five years, he was also a vice-president of Fantasy Records and a television producer and commentator. He was the author of several books including *The Jefferson Airplane and the San Francisco Sound* and *Celebrating the Duke.*

PETE HAMILL has been a columnist since 1965, a reporter for the *New York Post* and a contributor to the *Saturday Evening Post* and the *Village Voice*. He first covered Lennon's immigration fight in his column in the *New York Post*. His novels include *The Gift* and *A Killing for Christ*, and he has also written essays and screenplays.

J. HOBERMAN is a New York-based avant-garde filmmaker who has been writing about film since 1975. A film critic for the *Village Voice* since 1978, his work has also appeared in *American Film* and *Artform.*

STEPHEN HOLDEN has been a regular contributor to *Rolling Stone* for over ten years. Currently a pop critic for the *New York Times*, he is the author of *Triple Platinum*, a novel. Among the publications for which he has written are the *Village Voice*, *High Fidelity*, *Penthouse*, the *Boston Phoenix*, *Soho News*, *Playboy* and *The New Yorker.*

GREGORY KATZ first wrote for *Rolling Stone* in 1980. Currently a reporter for the *Boston Herald American*, he has also written for the *Chicago Tribune* and is the recipient of first prizes for feature writing from both the New England UPI and the New England Press Association.

DONALD KIRK is a freelance journalist based in Tokyo who has written for numerous publications. He is the author of two books on the Vietnam War, *Tell It to the Dead: Memories of a War* and *Wider War: The Struggle for Cambodia, Thailand and Laos*. He is also the recipient of the Overseas Press Club and George Polk awards.

ANNIE LEIBOVITZ is chief photographer for *Rolling Stone* and has been a regular contributor to the magazine since 1970. A portrait of John Lennon that she shot in 1970 was her first *Rolling Stone* cover. She was the editor of *Shooting Stars: The Rolling Stone Book of Portraits*, in which several of her photographs appear.

JAN MORRIS has been writing about cities for *Rolling Stone* since 1974; these essays were collected in *Destinations*. She writes frequently for numerous publications and is the author of many books including *The World of Venice*, *Conundrum* and the *Pax Britannica* trilogy.

ROBERT PALMER has been a contributor to *Rolling Stone* since 1969. He is the chief pop critic for the *New York Times* and the author of *Deep Blues*. His articles have appeared in the *Atlantic Monthly*, *Downbeat*, *Ethnomusicology*, *Journal of American Folklore*, the *Black Perspective in Music*, *Penthouse* and Boston's *Real Paper*.

JOHN PICCARELLA writes for the *Village Voice*, the *Boston Phoenix* and *New York Rocker*.

JOHN ROCKWELL has written frequently for *Rolling Stone*. He is the music critic for the *New York Times* and was its principal rock critic from 1974 to 1980. His articles have appeared in many publications including the *Oakland Tribune*, the *Los Angeles Times*, *Esquire*, *Saturday Review* and *Le Monde*.

JOEL SIEGEL contributed several articles to *Rolling Stone* in the early Seventies. He is currently the theater critic for WABC-TV (New York) and arts critic for "Good Morning America." He was the librettist for the musical *The First*.

SCOTT SPENCER is the author of *Preservation Hall* and *Endless Love*.

JANN S. WENNER is the editor and publisher of *Rolling Stone*, which he founded in 1967. His 1970 interviews with John Lennon were published first in the magazine, then later as a book entitled *Lennon Remembers*.

STUART WERBIN was a contributor to *Rolling Stone* in the early Seventies. His work has also appeared in the *Boston Phoenix* and *New Times*.

RITCHIE YORKE is the author of *The Led Zeppelin Biography; The History of Rock 'n' Roll;* and *Into the Music—the Van Morrison Biography*. He worked with John and Yoko for the "War Is Over! If You Want It" global peace campaign in 1969–70.

CREDITS

"In My Room" by Brian Wilson and Gary Usher, Copyright © 1964 Irving Music. "Aisumasen (I'm Sorry)" by John Lennon, Copyright © 1973 John Lennon. "One Day (at a Time)" by John Lennon, Copyright © 1973 by John Lennon. "Nobody Loves You (When You're Down and Out)" by John Lennon, Copyright © 1974 Lennon Music/ATV Music Corp. "What You Got" by John Lennon, Copyright © 1974 Lennon Music/ATV Music Corp. "There's a Place" by John Lennon and Paul McCartney, Copyright © 1965 Northern Songs Ltd. "Beautiful Boys" by Yoko Ono, Copyright © 1980 Lenono Music. "Cleanup Time" by John Lennon, Copyright © 1980 Lenono Music. "Dear Yoko" by John Lennon, Copyright © 1980 by Lenono Music. "I'm Your Angel" by Yoko Ono, Copyright © 1980 Lenono Music. "Watching the Wheels" by John Lennon, Copyright © 1980 Lenono Music. "Mother of the Universe" by Yoko Ono, Copyright © 1981 Ono Music. "Woman Is the Nigger of the World" by John Lennon and Yoko Ono, Copyright © 1972 Ono Music. "I Am the Walrus" by John Lennon and Paul McCartney, Copyright © 1967 Northern Songs Ltd. All rights for the U.S.A., Mexico and the Philippines controlled by Comet Music Corp. % ATV Music Corp. Used by permission only. All rights reserved. "You've Got to Hide Your Love Away" by John Lennon and Paul McCartney, Copyright © 1965. All rights for the U.S.A., Mexico and the Philippines controlled by Maclen Music, Inc. % ATV Music Corp. Used by permission. By arrangement with Unart Music Corporation. All rights reserved. Credits for the following songs: All rights for the U.S.A., Mexico and the Philippines controlled by Maclen Music, Inc. % ATV Music Corp. Used by permission. All rights reserved.

"Across the Universe" by John Lennon and Paul McCartney, Copyright © 1968, 1970 Northern Songs Ltd. "A Day in the Life" by John Lennon and Paul McCartney, Copyright © 1967 Northern Songs Ltd. "All You Need Is Love" by John Lennon and Paul McCartney, Copyright © 1967 by Northern Songs Ltd. "Ballad of John and Yoko" by John Lennon, Copyright © 1969 Northern Songs Ltd. "Cold Turkey" by John Lennon, Copyright © 1969 Northern Songs Ltd. "Crippled Inside" by John Lennon, Copyright © 1969 Northern Songs Ltd. "Don't Let Me Down" by John Lennon and Paul McCartney, Copyright © 1969 Northern Songs Ltd. "Everybody's Got Something to Hide Except Me and My Monkey" by John Lennon and Paul McCartney, Copyright © 1968 Northern Songs Ltd. "Getting Better" by John Lennon and Paul McCartney, Copyright © 1967 Northern Songs Ltd. "Gimme Some Truth" by John Lennon, Copyright © 1971 Northern Songs Ltd. "Girl" by John Lennon and Paul McCartney, Copyright © 1965 Northern Songs Ltd. "Give Peace a Chance" by John Lennon, Copyright © 1969 Northern Songs Ltd. "Glass Onion" by John Lennon and Paul McCartney, Copyright © 1968 Northern Songs Ltd. "God" by John Lennon, Copyright © 1971 Northern Songs Ltd. "Good Morning, Good Morning" by John Lennon and Paul McCartney, Copyright © 1967 Northern Songs Ltd. "Happiness Is a Warm Gun" by John Lennon and Paul McCartney, Copyright © 1968 Northern Songs Ltd. "I Found Out" by John Lennon, Copyright © 1970 Northern Songs Ltd. "Imagine" by John Lennon, Copyright © 1971 Northern Songs Ltd. "In My Life" by John Lennon and Paul McCartney, Copyright © 1965 Northern Songs Ltd. "Instant Karma!" by John Lennon, Copyright © 1970 Northern Songs Ltd. "Isolation" by John Lennon, Copyright © 1971

INDEX